International Management

International Management Cross-Cultural Dimensions

Richard Mead

First published 1994

Blackwell Publishers
238 Main Street
Cambridge, Massachusetts 02142
USA

108 Cowley Road
Oxford   OX4 1JF
UK

Library of Congress Cataloging-in-Publication Data

Mead, Richard.
    International management : cross cultural dimensions / Richard Mead.
        p.   cm.
    Includes bibliographical references and index.
    ISBN 0–631–18368–X. — ISBN 0–631–18369–8
    1. International business enterprises—Management—Social aspects.
2. Corporate culture.   3. Intercultural communication.   I. Title.
HD62.4.M4   1994   93–44708
658′.049—dc20   CIP

British Library Cataloguing in Publication Data

A CIP catalogue record for this book is available from the British Library.

Commissioning editor: Richard Burton
Desk editors: Sarah McNamee and Paul Stringer
Production manager and text designer: Rhona Richard

Typeset in 11 on 13pt Baskerville
by Graphicraft Typesetters Ltd., Hong Kong
Printed in Great Britain by BPC Wheatons Ltd, Exeter

This book is printed on acid-free paper

Contents

List of figures

List of tables

Preface

This book deals with international management. It focuses on the interpersonal skills needed to manage across national borders and shows how cultural factors influence behavior in the workplace and the negotiation.

Members of different cultures apply different priorities and values in making and implementing decisions. These differences are significant when the manager has to deal with members of another culture whether in superior–subordinate, peer, buyer–seller, negotiation, or consultancy relationships.

This theme is developed in the light of three questions:

- When should the manager take culture into account as a significant influence?
- When are other factors of greater direct influence?
- How does the manager weigh the importance of these different factors?

Illustrations are drawn from across the world and the first index indicates their scope. Most come from the Asian Pacific region (East Asia, including China, and South-east Asia). This region includes the world's fastest growing economies. It is likely to be of lasting importance to the future development of international business, as the 1993 Seattle summit of the Asia-Pacific Economic (APEC) forum indicated.

Structure

This book is organized to cover the various topics that make up the field of cross-cultural management as comprehensively as possible, but without presenting them as a list. Key topics such as communication are made the focus of a dedicated chapter, then elaborated in sections of further chapters. Some topics, such as culture and technology, are contextualized in a range of sections but are not centralized in any one chapter.

The five parts of the book consist of a total of 18 chapters. They are sequenced with the aim of giving the book logical development, as follows:

Part I Culture and Difference, deals with culture as a factor in explaining differences in work attitudes and relationships.

- Chapter 1 (Cross-Cultural Management) is introductory. It defines the notion of culture in management, and examines problems of managing cultural diversity.
- Chapter 2 (Doing Your Own Analysis) takes off from the practical concern of the manager to discover the specific features of the cultures with which he/she is dealing, and to assess their influence on the workplace. It deals with sources of information about the culture and with techniques for applying these to develop explanatory hypotheses.
- Chapter 3 (Comparing Cultures) focuses on the one data source not developed in the previous chapter; scholarly models. It discusses four standard models and assesses their value in making comparisons between cultures on a range of dimensions.

Part II Culture and Structure, examines culture as a factor in explaining how structures are built and implemented.

- Chapter 4 (Structures for Making Decisions) shows how scholarly models of culture can be applied to explaining variations in formal structures of organization. The importance of culture is balanced against other factors – including strategy, industry, and technology.
- Chapter 5 (Patronage Relationships) and chapter 6 focus on the role played by culture in determining how formal structures and systems are applied in practice. Chapter 5 shows when informal patronage relationships are a more important influence on decision-making than formal structures.
- Chapter 6 (Organizational Culture) examines the influence that national culture has upon the development of an organizational culture, and sees why the latter affects how formal structures are implemented. It deals with problems of changing the organizational culture.

Part III Culture and Relationships, focuses on the meaning of culture in day-to-day interactions between people from different cultural backgrounds.

- Chapter 7 (Cross-Cultural Management Communication) is pivotal. It shows how cultural priorities are expressed in communicative style. It ties together points raised in the previous chapters on communication as a process of implementing formal and informal structures, and builds a foundation for the chapters that follow.
- Chapter 8 (Motivation across Cultures) develops issues raised by chapter 7 in two respects. Effective communication is motivating (in part) when it reflects cultural priorities. Second, motivational systems are more likely to prove effective when they are appropriately communicated.
- Chapter 9 (Dispute) distinguishes different degrees of disagreement and shows that a dispute considered innocuous in one culture may generate serious complications elsewhere. Good communication helps avoid or resolve conflict, and bad communication may be causal.
- Chapter 10 (Negotiations) focuses on the importance of developing positive relationships with negotiation counterparts from another culture. Cultural factors influence the conditions under which you can trust and can expect to be trusted at different stages of the process.
- Chapter 11 (Culture and Ethics) deals with ethical differences from a general point of view. It discusses the development of ethical codes that can be applied pragmatically, and looks at the problems of identifying ethical norms in different cultures.

Part IV Culture and Organizational Policy, applies this foundation knowledge to different types of organizations.

- Chapter 12 (Family Companies) shows how attitudes towards and values practiced in the family company reflect the general business culture. The discussion centers on two contrasting types, the Southeast Asian (Chinese) and United States (Anglo) family companies.
- Chapter 13 (International Joint Ventures) illustrates the problems and opportunities that arise from business and cultural differences that arise in one common form of alliance, the international joint venture. Factors for success are discussed.
- Chapter 14 (Headquarters and Subsidiary) deals with the effect of cultural difference when the organizations are related within a multinational framework. It shows how both headquarters and subsidiary can benefit from contrasting priorities within their overlapping environments.
- Chapter 15 (Cross-Cultural Staffing Policies) examines issues of staffing multinational operations and problems of measuring expatriate success and failure, and the relative advantages of employing expatriate and local staff in different environmental contexts.

- Chapter 16 (Training for an Expatriate Assignment) takes up the practical implications that a given staffing policy has for training the expatriated manager and his/her spouse and dependants.

Part V Culture and Change, deals with the problem of how the manager recognizes cultural change and how he/she responds to it.

- Chapter 17 (Shifts in the Culture) asks when environmental change is significant, how and why a culture is modified, and how these shifts affect the company.
- Chapter 18 (Planning Change) deals with values associated with change and with cultural priorities in planning to make change. As the company is forced to react to an increasing rate of change in the environment, it adopts proactive strategies.

All chapters balance the theoretical and practical issues that arise in cultural analysis. All chapters have a section dealing with the managerial implications of points discussed, and an exercise. The Instructor's manual gives further exercises.

Who the Book Is For

This book has been primarily written for

- the management student; the book is recommended for MBA and executive classes, and some first-degree classes, that give an international slant to:

    - marketing;
    - organizational behavior;
    - project management;
    - joint ventures;

- the manager.

The development of international business means that today's management student is almost certain to work with members of other cultures during his/her career, and to need cross-cultural management skills. This is true not only for the expatriate but also the manager working at home.

In general, the working environment is becoming increasingly multicultural. Here are two examples. Ford's workforce in Germany consists of only about 50 percent native German speakers; the rest include Greeks and Turks – who have a long history of conflict. Second, the United States was by 1980 already the fourth largest Spanish-speaking nation in the world, and approximately 56 percent of the population of Miami had their origins in Latino-Spanish cultures.[1] Johnston and Packer (1987) calculated that between 1987 and the year 2000, 85 percent of net additions to the United States labor force would come from women and non-Caucasian men, particularly from Black, Asian, Hispanic cultures.

Mistakes in understanding the other person's culture can be expensive and even life-threatening; after the 1991 Gulf War, the RAF delivered pork sausages, luncheon meat, and bacon burgers to the millions of starving Kurdish refugees as part of its £20 million aid programme. They forgot that most Kurds are Muslims, who do not eat pork.[2]

Whether or not all cultures are converging to a point at which cultural differences are so slight that they can be safely ignored is a point taken up in the last two chapters. The practical answer for today is that this final convergence is still a long way in the future. Today's manager cannot afford to ignore evidence of difference. Cultural differences are real and how they are expressed can vitally affect the workplace.

Unique Features

In addition to covering the core topics common to most textbooks on cross-cultural management, the book has a number of original features. The expatriate manager is bound to be aware of apparent incongruities in the local behavior; chapter 2 shows the manager how to formalize these often unstructured impressions, analyze the other culture for him/herself and to develop a coherent explanation for the behavior of its members.

Business ethics (chapter 11) still tend to be discussed in terms of a single culture – usually American – rather than as a collision of values in different cultures. The culture of the family company (chapter 12) is often ignored but is useful for understanding its business-culture context.

Patronage relationships (chapter 5) are overlooked by almost every standard textbook. This bias gives an accurate reflection of management priorities in the United States and other Anglo cultures, where nepotism, for instance, is perceived as politically incorrect. But it overlooks realities in much of the developing world (and in many developed societies) where patronage is accepted and may often seem the most effective means of managing relationships. A Chinese entrepreneur, for instance, would almost never contemplate employing an outsider in preference to his own son. Whatever the cross-cultural manager may think of the ethics of patronage, he/she needs to recognize the phenomenon and be prepared to cope with its effects.

Ancillary Materials

The Instructor's manual contains:

- chapter outlines;
- main teaching points;
- class discussion questions;
- answers to exercise questions;
- supplementary exercises.

In addition it includes:

- transparency masters;
- test bank, of multiple-choice questions and true/false items for each chapter.

Notes

1. US Department of Commerce (1982).
2. 'Britain this week,' *The Economist*, April 13, 1991.

Acknowledgments

This book owes much to the support and encouragement of the Director of SasinGIBA, Professor Toemsakdi Krishnamra. Parts were drafted at the Kellogg School, Northwestern University, and at the Middlesex Business School, Middlesex Polytechnic (now Middlesex University). The comments and suggestions made by MBA students of these three institutions, in Thailand, the United States, and the United Kingdom, have had a major influence upon the contents of the text.

I am extremely grateful for the suggestions made by a wide range of scholars and business people; Mike Carroll, Lawnin Crawford, James Cumming, Tony Davison, Lee Gilbert, Vangie Holvino, Colin Jones, Hervey Juris, John Kelly, Kubi Luchterhand, Duncan McCargo, Norman McGuinness, Leslie Nathanson, John Ng, Michael Rabinovitz, Tom Reeves, Don Laurie Sugita, Gabriele Udeschini, Naufel Vilcassim, Shuo Watanabe. In particular, the following have read and commented upon chapters: F. Gerard Adams, Peter Bramley, Ian Brown, Daryl Chansuthus, Michael Forrer, Kullada Kesboonchoo, Robert McCann, John Sherry, Richard Williams.

Finally, I must express my appreciation of the enthusiastic and patient support given me by Richard Burton and other members of Blackwell Publishers and their readers.

Richard Mead
Simon Industrial and Professional Fellow
Manchester Business School,
The University of Manchester

Part I

Culture and Difference

1

Cross-Cultural Management

1.1 Introduction

A small Boston bank was acquired by an Italian bank. Senior Italian staff took over the top positions and soon exerted their authority. Relations between staff at all levels became more formal and responsibilities to superiors were differentiated more tightly than under the previous American management. Second, all the Italians were male, and were patriarchal in their relations with female employees. Third, the Italians showed no interest in long-term planning and left all planning decisions to their American subordinates.

Peter joined the bank a few weeks before the take-over. He had graduated from college three years before and had spent the interim working in advertising. After talking about the new management style with Bert, a long-term employee, he came to the conclusion that the greater differentiation reflected power distances wider in Italian than American culture.

"And another thing, management attitudes towards women. Isn't that also typical of Italian culture?"

"It's culture in part, perhaps, but it's also industry. Don't forget that in any country, banking is a masculine business and conservative. It's different to the media, you know."

"OK. But why don't they take more interest in planning? Is that culture too?"

Neither Bert nor anyone else could offer a solution. And this lack of interest in planning was surprising, particularly given the high needs shown by Italian culture to avoid future uncertainty (discussed in chapter 3).

But within a year the bank was resold. It became clear that the bank had been acquired by the Italians only for rapid resale, and hence the Italian management team had little interest in defining long-term goals. In this respect market values rather than cultural values determined behavior.

This case shows the practical importance of distinguishing how far culture and how far other factors are immediate determinants of behavior. If you had been a middle manager in this Boston bank, and had assumed that the disinterest in strategy was culturally conditioned, you might have invested your energy in "educating" top-management to the realities of American banking and needs for strategy. If you had guessed, correctly, that market conditions were the determining factor, you might have saved your energy and perhaps begun to search for another job.

The theme of weighing the direct importance of culture is pursued further below. This short chapter introduces the book. It has the following sections:

1.2 Why Are Cross-Cultural Management Skills Important?
1.3 Defining Culture
1.4 Managing Cultural Diversity
1.5 Implications for the Manager
1.6 Summary
1.7 Exercises

1.2 Why Are Cross-Cultural Management Skills Important?

Today's business world is increasingly global. Multinational firms produce and sell goods and services on an international basis, often far from the country of the headquarters. This often means establishing branches and subsidiaries outside their national boundaries; in 1990, the biggest private-sector firm in Singapore was General Electric – an American company. As firms such as General Motors, Ford, Rover, Volkswagen, and others have learned from Japanese competition, national markets are no longer safe. The point is being repeated in many other industries. By 1991, approximately 70 percent of all goods produced in the United States were exposed to international competition. This process of foreign involvement multiplies as companies in newly developing countries learn that to survive they also must produce and market on a world-wide basis.

This growth in multinational operations reflects wider political and economic ties, the formation of multinational trading blocks (for instance, the European Union, ASEAN), greater ease of transportation and the development of communications networks.

This means that the manager increasingly has to deal with individuals from other national cultures. He/she must develop skills and strategies for interacting with a range of individuals whose behavior is influenced by other cultural priorities. Every working manager is probably certain of having to deal with members of other cultures at various points in his/her career.

The international manager increasingly needs interactive skills of dealing with other people. In response to a survey conducted by Beamish and Calof (1989), human resource and other executives ranked communication skills as most important for positions of international responsibility, followed immediately by leadership skills, interpersonal skills, and adaptability/flexibility. Functional/technical strengths and technological literacy were rated lower (at 8 and 11 in a list of 12).

The other side to this coin is that the ethnocentric manager who is unable or unwilling to deal with members of another culture has increasingly restricted career opportunities.

A failure in an overseas posting damages the manager's sense of self-respect and could cost his/her job. In addition it costs the company money. Mendenhall et al. (1987) reviewed literature suggesting that "between 20 to 50 percent of personnel sent abroad return prematurely from their overseas assignments." In 1985 Copeland and Griggs calculated that expatriate failures were costing American companies $2 billion a year. More recent evidence suggests that each failure could cost between $250,000 to $1 million, "depending on the employee's salary, the location, and whether a family transfer was involved" (Caudron, 1992). The risks of incurring such costs are reduced when the company invests in training the manager for the assignment.

This need for international managers is recognized by business schools. Courses in international topics are now commonplace. Many schools also aim at attracting foreign faculty and students, establishing cross-registration agreements with foreign counterparts, and encouraging international research and consultancy.

Increasing priority is being given to teaching cross-cultural management skills at first-degree and MBA levels. These skills include the ability to communicate and interact with members of other cultures, which always implies learning about their cultural systems. In turn, this means developing a greater understanding of one's own system – without which objective comparisons are not possible.

Effective cross-cultural management means working *with* members of the other culture, tolerating differences so far as possible, and recognizing their priorities when developing shared priorities.

The manager cannot usually expect to force-fit members of another culture into his/her cultural norms. They cannot easily be made to accept his/her perceptions of reality as superior to values in their own culture. This is not a moral point, but a practical point. The history of colonialism shows that the great powers who made repeated attempts to enforce their value systems upon others eventually failed. The organization that attempts to impose its behavioral norms upon unwilling employees from another culture faces an uphill battle. (Chapter 6 examines policy for creating organization culture; chapter 14 deals with relations with local staff in a multinational subsidiary.)

1.3 Defining Culture

Scholars cannot agree on a single definition of "culture." The anthropological, sociological, and management literatures offer a host of alternative definitions. In a useful critical review Kroeber and Kluckhohn (1963, originally published as a monograph in 1952) discussed several hundred; there have been many additions since.

Contemporary studies sort into those that deal with culture as an *implicit* feature of social life (Geertz, 1973) and those that treat it as an *explicit* social construct. The emphasis chosen here reflects the concept of culture-as-implicit, and sees how values, beliefs, and attitudes influence behavior and relationships within the culture group. Hofstede's (1984a) definition is employed:

> the collective programming of the mind which distinguishes the members of one human group from another. . . . Culture, in this sense, includes systems of values; and values are among the building blocks of culture. (p. 21)

This implies:

- culture includes systems of values;
- a culture is particular to one group and not others;
- it is learned and is not innate; it is passed down from one generation to the next;
- it influences the behavior of group members in uniform and predictable ways.

The remainder of this section examines these implications.

1.3.1 Values, beliefs, and attitudes

Cultural *values* are defined as assumptions about "how things ought to be" in the society. They are often held at a preconscious level and may never be fully articulated. As such they are "ingrained," slow to change, and have the strongest influence on behavior (England, 1967). An example is the assumption held by some cultures (see chapter 3) that social hierarchy is important and should be respected.

Values may be distinguished from beliefs and attitudes. A *belief* is a conscious certainty that something exists, or is good, in the society. An example is the belief that wisdom is naturally acquired by experience, and that that the old are naturally wiser than the young. An *attitude* is normative – a conscious stance about how people ought to behave in society. For instance, "young people ought to pay deference to their elders."

Values, beliefs, and attitudes do not necessarily correspond. An illustration is provided by the upper-class student from a highly conservative society who leaves home to pursue university study in the United States. While there he acquires beliefs and attitudes about democratic and "classless" institutions; yet on returning home, very soon reverts to his old assumptions about the incapacity of his social inferiors to make decisions on his behalf. This reversion does not necessarily mean that his conscious stances are insincere. Rather, his basic values have never been modified.

Although the individual may not be able to articulate his/her values, they are the most sustained and they most influence his/her behavior. For this reason, the book focuses on values. It is argued that:

- the manager develops an understanding of values in the other culture by analyzing the behavior of its members;
- the manager builds skills in predicting behavior in the other culture by developing understanding of their values.

Chapter 2 proposes techniques for analysis of other-culture behavior.

1.3.2 Culture-as-explicit

The concept of culture-as-explicit focuses on such phenomena as:

- material culture;
- religion;
- political and economic ideology (Wuthnow and Witten, 1988).

The *material culture* produced within the group provides an oblique and sometimes distorted reflection of members' values. The professional anthropologist, sociologist, or art critic is trained to explain the relationship, and this highly specialized activity generally lies outside the province of the cross-cultural manager. Nevertheless, international managers are wise to achieve some basic knowledge of the material culture.

They are one jump ahead in Russia if they are able to quote Pushkin in Russian, and in Malaysia if they are able to eat *nasi goreng*, and in the United States if they understand the basic principles of baseball. The Latin-American cultures value their literature; when visiting Argentina, or Chile, or Brazil on business, reading something by their national writers is a useful way to prepare. Your hosts will appreciate your capacity to make intelligent comments and ask pertinent questions.

The material culture includes technology. Values influence the design, selection, and application of technology in the workplace. Several points in the book make clear that the use of technology influences behavior, sometimes overriding the effects of culture.

The *religion* practiced by the group may express values and clearly influences beliefs and attitudes. But religious practice is never an entirely reliable guide to behavior. A religious creed is idealistic and prescriptive rather than descriptive of actual behavior. For instance, Buddhism teaches moderation and abhors killing, but here is an educated Thai describing the people of his town:

> Characteristically, the Muang Petch people are suited to be *nak-leng* [patrons]. Killing and revenge is the name of the game, not necessarily based on any particular principle except for defending one's honour in the old way. We're quite extreme people which is strange considering that the people are mostly devout Buddhists.[1]

The same religious form may be practiced across a range of national boundaries; Catholicism is followed by majorities in Ireland, Spain, Poland, and the Philippines, but these cultures differ – as does the social significance of Catholicism within each.

Political ideology Political leaders commonly legitimize their regimes by claiming that their system provides a genuine expression of the majority culture; any admission to the contrary is extraordinary. However, constant political turmoil in much of the world suggests that the relationship between culture and the ideology proclaimed by political elites is often extremely tenuous.

The demise of Marxism across much of Eastern Europe in 1989 provides a striking example. It would suggest that:

- Marxism accurately reflected East European cultures before 1989. In 1989, these cultures changed radically, and Marxism was no longer adequate. *Or*

- Marxism had never accurately reflected East European cultures. The contradictions were no longer sustainable in 1989, when the political elites lacked the resources to enforce their will.

It is too early to give a definite answer, but the evidence seems to suggest that the people of these countries are reverting to behavioral patterns that predate Marxism, and hence the second explanation is preferred. This theme is taken up further in chapter 17, where problems of distinguishing superficial and significant shifts in the cultural and political environments are discussed.

When economic conditions reflect ideology, they can modify cultural values, but only when sustained over time. An economic/industry upsurge may inspire a new degree of optimism just as a slump causes a sense of depression, but these responses do not necessarily inspire cultural change. Culture is not an efficient predictor of economic development, and vice versa. For instance, Hofstede's (1984a) model (examined in chapter 3) shows wide economic disparities at the extremes of small needs to avoid uncertainty (Singapore, Jamaica), of great needs to avoid uncertainty (Japan, Guatemala), of small power distances (Sweden, Costa Rica), and of great power distances (Saudi Arabia, Sierra Leone).

1.3.3 Culture and the group

A culture is particular to one social group and not others, and this means that different social groups may respond to the same phenomena differently, and in similar situations behave differently. This happens when the social groups are organizations; for example, a company with an entrepreneurial culture might welcome a tariff reduction as an opportunity for competition whereas a mature and conservative company might perceive it as a threat. Here is an example in which different national cultures are involved.

The Japanese royal family is an important national institution, and in 1992 the question of the Crown Prince's marrying and producing an heir was a matter of great public concern.

> On one side of the broad green moat surrounding the Imperial Palace dwells a 32-year old crown prince who is eagerly searching for a bride. On the other is a free-swinging press corps that would love to report every detail of a royal romance.
>
> And yet, for nine months, all of Japan's media have rigorously honored a voluntary agreement not to report a word about the handsome young prince and his quest for a mate. In essence, the traditional Japanese desire for *wa*, or group conformity, has outweighed the universal reportial zeal for a story.[2]

How would the press treat this story in other countries? In the United Kingdom, the press were uninhibited in discussing their own crown prince's lack of a wife before his eventual marriage in 1981, and in assessing the qualifications of apparent candidates. They were no less unrestrained when the marriage broke down in 1992.

> Britain's royal family suffered another blow [on] Friday when tabloid newspapers said Prince Charles had been taped telling an old flame, a middle-aged married woman, that he loved and adored her. . . .
> The story set off a string of reports in the other tabloids, which are vying with one another to publish ever more lurid accounts of the reported breakdown of the 11-year marriage of Charles and Diana.[3]

The Japanese were constrained by far greater respect for the palace. The more individualist British showed little fear of embarrassing the social institution, and were driven by greater opportunities to compete.

Of course, these different behaviors cannot be explained only by values in the respective cultures. A full explanation would need to take into account such other factors as

- the power of the two palaces to protect themselves;
- the two newspaper industries, ownership structures, and relations between newspapers;
- expectations of the two newspaper-reading publics.

And although cultural influences might enter the equation here also, the point should be clear that environmental factors other than culture are always likely to be relevant and in some situations have a more direct bearing on behavior.

1.3.4   The limits to the group

The notion that a culture is particular to one group and not another raises questions about the limits to the group and hence to the culture. How accurately can one talk of an American culture when the United States includes a range of sub-groups claiming Caucasian, Black, Asian, Hispanic, Indian (etc.) American sub-cultures? And when should lines be drawn between Irish, English, Norwegian (etc.) Caucasian American sub-sub-cultures? And between Boston, New York (etc.) Irish Caucasian American sub-sub-sub-cultures? And so on.

Distinctions made sub-culture by sub-culture, region by region, class by class, city by city, block by block, make it difficult to generalize usefully for the entire national group. On the other hand, a general statement is of limited value in situations where sub-cultures have different priorities.

This ambiguity in the concept of the culture group has practical importance. Here are two examples. The difficulties that have arisen in creating a united Europe can be partly explained by the unwillingness of European enthusiasts to recognize the cultural differences that distinguish member nations and by their rushing to bridge these differences precipitously.

Second, the observer may need to change focus as events unfold, and this was shown before, during and after the Gulf War of 1991. Popular journalism often treats the Arabs as culturally homogeneous, and Arabs may themselves refer to the "Arab nation." They share classical Arabic – although spoken dialects of Arabic differ significantly. The great majority are Muslim (although belonging to many different sects).

It became clear that this monolithic concept was inadequate as preparations for fighting revealed varied interests and values expressed by Iraqis, Kuwaitis, Saudi Arabians, and Egyptians (who often distinguish themselves from the peninsular Arab peoples). During the fighting, Iraqi homogeneity was taken for granted. But the chaos that followed revealed cultural differences betweeen Kurdish Iraqis and Arab Iraqis, between the various Arab tribes that make up the population, and between adherents to Sunni Islam and Shi'ite Islam.

Viewed in these terms, the notion of "culture" is in part a construct created by the analyst for descriptive purposes. Similarly, the cross-cultural manager must be prepared to adjust his/her focus, sometimes equating the culture group with nation, sometimes with a supranational identity (for instance, Europe, the Arab world) and sometimes dealing with subnational ethnic, religious, and other groups (for instance Afro-Americans). This book adopts a similarly rough and ready solution to this problem of distinguishing cultural boundaries. The term "culture" usually refers here to a national culture (the American culture shared in common by Americans, the French culture by the French, etc.). But sub-cultures are differentiated where necessary.

1.3.5 Culture is learned

Culture is not programmed into the individual's genetic structure. It is learned – most intensively in the early years of life. By the age of five the individual is already an expert in using the language. He/she has also internalized values associated with:

- interacting with other members of the family;
- eliciting rewards and avoiding punishments;
- negotiating for what he/she wants;
- causing and avoiding conflict;

and so on.

These values are passed on by other members of the culture group. Culture is transmitted by parents, who are responsible for child-rearing and general enculturation; by other adults and institutions such as schools; and by peers (Berry and Cavalli-Sforza, 1986; discussed in Berry et al., 1992). Much of the transmitting and learning processes are unconscious.

The values become second nature and massively influence the individual's behavior in later life. They determine how the individual interprets the context of events that surround him/her; what he/she selects as important in the context, what needs to be explained and what can be taken as routine, and what can be edited out of consciousness as insignificant. They influence his/her behavior within an organization and expectations of others' behavior.

Because they have been acquired so early and often without conscious application, cultural values are extremely deep-rooted. They lie deeper than consciously acquired beliefs. This means that inevitable discrepancies between different cultures are often not consciously processed, and the causes of intercultural disputes are not resolved. The job of the cross-cultural manager is to raise differences to a conscious level where they can be consciously investigated.

1.3.6 Uniform and predictable influence

Their culture influences the behavior of members in uniform and predictable ways – within limits.

An understanding of the culture helps the manager predict behavior of typical members in normal situations. The general influence of childhood cultural learning does not obviate other psychological influences on individual and group behavior.

The individual's development is influenced by such other factors as:

- *gender stereotypes* Williams and Best (1982) carried out research into behavioral characteristics routinely associated with males and females across 25 countries; results showed large-scale differentiation in their respondents' views of how males and females behaved in all countries, and a broad consensus across countries;
- *sex–role ideology* while gender stereotypes reflect beliefs about the characteristics of males and females, sex role ideology communicates attitudes about how males and females *should* behave (Berry et al., 1992);
- *age* the individual's values shift as he/she grows older;
- *genetic transmission and development*;
- *social class.*

These factors, in addition to his/her culture and how that is learned, are vital influences on the individual's psychology and the choices that he/she makes in life. A focus on culture does not preclude psychology as an influence. The manager needs to develop psychological skills in order to predict how the individual will behave in different circumstances. But he/she cannot predict group behavior from their understanding of one person's feelings, experiences, etc. In general, psychological analysis is to the individual as cultural analysis is to the group.

All nations produce individualists as well as persons who prefer to express themselves within a group; all produce their workaholics, reclusives, extroverts, leaders, followers, etc. The manager cannot expect to deduce the predominant characteristics of the culture from the evidence provided by one member any more than he/she can restrict predictions of the individual's behavior to the culture model alone.

1.3.7 The importance of culture as against other factors

At no point does this book suggest that culture is the only significant determinant of behavior. On the contrary, other factors in the wider environment are always likely to intervene.

For instance, organizational decisions are influenced by:

- market factors, including demand for products and services; supply of capital, material, labor; the activities of competitors, opportunities, and threats;
- national and international economic factors;
- technology; needs for it; its availability, its implementation within the organization;
- industry values;
- laws and regulations;
- activities of trade unions, consumer groups, etc.;
- organizational culture;
- individual psychology.

The importance of culture can never be ignored, even when its influence is indirect. For instance, the demand for a certain range of products shows increasing instability, and management makes the decision to halt production of its older models and to rapidly switch to a new product line. This switch means investing in new plant and skills.

The decision might appear to be determined entirely by market factors – analysis of future market conditions. But it also reflects

- a strong willingness to plan for the future;
- a strong willingness to invest resources in future development.

That is, it reflects tolerances of risk and optimism that future time can be managed. These reflect values that cultures share in very different respects. A company situated within a different cultural context might respond to the same environmental events very differently – for instance, by channeling more resources into improving the quality of its existing product line, increasing its advertising budget, perhaps selling out.

In this case, culture may not cause the events in the market place, but it does influence how the two different firms respond to them.

When analyzing behavior within the workplace, the first problem for the manager is to decide how directly culture influences behavior, and how far it is peripheral to the explanation.

The introductory case gave one illustration. Here is a second. A Latin American exchange student was staying with an American family. He noticed that the mother of the family always sliced a joint of beef in two before baking it in the oven, and asked why "you Americans do that." The mother was unable to answer and asked her own mother, from whom she had learnt the habit; the grandmother also could not explain, and asked her sister. "Because when we were small, we didn't have a baking pan large enough to take a full joint, so mother cut it."

When he asked his question, the student took for granted that culture was the intervening variable. In practice, it turned out that although the behavior was learned (like culture) it owed nothing to group values, but was decided by entirely idiosyncratic circumstances.

1.4 Managing Cultural Diversity

The opportunities and difficulties of cross-cultural management are illustrated by the management of cultural diversity in work groups, when the group includes representatives from two or more cultures.

The successful management of diversity brings economic benefits. Cox and Blake (1991) argue that the organization's ability to attract, retain, and motivate people from diverse cultural backgrounds gives it competitive advantages in cost structures, creativity, problem-solving, and adapting to change.

Cultural diversity presents major opportunities for synergy. The term "synergy" refers to the output of two or more individuals or groups working in cooperation when this is greater than the combined output of their working separately.

The mixed-culture group offers a situation in which synergetic cooperation is possible. Members contribute a wider range of educational, professional, and cultural experiences than they would to a single-culture group. In appropriate circumstances they are more successful.

Shaw (1983) found that mixed groups outperformed homogeneous groups on complex problem-solving tasks.

In experiments with diverse and homogeneous groups over 17 weeks, Watson et al. (1993) discovered that when groups were newly formed, diversity constrained process and performance, but that in time the heterogeneous groups caught up and in some respects (identifying problem perspectives, generating solution alternatives) outperformed the homogenous groups. Overall performance remained the same for both; nevertheless, the implication is that where the task is open-ended and a range of alternative outcomes is desirable, the culturally diverse group is to be preferred.

This and other studies suggest that diverse groups need time to resolve process difficulties. Anderson (1983) examined group cohesion when both cultural and sexual differences needed to be overcome (Caucasian and Polynesian male and female managers). Eventually the experience of working together should significantly help break down racial, functional and organizational prejudices (Kanter and Mirvis, 1989, pp. 177–8). But synergetic effects can never be precisely calculated and the creation of a mixed-culture group is a risky undertaking. If successful, is is profitable both in terms of immediate results and the creation of goodwill for the future. If it fails, negative stereotypes are reinforced.

The group is more likely to be synergistic when members:

- value the exchange of alternative points of view;
- tolerate uncertainty in group processes;
- cooperate to build group decisions;
- respect each others' experiences and share their own;
- use the exposure to others' cultural values as a positive opportunity for cross-cultural learning;
- can overcome the misunderstandings and inefficiencies that result from members of different cultures working together.

1.4.1 Cultural and non-cultural influences on group commitment

The cultural profiles of the persons concerned influence how far they commit to the group's activities. Cox et al. (1991) experimented with groups of Asian, Black, Hispanic and Anglo American subjects; the former three represented collectivist, or group-centered cultures, and the latter an individualist culture. (The meanings of "collectivist" and "individualist" cultures are discussed further in chapter 3.) They discovered that

- groups composed of the collectivist individuals acted cooperatively more often than did the groups composed solely of individualists;

- under task conditions when cooperative behavior was expected from others, the collectivists tended to increase their level of cooperative behavior but the individualists did not. This pattern occurred in both single-culture groups and diverse groups.

This implies that management can increase the likelihood of synergy in a diverse group by adjusting the cultural mix. Management also controls a range of other factors that significantly raise the chances of success. It capitalizes upon cultural diversity by:

- enlisting top management's support for the group;
- setting a task that demands a creative and non-routine response (for instance, designing alternative solutions to a problem);
- giving the group time to overcome process difficulties;
- investing in diversity training; collecting, analyzing, and applying information pertaining to diversity-related issues (Cox and Blake, 1991);
- providing administrative support; facilities, opportunity to meet in work hours, etc.;
- rewarding commitment; working to overcome problems.

1.4.2   The alternative: ignoring diversity

Nevertheless, the successful management of diversity is not easy and may be expensive in terms of adjustment time, training costs, and mistakes. Cross-cultural relationships impose stresses and strains; members of different cultures value different priorities, and differences in language and culture can cause serious misunderstandings.

The escape from attempting to manage cultural diversity is to ignore it. This means that management:

- ignores cultural differences within the work force;
- down-plays the significance of cultural differences.

This strategy is followed when

- management lacks the skills and resources to handle diversity;
- the task offers no opportunities for deriving positive effects from diversity;
- the negative effects outweigh the positive effects;
- refusing to recognize diversity seems likely to minimize the negative effects.

This strategy may work when culture groups are assigned different tasks and beyond sharing essential resources are otherwise independent. (Thompson, 1967, refers to this as pooled integration.) But when groups and group members are reciprocally integrated and need to collaborate, deep-seated ambiguities arise from not recognizing cultural differences.

This strategy of ignoring diversity can easily fail, while the opportunities for applying it to competitive advantage are sacrificed (Adler, 1991, p. 104). We can go further and argue that as cultural diversity becomes the norm in many organizations, a failure to recognize and manage it courts failure, and may ultimately bring disaster.

1.5 Implications for the Manager

How can the material covered in section 1.4 above be applied to your organization? Answer these questions.

1. In what departments of your organization are a range of cultures represented?

    - What cultures are represented?

2. In each department, is this cultural diversity managed or ignored?

3. If it is managed,

    - what tasks are allocated to the diverse group?
    - what benefits arise from diversity?
    - what problems arise?
    - how could the diversity be better managed?

4. If it is not managed,

    - what are the obstacles to recognizing and managing diversity?
    - how could these obstacles be overcome?

1.6 Summary

This short introductory chapter has focused on the importance of developing cross-cultural skills and applying them to manage cultural diversity. Many of the themes discussed here are developed in greater detail in later chapters.

Section 1.2 showed *why cross-cultural management skills are important.* An increasing number of firms conduct their business on a global basis, and the manager needs cross-cultural skills in order to work with superiors, subordinates, peers, negotiation partners, and others in foreign-based organizations. The costs of poor intercultural relations are correspondingly growing.

Section 1.3 outlined the *definition* of *culture* applied in this book. Values (and to a lesser extent beliefs and attitudes) give a more precise indication of behavior in the culture group than do the explicit alternatives – including material culture, religion, and ideology. A culture is specific to a group, is learned, and in normal circumstances influences the behavior of members in uniform and predictable ways. In any given situation, the influence of culture has to be weighed against that of other factors.

Section 1.4 showed that when properly *managed, cultural diversity* brings great benefits to the organization. The process is not easy; simply assembling a multicultural group does not guarantee synergy. Some companies may choose to ignore the challenges posed by a multicultural workforce – but given the continuing globalization of business, this becomes an increasingly risky alternative.

1.7   Exercises

These exercises demonstrate how perceptions of reality are determined by values and needs. Just as individuals may share experiences but evaluate them differently, so members of different culture groups have different priorities.

Exercise 1

1. Write five lines of notes on the most significant *advantages* and *disadvantages* of living in your community. Write from the point of view of an above-average income member of the community.
2. Now imagine yourself into other roles, and write similar notes for each. Alternately, ask your colleagues to take on one of these roles and write notes.

    - a below-average income member;
    - a member of a racial minority;
    - a member of a religious minority;
    - the opposite sex/child/old person/disabled person;
    - a cyclist/pedestrian/driver/user of public transport;
    - a sports fan/art enthusiast/gourmet;
    - and so on.

3. Compare the sets of notes. You can expect each role to have listed very different priorities. The lack of common priorities illustrates how perceptions of the same reality differ, depending upon experience and needs, and the priorities of the group to which you belong.

Exercise 2

Behavior that is thought desirable and normal in one cultural context might be thought undesirable and deviant elsewhere.

1. Write a list of behaviors which members of your culture think desirable. Why might a member of some other culture perceive each of these as undesirable? In what sort of culture would each be thought of as undesirable?

    For instance, if you belong to one of the Anglo cultures, you might list "competitiveness" as desirable. But some other cultures equate competitiveness with aggression, and dislike it as likely to cause conflict and disruption. A culture that makes this interpretation places a premium on harmony and social cohesion.

2. Now list five behaviors that your culture considers undesirable. Why might members of some other culture perceive each to be desirable? What could this tell you about the other culture?

Notes

1. Piya Angkinand, "Of fear and honour," *Bangkok Post*, January 25, 1991.
2. T. R. Reid, "Silence wears thin on Japan's media in royal mating quest," *International Herald Tribune*, November 12, 1992.
3. Reuters, "U.K. press grinds out new grist on Charles," *International Herald Tribune*, November 14–15, 1992.

2

Doing Your Own Analysis

2.1 Introduction

This story says something about how Americans express their values:

> It might not be the same as having their art displayed at the US Capitol, but an exhibition of Barrington High School artwork in River North, Chicago's hottest gallery district, is closer to home and nearer to the students' hearts.
>
> By choosing to boycott an art competition sponsored by US Rep. Philip Crane (R-Ill.), who is opposed to federal funding of the arts, the students passed up a chance to have their work displayed in the halls of the capitol in Washington. But taking a stand has been worth it, some of the students say.
>
> "Stand up for what you believe in, and you can make a difference," said 14-year-old freshman Tim McLoughlin.[1]

This illustrates the American belief in individualism and in taking a stand for your beliefs, even when you are in a minority. Appearing in an American newspaper, it reinforces readers' cultural self-perceptions, and provides the outsider with an insight into that culture. And, as a later section shows, it illustrates the problems that arise in using secondary data – in this case, newspaper journalism – to investigate values.

The cross-cultural manager cannot always depend upon published research (discussed in the next chapter) in order to learn about the culture in which he/she is working. It may be undergoing rapid transformations that make all available findings outdated; or he/she is working with members of a sub-culture that has not been studied; or an organizational culture restricts the value of analysis of the national culture. When these conditions apply, the manager who needs to supplement scholarly analysis conducts his/her own informal research (Agar, 1980).

For precise answers to behavioral questions, fine-grained statistical methods are needed (Harrigan, 1983). But few managers have the time to conduct large-scale research into culture. The data sources and methods discussed here provide answers that may be rough and ready, but are often adequate.

The chapter shows how to do such analysis. It is organized as follows;

2.2   Stereotypes and Generalizations

Human beings need to generalize about their environments in order to operate efficiently. For instance, suppose that you are going into a meeting with a new group of employees. You prepare yourself on the basis of your

- assumptions about their past experiences, qualifications, capacities;
- predictions of their needs;
- experiences with similar groups.

And if you made no such generalizations and treated them as an entirely new phenomenon, your meeting with them would last a very long time before you eventually decided on what action was required.

The cross-cultural manager likewise needs to make generalizations about members of the other culture. But this is not easy when he/she lacks understanding of their values and experience of their typical behavior.

One way of generalizing about other people is to stereotype them on the basis of their ethnic identity, culture, occupation, age, sex, etc. Stereotyping – using fixed images – is normal when faced with a new reality. Ratiu (1983) found that all the 250 young executives in his research sample used cultural stereotypes to some degree. The "most international"

> use them self-consciously and tentatively, as if recognizing the stereotype as no more than a temporary hold on an elusive reality. . . . The other managers use cultural stereotypes unself-consciously and conclusively, suggesting that the stereotype is indeed a valid and stable categorization that is somehow inherent in the world "out there." (p. 142)

But the stereotype is *not* inherent in the world "out there." The manager is unlikely to be effective when he/she continues to respond to the other culture in terms of stereotypes, even in the light of experience. As Ratiu indicates, the best managers break their dependence on stereotypes as early as possible.

This section deals with the problems of ethnocentric stereotyping, when the individual measures some other culture in relation to his/her own (LeVine and Campbell, 1972). It develops techniques for making flexible interpretations that reflect and rationalize growing experience. It maps out a comparative approach, by which the individual analyses the other culture objectively, in terms of its members' own needs and beliefs, which may differ radically from his/her own.

2.2.1   Inflexible stereotyping

Inflexible stereotypes are generalizations that do not allow for change or exceptions to the norm. They lump together all members of the stereotyped group, regardless of objective evidence.

Here is an example; a British–American study group arranged by the then British Prime Minister, Mrs Thatcher, to consider German reunification, resulted in a memorandum on the German character. Listed German characteristics included

> unsensitivity, self-obsession, a strong inclination to self-pity and a longing to be liked. Others mentioned were: *angst*, aggressiveness, assertiveness, bullying, egotism, inferiority complex, sentimentality. Two further German traits were cited as reasons for concern about the future: a capacity for excess, to overdo things and a tendency to over-estimate their strengths and capabilities.[2]

National and ethnic stereotypes are long lasting, and survive political and international upheavals. Many of the stereotypes that Eastern European nations have of each other predate the Communist takeovers of the late 1940s and the 1939–45 war.

> Beyond Poland's borders there is a common view that all Poles are lazy crooks. East Germans are regarded as potential Fascists, Czechs as snobs, and Hungarians as stubbornly weird. Outsiders, like the Vietnamese Gasterbeiter, have borne the brunt of the region's intolerance. (Glenny, 1990, p. 7)

Within the region, prejudices against outsiders were exploited by the ruling Communists as a means of deflecting attention from the political and economic deficiencies of their regimes. Romanian and Jewish minorities were most commonly targeted.

Stereotyped thinking disregards evidence that contradicts the fixed image, or distorts it to fit. Suppose that "everyone knows" that members of Culture A are poorly motivated. How does the stereotyper deal with a member of A who works 16 hours a day? These explanations for the disparity between stereotype and reality all try to protect the stereotype intact and to disvalue the individual case:

"It's not real work. It's just routine that anyone could do."
  "That's just to create a good first impression. After a couple of weeks he'll give up trying, like all the rest."

When the individual cannot be fitted within the stereotype, the stereotyper can take the route of distinguishing him/her from apparently similar persons.

  You're not like those other whites/blacks/men/etc.

This appears to be treating the individual as favored and a special case. But the stereotyping is not weakened; rather it is still assumed that "those others" will conform to it.

These examples show negative stereotyping. But positive stereotypes that patronize can be equally misleading. Assumptions that all members of Culture A are "cute," "hard working," "honest," etc., show similar lack of thought and may be as costly when contradicted by an individual instance.

2.2.2 The costs of fixed stereotyping

Fixed stereotyping is offensive; it can also be expensive. Changes in the international business environment over the past decade indicate how dangerous it can be to stereotype the business acumen of business people from less developed countries on the basis of historical experience.

  Similarly, the businessman who assumes that women are incapable of sustained logical thinking or forceful action may be unpleasantly surprised by reality. Laffin (1982) discusses the factors that led the Argentinian leaders to invade the British possessions of the Falkland Islands in 1982. When they underestimated the determination of British Prime Minister Margaret Thatcher, they

  made a major sexist miscalculation. . . .
    This error of judgement is understandable, because Argentinian men, from the president down to a schoolboy, are victims of machismo. . . .
  [When Mrs Thatcher became leader of her party and then Prime Minister]

the Argentinian generals assumed that she was the result of a compromise made by strong men with equal following. Therefore, she would be dominated by the men who had put her into the leadership.

The Galtieri Junta reasoned that no woman would want war; further, no woman could politically direct a war. Accustomed to facing down and conquering women in their own society, the Argentinian leaders really believed that Mrs Thatcher was the weak link of the British government. (p. 17)

The Argentinian defeat in the war, and the subsequent ousting of the Junta showed that this was an expensive mistake.

2.2.3   Creative generalizations

The manager who generalizes creatively is continually readjusting his/her conceptual map of the other culture in the light of new evidence. The more sophisticated the generalization, the better it can handle new information.

Stereotyping is static when it force-fits experiences into given explanatory categories. Effective generalization is dynamic because experience serves to modify the explanatory categories. It helps to

- explain the causes of the behavior that is of interest, including the conditions for it to happen and not happen, and the factors upon which variations depend;
- explain the consequences of the behavior;
- predict circumstances under which similar behaviors, with similar causes and consequences, can occur.

The differences between fixed stereotyping and creative generalizing are shown in table 2.1.

2.3   The Process of Analysis

The cross-cultural manager builds creative generalizations through a process of cultural analysis. This process has six stages:

Stages in cultural analysis

1. identifying behavior which seems incongruous and has to be explained;
2. collecting data about the incongruous behavior;
3. developing a set of hypotheses to explain this behavior;
4. testing these hypotheses;

Table 2.1 Fixed stereotyping vs creative generalization

	Fixed stereotyping	*Creative generalization*
Attitude to the other culture	Static, inflexible	Dynamic, flexible
Attitude to new experience	Selective	Explanatory
Attitude to experience that contradicts the stereotype/ generalization	Disregarded	Applied
Attitude to the stereotype/ generalization	To be protected at all costs	Always liable to modification
Source of the stereotype/ generalization	Received	Created

5. selecting the most likely hypothesis; this gives a working generalization about the other culture;
6. in the light of further experience, correcting the hypothesis.

These stages are discussed in the remaining sections.

2.3.1 Incongruity

The newcomer to a culture is most likely to notice and to question such behavior in the local culture that appears unusual and unexpected – in terms of his/her own culture.

For example, Reddy (1989), an Indian anthropologist, conducted a study of a Danish village – perhaps the first study ever made by a Third World anthropologist in an industrial country. The village demonstrated

> an almost complete lack of community ... Some people did not know their neighbours, let alone go constantly in and out of each other's houses, as they do in the professor's region in India.
>
> To an Indian, used to close relations with an extended family, the Danish family was hardly recognizable. Children, he considers, are brought up to be independent and lonely. The accent on individualism, he suspects, is one reason why, when young adults begin to pair off with each other, they find it hard to stay together: their egos get too easily in each other's way.[3]

Reddy questions behavior that is incongruent in terms of the norms taken for granted in his own culture. Similarly, the cross-cultural manager might soon begin to notice the following when they do not correspond to behaviors in his/her own culture:

- how members of the culture greet each other;
- how they behave in the presence of superiors and subordinates;
- how decisions are taken and communicated;
- how conflicts erupt and how they are resolved;
- how much importance is given to starting work promptly on time, and arriving on time for an appointment;
- what factors motivate performance.

The analyst identifies and questions the following modes of behavior.

- That which occurs within the local culture but does not occur within his/her own culture. For instance, Asian cultures such as India, Sri Lanka, Thailand, Laos, Cambodia often greet each other by placing the palms of their hands together at the level of their eyes in a gesture of respect. This gesture (known variously – for instance, as *namaste* in Hindi and *wai* in Thai) is not used by Westerners in their cultures.

- That which occurs within both the local and his/her own cultures, but has a different significance within each. In Western cultures, holding hands by a couple in public usually indicates an intimate relationship. This is still not normal between adult males. In India, a married or engaged couple do not usually hold hands, but a male couple – friends or male relatives – commonly do.

- That which occurs within his/her own culture but apparently not in the local culture. The problem then is to discover what alternative forms of behavior substitute to express the same meaning. The Thai manager coming to an Anglo country realizes that his *wai* is not appropriate within this different context. Under what circumstances should he/she express a greeting by behavior (such as shaking hands, an embrace, a slap on the back, a salute, a wave), perhaps supplemented by a verbal greeting only (an informal "Hi," a more formal "How do you do?").

2.3.2 Rationality, non-rationality, and irrationality

The ethnocentric manager assumes that only behavior reflecting values found in his/her culture is rational, and so should be common to all other cultures. When members of the other culture fail to behave in accordance with his/her models, he/she condemns their behavior as irrational.

This position is false. All cultures survive and adapt because they are essentially rational, but this does not mean that the same models of rationality apply. What is rational behavior in one context may not be in another.

However, we should not go to the reverse extreme and assume that all behavior performed by the members of the other culture is rational in their own terms. All societies use sanctions to punish and correct members who do not conform. The existence of institutions for those labeled criminal or insane shows that not everyone succeeds in behaving according to the rules and norms.

The cross-cultural manager needs to adopt a comparative attitude towards cultural differences and to distinguish when local behavior seems rational, and when irrational, in terms of local values. Three cases illustrate dimensions of this problem.

First: New York banks commonly set aside private dining rooms for the use of their senior executives and directors. One bank decided to renovate its dining suite, then encountered resistance from its executives when they were requested to lunch with junior executives in their dining room (where the cuisine was the same). Top management only overcame this difficulty by fitting up a vacant room for temporary accommodation until the regular suite had been restored to its previous glory.

Second: a few years ago, a successful Thai businessman used to attend meetings escorted by an entourage of aides who contributed very rarely, and only when asked point blank for a technical detail which had escaped his prodigious memory. This practice was expensive; the aides were taken away from their regular duties and when the venue was overseas, the businessman covered the costs of their travel and accommodation.

Third: a British manufacturer signed a deal with a local supplier, then suffered a number of financial reverses which made it imposssible for him to pay for the contracted goods. Frustrated and angry, he reacted by publicly accusing the supplier of welching on the deal, although all the evidence pointed in the opposite direction, and then by insulting him at a local chamber of commerce meeting. The supplier took him to court and successfully sued for defamation of character.

The first two cases describe behavior which may appear irrational to the outsider. But if by irrationality is meant illogical behavior not directed towards desired ends, the term is inappropriate here.

The bankers' dining room indicates their status in the organization, buttresses the morale of those lucky enough to use it, motivates junior executives aspiring to join the privileged elite, and flatters and impresses visitors. All in all, it is good for business, and given the values that the culture associates with earned privilege, conforms to the culture's notions of rationality.

The entourage with which the Thai businessman surrounded himself might appear a matter of personal vanity. But this behavior was rational within the cultural context. He demonstrated to his negotiation counterparts that he controlled a large organization, loyal to his person. This symbolic demonstration of power and dependability was easily understood by other South-east Asians.

In the third case, the British manufacturer's behavior was irrational in terms of local values. His problems had arisen from his dealings with other persons, not this particular supplier. His actions did nothing to relieve the cause of frustration, and landed him in court, thus multiplying his difficulties.

Whereas irrational behavior bears no relationship to desired ends, rational and non-rational behaviors are consciously aimed at achieving these ends. Rational behavior is logically linked to them, and this is apparent both to the performer and to others who understand the ends and the means used to achieve them. Non-rationality is an ascriptive category; if I do not understand the connection between your behavior and ends but can still assume that there must be a link, I label your behavior non-rational.

This has important implications for the cross-cultural manager. In time he/she aims to develop a double vision; identifying what is non-rational to him/herself but rational in local culture terms, and how far his/her own "rational" behavior is non-rational in local terms.

2.3.3   Symbols

The first two cases above involve the skilful use of symbols. A symbol can be defined as any object or event that refers to some other thing. Symbolism involves three elements; the symbol itself, what it refers to, and the relationship between symbol and referrant (Leech, 1976). And the audience must be competent to recognize and understand the relationship.

In these instances, the executive dining room and the team of silent aides both make statements about the possessor's authority and power. They are effective because the symbolic communication is recognized and respected by the intended audience.

Symbols are sometimes contrasted to "substance" as though only the latter had lasting meaning. For instance, a writer in an American newspaper commented on the appointment of a new governor of the Bank of England:

> the change of the guard . . . is more a matter of symbols than substance.
> . . . Mr George has to date confined himself to pronouncements on detail.

Last month he polished up his image as a hard-liner on inflation by announcing that he would forego a raise through his five-year term. He also set a more egalitarian tone to management by rejecting his traditional due in the company car, the governor's Rolls Royce, in favor of his Jaguar.[4]

But when symbolic behavior is respected and creates authority, the distinction between symbol and substance disappears:

The consensus is that greater power lies within reach of Mr George, but it will take years and numerous changes within the bank to bring it out of its long period of isolation.[5]

Industries such as television, advertising, and public relations are principally concerned with creating symbols. Considerable sums are invested in creating symbols that appropriately communicate organizational messages to employees, business partners and customers. In 1991 British Telecom planned to spend £60 million

changing its image from a "fuddy-duddy state industry" to a "new thrusting commercial organization."

The money will be spent over three years embellishing stationery, buildings, 95,000 telephone boxes and 70,000 vans, and providing polka dot dresses and designer overalls for staff with a logo designed to depict a dynamic and caring company.[6]

To a great extent, all managerial roles are centrally concerned with creating and interpreting powerful symbols (Pfeffer, 1981; Smircich, 1983). Managers influence other people by using symbols that have meaning to these persons and that motivate them towards desired ends. Hofstede (1984b) writes that

[a]n example of such a symbol is a memorandum written by the manager to announce a change in procedure. Its effect depends on a complex set of pre-programmed interpretations by the receivers; whether they can read, whether they understand the language used, whether they respect the legitimacy of this decision by this manager, whether they consider the style of the memo appropriate to their status, whether they are accustomed to react on written messages, whether they consider themselves as competent to take the requested steps, etc. (p. 82)

Managers tend to take for granted the rationality of the symbols they commonly use in their own cultures. An Anglo manager selects the memo as the most "efficient" way of communicating a message, and therefore its use seems obviously rational, and hence may not be aware of it as a symbol. But the memo is efficient, and rational, only so long as the conditions listed by Hofstede apply in this particular cultural context. Where face-to-face communication is a more efficient means of persuading peers and immediate subordinates, sending instructions by memo is likely to be resented as rudely impersonal. And so here the memo is *not* the most efficient or rational means of managing change.

Symbols rooted in some other culture appear exotic (Gregory, 1983, p. 364). The significance of a symbol in some other culture is obscure to the outsider unless he/she understands the context from which the relationship between symbol and referrant derives its meaning. The manager should beware of dismissing a symbol in the other culture as "irrational," merely because it does not have a referrant in his/her culture, or has a different referrant. The important point is to ask what meaning it conveys within the culture to which it is rooted.

2.4 Using Data

Workable hypotheses designed to explain apparently incongruous behavior are developed on the basis of data that have been systematically collected. Collection is systematized by using a framework of categories.

Framework for systematizing data

- *What* typically happens; the behavior (e.g., giving an order, displaying courtesy) and streams of related activities (e.g., the process involved in implementing a plan, initiating a project, corruption).[7]
- *How* the behavior is typically performed.
- *Who* typically participates.
- *How* do the participants typically contribute.
- *What* implements, data, etc. are typically employed.
- *Where* the behavior is typically performed.
- *When* the behavior is typically performed.

This framework does *not* include an obvious eighth category:

- *Why* does the behavior occur? What are its overt purposes and goals? What other functions does it serve?

These other functions may be hidden from participants themselves. For instance, when shopkeeper and customer haggle over the price of a good in a small neighborhood shop – the norm in some cultures – they are doing more than just fixing a fair price. They are also maintaining a social relationship, a vital activity in a collectivist culture but less significant where values are more individualist. But except in the unlikely event that shopkeeper and customer are also trained sociologists, they would not be expected to offer this explanation of their behavior.

Discovering *why* is the reason for conducting the analysis at all; but answers to *why* questions are essentially hypothesis-building, and so are dealt with in section 2.5.

2.4.1 Analysis of a greeting

How this framework is applied can be demonstrated by considering in a specific context the first point listed in section 2.3,

- how members of the culture greet each other.

It has been noted that greetings in Thailand are made by a *wai*. The gesture is unlike anything seen in the West, and Westerners are quick to question its equivalence to a handshake. The framework can be used to generate relevant data about the *wai*.

- ***What*** *typically happens?*
  An individual (or individuals) makes a *wai* to some other individual (or individuals). Inanimate objects which have major symbolic import-ance – such as a religious shrine or a spirit house – may be *wai*ed.

  When the *wai* is made at the beginning and end of a social en-counter (see *When* below) it is usually accompanied by an appropriate speech act: for instance, *sawadii* – used both as a greeting and leave-taking;

- ***How*** *is the* wai *made?*
  The person wishing to make a *wai* first catches the eye of the recipi-ent. The palms of both hands are placed together. The person making the *wai* shows particular respect by bowing the head and positioning the hands so that finger tips are adjacent to the top of the nose, or even between the eyes. The deeper the *wai*, the greater the degree of respect shown. But this must be appropriate, given the relation-ship between the persons and the occasion.

- ***Who*** *makes the* wai?
  The junior first makes a *wai* to the senior and the senior recipro-cates. Age often, but not always, determines seniority. For instance, in one company, the supervisors regularly *wai* their factory manager first, although he is young enough to be their son – but he is a close relative of the owner. They also *wai* his wife first – and she is even younger.

  Persons of equal social standing and seniority perhaps only *wai* each other on formal occasions or when meeting after a long absence; when they do, they make their *wai*s at the same time.

*Wai*s are exchanged between persons who already have a relationship or expect to have a relationship – for instance, are being newly introduced or introducing themselves.

A *wai* has to be acknowledged. Usually it is reciprocated by an answering *wai* and when the persons are close in seniority and rank, a failure to reciprocate may be highly insulting. But there are exceptional cases, when reciprocation is not expected. For instance; when senior and junior are widely differentiated by age and rank – such as in a restaurant – an acknowledgement such as nodding is sufficient.

- **Where** *is the* wai *made?*
  A *wai* is made both when you are in physical proximity to the other person, and at a distance – for instance, across a room.

  In a formal presentation, the speaker may *wai* his/her audience at the beginning and end. Television newsreaders also wai their audience;

- **When** *is the* wai *made?*
  When the persons are meeting in a "polite" or formal encounter, the *wai* is made both at the beginning and at the end, on leave-taking. A *wai* is not always expected when the persons meet on a daily basis – for instance, the boss and his/her secretary; but when they are appropriate, they are exchanged only at the first meeting of the day. *Wai*s are also made by a junior to express thanks for a significant gift or favor.

2.4.2 Sources of data

Second-hand insights help the manager develop a functional understanding when they describe routine behavior and values that he/she can expect to experience. They are of less value when they describe freak behavior or reflect fixed stereotypic thinking and bias. The practical problems that arise are discussed throughout this section.

Sources of information about the society and culture include:

- agencies, reports, etc.;
- journalism; newspaper stories and magazine articles; television and radio; other media;
- other outsiders, including other expatriate managers;
- members of the local culture;
- scholarly analysis – discussed in the next chapter.

All present disadvantages as well as advantages. The manager does not accept a source without question, and is continually supplementing and checking information derived from one source against others (Goodman and Kruger, 1988).

2.4.3   Official bodies, reports, etc.

Technical information, and often cultural data, is offered by the following:

Official bodies, including:

- your country's department of commerce/foreign trade, foreign ministry;
- the other country's embassy, consulate, trade missions, trade associations; for instance, the Japanese External Trade Organization (JETRO);
- international organizations; agencies of the United Nations; the International Trade Association (ITA); the International Monetary Fund (IMF);
- international banks, that are represented in the other country; for instance, the Asian Development Bank;
- trade/professional associations.

Reports, etc., including:

- reports issued by the agencies listed above;
- specialist reports; for instance, *The Economist* "Country Reports;"
- specialist year books;
- the financial press (e.g., *Financial Times, Wall Street Journal,* and their regional editions);
- conference and seminar reports;
- trade publications;
- in-house material published by companies in the other culture; e.g., company reports, newsletters, etc.

Some of these sources provide information free; others may prove expensive. They should all be used with an eye open for conscious or unconscious bias. For instance, the prime purpose of government agencies is to represent their national interests; and statistical information is often open to a number of interpretations other than that supplied.

2.4.4   Journalism

Journalism seldom meets the needs of scholars, but often provides the working manager with useful insights. So long as he/she is alive to the problems that it offers, it can be usefully applied. The focus is on print journalism, although the same points apply to television and radio journalism.

Journalism offers the advantages that:

- the supply of material is continuous;
- the material has immediacy, and is up-to-date;
- material that includes lengthy quotation may give insights into the thinking of insiders.

However, it provides only secondary data, and thus presents interpretation difficulties (Dobbert, 1982, pp. 180–3). A story reflects bias – of persons quoted, journalists, editors, proprietors, the predicted audience.

This bias may be witting or unwitting. An example of deliberate bias is provided by the excerpt used in the introductory case. This story reflects editorial opposition to the politician in question, and support for the federal funding of the arts. (A newspaper sympathetic to his views might have taken a very different approach towwards these events – or ignored them altogether.)

Unwitting bias creeps in when the journalist is describing events in some other culture than his/her own, and hence is processing them in terms of his/her own cultural viewpoint.

An example is provided by an interview conducted by an Italian woman journalist with Iceland's President, Ms Vigdis Finnbogadottir. The questions and answers make clear that the two women come from cultures that view women's role very differently. The reporter suggests

> by electing you the Icelanders have expressed a tribute to the memory of their mothers and to the women who waited for a lifetime the report of a warrior's boat . . .[8]

She makes clear her own feminist concerns and her question says more about the role of the woman and mother in Italian culture than about Icelandic values. (The President goes on to explain why Scandinavian women have always had an important role as administrators and why feminism has nothing to do with it.)

Because journalism is interpretive, the manager who used it to uncover cultural values needs to keep in mind the following: First, most journalism focuses on behavior (events) rather than values. But a unique event does not help you predict future behavior; an understanding of the values does. Hence, journalistic descriptions of events should be read critically, always asking yourself what values generate them.

Second, journalism often focuses on aberrant behavior. Behavior is aberrant when it is untypical and hence gives a negative reflection of values. In a culture that rewards honesty in dealing with state authorities, the politician who fails to pay his/her taxes makes the front page but the honesty of colleagues who do is ignored. So when the story focuses on untypical behavior, it may be primarily of interest because of any explanation it gives as to *why* the event is unusual. In such a case, you discover the culture by inferring the norms that make the event news-worthy, not through the event itself.

Third, a story must be read in terms of its context. It may reflect values that are typical of the culture but are manifested in behavior considered extreme within the *specific* context. The introductory story gives an example; 14-year-old Americans do not normally express fundamental attitudes so forcefully.

Fourth, journalism is ephemeral; most newspaper stories are "dead" the day after publication. (In contrast, academic studies have a longer shelf-life.) And newspaper readers want crisp, succinct stories. These market pressures can lead to journalists oversimplifying complex issues and assuming greater certainty in their reporting than is justified; X is certainly going to happen, prevailing values are certainly Z.

2.4.5 Outsiders

Outsiders who can supply useful data consist of persons who have worked and socialized with members of the group, either in the local environment or elsewhere (Dean, Eichorn, and Dean, 1967, p. 285). They know the culture well, but have not become entirely assimilated, and are capable of making objective assessments. Their ability to make friendships with members of the other culture does not impair their capacity to make discerning and articulate analyses.

Useful outsiders include persons who can be tapped before you travel to the other country – such as members of your own organization who have previously worked in the culture, consultants, faculty from university departments and research institutes (and not limited to management schools).

The manager at post consults diplomats and senior business people. But he/she is wise not to restrict sources to those dealing with the local culture from positions of power and influence. Cultivate journalists and visiting academics. In some societies priests and missionaries may be helpful. Talk to visiting students and volunteers who know the culture from a lower social level, and to the newcomer who may be alive to subtleties which the jaded long-termer no longer clearly perceives.

Using outsiders presents both *advantages* and *disadvantages*. The *advantages* are:

- as non-members of the culture, they are more able to be objective about features which members take for granted;
- when they are also members of your culture and share your own values, you have a common base from which to evaluate the other culture;

- when they are also members of your own culture, you share with them a common language, which may not be the case with members of the local culture;
- you can learn from their mistakes;
- there is less risk of upsetting local sensibilities by asking unintentionally offensive questions.

The *disadvantages* are:

- outsiders make mistakes, which may not be apparent to either them or you;
- they do not see the big picture; they blow insignificant details out of proportion;
- they may adopt fixed stereotypes about the other culture;
- particularly when they do not speak the local language, outsiders can never entirely share and understand the values.

Beware of depending upon outsider groups that are radically isolated from the host culture. In the worst cases, they are prey to a siege mentality that expresses itself in paranoia and negative stereotyping. Their isolation is worsened when their only sources of "real" information about local events are official government sources, for instance at ministry levels.

The expatriate manager who ignores grassroot cultural values is out of touch with his/her end-markets. This was demonstrated in Iran during the 1978 revolution. Even a few weeks before the Shah's overthrow, many expatriate companies continued to accept the government's assurances that all was well, and ignored the evidence of a fundamental crisis at lower levels in the society (Gillespie, 1989). They had been well-briefed by senior officials, but knew nothing of attitudes held at street level.

2.4.6 Observing insiders

Methods of discovering how insiders experience their culture include the following:

- trial-and-error participation; for instance, by participating with insiders in performance of a task, where appropriate;
- observation;
- interviewing and questioning.

This section focuses on participation and observation.

Participant observation is usually an essential prerequisite to interviewing and is a strategy that facilitates further data gathering (Bernard,

1988, pp. 150–1). By observing actively, the analyst begins to formulate answers to such questions as:

- *What* is the task?
- *Who* typically performs the task? What different roles do the participants take and who decides? Who is excluded and why?
- *Who* communicates with whom in performing the task and how?
- *How* is the task performed? What counts as acceptable performance? What technologies are used?

Observation (like all methods of data analysis) needs to be organized so that you collect an adequate and manageable quantity of appropriate data and analyse it appropriately. This involves deciding on:

- a setting for observations;
- times and duration for observations;
- a method of recording and codifying observations (Reid, 1982);
- a method for assessing the reliability (and typicality) of observations (Hartmann, 1982).

By participating, the analyst is able to supplement observation by listening to the participants' communication while they perform the task – assuming understanding of the language. But proximity is not necessarily advantageous, and participants are likely to modify their behavior (consciously or unconsciously) when they know they are being watched.

2.4.7 Relationships with insiders

You hope to glean information about behavior within the organization that your informant would prefer not to be repeated to other persons and in particularly not to superiors; the most valuable data may be framed by such moves as "I don't suppose I should really be telling you this" or "Don't tell her I said this for goodness sake" (Hitchcock, 1983, p. 30).

Ethical considerations and the need for trust influence how far the researcher makes clear the real reason for his/her investigating the experiences of informants. Their social and educational experiences influence their attitudes towards an outsider "researching" and "asking questions." In some societies your openly adopting a "research" role automatically makes you the object of suspicion. But when you develop a relationship that seems entirely based on friendship and the other person only later discovers your true reason for asking those "innocent" questions, his/her sense of outrage at being manipulated may rebound to your disadvantage (Hammersley and Atkinson, 1983).

2.4.8   Advantages and disadvantages of using insiders

Insiders, who can answer questions about the behavior that interests you include both those who typically participate and non-participants. Learning from interviewing members of both these groups presents *advantages* and *disadvantages*.

The *advantages* are:

- as members of the culture, they have more information available than do most outsiders;
- they can explain behavior in terms of the local culture;
- they can help correct hypothesis;
- they avoid outsider stereotyping;
- they are more likely to see the big picture.

The most obvious *disadvantage* is that members of the other-culture group fear you as an outsider and are reluctant to discuss their behavior. Ideally, you have the time in which to develop a trusting relationship so that their suspicions fade.

The reverse situation, in which members of the culture appear over-eager to discuss their behavior and their values, also presents difficulties. What sub-groups are anxious to confide in foreigners, and why? What axes do they have to grind? How far can their descriptions be taken at face value? This problem is most acute in totalitarian societies where self-elected spokespeople have been primed to feed you misleading information, and to discover the identity of other sources that you may have.

Third, members may disagree radically on what are the norms of behavior and on how statistical data should be interpreted. Here are excerpts from two letters, written by Hongkong Chinese and published in local newspapers.

> [1] Expatriates are always complaining that Hongkong Chinese are rude and badly behaved. I would like to say that this is not so. Chinese do not consider their behaviour rude or their habits and traditions disgusting. We have grown up accepting local behaviour as normal and we see nothing wrong with our ways of living.

and

> [2] I, being 100 percent Chinese, am disgusted with the appallingly rude manners of Hongkong Chinese. Therefore, it is not only foreigners who complain. Local people do, too. People spit, litter, queue-jump and push,

smoke in non-smoking areas, shout instead of talk, eat with their mouths open and talk with their mouths full; the list is long and disgraceful.[9]

Which of these letters reflects the norm? Radical disagreement among members should indicate the need for further research.

Fourth, members fail to notice features that they take for granted, even when these are conspicuous to the outsider whose culture does not share them.

Fifth, the insider behaves differently with members of his/her own culture and with outsiders – such as the analyst. The more sophisticated the insider, the more likely to adapt his/her behavior to approximate to the cultural stereotype that he/she has of your value system. In practice, the analyst may need to distinguish between:

- members' ideals of their behavior;
- members' perceptions of their actual behavior;
- members' ideals of how the outsider should interpret their behavior;
- members' perceptions of how their behavior appears to the outsider.

Just as members' ideals may be impossibly high, so their attempts at the difficult task of objective self-analysis may seem as unrealistically bleak. For instance, a report issued by the Philippine senate discussed the strengths of the Filipino culture; sensitivity to other people's feelings, family orientation, joy and humor, flexibility, adaptability and creativity, hard work and industry, faith and religiosity, an ability to survive.[10] Then, extraordinarily for an official document, it listed perceived weaknesses; extreme personalism, extreme family centeredness, lack of discipline, lack of initiative, a colonial mentality, lack of self-analysis and self-reflection, and envy for, or blaming, someone else. As a commentator suggested, this "stunning candor" paints a dismal picture.[11] But these weaknesses are by no means unique to the Filipino character, or to the Asian.

2.4.9 Techniques of informal questioning

The analyst needs to develop informal techniques for effectively questioning insiders. These skills are necessary when collecting information about the target behavior, and when testing and correcting explanatory hypotheses.

Questioning often proves the most rewarding means of getting information from insiders who are flattered by the attention. But it also poses the greatest difficulties.

For example, in a country where organizations have very hierarchical structures, the superior may be expected to have the answers, not to need to ask questions. When the cross-cultural manager is perceived to have this superior status, he/she has the problem of enquiring about local behavior without seeming incompetent and damaging his/her status.

The analyst establishes good faith as an observer by making clear that he/she does not ask questions in order to censor or punish. This may mean enquiring indirectly for explanations from individuals other than those directly concerned in the behavior.

In direct questioning, the *form* of the question is crucial. The analyst wants to understand the behavioral event within its context and the values that it reflects; but a "Why . . .?" question asking explicitly for meaning is unlikely to elicit this information. This is partly because human beings generally seem to find "Why . . .?" questions harder to answer than "What . . .?" and other questions, and it is not easy to explain the reasons for those kinds of behavior which are taken for granted as the natural and rational way of doing things. Section 2.4 discussed the example of haggling in a shop. The participants may easily explain their behavior as the best means of agreeing on a mutually satisfactory price, but are unable to articulate the deeper function of maintaining social relationships.

Second, a "Why . . .?" question fails to get a satisfactory answer when it is interpreted as coercive. A local subordinate may be worried by a direct request for an explanation, and answer only in terms that seem most likely to appease. This inhibition does not produce good-quality data.

2.4.10   Question types

Interviews designed to discover meaning inferentially and indirectly commonly begin with a *framing move*. This statement contextualizes the questions that follow, establishes good will and gives a reason for the interview.

For example, suppose that the analyst was interviewing the Thai manager who attended negotiations accompanied by his silent entourage – described in section 2.3.2 above. (This illustration is applied to all question types described here.) An appropriate move might be:

> *Frame:*   "Congratulations on your success. I'm very interested in your strategy because we do things differently in Country X, and it seems we have something to learn."

Question types that elicit descriptions of behavior include the following (Spradley, 1979):

Survey question:
inviting the other person to
introduce a wide range of
themes, any of which can
then be pursued by further
questioning.

"I guess there are definite
advantages to having a number
of aides with you."

Situation question:
checking when and where the
behavior is appropriate.

"There must be some negotiations
when their silent support is an
important factor."

Example question:
asking for illustrations of
the behavior.

"I guess there must have been
times when you find yourself
facing a single individual, when
your aides cannot play an active
role."

Contrast question:
deriving information by
discovering where alternatives
are and are not appropriate.

"In your experience, would there
be any advantages in negotiating
on your own?"

Checking question:
checking whether or not your
understanding of the
information (or data obtained
previously) is accurate.

"I guess you prefer to bring a
team because of what this says
about the organization, is that
right?"

Survey questions are open, giving wide opportunities for free interpretation, and are posed first in the interview, and at other points to open up the topic. The ordering of situation, example, and contrast questions is determined by topic development. Checking questions are closed, often asking for yes/no responses. They tidy up details and wrap up a topic.

This short list is obviously not exhaustive, and experience shows the analyst what other question types are non-threatening and elicit useful information. But so far as possible "*Why?*" questions are avoided.

"Why do you go into negotiations supported by a team of aides who remain silent?"

A direct "*Why?*" question is often more threatening than a corresponding indirect form.

Finally, the analyst who needs to take notes asks permission, then makes them inconspicuously, writing up these minimal jottings later in private. Even if an informant agrees to make a video or audio recording, this may not be satisfactory. Most people who are inexperienced in giving recorded interviews "freeze" when automatic recording equipment is produced, and consciously or unconsciously edit their contributions. Secret recording is unethical and should not be made. If it is discovered, the analyst loses the trust of the informant and all other persons who come to learn of the incident.

2.4.11 The status of the norms

Informants indicate whether an instance of behavior is typical (and so may reflect values deeply held by members of the culture group) or untypical. Untypical behavior may be in breach of formal rules or informal social norms.

Informants are often uncertain whether a breach is of rules or norms. When they explain "we always/never do X" or "we should/should not do X," which of the following applies?

- *Level 1* Compliance is enforced by national law, and non-compliance is punished.
- *Level 2* Compliance is enforced by rules of the institution, and non-compliance is punished. For instance, company regulations enforce that, on pain of a fine and dismissal for repeated violations, employees arrive on time for work, sing the company song, clean off work surfaces before going home, etc.
- *Level 3* Compliance is enforced by social pressure and non-compliance attracts non-legal sanctions. A company that does not impose regulations making employees clean their work surfaces (as for Level 2 above), might still enforce compliance through the company culture and its members' sense of how they should behave.
- *Level 4* Compliance with X is customary, and enhances the sense of community, but non-compliance is not sanctioned; for instance, preparing specific types of food to celebrate festivals – haggis for Burns' Night in Scotland, turkey for Thanksgiving in the United States.

Behavior acceptable in one culture may be assessed differently in another. In Saudi Arabia, women have always been forbidden by customary practice to drive cars. In 1991 opposition by Saudi women to this restriction so enraged the Saudi government that this ban was converted into a civil law.[12] In the United States it is usual that they do – but American women soldiers based in Saudi Arabia during the 1991 Gulf War were ordered by their high command to drive only when on duty.

In most countries, your carrying a large package on the subway during the rush hour might be considered anti-social and be sanctioned by scowls and reprimands. This social offence is not normally criminalized. But in Singapore

> when the new subway opened, it came equipped with a list of prohibitions. Smoking and playing radios or musical instruments are banned. So are eating or drinking, bringing animals, carrying "large" luggage, hawking, and resting feet on the plastic seats. All carry a S$500 [about US$288] fine.[13]

There are practical reasons for checking the level of the norms. The analyst establishes the rewards for compliance and the penalties for non-compliance. This can save expense and embarrassment, and helps build relationships with cultural insiders. Finally, there may be some norms that the analyst, as an outsider, is not expected to follow – or is even expected *not* to follow. When compliance is optional, it is useful to discover whether compliance will win respect or not.

2.5 Developing, Testing, and Selecting the Hypothesis

The assembled data are applied in the generation of an informed hypothesis that explains the behavior in question. This process involves:

- developing a set of alternative explanations; for instance, initial research into the Thai *wai* (section 2.4.1) might suggest the alternatives:

    (a) the *wai* has the same significance as the handshake in the United States;
    (b) the *wai* expresses affection and friendship;
    (c) the *wai* expresses respect within a hierarchical system;

- evaluating each alternative in terms of what is already known about the other culture;

- testing each with informants;

- discarding those alternatives that cannot be substantiated by further understanding and the advice of informants (but they may have to be reconsidered if the selected explanation should later be proved false); the first two explanations offered above are discarded because

    (a) norms determine who first makes a *wai* (the junior, as determined by age and status); but (usually) either party can initiate the handshake;

(b)   the *wai* is a respect marker rather than a friendship marker (and also functions for greetings and farewells, to show gratitude, to make an apology); married couples and parents and children seldom *wai* each other, except on very formal occasions;

- selecting that alternative which seems best to explain the data. To return to the example; Thailand is a hierarchical society, in which seniors and juniors are differentiated by wide power distances maintained throughout their relationships. Norms for social intercourse are fixed and generally known. The third alternative, that (c) the *wai* expresses respect within a hierarchical system, fits neatly within the total picture of Thai culture. The *wai* both reflects and reinforces social differentiation on a vertical basis.

The selected alternative should be able to provide a flexible generalization about the culture that answers a question *why?* – in this instance, why is the *wai* significant. It should lead the analyst to directly confront cultural values.

The explanation given for the *wai* associates an apparently trivial aspect of behavior with a significant feature of Thai culture. It leads the analyst into asking further questions about how differentiation is expressed more directly in the organization – for example, in communicating between superior and subordinate, directing and controlling subordinate activity, cooperating with peers. These aspects of work relationships in both high- and low-power distance cultures are discussed throughout the book.

2.5.1   Testing

The hypothesis is tested against additional data. Specific tests can be made by examining exceptional instances in which the behavior is *not* appropriate (and when the question then arises as to what behavior would be appropriate). This may be illustrated by negative questions asked of the Thai *wai*:

- *How* is the *wai never* performed?
  It is never performed with the hands at waist height.

- *Who never* makes a *wai*?
  Monks do not make, return, or acknowledge *wai*s. (They are expected to be indifferent to such worldly matters as social status.)

- *Who* is *never* made a *wai*?
  Children are never *wai*d first by an adult, unless they have great rank – for instance, royal princes and princesses. The only animals

to be *wai*d are those with unusual symbolic importance – for instance, the royal white elephants.

- *Where* is a *wai never* made?
  (There are probably no places in which a *wai* is absolutely inappropriate.)

- *When* is a *wai never* made?
  (There are probably no times at which a *wai* is absolutely inappropriate.)

2.5.2 Correcting

The hypothesis is corrected when new data and examples of the behavior in new contexts demonstrate that it is inadequate and needs revising. This process of constantly modifying earlier explanations is necessary in order to develop a real and deep understanding of the culture.

When the original hypothesis is shown to be inadequate, the cause of the fault is identified by returning to the model set out in section 2.2.5 and, starting at the lowest level, checking up succeeding levels:

1. Has the generalization been tested appropriately?
   If the answer is "yes," go one level higher:
2. Has the best alternative been selected?
   And again, if the answer is "yes," ask:
3. Have the hypotheses been developed appropriately?
   And at the next stage up:
4. Has adequate data been collected?
   And if the answer is again "yes," the analyst must deal with new incongruity. In effect, this means going through the process again: collecting new information, developing alternative hypotheses, selecting the best, testing.

2.6 Implications for the Manager

1. Develop creative (and hence flexible) *generalizations* about the other culture. Develop these by:

   - recognizing behavior in the local culture which seems to you incongruent;
   - collecting information about this behavior and its causes and predictable repercussions;
   - developing hypotheses to explain this behavior in terms of your existing understanding of the local culture;

- selecting the best hypothesis – which gives you a workable generalization to explain behavior in the other culture;
- testing the generalization;
- correcting the generalization in the light of further experience.

2. In order to explain incongruous behavior, the manager collects information about it under these headings:

- *What* typically happens?
- *Who* is typically involved?
- *How* is the behavior typically performed, and how do the participants contribute?
- *Where* does the the behavior typically occur?
- *When* does the behavior typically occur?

3. Bearing in mind the problems that each of these sources presents, collect and analyse data from:

- official bodies and reports;
- journalism;
- outsider informants;
- insider informants.

4. When interviewing *insiders,*

- ask for information about behavior and experience; avoid asking for values;
- use a range of non-threatening question forms that do not exploit your managerial status;
- try to avoid asking *why* questions;
- check the status of norms described.

5. Test the selected hypothesis with informants:

- When members of the culture discuss their behavior and values, look for differences between their ideals, their values as practiced, and what they think you ought to know or wish to know.

2.7 Summary

This chapter has dealt with the problem of learning and interpreting another culture in terms of its own priorities. Informal cultural analysis is conducted in order to supplement published research, which may not adequately explain the cross-cultural manager's own situation.

Section 2.2 argued that efficient *generalizing* leads to the development of a flexible model of the other culture, whereas *fixed stereotyping* restricts creative responses. Section 2.3 set up a model for doing *analysis.* Behavior that needs explaining includes incongruency, when the link with desired ends is not apparent. Management is often symbolic, and the rational meaning of a specific symbol may be unclear to the cultural outsider.

Section 2.4 focused on collecting and *using data.* Sources of information include official bodies and reports, journalism, cultural outsiders, cultural insiders. The analyst can learn from insiders by participatation and observation, and interviewing. Techniques of informal questioning were examined. It was suggested in conclusion that the analyst needs to check the status of norms described. Section 2.5 dealt with problems of *developing, testing and correcting hypotheses* to explain target behavior in the other culture.

2.8 Exercise

This exercise gives practice in analysing culture.

Part 1

(a) Take any one of the case examples used in this chapter – for instance, Barrington High School (section 2.1), the Danish village (section 2.3.1), the bank dining room (section 2.3.2). Decide on what aspect of the behavior described particularly interests you.

(b) Review the list of question types given in section 2.4.10:

- frames;
- survey questions;
- situation questions;
- example questions;
- contrast questions;
- checking questions.

(c) Assume that you are a cultural outsider interviewing a protagonist in one of these situations (a pupil, villager, banker) and prepare a list of questions that will help you understand the target behavior.

Part 2

(d) Now take the case of a colleague's place of work. Identify an aspect of typical behavior that you do not fully understand, and prepare a list of questions.

(e) Use these questions to interview your colleague. Aim to reach a full understanding of the target behavior – but without asking any *"why?"* questions.

Notes

1. "Barrington High School's teenage artists plan show to voice protest," *Chicago Tribune*, April 23, 1991.
2. "The memo on German reunification," *Independent*, 16 July, 1990.
3. "An Indian in Hvilsager," *The Economist*, January 25, 1992. The English language version of Reddy (1989), *Danes Are Like That*, was unpublished as of January 1992.
4. Erik Ipsen, "Clout at Bank of England?," *International Herald Tribune*, July 1, 1993.
5. Ibid.
6. Roland Gribben, "'Fuddy-duddy' BT is no more," *Daily Telegraph*, March 21, 1991.
7. This system of categories has many forbears. It is adapted in part from a scheme developed by the pioneering anthropologist Bronislaw Malinowski (1884–1942); see Malinowski (1964). For a more recent system, see Lofland (1971).
8. "Donna al potere nei paesi Nordici" (Women holding power in Nordic countries), *Corriere della Sera*, May 15, 1991. I am grateful to Gabriele Udeschini for these insights.
9. "Other voices," *Asiaweek*, March 1, 1991.
10. Philippine Senate, "The Moral Recovery Programme: building a people – building a nation," May 1988.
11. James Clad, "Naming the good, the bad, and the ugly of a nation," *Far Eastern Economic Review*, 22 September 1988.
12. "King Fahd's Privy Council," The Economist, November 17, 1990.
13. Kenneth L. Whiting, "Where rules are rules," *Bangkok Post*, Associated Press, March 13, 1991.

3

Comparing Cultures

3.1 Introduction

A magazine reports outsider impressions of the Swedes.[1] They appear humourless compared, say, to the British. The Turkish immigrant arriving at Stockholm's main railway terminus is stunned by the silence. They are reputed to value rationality and to suppress strong emotions. They seldom lose their tempers, and don't shout.

These outsider impressions have now been substantiated by a scientific study. A Swedish professor of ethnography has found that

> 24 percent of adult Swedes admitted to being moved to tears when their prime minister, Olof Palme, was murdered in 1986. This compares with 53 percent of adult Americans who said they cried when they heard of the killing of John Kennedy ... About half as many Swedes as Italians and Koreans (and far fewer Swedes than Finns) admit to losing their temper easily ...
>
> Psychological tests suggest that the Swedes in general are more introverted than other Europeans or than Americans, which helps explain why Swedes see shyness as a positive trait and talkativeness as a negative one.

This example draws comparisons between behavior in different societies. Specifically, it

- describes anecdotal evidence of typical Swedish behavior, as experienced by outsiders;
- provides "scientific" and quantitatively-based evidence of difference.

The previous chapter dealt with the problems of the cross-cultural manager who does not have access to published research and must do his/her own analysis of the local culture. This chapter deals with applications of published research, and focuses on the value of comparative studies. It has the following sections;

3.2   Modeling Cultural Orientations

Kluckhohn and Strodtbeck (1961) designed a comparative model that has been widely influential. They argued that although cultures may change slowly over time, they are essentially stable, and members of a culture group exhibit constant "orientations" towards the world and humankind. Different culture groups exhibit different orientatations, and may be compared on this principle.

Their model distinguishes six basic orientations; these pose questions about the target culture group's perceptions of the human condition, and presents a range of variations, or possible answers, in response to each. As presented here (see table 3.1), the model applies developments proposed by a range of other writers since its original formulation (see, for instance, Evan, 1974; Adler, 1979; Neghandi, 1983):

Table 3.1 Kluckhohn and Strodtbeck's (1961) six basic cultural orientations

Orientations	Range of variations
What is the nature of people?	Good (changeable/unchangeable) A mixture of good and evil Evil (changeable/unchangeable)
What is the person's relationship to nature?	Dominant In harmony with nature Subjugation
What is the person's relationship to to other people?	Lineal (hierarchical) Collateral (collectivist) Individualist
What is the modality of human activity?	Doing Being in becoming Being
What is the temporal focus of human activity?	Future Present Past
What is the conception of space?	Private Mixed Public

Each orientation of this model is illustrated first by some aspect of mainstream culture of the United States and then from other cultures. This profile of United States culture is personal; a similar interpretation is made by Kohls (1984, p. 25).

The nature of people

Orientation	US variation
What is the nature of people?	A mixture

Mainstream United States culture is optimistic in so far as it is assumed that any achievement is possible if worked for, and that humanity is ultimately perfectible – as the millions of self-help books and videos marketed every year demonstrate (Schein, 1981). But this assumption of perfectability does not mean that the American is equally optimistic about his/her opposite numbers in day-to-day encounters. The fact that the negotiating team regularly includes legal staff implies fear that the other party will renege on a deal if given a loophole.

Many Europeans take a more pessimistic approach towards human nature. They show a greater suspicion of experts, and assume that human motivations are more complex than do Americans. This is reflected in a preference for more complex cognitive models of behavior and hence more complex structures than are found in American organizations (Cooper and Cox, 1989).

Relationship to nature

Orientation	US variation
What is the person's relationship to nature?	Dominant

Up until recently, United States culture has generally perceived the human as separate from nature, and entitled to exploit it. Such activities as mining, damming rivers for hydro-electric power, analysing and planning to control weather patterns, genetic engineering, all show a need for dominance. But recently, the public has become more conscious of needs to preserve the environment, and this is reflected in corporate marketing policies and the development of "recyclable" and "biodegradable" products.

More generally, perceptions of dominance are reflected in a readiness to manage human psychology, and human relationships. An example is provided by policy designed to adjust an organizational culture.

In comparison, Arab culture tends to be highly fatalistic towards attempts to change or improve the world. Humanity can do little on its own to achieve success or avert disaster. This is shown by the 1990 case of a tunnel that collapsed in the Muslim holy city of Mecca (Saudi

Arabia) during the annual pilgrimage. In the resulting panic, over 1,400 pilgrims died.

> Saudi officials insisted earlier yesterday that "the will of God" rather than sabotage or incompetence had led to the disaster. . . .
>
> "It was God's will, which is above everything," King Fahd told Saudi security officials. "It was fate. Had they not died there, they would have died elsewhere, and at the same predestined moment." While the King's statement may soften the embarrassment of the Saudi authorities, who are supposed to protect the Mecca pilgrims, it is unlikely to be accepted so easily by other Muslim states. Egyptians, Indonesians, Malaysians and Pakastinis were among the dead.[2]

Relationship to other people

Orientation   *US variation*
What is the person's relationship   Individualist
    to other people?

United States culture values individualism and perceives fulfilment as gained through personal achievement. Maximizing one's opportunities and capacities becomes a moral imperative. But although Americans pride themselves on their respect for individual liberty, many American corporations (particularly in such traditional sectors as banking and insurance) are markedly hierarchical. By comparison, in collectivist Japan,

> even a chief executive whose company bears his name knows he must balance personal desires against the harmony of the group. . . . "In North America," says Noritake Kobayashi, dean of the business school at Keio University, "the boss is the boss, and he gives orders. Here, that can be very dangerous."[3]

Human activity

Orientation   *US variation*
What is the modality of human   Doing
    activity?

Stewart (1972) claims that United States culture does not provide clear means of achieving self-identification other than through action and performance, and so goal-attainment becomes a means by which you distinguish yourself apart from the group. Because other persons should be able to recognize this achievement, it has to be visible and measurable. Thus financial wealth provides one measure of successful activity. Within the organization, employees are motivated by promises of promotion and status symbols overtly associated with rank such as a superior company car and a luxuriously fitted office.

Buddhist cultures in South-east Asia which adhere to beliefs in reincarnation hold that the individual is born into his/her present status and circumstances by virtue of meritorious acts performed in a previous life and that struggle in this life may be pointless. By avoiding sinful acts and by maintaining the harmony of present circumstances, you help your chances of being born into a higher position in your next reincarnation.

Human activity

Orientation *US variation*
What is the temporal focus of Future
  human activity?

The United States is commonly held up as a future-oriented society which believes that the future can be planned and controlled. Moreover, the future is bound to be better than the present just as the present must be an improvement on the past (Kluckhohn and Kluckhohn, 1947). But this orientation may be short-term. One survey asked American chief executive officers (CEOs) to judge their firms' time horizons against other American firms, European firms, and Asian firms (Poterba and Summers, 1991). The respondents thought their companies less short-sighted than their American counterparts, but more short-sighted than their European competitors, and even more so than Asian competitors.

Past-oriented cultures base their decisions on lessons learned from the past. Their members are more likely to resist constant innovation in structures and procedures – unless the innovation has precedent. In the 1960s the People's Republic of China was convulsed by a "cultural" revolution which seemed to represent a radical break with history. But Terrill (1984) shows that criteria for what was and was not revolutionary were rooted in the past.

> Chinese tend to think that everything that can happen has happened, and that moral conduct consists of repeating the correct performances of the past. Jiang and Mao were going to insist that henceforth the past ... was going to be *their* past, the few short decades since the 1920s. (p. 244)

Past-oriented cultures also pay greater respect to age. A Japanese-American manager suggests

> If you're having any trouble with a government department in Japan, take along someone who is really old. Japanese bureaucrats really respect old

people. When I had a problem, I took along a pensioner who used to work for my company and he explained my situation.[4]

Conception of space

Orientation   *US variation*
What is the conception of space?   Private

In general, the United States employee feels some inhibition about entering the office of a colleague when the door is closed; it is usual to tap on the door, even if this is immediately followed by trying the handle without waiting for an invitation to enter. Notices outside conference rooms warning "Meeting in progress" are interpreted as directives to stay out.

Only very close friends enter each others' houses without warning. More distant acquaintances ring the door bell or even telephone in advance to ask if a visit is appropriate.

In Germany, office space is perhaps even more private than in the United States. Germans often dislike open-plan offices and prefer to work in their offices with doors closed.

At the opposite extreme, space is mostly public in the People's Republic of China. The authorities work hard to stamp out the game of mah-jongg, which is usually played for small stakes behind locked doors.

> Western countries also control gambling, but Shanghai is one of the few places in which authorities try to change social habits and ban small-scale betting in the privacy of the home. . . .
>
> One reason for the authorities' zeal . . . may be that privacy is not a well-known concept in China, and even the expression in Chinese for privacy is usually used in a perjorative sense, to hint at selfishness or secretiveness.
>
> Still, even if they don't always value privacy, many ordinary Chinese value their small-stakes mah-jongg.[5]

3.2.1 Counter-examples

As you read the section above, you may have thought of counter-examples that contradicted each of the points made. But these do not invalidate the model. Social anthropology does *not* claim that all members of the culture group practice the same behavior all the time. Any culture is diverse; its members differ in their values and behavior.

The contradictions to predominant mainstream values also contribute to the total mosaic of United States culture. They tell us that a profile based only on predominant variations is inadequate, and does not fully

Table 3.2 Modified system of basic cultural orientations: predominant and subordinate variations

Orientation	*US variations*
What is the nature of people?	A mixture of good and evil *over* Good (changeable over unchangeable) *over* Evil (changeable over unchangeable)
What is the person's relationship to nature?	Dominant *over* In harmony with nature *over* Subjugation
What is the person's relationship to other people?	Individualist *over* Lateral *over* Hierarchical
What is the modality of human activity?	Doing *over* Being in becoming *over* Being
What is the temporal focus of human activity?	Future *over* Present *over* Past
What is the conception of space?	Private *over* Mixed *over* Public

Source: adapted from Evan (1974)

describe United States values in all circumstances, for all groups of the population, and at all times. The modified system (table 3.2), adapted from Evan (1974), distinguishes predominant from subordinate variations.

These subordinate variations are significant when

- analysing the behavior of cultural sub-groups;
- analysing mainstream groups in abnormal situations.

3.2.2 Applying comparative models

The Kluckhohn–Strodtbeck model has definite weaknesses, so far as the manager is concerned:

- the authors were not centrally concerned with management studies, and the implications for management have not been fully demonstrated;
- the orientations and variations are imprecisely defined;
- interpretations are bound to be subjective.

Nevertheless, it provides a useful illustration of comparative analysis, and these points emerge:

- in *general* terms, cultures can be compared along distinct dimensions;
- comparative models can be applied to cross-cultural management;
- analysis of predominant variations within the national culture does *not* accurately predict, in all respects,

    (a)   the values of sub-cultural minorities;
    (b)   the values practiced in different industries and organizations;
    (c)   values reflected in extraordinary circumstances (for instance, behavior when a building catches fire).

In sum, a general issue has to be faced when using multi-dimensional models that compare cultures. General comparability may be adequate for most purposes, but does not justify the manager proposing exact equations.

Any one dimension carries different connotations when it is applied to different countries – because the total profile differs. For instance, individualism is reflected differently in Culture A and Culture B. In Culture A, individualism may be associated with, say, perception of people as generally good and the future as the temporal focus; but in Culture B, with perceptions of people as evil and the past as the temporal focus.

Hence there can be no exact point of comparison.

But despite this qualification, comparative models are still useful. They offer the manager insights which can form the bases of working hypotheses, to be validated by informal research – as the previous chapter demonstrated.

3.3　Cultural Contexts

Supposing a visitor enters your office and remarks, "It's cold today." As it stands, this utterance is open to a range of interpretations:

(a)   That's an improvement on the recent hot weather.
(b)   That's a disappointment after the recent hot weather.
(c)   The heating should be turned up.
(d)   The heating is turned too high, given temperatures outside.

And there are many others. But how do you correctly identify the speaker's intended meaning? The short answer is that you interpret by referring to social and situational cues. If he had complained the previous day of the excessive heat, interpretation (a) may be appropriate. If it is usual in your group that people enjoy the heat, then select (b). If the heating is already turned excessively high, then ignore (c), and consider (d). And so on.

3.3.1 High- and low-context cultures

This point, that we interpret and create communications in reference to the context, serves as a simple analogy to the basic argument developed by Hall (1976). Hall deals with the individual's search for meaning in relation to the culture within which he/she is reared.

Your cultural experience determines your understanding of the context and how you structure your life; and cultures vary in how they program their members to depend upon the context when communicating, and more broadly, in developing relationships. Thus the "hidden dimensions" of context influence the expression and reinforcement of shared values.

Hall distinguishes between *high-context* and *low-context* cultures.

In high-context cultures, the external environment, situation, and non-verbal behavior are crucial in creating and interpreting communications. Members of the culture group are programmed from birth to depend heavily upon covert clues given in these contexts when they communicate; that is, meaning is communicated implicitly. In languages spoken in high-context cultures (such as Arabic, Chinese, Japanese) subtlety is valued and much meaning is conveyed by inference. In low-context cultures, the environment, situation and non-verbal behavior are relatively less important, and more explicit information has to be given. A direct "blunt" communicative style is valued, and in management communications, ambiguity may be sanctioned. Members depend less on their internal skills of correcting for distortions or omissions of information in messages.

High-context cultures tend to have the following characteristics.

- Relationships between individuals are relatively long lasting, and individuals feel deep personal involvement with each other.
- Because so much is communicated by shared code, communication can be economical, fast, and efficient – particularly in a routine situation. High-context cultures fully exploit the communicative context. The Japanese

> talk around the point. [They] think intelligent human beings should be able to discover the point of discourse from the context, which they are careful to provide. . . . The United States, having its roots in European culture which dates back to Plato, Socrates, and Aristotle, has built into its culture assumptions that the only natural and effective way to present ideas is by means of a Greek invention called "logic."
> (Hall, 1983, p. 63)

Communication in high-context cultures is an art form that consciously employs a far wider palette of communicative expression than is usual in Anglo cultures. For instance,

> [m]any Japanese are convinced they can communicate with each other without words at all. "Haragei," it is called, or "belly language."
>
> Because of the country's cultural homogeneity, it is argued, Japanese somehow can convey their intentions through penetrating stares, casual glances, occasional grunts and meaningful silences. As a rule, foreigners are beyond such communication . . .[6]

Similarly, Connerton (1989, pp. 79–82) finds cases of Sicilian and Napolitan communities able to carry on entire conversations by dumb show and gestures alone.[7] He cites a vocabulary listing about 150 gestural items used by Southern Italians.

- People in authority are personally responsible for the actions of subordinates. In practice, this places a premium on loyalty to superiors and subordinates.

- Agreements tend to be spoken rather than written. This can mean that a written contract is no more than a "best guess." In Japan,

> after a contract has been signed, the Japanese will request a meeting at which they ask for changes, which usually means that the American company representative in Japan must contact US headquarters for approval. The American reaction is one of indignation or distress because Americans regard a contract as binding, a stable element in a changing and uncertain world. Many Japanese contracts have a clause that says if the situation changes the contract will be renegotiated. Even if the clause is not there, they will expect to change if the situation changes. For the Japanese, if conditions change, everything changes. (Hall, 1987, pp. 128–9)

- Insiders and outsiders are tightly distinguished; outsiders include, first, non-members of the family, clan, organization, etc., and foreigners. In 1990, Japanese women were encouraged by their Finance Minister

> to bear more children to avoid "contaminating" Japanese society with *jappayuki* (immigrant workers). . . . Some senior leaders of the ruling Liberal Democratic party say they favor restricting sales of contraceptives.[8]

The worry that "the country might become flooded by foreigners with strange customs" forced parliament to enact harsh new curbs against the immigration of unskilled and illegal Asian workers. In 1993 the Labor Ministry calculated there were 280,000 illegals, most from Thailand, then from the Philippines, Pakistan, Sri Lanka, Bangladesh, and the Middle East. By then, Japan had discovered another pool of workers, descendants of its own people. In 1989,

> laws had been changed to allow entry to any foreigner with parents or grandparents in Japan, and the number of workers fleeing the troubled economies of Brazil and Peru rose sharply.[9]

These Latin-Japanese did not have an easy ride. They looked Japanese, but such behavior as talking loudly and public embraces, and their troubles with the language, marked them out as different.

> "The people of Japan do not respect us," said Roberto Iskizuka, 26, a former automobile worker in Sao Paulo . . . "The Japanese treat us like some kind of inferior race." . . .[10]

- Cultural patterns are ingrained, and slow to change.

Low-context cultures tend to have the following, opposite, characteristics.

- Relationships between individuals are relatively shorter in duration, and *in general* deep personal involvement with others is valued less. In practice, low-context countries tend to be more heterogeneous, and prone to greater social and job mobility.
- Messages must be made explicit, and the sender can depend far less on the receiver inferring the message from the context. Members of the culture group are relatively unconditioned in non-verbal communications codes.
- Authority is diffused throughout the bureaucratic system and personal responsibility is difficult to pin down.
- Agreements tend to be written rather than spoken. Low-context countries treat contracts as final and legally binding. They place greater reliance on written legal systems to resolve disputes – which is reflected in the size and structures of their legal professions; 1987 figures credited the United States with 279 lawyers per 100,000 people, the United Kingdom with 114, West Germany with 77, France with 29, and Japan with only 11.[11]
- Insiders and outsiders are less closely distinguished. This means that foreigners find it relatively easier to adjust, and that immigration is

more acceptable. In the United States and Brazil for instance, (legal) immigrants are encouraged to take nationality.
- Cultural patterns are faster to change.

3.3.2 Applying Hall's model

Hall builds his model on qualitative insights rather than quantitative data. He does not attempt to precisely rank different countries in terms of high- or low-culture contexts. But we can expect to find high-context cultures in Japan, China, Korea, Vietnam, and other Asian countries, countries around the Mediterranean and in the Middle East. Low-context countries include the United States, Scandinavian countries, Germany, and Switzerland.

These informal placings indicate tendencies only. No country exists exclusively at one end of the scale, and all countries exhibit high-context cultural behavior and low-context cultural behavior. All countries are likely to include sub-cultural groups that deviate markedly from the general orientation, at least in some activities. For instance, the low-context, Anglo countries include associations with restricted membership such as Rotary and the Masons; their personal relationships give members access to power and influence both within the association and more generally in society.

France exemplifies a country whose culture is a mix of high- and low-context institutions and situations. Insiders to the culture group and outsiders are closely distinguished, and great importance is associated with speaking the language correctly and appropriately. But the impersonality of both public- and private-sector bureaucracies is more typical of low-context cultures.

The model provides insights into the values that determine how a range of management functions are performed across cultures. For instance, the high-context emphasis on personal relationships means that when negotiating in these cultures, you can expect to invest considerable time in building trust with your opposite number. Only when you feel comfortable with each other can you expect your business to proceed with any rapidity. But in low-context cultures where personal involvement with your negotiating partner is less important, and your identity as representative of a particular business interest is relatively more so, you can expect to move quickly into negotiating prices and concessions.

3.4 Culture, Status, and Function

Cross-cultural research conducted by André Laurent and colleagues shows attitudes towards organizational power differing across cultures. Laurent

(1983) examined the attitudes of managers in nine European countries (Switzerland, Germany, Denmark, Sweden, United Kingdom, Netherlands, Belgium, Italy, France) and the United States. He focused on four parameters; perceptions of the organization as political systems, authority systems, role formulation systems, and hierarchical relationship systems.

Further work (Adler, Campbell, and Laurent, 1989) collected data from the People's Republic of China, Indonesia, and Japan, thus enabling comparisons to be made with Asian Pacific countries.

Laurent saw management as an implementation process by which managers expressed their cultural values in explicit management decisions. Considerable variances were found across the different national groups examined. For instance, they perceived the political significance of managerial status very differently. In response to the statement, "through their professional activity, managers play an important role in society," the percentages in agreement were as follows:

Denmark	32%
United Kingdom	40%
Netherlands	45%
Germany	46%
Sweden	54%
United States of America	52%
Switzerland	65%
Italy	74%
France	76%

Source: Laurent, 1983, p. 80

In France and Italy, therefore, the manager carries his status over to general. The manager is very conscious of his/her social influence. But Danish and British managers enjoy less social power, and are less able to carry their organizational status into other activities. The British manager who is also a member of a local football club may find himself playing under the captaincy of his works foreman; his French or Italian equivalents would be most unlikely to accept this situation. French and Italian managers think of authority as the property of the individual office-holder. At the other end of the spectrum, managers see it more as an attribute of the role or function.

3.4.1 Hierarchy

Cultures that value hierarchical structuring as a means of maintaining social cohesion impose severe restrictions on communication flow. This affects what information is communicated, how it is communicated, and to whom. In response to the statement, "In order to have efficient work relationships, it is often necessary to bypass the hierarchical line," the national groups responded thus in *disagreement*:

Sweden	22%
United Kingdom	31%
United States of America	32%
Denmark	37%
Netherlands	39%
Switzerland	41%
Belgium	42%
France	42%
Germany	46%
Italy	75%
People's Republic of China	66%

Source: Laurent, 1983, p. 86; Adler et al., 1989, p. 64

Where non-hierarchical communication is tolerated and encouraged, the individual does not need to seek permission from superior levels in order to bypass the hierarchical line, and information can be channeled quickly around the organization. But there may also be disadvantages. It may not be easy to distinguish "official" and "unofficial" information, and the superior may feel his/her authority compromised. On the other hand, where bypassing is sanctioned and all communication has to be routed up and down the hierarchy, the process may be slower. Access to information is restricted. On the other hand, the status of the information communicated, and the authority of the individual and of his/her superiors and subordinates, is far less ambiguous.

Culture is not the only factor to influence how far non-hierarchical communication is tolerated. An entrepreneurial project-based organization is more likely to value unofficial channeling than is, say, a bank, in which routine is expected and the precise status of a message must be apparent.

The cross-cultural implication is that mixed-culture workforces might easily be drawn into conflict. For example, in the interests of efficiency and speed, Swedish employees working in a typical Italian company naturally attempt to by-pass hierarchical lines and make direct contact with information sources located elsewhere in the organization. But their Italian boss perceives their lack of respect for hierarchical lines of behaviour as insubordinate and threatening to the structure (Adler, 1986, pp. 33–4). And Italians workers in a Swedish firm are censored for lack of motivation and initiative when they refuse to approach an information source in some other unit.

Italians value the security of knowing precisely the rights and limits of their authority. They know who communicates with whom on what topics, and how these communications will be handled. Hence the Italian organization tends to be pyramidic, with clearly differentiated hierarchical ranks and power centers. The Swedish organization, on the other hand, may have a number of power centers.

3.4.2 The manager as expert versus the manager as facilitator

Laurent (1983) asked managers to respond to the statement, "It is important for a manager to have at hand precise answers to most of the questions that his subordinates may raise about their work." The Asian Pacific managers agreed with this statement far more strongly than did their Western colleagues. Percentages in agreement were:

Sweden	10%
United Kingdom	27%
United States of America	18%
Denmark	23%
Netherlands	17%
Switzerland	38%
Belgium	44%
France	53%
Germany	46%
Italy	66%
Indonesia	73%
People's Republic of China	74%
Japan	78%

Source: Laurent, 1983, p. 86

The Asian Pacific managers think the manager should be a specialist able to provide convincing answers to technical questions. And subordinates cannot challenge these without incurring social sanctions. Hence subordinates value advice from their manager above that given by peers, whatever its quality. Furthermore, they may restrict questions to topics on which they know that the manager is technically competent to answer.

The manager who cannot answer subordinates' questions loses status. Because the unity of the group depends on the manager's maintaining his/her hierarchical position, his/her loss of status would endanger the security and stability of the entire group, and so also the interests of its individual members. Thus it in the subordinates' interests to maintain the manager's status.

This means that the technical efficiency of the organization is heavily dependent on the efficiency and professionalism of its superior. But even a technically inefficient superior is accepted for as long as he/she satisfies the group's aspirations in other ways and works for its harmony.

In cultures such as Indonesia managers tend to be promoted because they are best able to project an image of specialist expertise and have status. They may not be skilled or trained as general managers (in the North European sense, as facilitators, coordinators, fixers, decision-takers, etc.), and increasingly their technical expertise becomes dated as they become primarily occupied with managerial problems. Hence, their efficiency both as technicians and as managers is apt to deteriorate.

Swedes think the manager should know how to get a problem solved. He/she does not need to be an expert in all aspects of the unit's work, but by implication, should be able to tap sources of expert power, perhaps elsewhere in the organization.

The Swede is relatively less inhibited than the Indonesian or Chinese about approaching an outsider to the work unit for advice if this person seems able to supply help not forthcoming within the unit. This has cross-cultural implications. The Swede working in an Indonesian organization may be as frustrated by what he/she perceives as inefficiency when Indonesian co-workers refuse to ask an outsider, or insider outside the chain of command, for help. And when he/she does make such an advance, they are drawn to censor his/her apparent lack of loyalty and respect.

Whereas the Swedish manager uses hierarchical structuring as one way of facilitating problem-solving and organizing tasks, the Indonesian values it as a means of signalling who has authority over whom. So when planning a project, the Swede first identifies the necessary functions then looks for the right people to fill them. But the Indonesian places most value on social harmony and assesses the potential of a project on the basis of who will be involved in the different positions. In Indonesian terms a group of people who do not observe the proper social priorities and protect their group interests, place their individual interests at jeopardy and cannot be expected to work together efficiently. This affects not only the project at hand but their future relationships (Vroom, 1981).

3.5   Culture and the Workplace

Hofstede's research goes further in showing how the underlying values of the culture group permeate through to affect relationships, and work and social values. This chapter focuses on his early research (Hofstede 1980a, 1980b, 1983a, 1983b, 1984a, 1984b). This demonstrates that:

- work-related values are *not* universal;
- national cultural values are likely to persist, even when a multinational tries to impose the same norms on all its branches;
- local values determine how headquarters regulations are interpreted;
- by implication, a multinational that insists on imposing the same organizational norms is in danger of creating unnecessary morale problems and inefficiencies.

Hofstede's research compares work-related attitudes across a range of cultures. This has been presented in a number of papers and a book, *Culture's Consequences: International Differences in Work-Related Values* (1980a). The comments made here are based on the abridged paperback edition (1984a). An extension (1991) of this work is discussed in chapter 17.

Hofstede (1980a, 1984a) surveyed 116,000 employees (at a range of managerial and non-managerial levels) in IBM branches and affiliates, in 50 countries and three regions (East Africa, comprising Ethiopia, Kenya, Tanzania and Zambia; West Africa, comprising Ghana, Nigeria, and Sierra Leone; and Arab countries, comprising Egypt, Iraq, Kuwait, Lebanon, Saudi Arabia and the United Arab Emirates).

Comparisons between the different cultures were plotted across four dimensions, largely independent of each other. These are:

- *power distance*: the distance between individuals at different levels of a hierarchy;
- *uncertainty avoidance*: more or less of a need to avoid uncertainty about the future;
- *individualism versus collectivism*: the relations between the individual and his/her fellows;
- *masculinity versus feminity*: the division of roles and values in society.

3.5.1 Power distance

This dimension deals with the desirability or undesirability of inequality, and of dependence versus interdependence. It indicates how the culture adapts to inequalities among its members. In some cultures, natural physical and intellectual differences generate wide economic, political, and social inequalities which may eventually be perpetuated on a hereditary basis. Other cultures try to narrow power distances between its members. For instance, the British actress Glenda Jackson argued (in her persona as a Labour Party Parliamentery candidate):

> We are none of us born equal. . . . The first duty of a society that claims to be civilised is to attempt to bring a combination of resources to balance up that basic inequality.[12]

The dimension shows how far the culture tolerates and fosters pecking orders, and how actively members try to reduce them.

Where power distances are low, students value independence rather than conformity. Hierarchical relationships are perceived as convenience arrangements rather than as having existential justification. Managers like to see themselves as practical and systematic, and they admit a need for support. They are more likely to make decisions only after consulting with subordinates. Subordinates dislike close supervision and prefer a

Table 3.3 Key to the countries and regions in Figure 3.1

ARA	Arab countries	JAM	Jamaica
	(Egypt. Lebanon. Lybia. Kuwait.	JPN	Japan
	Iraq. Saudi-Arabia. U.A.E.)	KOR	South Korea
ARG	Argentina	MAL	Malaysia
AUL	Australia	MEX	Mexico
AUT	Austria	NET	Netherlands
BEL	Belgium	NOR	Norway
BRA	Brazil	NZL	New Zealand
CAN	Canada	PAK	Pakistan
CHL	Chile	PAN	Panama
COL	Colombia	PER	Peru
COS	Costa Rica	PHI	Philippines
DEN	Denmark	POR	Portugal
EAF	East Africa	SAF	South Africa
	(Kenya. Ethiopia. Zambia)	SAL	Salvador
EOA	Equador	SIN	Singapore
FIN	Finland	SPA	Spain
FRA	France	SWE	Sweden
GBR	Great Britain	SWI	Switzerland
GER	Germany	TAI	Taiwan
GRE	Greece	THA	Thailand
GUA	Guatemala	TUR	Turkey
HOK	Hong Kong	URU	Uruguay
IDO	Indonesia	USA	United States
IND	India	VEN	Venezuela
IRA	Iran	WAF	West Africa
IRE	Ireland		(Nigeria. Ghana.
ISR	Israel		Sierra Leone)
ITA	Italy	YUG	Yugoslavia

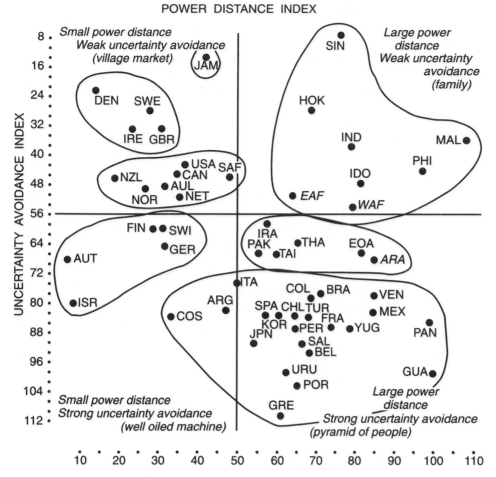

Figure 3.1 Uncertainty avoidance × power distance.
(*Source*: Hofstede, 1983b)

participative superior. They are relatively unafraid of disagreeing with the boss. They find it easier to cooperate with each other, and interdependence is stressed. In the wealthier low(er) power distance cultures, technical education is perceived as a means of acquiring expert power rather than of signalling social status.

Where power distances are high, the opposite conditions are found. Employees manage their work according to what the manager wants – or they intuit he wants. Managers are seen as showing relatively little consideration but like to see themselves as benevolent decision-makers. Coercive and referent power is stressed over reward, expert, and legitimate power.

Hofstede's findings for power distance are shown in figure 3.1 on the horizontal axis. This shows power distances least in Austria and Israel and greatest in Malaysia. (These plots have the advantage of showing groups of countries in relation to each other on more than one dimension. For instance, note the proximities in all three figures of the plotted indices of the Scandinavian countries, the Anglo countries, Latin and Central American countries, and the South-east Asian countries.)

Power distances are relatively very low in the Scandinavian countries, where conscious efforts are made to eliminate inequalities; a journalist describes how the Scandinavian ideal that no one should succeed too far and no one should slip too far behind;

> all should seek the middle ground. . . . In Norwegian schools, grades no longer exist for pre-teen students, and the message in classrooms throughout the region – nurtured as much by the absence of reward and the example of life around them as by any overt policy – is that to be average is to be safe.[13]

These non-elitist values and the lack of a need to compete are expressed in all-embracing welfare state system which protects the individual from cradle to grave. In industry the traditional barriers between management and workforce have broken down to a far greater extent than elsewhere. Workers' rights to participation and codetermination in Norway date back to the last years of the last century, and employees in companies with at least 50 employees now have the right to elect one-third of the member of the board.

3.5.2 Uncertainty avoidance

This dimension measures how far different cultures socialize their members into accepting ambiguous situations and tolerating uncertainty about the future. Members of high uncertainty avoidance cultures appear anxiety-prone and devote considerable energy to "beating the future."

The connotations of low needs to avoid uncertainty include lower anxiety and job stress, a greater readiness to take risks, and less emotional resistance to change. For instance, the introductory story shows the tendency of Swedes to suppress emotion. They tend to prize the rational above sentiment and

> [t]his attitude . . . also sets the tone for Swedish politics and business life. Swedish firms are avid appliers of new technology and ruthless in scrapping what is old and inefficient. Trade unions, which are often represented on the boards of companies, often do not oppose job cuts if there are rational arguments to back them.[14]

In these cultures, managers are more likely to be of lower average age in higher-level jobs. Little virtue is attached to loyalty to the boss. Management careers are preferred over specialist careers, and the professional manager does not feel constrained to develop technical expertise in the field that he/she manages. Inter-organizational conflict is considered natural, and compromise is an accepted route for reconciliation. The manager is prepared to break formal rules if necessary. For instance, he/she is prepared to by-pass hierarchical structures to communicate with a superior or peer if the need arises. Foreigners are accepted as managers with relatively little suspicion.

The opposite conditions apply in countries with high needs to avoid uncertainty, employees place a premium on job security, career patterning, retirement benefits, health insurance. There is a strong need for rules and regulations; the manager is expected to issue clear instructions, and subordinates' initiatives are more tightly controlled.

In Japan, the occupational elite can hope for lifetime employment with one employer – and are generally glad to take it. In response to a question about cultural problems that arise when dealing with European and Japanese employees, the CEO of Nomura Securities exemplified the company's different employment systems.

the American employment system at Nomura is by contract. Under that system, we are prepared to pay the best possible price now. The Japanese employment system, in contrast, is very traditional – step-by-step. Our Japanese employees give up part of today's salary to enjoy guarantees of future employment and income. Every few years, everyone gets promoted at the same time. If our American employees would accept the Japanese system, we would be glad to offer it. But as of today, no American has signed up for it. (Schrage, 1989, p. 74)

3.5.3 Individualism versus collectivism

This describes the relationship between the individual and the group to which he/she belongs. Individualist cultures stress individual achievements and rights and expect the individual to focus on satisfying his/her own needs. Competition is expected. Note, for instance, the readiness with which Americans go to court in order to test their individual rights both against authority and each other. Individual decisions are generally prized above group decisions, and the individual has a right to thoughts and opinions which differ from those held by the majority. Social philosophies tend to be universalistic rather than particularistic, and order is associated with the needs of society rather than with those of a particular community. The manager lacks emotional attachment to the

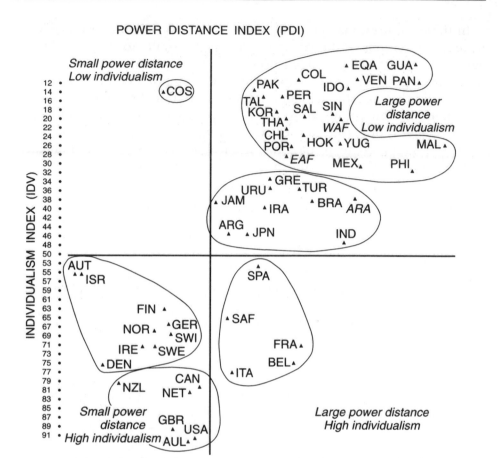

Figure 3.2   Individualism × power distance.
(*Source*: Hofstede, 1983b)

company, and his/her involvement is essentially calculative. He/she aims for variety rather than conformity in work.

The degree of the person's individualism or collectivism affects their performance within a group. Earley (1993) discovered that his collectivist subjects (Chinese and Israelis) performed less effectively when working in an individual or outgroup context, whereas individualists (Americans) who thought they were working in either an in-group or out-group performed less well than when working alone. The implication for the manager is that culturally diverse groups are more likely to be synergistic when the potentially disparate actions of multiple in-groups are coordinated.

In collectivist cultures, the distinction made between in- and out-groups means that altruism may be restricted to members of one's group. After a plane crashed in Thailand the local people scavanged the possessions of the 223 dead. A farm woman claimed that she and her neighbours had a right to whatever fell from the sky onto "their place."

> "We deserve what we got. Why should we give it to the police who did nothing?" . . . Like the other people of the valley, whose only living is what they can get out of the soil, the woman said she had a right to also harvest what fell upon the ground. . . .
> In a dozen conversations no-one expressed any remorse for joining in the looting . . . Rather, the looters spoke with pride of how quickly they responded to the situation and how much better they were at handling the local terrain than police and emergency workers. . . . Some looters lost the fruits of their labour to policemen, whom they accused of taking the valuables for themselves.[15]

A high premium is placed on group loyalty, and loyalty is valued above efficiency. In Japanese universities, students give club membership a higher priority than academic achievement. They

> will choose classes at which attendance is not taken so they can devote more time to club activities. Indeed, clubs are so important that prospective employers scrutinize not grades but club memberships. . . . [A company spokesman said]. "If a student was a captain of the club, then he is likely to be trained in harmonizing the team to produce good teamwork and to work under pressure. We don't require them to submit grades. . . ."[16]

Different attitudes towards individual achievement were shown by Americans and the more collectivist Saudi Arabians in response to the feat of a Saudi pilot during the 1991 Gulf War.

> Captain Ayad al-Shamrani, the Saudi fighter pilot lionised by US television networks for his double kill on Thursday, is an unsung hero in his native land.
> The short bearded ace, whose F-15 interceptor shot down two Iraqi Mirage F1s off Saudi Arabia's Gulf coastline, made guest appearances on US television broadcasts.
> But in the Arabic newspapers of conservative Saudi Arabia, where sensationalism is taboo, Shamrani was unnamed and his feat was hidden in the stolid language of the official military communication.
> "One of our planes engaged the enemy aircraft and shot down both of them. Our planes returned safely to base," said the Riyadh daily "al-Riyadh."[17]

3.5.4 Masculinity versus feminity

In masculine cultures sex roles are sharply differentiated, and traditional masculine values such as achievement (defined in terms of recognition and wealth) and the effective exercise of power determine cultural ideals. Managers are less attracted by a service ideal. Decisions by the group rather than the independent decision-maker are respected. Men are expected to be assertive and competitive.

In feminine cultures sex roles are less sharply distinguished, and little differentiation is made between men and women in the same job. For instance, Scandinavian men are accepted in roles that may elsewhere be associated with the feminine role – primary-school teaching, nursing, and house-husbanding (while the wife goes out to work). The dominant values are those usually identified with the feminine role. Achievement is measured in terms of the living environment and human contacts rather than of power and property, and motivation is less. Members stress relating to others rather than competing. Individual brilliance is suspect and the outsider and anti-hero are regarded sympathetically. The company's interference in private life is rejected.

Masculinity is sometimes expressed in sexist behavior. For instance, in Japan (the most masculine),

> Sexist advertising is commonplace . . . J R East Co., a big railway company, promotes ski vacations with a cartoon skier slaloming between a woman's bikini-clad breasts.
>
> Other Japanese advertisers often use more subtle forms of sexism. Images of doe-eyed, complacent women are common advertising. Household appliances are sometimes touted with the phrase, "So simple a woman can operate it."
>
> Japanese advertisers seem genuinely puzzled that anyone would question their ads. "Don't you feel there is some kind of connection between nude women and whisky?" asked a Suntory spokesman as an associate unrolled a revealing calendar.[18]

But Hofstede is measuring far more than degrees of sexism. He is concerned, primarily, with the importance of work. The more masculine the culture, the greater the importance associated with work and work relationships. The first-place ranking given to Japan in Hofstede's study is supported by England's (1986) study showing that Japanese employees agree more strongly that "work is . . . central in life" (scoring 7.78 on a range of 8.0) than do comparable Americans (6.94) and Germans (6.67). A survey conducted among Japanese businessmen revealed that 77.5 percent chose drinking with business colleagues as their favorite activity outside work.[19]

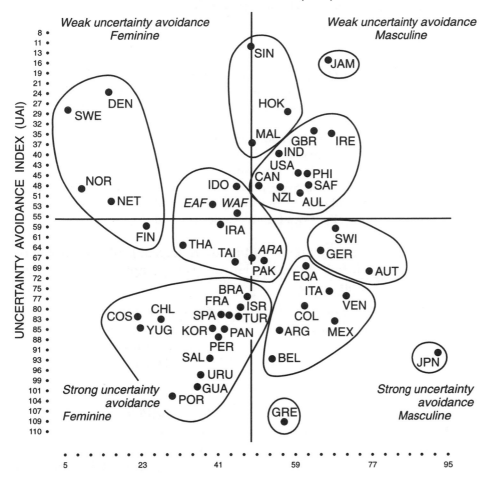

Figure 3.3 Uncertainty avoidance × masculinity.
(*Source*: Hofstede, 1983b)

3.5.5 Evaluating Hofstede's model

Hofstede's analysis is vulnerable on a number of counts (see comments and references in Jaeger, 1986).

First, it assumes that national territory and the limits of the culture correspond. But cultural homogeneity cannot be taken for granted in countries which include a range of culture groups or with socially dominant and inferior culture groups: the United States, Brazil, Switzerland (French, German, Italian, Romansch cultures); Belgium (French, Flemish cultures); Italy (Milanese northern and Sicilian southern); Spain (aristocratic Catalan and peasant Castillian).

Cultural heterogeneity within one country can have practical implications. For instance, the marketing manager makes a serious mistake if he/she assumes that the tastes of French Canadians and English Canadians coincide.

> "[French Canadian] Quebeckers consciously wish to be distinct and they reward with their business brands and products that recognise this distinctiveness," said Coca-Cola Canada's vice president of marketing, Dave Sanderson. . . .
>
> The fast-food chain McDonald's has adjusted its menu in Quebec to include poutine, a French Canadian dish consisting of fried potatoes covered with cheese curds and brown gravy.
>
> "We're seeing regions like Australia, Europe and Latin America becoming more outward-looking. . . . But the Quebec market these days is focusing inward upon itself," Coca-Cola's Sanderson said.[20]

Second, there are conceptual and methodological problems. Some of the connotations listed above overlap or even paraphrase each other. For instance, we find

	Low-power distance	*High-power distance*
1.	Students put high value on independence	Students put high value on conformity

(Hofstede, 1984a, p. 92)

and

	High masculine	*Low masculine*
25.	Belief in the independent decision-maker	Belief in group decisions.

(Hofstede, 1984a, p. 200).

This means that an example of "independent" non-conformism with group norms could be explained either in terms of low-power distance (suggesting that other connotations of low-power distance apply), or in terms of high masculinity (suggesting that other connotations of high masculinity apply).

Further, not all important value dimensions are represented (Triandis, 1982), and the structure of those four dimensions that are used can be challenged. The Masculinity/Feminity dimension is perhaps misnomered; it invites interpretation in terms limited to sexism. (This point is implicit in Sekaran and Snodgrass, 1989.) Yeh (1988) suggests that the two dimensions actually reflect "physical" and "social" needs. The Individualism dimension appears to be defined primarily in terms of a perception of the private self, and a need to achieve. But other interpretations are possible. Czarniawska (1986) refers to individualism in the United States as "competitive individualism" (p. 325) and above all a question of competition in preference to cooperation; but she characterizes individualism in Poland (before the collapse of Communism) as a struggle against the impersonal state. Brummelhuis (1984) explains the Thai concept in terms of needs for independence from authority.

> The individual's preoccupation is not so much with self-realization and autonomy as with adaptation to the social or cosmological environment. If a notion of Thai individualism is to have any specific meaning it is in designating that particular mode of retreat, avoidance and distrust [of authority], which colours so many forms of behaviour and social relationships. (pp. 44–5)

These examples indicate the problems that arise in applying a single concept of "individualism" across cultures. Similarly, "collectivist" behavior in one context might have other connotations elsewhere. Yeh (1989) points out that the Japanese are loyal to their organizations and the Chinese to their families. In Japanese terms, then, a Chinese employee who places his collectivist family interests over the interests of the organization is disloyal and cannot be fully trusted.

Third, the research is in itself culture-bound (Roberts and Boyacigiller, 1984). The results inevitably reflect the methodology used, and hence the cultural bias of the researchers. The team was composed of Europeans and Americans. And thus many of the questions asked and the analysis made of the answers reflect Western concerns and have had less relevance to other cultures. Hofstede (1991, ch. 7) himself argues that this imposes a limitation on the effectiveness of the research instrument.

Fourth, in some instances the findings may be out of date. An extreme example is provided by the country "Yugoslavia" – which no longer exists, and broke up in part because of cultural incompatabilities. In general, though, there is no reason to suppose that the great majority of the cultures surveyed have changed radically. This question is discussed further in chapter 17.

Fifth, Hofstede's informants worked within a single industry (the computer industry) and a single multinational. Robinson (1983) points out that the values of IBM employees are unlikely to be typical of their countries, and that certain social classes (for instance unskilled manual workers) are altogether excluded.

However, these objections are dwarfed by the importance of Hofstede's work in relating different cultures and applying cultural analysis to practical management problems.

- The choice of informant population poses some problems in generalizing to other occupational groups within the target populations (as we saw in the fourth point listed above) but it also offers a signifi-cant advantage. The population is controlled across countries, which means real comparisons can be made.

- The dimensions of power distance, uncertainty avoidance, individu-alism, masculinity, tap into deep cultural values and allow significant comparisons to be made between national cultures.
- The questions asked of the informants (reflected in the connotations listed) express issues of immediate concern to the cross-cultural manager.
- No other study compares so many other national cultures in so much detail. Quite simply, this is the best we have.
- Hofstede's work provides the manager with a framework of guide-lines and hypotheses against which to measure his/her own analysis. In the words of Westwood and Everett (1987), it is

> useful heuristically as a starting point for further investigation of cul-ture and cultural variation, particularly for more qualitative research and analysis. (p. 201)

Applied intelligently and not slavishly, it provides the cross-cultural manager with an essential instrument, and a starting point for doing his/her own analysis.

3.5.6   Applying Hofstede's model

Hofstede's research findings are invaluable when applied as a general model which needs to be interpreted in terms of your *specific* situation. They are likely to be misleading if applied literally in all circumstances. In other words, look for both similarities *and* differences between your situation and that of Hofstede's research sample (within the same coun-try), and decide how the differences affect your application of the model.

In particular, look for

- sub-cultural differences;
- industry differences;
- differences arising from the organizational culture.

Hofstede's research indicates which orientation *most* members of a culture group are likely to adopt in routine situations. It maps out ten-dencies, and does not make hard-and-fast predictions that will apply in all cases. This drives home the point that cultures differ in relative, not absolute, terms. The fact that Indonesian culture is essentially collectivist does *not* mean that appropriate behavior in Indonesia is never appro-priate in the United Kingdom, for example, or vice versa.

It is a mistake to assume that these research profiles describe only the values accepted by the power elite or by those who seem most likely to benefit from their expression. A member of a more feminine culture might expect that in a masculine culture, such as Japan, the majority of women would be angrily opposed to the dominant culture. But this is not the case:

> [a] survey of female seniors attending 561 universities and junior colleges in the Tokyo area shows that coeds not only expect sexism in the workplace, most of them don't seem to mind it.

- More than 91 percent said they would not mind being treated as "office flowers." . . .
- Over 66 percent said acting like an office flower would make the atmosphere more pleasant.
- . . . 60 percent said they'd be happy in a situation where the man goes to work while the woman stays home.[21]

That is, the majority endorse their shared culture, even though an insider might perceive that they are its victim.

If the manager comes from an individualist culture, the advantage of social and organizational structures which encourage self-expression and achievement seem to outweigh the dangers of social alienation and competition within the group. But a member of a collectivist culture values social harmony and his/her identity as a member of the group; he/she has no good reason to express individualism if it means surrendering these advantages.

3.6 Implications for the Manager

Compare an organization that you know well in *your own culture* and a similar organization in *some other culture.*

1. Review the Kluckhohn and Strodtbeck model (section 3.2) and apply it to the cultures of the two organizations.

    - Review each orientation.
    - Design profiles for both organizations, distinguishing both predominant and subordinate variations.
    - Identify significant differences in the variations descriptive of the two organizations.

2. Review Hall's explanations of high- and low-context cultures (section 3.3) and apply it to the cultures of the two organizations.

   - Given your analyses, what differences do you find in:

     (a) management-staff communications?
     (b) the formation and activities of work-groups?
     (c) relations on a vertical axis?
     (d) relations on a horizontal axis?

3. Within *your-own-culture* organization,

   (a) which of these is likely to be rewarded?
   (b) which of these is likely to be punished?
   (c) which of these receives neither reward nor punishment?

   - The individual follows his/her job specification to the letter, whatever the task.
   - The individual departs from his/her job specification when this seems more likely to accomplish the task.
   - The individual follows authorized reporting procedures, whatever the task.

4. Answer the questions asked in (3) for *your-own-culture* organization.

   - Explain any differences in your answers for the two organizations.

5. From your understanding of *your-own-culture* organization, how far does it fit Hofstede's profile of the culture (or a close culture)? What evidence can you find for disagreeing with Hofstede and arguing that:

   (a) power distances are significantly wider/narrower than as plotted?
   (b) needs to avoid uncertainty are higher/lower?
   (c) relationships are more collectivist/individualist?
   (d) perceptions of role are more masculine/feminine?

   - How do you explain any variations from the profile?

3.7   Summary

This chapter has examined various models making cross-cultural comparisons on a range of dimensions. Section 3.2 discussed the Kluckhohn–Strodtbeck model of *cultural orientations*. Section 3.3, *cultural contexts*, examined Hall's notion that cultures vary in how they program their members to depend upon the context when communicating and developing relationships. He distinguished between "high-context" cultures, in which members depend upon implicit clues, and "low-context" cultures, in which members place greater reliance upon explicit information.

Section 3.4 examined Laurent's concepts of *culture, status, and function*, and then showed the implications these have for explaining different priorities given to technical expertise and facilitating skills. Section 3.5, Culture and the Workplace, examined Hofstede's early model in detail. The parameters of power distance, uncertainty avoidance, collectivism/individualism, and masculinity/feminity were illustrated. The strengths, weaknesses, and mode of application by the manager were discussed.

3.8 Exercise

This exercise practices applying models discussed in this chapter.

Use it to decide whether the behavior described in the last sentence of each of the following is typical *or* untypical *within the cultural context, and explain your answers by referring to the relevant model or models.*

(a) Your management career is based on your success as a facilitator. You are posted to the marketing department of your company branch in Indonesia. You are asked a technical question that relates to marketing, to which you do not know the answer. You respond, "I don't know." Your plain-speaking is highly respected.

(b) In the United Kingdom, you decide to promote a junior manager to a senior post. She is a poor communicator and is unqualified – except that her father is an influential politician. This promotion is happily accepted by other employees because it seems likely to benefit the company.

(c) At company headquarters, you form a mixed-culture work team consisting of Japanese men and Swedish women, and chaired by a woman. These persons have been temporarily borrowed from your subsidiaries in Tokyo and Stockholm. The team is neither compatible nor productive.

(d) You are posted to a newly acquired subsidiary in Italy. You discover that your peer's subordinates are unwilling to come to you for help even though they know that your technical skills will enable them to solve their problems.

(e) In Australia, the great majority of your employees opt to take lower salaries in return for guarantees of lifetime employment.

(f) In Pakistan, an employee asks the help of a local manager in your subsidiary to solve a family problem with his (the employee's) brother-in-law because he (the manager) is "an important man in the community."

(g)　In Sweden, your subsidiary is losing money. You decide to introduce new technology, which means scrapping the previous technology, retraining many of the workforce and changing their work assignments. You explain your proposals in detail to the union. The union accepts them without demur.

Notes

1. "Cool as a Swede," *The Economist*, May 6, 1989.
2. Robert Fisk, "1,400 pilgrims killed in Mecca tunnel," *Independent*, July 4, 1990.
3. Karen Lowry Miller, "How Japan vaccinates its CEOs," *Business Week*, April 1, 1991.
4. I am indebted to Ms Laurie Sugita for this example.
5. Nicholas D. Kristof, "Can Communists Beat the Red Dragon?," *International Herald Tribune*, February 26, 1992.
6. Clyde Haberman, "Some Japanese (one) urge plain speaking," *New York Times*, March 27, 1988.
7. Connerton (1989) cites Efron, D. (1941).
8. Robert Whymant, "Populate or perish call to Japanese," *Daily Telegraph*, June 13, 1990.
9. Steven R. Weisman, "In Japan, the Brazilian 'Cousins' get no respect," *International Herald Tribune*, November 7, 1991.
10. Ibid.
11. Figures produced by the Ministry of Justice of Japan, 1986, reported in "A law unto itself," *The Economist*, August 22, 1987.
12. Helen Fielding, "The votes that live on the hill," *Sunday Times*, June 16, 1991.
13. Tyler Marshall, "The Scandinavian good life: would a few hurdles hurt?," *International Herald Tribune*, December 15, 1988.
14. Alan Elsner, "Research says Sweden can banish emotion from life," Reuter, *Bangkok Post*, January 30, 1989.
15. Reuter, "Thai looters' proud harvest," *Sydney Morning Herald*, May 31, 1991.
16. Susan Chira, "For Japanese students, club spirit outclasses good grades," *International Herald Tribune*, June 30, 1988.
17. Reuter, "Saudis keep air force ace out of limelight," *Bangkok Post*, January 26, 1991.
18. Damon Darlin, "Advertising: commonplace sexist ads raise only a few eyebrows in Japan," *Wall Street Journal*, April 19, 1989.
19. Associated Press, "Workaholics rule," *The Nation* (Bangkok), March 24, 1992.
20. Christine Tierney (Reuter), "Pleasure-seeking Quebec is truly distinct within Canada," *Bangkok Post*, February 24, 1992.
21. Emily Thornton, "Japan: sexism OK with most coeds," *Fortune*, August 24, 1992.

Part II

Culture and Structure

4

Structures for Making Decisions

4.1 Introduction

An extreme example of a flattened company hierarchy and high employee participation is provided by a thriving Brazilian manufacturer of industrial equipment, Semco. The owner, Ricardo Semler, created a structure in which

> most employees decide their own salaries. Their bonuses, which are tied to the company's profits, are shared out as they choose. Everyone, including factory workers, sets his own working hours and groups of employees set their own productivity and sales targets. . . . There are no manuals or written procedures. Workers choose their own boss and then publicly evaluate his performance. . . . Big corporate decisions, such as diversifications and acquisitions, are made by all employees.[1]

Hofstede's (1984a) model shows that Brazilian values are relatively high-power-distance and collectivist. The company therefore seemed to buck the norms of the culture, at least in terms of power distance.

> Semco's unique management style would be radical anywhere, but in Brazil, where authoritarian bossism remains in fashion, it looks even more bizarre.[2]

The company survived in part through strict budgetary controls. And because employee earnings were directly linked to profits, the peer pressure to contribute and not to abuse privileges was enormous. Thus collectivist norms were applied and reinforced.

This suggests that the structure adopted by an organization and implementation procedures may be influenced by a number of factors; in this case, by the entrepreneur's personality and beliefs, by needs for financial control, and by culture.

The problem for the cross-cultural manager is to identify:

- how far culture is a factor in determining priorities of structural design and their implementation;
- the importance of culture as against other factors.

The chapter discusses this problem of formal structure. (Informal structures are dealt with in the next chapter.) It has the following sections:

4.2   The Functions of Structure
4.3   Influences Other than Culture
4.4   Culture and Structure
4.5   Bureaucracy
4.6   Implications for the Manager
4.7   Summary
4.8   Exercise

4.2   The Functions of Structure

The Oxford English Dictionary defines a structure as the

> arrangement or the interrelation of parts dominated by the general character of the whole.

An organizational structure is a system for dividing and coordinating responsibilities allotted to its members.

Structures have the following functions.

- *Assigning responsibilities*   Each member of the organization is given responsibilities for performing specific tasks. Related responsibilities are assigned to the same unit or department on the basis of the skills needed to perform them.
- *Assigning relationships*   The tasks assigned to the member are coordinated with those assigned to other members, who have been delegated the same or complementary tasks. Formal relationships determine who plans whose responsibilities, who controls whom, who reports to whom, who works with whom, etc.

In all organizations, certain responsibilities and relationships are *permitted* and enforced. For instance, B must perform task X and report to Supervisor A. Other responsibilities and relationships are more or less *proscribed*; B must not (or ideally should not) interfere in task Y and not report to Supervisor C. So within the organization, members are constrained to certain sub-sets of interactions. The formal structure communicates the restrictions on these subsets. But the culture of the organization and more general context decide how these constraints are applied. Where management perceives a need for tight control, constraints are enforced to the letter by rules and routines.

The manager selects and applies within his/her organization those structures which seem most likely to answer these questions as effectively as possible.

- How can the mission and goals of the organization be achieved? How can the direction of the organization be maintained?

- How can members' individual efforts be aggregated so that they contribute productively to achieving the organization's goals? How are individual jobs related to each other?

- How can members' needs be satisfied so that they are motivated to contribute productively?

Every organization has to deal with the implications of all three questions. But they will be prioritized differently. When the second is emphasized, the structure is mechanistic; when the third is emphasized and the importance of individual initiative is recognized, a more organic structure is implemented.

4.2.1 Mechanistic structure

The structure is mechanistic and normative when its members are treated like parts of a machine. It is designed to give top management greater control over their subordinates' activities, and thus to make these activities more predictable. Management calculate that the organization operates most efficiently when tasks are planned in detail and routinized, and restrictions on responsibilities are highly specialized. The creation and maintenance of this bureaucratic machinery is the primary role of the support staff. Typically, departments are organized on a functional basis. Opportunities for individual initiative are highly restricted.

In appropriate conditions, the machine organization is efficient. These conditions include the organizational goal – when the work demands routinized efficiency rather than creativity – for instance, in a steel plant, a national postal service. And there must be a pool of labor whose educational, cultural, and other experiences and needs precondition them for working within this structure.

4.2.2 Centralized structure

The mechanistic structure may also be highly centralized. An organization is centralized when units and individuals are dependent upon decisions taken by a single person (or small group). Communication is limited to formal structures, and this means it may be slow.

In a large and complex organization, centralization places too much responsibility on one person, who is unlikely to be expert in all the organization's activities or to have access to all necessary information. But some companies benefit from centralization. This applies not only to small family companies but also to much larger organizations. Hewlett-Packard in 1982 was faced with coordination problems and centralized research, marketing, and production, which had previously been dispersed among autonomous divisions.[3] By 1988 the company had more than recovered its previous market position.

In general, centralization is attractive when

- speed in responding to changes in the environment is of low priority; relevant factors in the environment are stable;
- there is no need to push decision-making down to lower levels in the organization;
- time spent in communicating messages up and down the hierarchy can be reduced to an acceptable minimum;
- coordination between departments has to be highly regulated;
- a multinational headquarters needs to retain control over subsidiaries, for instance when marketing a global product that must meet the same specifications in all markets; Coca Cola headquarters in Atlanta has recently strengthened its centralized control over subsidiaries, particularly in South-east Asia;
- there is a sense that decision-making cannot be entrusted to lower levels. Northcraft and Neale (1990) note that

> [r]isk often tends to centralize decision-making. Where the consequences of making poor decisions are great, top management will be unlikely to give up control. (p. 676)

The environmental factors that foster this sense of insecurity can include culture, and a high need to avoid uncertainty.

Decentralization is attractive when speed in communicating and responding to change is essential, and when top management feels less need for tight control. When an organization needs to operate in diverse markets, it diversifies. This means creating a number of power sources, building bridging structures giving greater opportunities for communication between departments, and so far as possible pushing decision-making down to lower levels. For instance, a multinational which replicates headquarters structure under regional managers reflects pressures for regional diversity.

In 1991 the loss of $10 billion led IBM to decentralize many of its decision-making systems on an international level. ICI decentralized its chemicals and pharmaceuticals divisions when they showed themselves no longer sufficiently rapid in reacting to what was happening in the world.

Those functions which are centralized when the overall structure is otherwise decentralized are flagged as essential to maintain the necessary minimal degree of homogeneity; Handy (1985) notes that

> where the only central department is finance implies that this is the only form of uniformity that is crucial in comparison with the pressures for diversity. (p. 306)

4.2.3 Organic structure

Organic structures are developed when the organization places a priority in flexibility, for instance when it must continually adjust to sudden shifts in the environment. Knowledge and experience is valued more than organizational rank. Formal and informal communication links are fostered at all levels, between centers of expertise in order that information can be shared as widely as necessary. To the extent that the manager relinquishes control over his/her subordinates, the outcomes of their activities are less predictable. The organic structure is given complex expression in the form of the matrix, discussed in section 4.4.4.

A successful organic structure motivates the commitment of its members. Their knowledge and skills are rewarded, and they influence how systems are implemented. They are motivated by their meaningful relationships with each other and with the organization as a whole (Trompenaars, no date, p. 32). The structure provides opportunities to satisfy both individual and group needs.

Individual and group needs are significantly influenced by culture. But before discussing the significance of culture, this chapter now examines factors *other than* culture that help determine the organization's choice of structure and how that structure is implemented.

4.3 Influences Other than Culture

Culture is not the only factor to influence what structure the organization adopts and how that structure is implemented. The introductory case gave an example showing the importance of an individual's personality. Here, these other factors are discussed:

- strategic factors;
- industry factors;
- size;

- technology;
- the complexity of the task.

4.3.1 Strategic factors

Chandler (1962) concluded from his history of United States business that strategic issues determine structure. A company that does not adapt its structure in order to meet new strategic needs quickly grows inefficient. Strategic needs are largely influenced by environmental factors. For instance, markets have changed and the company decides to expand into (or retreat from) new geographical regions, functions, and product lines. New constraints are set by changes in the economic, political, and ethical contexts. New sources of materials and labor emerge or old sources dry up.

The old structure is no longer able to cope with these pressures, and a new culture seems likely to provide the necessary administrative and cultural reforms.

An example is provided by the case of the Swiss multinational Ciba-Geigy (Kennedy, 1993). Public reactions to an environmental disaster in Basle (for which the company was not responsible) persuaded top management that the ethical context was now insecure for a chemical and pharmaceutical manufacturer. More attention had to be paid to social responsibilities outside the firm and to developing an organizational culture of responsibility within. A photographic film business was sold off and the company decentralized, making each of the 14 new divisions responsible for its own strategic planning, performance, and results. More individual initiative was encouraged throughout. The mandatory retirement age was lowered from 65 to 60.

This case shows how strategic issues cause a company to review its options for vertical structuring. Choices are made between the following.

- *A functional structure* for instance, departments of marketing, finance, production, etc. This option is selected when the company produces a very limited range of products or services, and finds it useful to concentrate functional experts within corresponding units.
- *A product structure* for instance, departments for Product 1, Product 2, etc., each product department including managers responsible for marketing, finance, production, etc. This option is selected when the company produces a wide range of products and services.
- *A client structure* departments are organized in terms of the clients they serve – for instance, wholesale, retail.
- *A matrix structure* the individual reports to two superiors, for instance a project manager and a functional manager (discussed in section 4.4.4.).

- *A divisional structure* headquarters is mainly concerned with strategic issues, and general managers at divisional level are responsible for profits in their divisions, each of which is a self-contained profit center. Divisions may be geographically or product based – Asian division, European division, etc.; toiletries division, food division, publishing division, etc. The division adopts a functional or product structure.

A strong single-owner has relative freedom to enforce a personal interpretation of differentiation needs and to define structural priorities. The introductory case gave an example.

In the entrepreneurial organization, influence typically spreads from the central figure along functional and specialist lines; Handy (1985) labels it the "power" culture. Formal structuring may be relatively weak. But an organization that offers its members security and predictability (and has a "role" culture) is built around structures that reflect needs for rules and systems. In time the organization may evolve from the first to the second state, particularly as its markets mature, and assuming that the process is handled successfully, its structures are correspondingly adapted.

4.3.2 Industry factors

A structure that meets the needs of any one of these organizations may not suit the others:

- a traditional government bureaucracy;
- a high-technology producer;
- a private law firm;
- an advertising agency;
- a hotel.

For instance, the law firm may consist of a number of partners who work relatively independently of each other, conjoined only by their needs to share a stock of shared resources (premises, clerical assistance, etc.). Goals are formulated loosely; to provide legal services, perhaps in a specific area of law. The activities of one partner have very limited impact on the activities of others, provided that they are ethical and legal, and except in so far as they affect profit margins.

Drucker (1988, p. 46) suggests that information-based organizations (for instance, hospitals) depend increasingly on the inputs of independent specialists who route their communications directly, rather than through superiors. This has the effect of rendering whole layers of middle-management redundant, and hence of flattening the organization.

At the opposite extreme, the government ministry requires that responsibilities and relationships be precisely formulated; and a hierarchical structure, that drastically reduces opportunities for independent initiative, is more appropriate. A study of US government public personnel agencies and finance departments suggested that when administrative authority is invested in expert personnel, there is a tendency to generate tall hierarchies with narrow spans of control (Blau, 1968).

From evidence drawn from Western Europe, Child (1987) argues that the firm which produces a single product will control and coordinate its members through an integrated hierarchy. A multi-divisional firm or holding company controls at arm's length and uses a looser, semi-hierarchical mode. Joint venture partners and other "co-contracting" firms control the joint venture through agreed specifications and deadlines, and depend upon trust relations. Licensing and franchising firms control their franchisees through formal financial agreements and monitoring of service standards.

4.3.3 Size

Size influences needs for vertical differentiation. For instance, a product structure permits greater growth than does a functional structure; a common response to success within a functional organization is to restructure adopting a product structure. A divisional structure organized on a geographical basis reflects at least a wide international network and often multinational interests.

When a company is first established, it may consist of very few members and precise differentiation of roles and relationships is important. But as it grows, these have to be formalized. A Bangkok-based Belgian Thai joint venture grew from two to 300 employees in three years. Organizational goals were spelled out clearly from the start, but there was an almost total lack of detailed job descriptions, and of coordinating systems. Initially of course, there were few problems. But over time, line and staff units increasingly conflicted over their areas of responsibility. Management style was firmly cast in an entrepreneurial style, quick to respond to changes in the external environment, but relatively uncaring of organizational difficulties.

After three years, top managers were forced to channel their energies away from routine operations and into arbitration between units; and eventually, into a structural overhaul.

4.3.4 Technology

The introduction of technology may profoundly affect relationships between members. For example, when staff take data and instructions from a computer model rather than from supervisors, supervisors become redundant. The removal of this managerial layer has the effect of flattening the structure.

Alter (1980, pp. 95–6) suggests that the introduction of information technology (particularly in decision systems) has such benefits as

- improving personal efficiency and problem-solving;
- improving interpersonal communication, by creating standard data and operating procedures;
- increasing organizational learning and understanding through experience;
- increasing organizational control.

Bahrami and Evans (1987) show the practical implications. They describe an organizational innovation developed by successful high-technology firms in California's "Silicon Valley," the "stratocracy." Unlike the traditional organization it is designed to focus on short-lived opportunities and in fluid environments, rather than on long-term markets within a stable environment. In the stratocracy, rather than in the bureaucracy:

- job designs foster multiple roles, rather than specialization;
- departments are fluid, rather than separated by formal boundaries;
- decision-making is centralized and decentralized, rather than top down;
- staff functions support productive functions, rather than standardize their operations;
- control is administered through the organizational culture, rather than by formal rules;
- rewards are determined by accomplishments and expertise, rather than by span of control and seniority.

4.3.5 Complexity of the task

The complexity of the tasks allocated to members of the organization influences their needs for supervision, and hence influences how the structure is implemented.

Assume, first, that manager A is responsible for supervising two subordinates, B and C, and second, that this situation applies:

- the task is close ended; there is only one way of correctly performing it, and one correct outcome;
- A has expert knowledge of how the task should be performed;
- B and C do not have this expert knowledge;
- in this cultural context, tight control is welcomed. The previous chapter showed that where power distances are large, close supervision is positively evaluated, and the superior is expected to be directive.

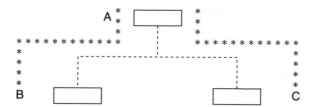

Figure 4.1   Vertical communication in a simple hierarchy.

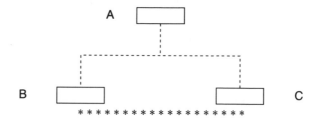

Figure 4.2   Horizontal communication in a simple hierarchy.

A invests time in giving instructions, suggestions and advice, and checking B and C's understanding. B and C may take little or no part in planning the task, deciding what procedures are to be used, what performance criteria are appropriate, and when these criteria have been met. A is responsible for controlling the information flow.

This structure is shown in figure 4.1; the heavy lines indicate the communicate focus, which is on a vertical axis. But when the cultural context does *not* welcome tight control, and where close supervision is *not* positively evaluated, this strong vertical control may have to be modified.

For instance, when

- the task is open-ended and there are many possible outcomes;
- B and C know more about how to accomplish the task than does A;
- B and C must collaborate in order to accomplish the task;

it becomes increasingly important that B and C are able to communicate efficiently, and A's access to either B or C is less important. In figure 4.2, the heavy line indicates that the communicative focus is on the horizontal axis.

This relationship is reinforced in cultural contexts where tight control by the superior is not welcomed. Hofstede's (1984a) model shows that in small power-distance cultures, close supervision is negatively evaluated, and a participative superior is preferred.

These examples show that the basic superior–subordinate structure incorporating A, B, and C is implemented differently in different situations. The nature of the task and the culture are both factors influencing how the structure is implemented.

4.4 Culture and Structure

Here we look in greater detail at how the participants' cultural values and needs modify how a structure is implemented, and may indirectly influence what structure is chosen.

4.4.1 Weighing culture as against other factors

The problem of weighing culture as against other factors is illustrated by Lincoln (1989). An objective comparison of Japanese and United States organizations showed that in both countries, employees were less committed and less satisfied in taller firms, and more so in flatter firms. And because no significant difference could be found on this dimension across the two countries, culture appeared *not* to be a factor in influencing motivation.

Lincoln also demonstrated that the Japanese firms had more levels of structure; by implication, then, Japanese employees were *in general* less happy in their work than were their American counterparts. However, relations between superiors and subordinates differed markedly. These differences reflected cultural differences; and significantly, may not be shown up in when organizational charts are compared on a strictly objective basis (the number of employees, the number of levels, etc.).

For instance,

- American subordinates were far less likely to socialize with their superiors and work-groups outside work hours than were their Japanese equivalents;
- American subordinates were less tolerant of close supervision and resented narrow spans of control.

And, in conclusion,

> frequent supervisor-subordinate interactions have a positive quality in Japanese work settings which is missing in the U.S. While American manufacturing employees keep their distance from supervisors, Japanese employees seek such contact and through it develop stronger bonds to the work group and the organization as a whole. (Lincoln, 1989, p. 96)

This suggests that the employee is better motivated by a structure that reflects his/her values in regards to superior–subordinate–peer relationships – but on condition. The condition is that the structure should be interpreted appropriately, and in terms of the cultural context.

This point is underlined when we see how structures are traditionally implemented in large Japanese organizations. Top management provides "top down" strategic guidance, which gives a framework within which policy details are formulated. Middle-level managers and below contribute "bottom-up" enthusiasm; for instance, quality circles make suggestions for modifications and perhaps for new products. These are reviewed by top management, and may eventually stimulate new strategy. Thus influence moves in both directions.

But this does not mean that formal authority is delegated downward. In their study of 50 Japanese organizations, Azumi and McMillan (1981) found that strategic decision-making processes tended to be centralized, regardless of organizational size and technology, and that strategic decisions were taken by top management.

In traditional United States organizations, on the other hand, criteria of structural rationalism are still treated as superordinate, and opportunities for "bottom-up" influence are very restricted.

All this tells us that a given structure should not be interpreted too mechanically, as though fully encapsulated by an organizational chart. For instance, there can be no simple answer to the traditional question, what is the ideal span of control. How a given span translates into practice depends on needs for autonomy, access to the manager, and degree of task specialization. That is, the relationships modeled by the chart must be observed in action before the structure can be fully analysed.

This discussion is best carried forward by applying three of the research analyses reviewed in the previous chapter. Sections 4.4.2–4.4.4 and section 4.5 apply the work of Kluckhohn and Strodtbeck, Laurent, and Hofstede.

4.4.2 Applying the Kluckhohn and Strodtbeck model

It will be recalled that the Kluckhohn and Strodtbeck model includes the following:

Orientation	*Variations*
What is the person's relationship to other people?	Hierarchical
	Lateral
	Individualist

These variations influence preferences for structure. Members of a culture characterized by lateral relationships are likely to feel at home

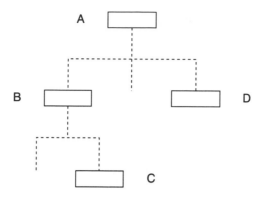

Figure 4.3 Relations in a hierarchy.

in tall organizations where power flows down the hierarchy (see Figure 4.3).

C receives instructions from B (and never D), and B derives his authority from A, and C communicates with A only through B. Similarly, B and D do not directly communicate except in so far as they are licensed to do so by A.

A tendency towards collaterality translates into a preference for flat structure.

By definition, no structure permits absolute individualism, where individuals are free to define and achieve their own ends without any regard to the interests of other members. But greater degrees of individualism can be perceived in a law firm, for instance, where the individual is the central point and members are relatively free to select their own cases.

4.4.3 Applying Laurent's findings

The chapter 3 discussion of Laurent's work (1983; with collaborators, 1989) drew attention to different values attached towards communicating within and across the vertical line of control.

Figure 4.4 shows a structure in which B feels free to communicate directly with C, and C with B, even though this means bypassing C's direct superior. For instance, B may have expertise which is essential to C in order to complete a task, and direct communication is more likely to result in efficient work than routing messages through A. The decision to by-pass is influenced by cultural values: Laurent (1983) found that only 22 percent of his Swedish respondents disagreed with the statement "In order to have efficient work relationships, it is often necessary to bypass the hierarchical line" (p. 86), as against 75 percent of his Italians.

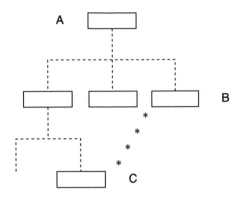

Figure 4.4 Bypassing the hierarchy (1).

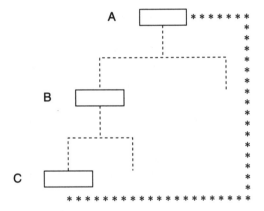

Figure 4.5 Bypassing the hierarchy (2).

But this does not mean that the high-power distance organization in Italy is necessarily working at sub-optimal efficiency. If it were flattened, its members would no longer enjoy the security of precise reporting relationships – which their culture teaches them to value. The ensuing confusion and conflicts (in a culture which works hard to avoid organizational conflict) would cancel out any benefits derived from faster formal communication.

Similarly, in figure 4.5, C bypasses an immediate superior, B, in order to communicate with their common superior, A.

Of course, in all cultures B might resist this practice, but this resistance is least in such cultures as Sweden, Netherlands, and the United States (all of which Hofstede (1984a) classifes as low-power distance). It is strongest in Japan, the People's Republic of China and Indonesia (high-power distance) where a premium is placed on maintaining the

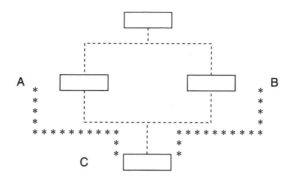

Figure 4.6   The matrix.

hierarchical integrity of the organization, even when this slows down or hinders operations.

4.4.4   The matrix structure

Laurent's findings apply to functions of the matrix structure. Unlike in other structures where each individual reports to one superior, in the matrix he/she reports to two (see Davis and Lawrence, 1977). The matrix is often the chosen alternative of project-focused companies (such as NASA, and many engineering and construction companies), where relationships and responsibilities are always likely to be modified as each new project is contracted.

Figure 4.6 represents a matrix structure, in which C reports to both A and B. For instance, C is a project engineer, and reports to both project manager A and engineering manager B.

The matrix involves a balance of power and joint decision-making between functional departmental heads (Galbraith, 1971). For instance, they must be able to collaborate on budget plans, and agree on dual reporting relations. Matrix structures work well when their members are prepared to cooperate, share information in a relationship of inter-dependence, collaboration, and trust.

But because they depend so heavily on mutual trust and a willingness to share resources, including information, matrix structures are difficult to operate effectively, and may always pose problems. Burns and Wholey's (1993) study of United States hospitals that had abandoned matrix structures found that the most common reasons were financing problems, turnover and staffing problems, and conflicts between physicians and nurses.

In which cultures are matrix structures least likely to succeed? When members have high needs to avoid uncertainty, they are uncomfortable with dual reporting procedures. In high-power distance cultures, employees prefer hierarchical lines of control and communication, and are relatively reluctant to trust their peers – as A and B must, as figure 4.6 showed. Laurent's (1981) data indicate that "rejection of the dual-boss principle appears much stronger in the Latin cultures [France and Italy] than in others [Northern Europe and the USA]" (p. 108).

The matrix is most likely to succeed in cultures where there are low-power distances and low needs to avoid uncertainty – for instance, in Anglo and Scandinavian cultures. Poulsen (1988) claims that Scandinavian companies succeed when employees and management see themselves as peers, control is loose and manners informal, "close to disrespectfulness"; this style "is something rarely found in the USA, Japan, France or West Germany" (p. 230).

And in this cultural context, the matrix serves to reduce conflict and to positively harness the contradicting interests of different departments (for instance, sales, and production) rather than to create conflict.

Multinationals may decide to establish matrix structures when local executives have to report to both a local manager and an expatriate manager. The expatriate may be briefed to train his local counterpart; in practice, he/she is perceived to be protecting headquarters' interests. When the headquarters' point of view always takes precedence over local feelings and the supposed equality of the expatriate and local is transparently false, the loyalties of local executives are seriously strained. Their career needs lead them to treat the expatriate as boss, and their cultural identity to identify with the local.

Hari Bedi tells of the anguish of a local Malaysian manager when his multinational headquarters imposes a matrix, or "two-boss system."

> [T]he new system would effectively take away much decision-making responsibility from the local manager. He would become a figurehead. Haleem's boss would no longer be the real boss and instead he would have to refer most matters to the regional office. Other employees shared Haleem's concern. They felt that the downgrading of their boss's position would seriously affect the standing of the company in the community.[4]

This demoralizing situation is further worsened if

- the expatriate boss is assigned when the local boss has already held the position for some time on his/her own; the local appears to have been demoted and his/her authority is undermined among other local staff;

- the expatriate boss is younger than the local boss. In Asian societies, where age is respected, the elder loses face by sharing authority with a younger person;
- the expatriate is less experienced.

4.5 Bureaucracy

Although the terms "bureaucracy" and "bureaucratization" have come to have negative connotations, Weber and other early sociologists used them in a neutral sense to describe how modern organizations operate. And no company can work efficiently without some bureaucratic division of labor and responsibilties.

Weber's (1947) "ideal" bureaucracy is rule-governed. Rules determine the following.

- *Job specifications* The bureaucrat is expected to perform specified duties, and to refrain from meddling in the duties allocated to others. He/she fills a particular specialized function which complements functions performed by other members of the organization.

- *Reporting relationships* Relationships with superiors, subordinates, and peers are regulated.

- *Remuneration* Pay and allowances (including sick pay and pensions) are structured for all members of the organization according to their rank and duration of service, and the emoluments paid for any given job are typically detailed in the job specification.

- *Entry to the organization* Qualifications for entry (which usually include examinations passed and certificates held) are specified. Age restrictions also apply. The bureaucrat is appointed on the basis of his/her knowledge and professional expertise.

- *Criteria for promotion, rewards and punishments.*

- *Exit from the organization* The bureaucrat must retire by a certain age, for instance 65.

Bureaucratic organization is impersonal in that the rules apply to all members, whatever their identity (social status, family relationships, etc.) outside the organization. The bureaucrat is employed to serve the organization's interests rather than his/her own.

The term "bureaucracy" is sometimes thought to refer only to government and state organizations. But both public and private organizations adopt bureaucratic rules in order to make members' behavior predictable and to reduce uncertainties. So a culture that has most need for these rules creates bureaucratic structures that most nearly approach the ideal model.

Needs for degrees and types of bureaucratic organization are influenced by factors other than culture, and by culture. The non-cultural factors were discussed in section 4.3 above: strategic factors, industry factors, size, technology, task complexity. Here we focus on culture.

4.5.1 Bureaucracy and culture

In practice, of course, bureaucracies very seldom (perhaps never) fit this "ideal" model at all points. The factors discussed in section 4.3 are all likely to influence not only what structure is adopted but how bureaucratic priorities are implemented. This section sees how culture determines how the bureaucratic "ideal" is interpreted in practice.

Hofstede (1984a, pp. 215–18) models four bureaucratic types, which roughly correspond to the four variations found on the power distance and uncertainty avoidance indices. That is, the four types exemplify:

- large-power distance + large uncertainty avoidance cultures;
- small-power distance + small uncertainty avoidance cultures;
- small-power distance + large uncertainty avoidance cultures;
- large-power distance + small uncertainty avoidance cultures.

He argues that each is *likely* to be favored above the others in a specific cultural setting, all other things being equal. This prediction should not be interpreted as an absolute; in practice of course, any one society (probably) includes examples of all four types and variations on them. Family companies can be found across the world. A multinational is likely to replicate significant features of its own structure when it establishes subsidiaries, wherever they are located.

Further, it cannot be assumed that bureaucratic styles in cultures near to each other on these two indices will approximate closely. For instance, the United Kingdom and the United States are both found within the low-power distance + low uncertainty avoidance group. But, as Neghandi (1979) notes,

> "modern" systems of management in British and American origin have a great deal in common. . . . [Nevertheless] it is perhaps possible to distinguish between, on the one hand, an "American" style of rather authoritative decision-making but at the same time rather status-free, informal intercourse between superiors and subordinates, and on the other hand, a "British" style of participative management accompanied by relative formal relations in the social sphere. (pp. 326, 328)

These objections aside, Hofstede's model provides the cross-cultural manager with a useful framework on which to base his/her initial hypotheses about the structure and management style of the other-culture

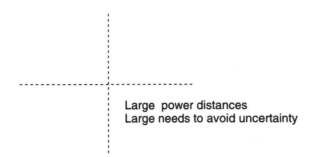

Large power distances
Large needs to avoid uncertainty

Figure 4.7 The full bureaucracy.

organization. The manager conducts his/her own research in order to verify the appropriacy of Hofstede's analysis to the particular organization. Where the model does not fit, the manager looks for factors to explain why not, and proposes and tests alternative hypotheses.

4.5.2 The full bureaucracy

An organization adopts bureaucratic rules in order to make members' behavior predictable and to reduce uncertainties. So a culture that has most need for these rules creates bureaucracies that most nearly approach the ideal type. Hofstede names these "full" bureaucracies. Relationships between members, and the procedures required to perform tasks correctly, are highly regulated. Typically, members respect the unequal distribution of power and the right of superiors to enforce rules, and they have a strong need to avoid ambiguous procedures. Greece, Japan, Portugal, France, Turkey, Mexico, and other Latin American countries belong in this large power distance, strong uncertainty avoidance category (see figure 4.7).

This applies the relationship shown between superior and subordinates shown in figure 4.1. Opportunities to communicate bypassing the hierarchy are rare; perhaps departments communicate only at the highest levels. Functions are tightly distinguished. Vertical communication is the norm and line authority is prioritized. Any criticism of higher levels is likely to be communicated upward only through informal channels and third parties.

Aiken and Bacharach (1979) find significant differences between Belgian local government bureaucracies in Flemish areas (Dutch culture – hence smaller power distances and weaker needs to avoid uncertainty) and in Walloon areas (French culture). The former are characterized by greater reliance on interpersonal mechanisms for social control, less use of impersonal rules and procedures, less routine work, and more short-circuiting of official channels.

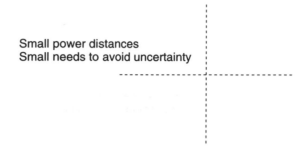

Small power distances
Small needs to avoid uncertainty

Figure 4.8 The market bureaucracy.

The Walloon organizations seemed to be characterized by greater rigidity and various characteristics that one associates with Weber's ideal type of Bureaucracy while the Flemish organizations tend to be more flexible and less bureaucratic. (p. 240)

Crozier (1964) analysed four basic elements in French bureaucracy;

- the impersonality of the rules – members have a low tolerance of ambiguity, reflecting high needs to avoid uncertainty;
- the centralization of decisions;
- strata isolation – senior officials (who have passed the baccalaureate) from junior officials, reflecting high-power distances;
- the development of parallel power relationships.

He found one French organization

in which only the director and his assistant were able to make changes in the factory. But their power, which was theoretically great, was held completely in check by the inadequacy of the power structure we have analyzed. ... In the French pattern, authority is helpless against subordinates because it cannot discriminate among them. Authority in Russia disposes, on the contrary, of all the necessary tools with which to interfere in subordinates' affairs. This is well accepted by the subordinates themselves, who do not object much to such arbitrary discretion. (p. 228)

4.5.3   The market bureaucracy

On the other hand, bureaucratic structures tend to be weakest in cultures marked by small power distances and weak needs for uncertainty avoidance. Members place more reliance on personal relationships and depend less on place in the bureaucratic hierarchy. They have relatively greater control over how they perform their tasks. Hofstede describes this form of implicit structure in terms of a market, where power is less centralized and emanates from a number of sources (see figure 4.8).

Market bureaucracies include the United Kingdom and the United States and other Anglo countries, South Africa, Norway, Ireland, Sweden, the Netherlands. Members negotiate for power and influence, creating alliances by trading support and the threats of reprisals if support is not forthcoming; "you scratch my back and I'll scratch yours, but if you give me trouble you can expect trouble in return." These informal alliances may cross departmental lines, as figures 4.4 and 4.5 illustrate.

It is not surprising that matrix structures are most successful in these cultures. Burns (1989) argues that the matrix

appears to be, in part, an outcome of political compromise between professional groups vying for power and control over resources. (p. 366)

In other words, the matrix succeeds in cultural contexts where compromise and competition between organizational units and peers are most easily tolerated.

Power differences are small but this does not mean that members of the organization undervalue the attributes of power. On the contrary, symbols of rank can assume exaggerated importance – perhaps just because functional differences are so slight. In an American insurance company, junior clerical staff worked in a large open-plan office in which each individual's work space was precisely regulated and marked off by screens, and senior grades enjoyed several square inches more than their juniors. Persons who arrived before work in order to move their screens a few inches further apart made themselves extremely unpopular with their colleagues, who perceived their rights to be infringed.

A further example is provided by another American company which symbolized rank by the cars it provided its members; senior officers who drove were allotted more expensive models, subordinates less expensive models. A new CEO decided to "rationalize" by stopping this practice. Instead, all staff were paid car allowances, again graded. By privately supplementing his allowance, an Assistant Finance Officer was able to afford a Porsche whereas his superior, the Director of Finance, drove an old Chrysler. So ranking was still signaled symbolically within the company by the car allowance paid. But the make of car driven had greater symbolic importance to outsiders.

Contacts are forged by working closely with members of other units on joint projects, or even by working in a number of departments during a career with the organization. DiPrete (1987) made a study of mobility within bureaus of the US Federal Government and found significant evidence of individuals crossing organizational boundaries, between professional and administrative jobs. This implies relatively low needs to avoid uncertainty both on the part of those prepared to make such moves, and those prepared to work alongside rotating staff.

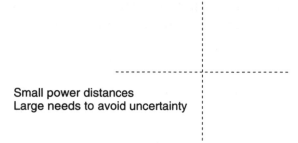

Figure 4.9 The workflow bureaucracy.

4.5.4 The workflow bureaucracy

Between these two extremes lie the workflow bureaucracies typified by Germany, Switzerland, Finland, and Israel, and the personnel bureaucracies, typified by the South-east Asian countries. The organizational structures of workflow bureaucracies place more emphasis on regulating activities than relationships. Hofstede compares them to well-oiled machines.

The need to avoid uncertainty is relatively much higher and requirements for job performance are tightly specified, but power distances are low (see figure 4.9). Note for instance that in large German companies executives and workforce may share common canteen facilities, whereas in Russia, different facilities may be provided for up to six different grades. And in Germany, unions, management and government find it relatively easy to cooperate and avoid conflict – for instance, in organizing training programs (Hilton, 1991).

Child and Kieser (1979) argue that typically, German top managers centralize their power to a greater extent than do their British equivalents. Similarly, Haine, Ghiselli, and Porter (1966) found that German departmental managers are more likely than their British equivalents to find that decisions are being taken over their heads. They comment

> It is not surprising therefore that they perceive themselves as having significantly less discretionary authority attached to their roles . . . and that they are perceived by their colleagues as having less influence within their companies . . . (p. 362)

4.5.5 The personnel bureaucracy

Personnel bureaucracies occur in collectivist cultures where power distances are wide; for instance, West and East Africa, India, and the Asian Pacific countries of Indonesia, Philippines, Malaysia, Hong Kong, Singa-

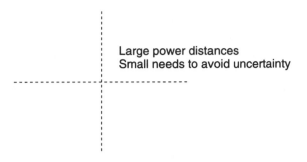

Large power distances
Small needs to avoid uncertainty

Figure 4.10 The personnel bureaucracy.

pore. Hofstede likens them to the oriental family. The organization is typically built around a strong leader who controls by direct supervision, and authority is associated with this individual rather than with the organization or his/her rank (as in the full bureaucracy).

In a United Nations report, Ross and Bouwmeesters (1972) describe patterns of authority in tropical African companies.

> Where delegation of authority does occur, it is usually confined to relatives (in private enterprises) or persons with whom top managers have political ties (in public enterprises). . . . mistrust of those not related by ties of kinship or ethnicity limits the possibilities of delegation and teamwork. (p. 72)

Ethnic, tribal, clan and family ties are likely to be significant factors in how the structure is implemented. A study by Scott et al. (1979), comparing authority systems in US and Nigerian organizations, noted that despite important similarities, only one US respondent mentioned race as a factor that determined rewards and sanctions. But

> well over half of the respondents in both the Nigerian hospital and tobacco company mentioned ethnic or tribal identity as effecting their organizational sanctions. Apparently tribal loyalties were a sufficiently strong force to intrude themselves in important ways into the functioning of these Nigerian organizations. (p. 181)

Ranks are tightly differentiated and promotion is restricted. But roles are specified less precisely, and workflow is less restricted. Neghandi and Prasad (1971) found that Indian organizations tended to have many more hierarchical layers than did American subsidiaries in India, but fewer control systems on production. The manager needs to show greater intelligence and expertise than his/her subordinates in order to secure and maintain their loyalty. If a candidate for promotion lacks these qualities, then he may well be disqualified.

The same point applies in relations between peers. The individual who refuses to behave according to his/her bureaucratic role may be perceived to be "stepping out of place," and endangering the structure. Writing in an Indian newspaper, an Indian manager makes the point:

> Lack of knowledge of one's role and that of others one comes in contact with is one of the foremost causes of employee and organizational ineffectiveness. . . . Relationships often fail due to misunderstandings and lack of role clarity, as can be seen in the example of an old employee trying to play the role of adviser to a new employee who misinterprets this as being "bossed" by one who has no business to do so![5]

Where labor is cheap, a trusted manager may be rewarded with additional staff. Hence size of his/her department and the number of staff over whom he/she exercises control has symbolic value, indicating his/her importance.

Chung et al. (1989) dispute Weber's insistence that modern bureaucracies must be essentially impersonal and mechanistic in order to develop and continue capitalism. They argue that Confucian principles of respect for family members and a "ceaseless pursuit for perfection" exert important influences in Chinese and East Asian cultures (p. 315). The development of Asian business is facilitated by the local emphasis on the well-being of employees and the quality of work-life, and a philosophy of improvement.

Fukuda (1983) argues that Hong Kong Chinese companies depend less on informal channels of communication in order to achieve a free flow of information than do Japanese companies. The Chinese manager hoards information that he considers of no direct relevance to others.

> On this ground, it is doubtful whether the decision-making processes of Chinese management can be truly regarded as collective (at least in the Japanese sense). Based on these observations, the decision-making system adopted by many Chinese firms may well be characterized by what I call the "top-down" narrowly-collective process of decision-making. (p. 42)

4.6 Implications for the Manager

Compare an organization that you know well in *your own culture* with a similar organization in *some other culture*.

1. In each of the two organizations:

   - which of these is likely to be rewarded? Which of these is unlikely to be rewarded?

     (a) the individual follows his/her job specification to the letter, whatever the task;

     (b) the individual departs from his/her job specification when this seems more likely to accomplish the task;

     (c) the individual follows authorized reporting procedures, whatever the task;

     (d) who the individual reports to in any given situation depends upon the task.

   - What formal and informal communication networks are used? Who reports to whom in theory and in practice? Who negotiates with whom in order to complete a task?

   - How far can differences in your answers for the two organizations be explained by cultural differences?

2. In what respects can differences between the organizations be explained by

   - strategic factors?
   - industry factors?
   - size?
   - technology?
   - complexity of the task?

3. Which organization shows

   (a) greater differentiation of functions?

   (b) more formal systems for controlling performance?

   (c) more integrating control mechanisma?

   (d) more processes for coordination and communication?

   - How can these differences be explained?

   - How far are cultural differences significant in explaining these organizational differences?

4. For similar departments in the two organizations, compare and contrast the following.

   - *Relations between peers* How much assistance do they give each other in their work? How easily do they cooperate? Over what issues do they come into conflict? How much do they socialize outside the workplace, and how does this affect job performance? What factors *other* than culture influence their relationship?

• *Relations between superior and subordinates* How much supervision do the subordinates desire, and how much does B give? How much freedom do subordinates have to plan, implement and evaluate their work? Who initiates communications? How much do they socialize outside the workplace, and how does this affect job performance? What factors *other* than culture influence their relationship?

4.7 Summary

This chapter has examined influences on the formal structure adopted by the organization, of which culture is only one.

Section 4.2 dealt with the *functions of structure* and focused on needs to organize responsibilities and relationships. Concepts of mechanistic as against organic structure, and centralized as against decentralized structure were examined.

Section 4.3 took up a theme developed throughout the book; the problem for the cross-cultural manager is to differentiate the importance of culture as against *influences other than culture* in determining priorities in structural design and implementation. These other factors were separated out; and then section 4.4 focused on the significance of *culture* for *structure*. Comparisons of structures derived from objective and statistical analysis are unable to show how a given structural type is experienced and implemented within a particular setting.

Section 4.5 went on to see how the need to rationalize roles and relationships fosters the development of *bureaucracy*. Hofstede's (1984a) analysis suggests that the variable of culture is an influence on how bureaucractic norms are interpreted in different contexts.

4.8 Exercise

This exercise involves role-playing first the resolution to a grievance, and then the design of structures aimed at preventing such conflict reoccurring in the future. The exercise is a pair and class activity.[6]

1. The class divides into pairs. Each pair consists of:

   • the sales manager;
   • the production manager.

   You work for a small engineering company. Read your roles, which are as follows:

Sales manager The production manager never cooperates with you when you have a rush order. You have to fight with him/her every time you want to make a change in the production schedule. You can't understand why he/she won't be more cooperative. After all, if you can't collaborate to keep your customers happy, you will both be out of a job! You have requested a meeting with the production manager to confront him with this problem.

Production manager The sales manager never cooperates with you when there's a rush order. Every time he/she expects you to change the production schedule, and entirely overlooks the problems you face in procuring materials, tooling up, organizing work details, etc. If you have to rush an order ahead of schedule to get it finished, you cannot guarantee quality, and other scheduled jobs are delayed, which affects other customers. After all, if you can't collaborate to keep your customers happy, you will both be out of a job! The sales manager has requested a meeting with you today in order to resolve this problem.

2. Each pair: develop any further data you need about a recent incident in order to give your role-play greater realism.

(About 10 minutes.)

3. (a) *All* sales managers meet together to discuss your problems and strategy.

   (b) *All* production managers meet together to discuss your problems and strategy.

(About 7 minutes.)

4. Each pair: *role-play* and negotiate a solution to the immediate grievance.

(About 12 minutes.)

5. (a) *All* sales managers meet together to discuss the solutions you have just negotiated. How can such problems be prevented in the future, assuming that the company is operating within

   • a *market bureaucracy*?
   • a *full bureaucracy*?

   (b) *All* production managers meet together to discuss the solutions you have just negotiated. How can such problems be prevented from reoccurring in the future, assuming that the company is operating within

   • a *market bureaucracy*?
   • a *full bureaucracy*?

(About 12 minutes.)

6. *Pairs 1, 3, 5, 7, etc.*   Assume that your company is operating within a *market bureaucracy.*

Pairs 2, 4, 6, 8, etc.   Assume that your company is operating within a *full bureaucracy.*

All pairs: roleplay as follows   Design a structure/formal rules/informal rules which will prevent such problems reoccurring in the future – *given your cultural context.* Your recommendations will be passed on to the responsible authorities within the company for their decision.

(About 15 minutes.)

7. *Full class discussion*   Compare and contrast your recommendations.

Notes

1. "Diary of an anarchist," *The Economist,* June 26, 1991. See also Semler (1991).
2. Ibid.
3. Jonathan B. Levine, "Mild-mannered Hewlett-Packard is making like Superman," *Business Week,* March 7, 1988.
4. Hari Bedi, "Top vacancies," *Asiaweek,* December 4, 1987.
5. Dr V. V. R. Sastry, "Know thy role," *Times of India,* May 29, 1991.
6. This exercise is based on unpublished teaching material written by Ms Daryl Chansuthus. I am grateful for permission to adapt it.

5

Patronage Relationships

5.1   Introduction

A home-based United States firm opened negotiations with a Malaysian public-sector organization. At first, American executives dealt directly with the chairman. Then, the chairman fell unexpectedly sick and was taken to hospital.

The American executives faxed their sympathies to the managing director. Taking for granted that he would assume executive control in his chairman's absence, they directed all communications to him.

However, all their messages met with the same response: nothing could be settled definitely until the chairman was back at his desk. But the chairman was already recuperating and the prognosis was good; could he not be approached at home? Unfortunately not; he had given strict instructions that he was not to be bothered with business matters until his recovery was complete.

Frustrated, the Americans considered breaking off negotiations. A company so dependent upon one person seemed unlikely to prove an efficient business partner.

They discovered only after the chairman's return to work that the young general manager, nominally subordinate to the managing director, was the son of a personal friend of the chairman, and enjoyed more direct access. In fact, he had been visiting the chairman on a daily basis, briefing him informally on events in the office. Because he feared losing face, the vice-chairman had been unwilling to redirect messages from the American firm down to his subordinate for rerouting to their common superior. And neither the general manager nor the chairman had been aware of how urgently the American firm needed to contact him.

The American executives assumed that formal structures of control determined actual reporting relationships, and that these were accurately modeled by the organizational chart. They failed to look for informal links which transcended formal structures. In the event, the general manager enjoyed a patronage relationship with the chairman, that excluded the vice-chairman from effective control.

Supposing the Americans had identified the importance of this patronage relationship, how might they have overcome their communication problem? Some pretext for communicating with the general manager would have given them the license to discreetly copy to him all messages ostensibly addressed to the vice-chairman. Thus communication with the chairman would have been maintained without forcing the vice-chairman to lose face.

This chapter examines the importance of informal links in both the public and private sectors, within and between organizations. It focuses on patronage relationships, which develop differently in different cultural contexts. When they override formal structures, they pose particular difficulties for the outsider who does not recognize them.

Informal relationships generally and patronage relationships in particular affect not only the interests of the persons concerned. They significantly influence:

• priorities in investing resources;
• priorities in recruiting, selecting and promoting staff;
• priorities in interpreting organizational structures and systems.

And when the cross-cultural manager has to deal with political, public-, or private-sector organizations in which the selection of such priorities processes is determined by informal relationships, he/she needs to understand how they work.

The chapter has the following sections:

5.2   Informal Relationships and Patronage

Informal relationships are distinguished here from those formalized by rational bureaucratic processes. When two members of a company get on well together, take their lunches together, and spend weekends together, their relationship is *informal*. The responsibilities that link manager and assistant manager in a *formal* relationship are defined by the organizational structure and expressed by their job descriptions, the organizational chart, and organizational practice.

Formal and structured relationships have been dealt with in chapters 3 and 4, and need not concern us further here.

Of course, persons in a formal relationship may also enjoy informal ties – as in the introductory story. When this is the case, an effort must be made to distinguish behaviors caused by their exercising their official and unofficial capacities. This may not be easy, and the problems that ensue go some way to explaining why informal influence is so abhored by the rational bureaucratic mentality – as we see.

Two types of informal relationship are distinguished:

* *patronage* relationships (discussed throughout all sections saving only 5.2.6);
* *friendship* relationships (discussed in section 5.2.6 only).

5.2.1 Patronage relationships

Patronage relationships include a patron and at least one client. They are vertical; the patron plays a relatively senior role – both within the relationship and in other interactions, and the client the junior. The patron secures and rewards the client's loyalty and service, and the client reciprocates, each contributing such resources as he/she controls. The decision by social superior and subordinate to enter this type of relationship reflects, on the part of each, perceptions of

* need for resources, controlled by the other and otherwise unobtainable;
* social distance;
* an opportunity to bridge this distance, at least on a personal level, and hence to satisfy the need (Kahn, 1988).

Patronage relationships are *personalized*, in the sense that patron and client freely choose each other; they can therefore be distinguished from relationships of formal authority and manipulation, in which the relationship is determined by organizational criteria and compliance is enforced.

They serve as a means to *distribute resources*. Different types of resources are exchanged. The patron probably has access to such economic and instrumental resources as money, work opportunities, choice of work detail, a contract, service.

Social resources include support and protection, information, votes and support. For instance, the patron is obliged to protect his/her clients against the forces of impersonal bureaucracy and outsiders, perhaps even when these outsiders represent legally constituted authority.

This point was demonstrated in 1992, when the United States and United Kingdom concluded their investigations into the 1988 bombing of a Pan Am plane over Lockerbie in Scotland, and named as suspects two members of the Libyan security services. They requested that Colonel Gadaffi's Libyan government surrender the two for trial. Gadaffi refused. He had good cause to comply with these demands, but

> some of his most powerful henchmen are opposed to handing them over, among them Major Abdelsalaam Jalloud, the de facto second-in-command. One of the accused belongs to Jalloud's tribe, the powerful Magaref; under bedouin traditions, a tribal leader must fight to the death for his members.[1]

And by implication if their positions were reversed, the clients would be expected to fight no less fiercely to protect their patron. That is, the clients give loyalty, service, information, and protect their patron's interests.

Other resources include personal and sexual favors, and psychic rewards such as loyalty and trust.

The decision to exchange resources is based upon perceptions of interest. The patron needs the client's loyalty and service, and the client needs protection, opportunities to work, etc. By implication, then, patron and client are conjoined in a relationship of mutual dependency. The relationship may be unequal but cannot be characterized as autocratic, and the patron who exploits his/her clients is courting disaster (Thompson, 1989, p. 325).

5.2.2 Reciprocity

Exchanges are usually made between *dissimilar* resources. That is, a vote is unlikely to be exchanged for a vote. By virtue of their different social roles, the patron and client have access to different resources, and the patron commands greater resources than does his/her clients.

Given this, a problem arises; how can patron and client enter into a "reciprocal" relationship when the sums of their resources are in imbalance?

The relationship should not be perceived as a simple commercial transaction. Each side expects to obtain from it what is not otherwise available. Symbolic offerings – such as expectations of protection and service – may be significant. Legg (no date) argues that the requirement of reciprocity need not mean "balance" on one-for-one exchange in objective terms, but merely balance in terms of a series of "mutual expectations." . . . There can be no mutual standard of value against which to judge the goods exchanged because the subjective assessment of each partner is the determinant. The evaluation of the offerings is derived from the actors' personality systems and the cultural norms governing the particular type of exchange. (p. 13)

The contribution that each makes may be of little value to him/herself but significant to the other. For instance, a political patron signs a letter on behalf of his client's son who wants a government job. The client reciprocates by making sure his family members vote for his patron at election time.

The comparative worths of the resources being exchanged may never be explicitly measured by the participants, and the contribution made by one side is often not made conditional upon an immediate and equivalent contribution made by the other. Conditions such as "if you find my son a job I'll vote for you in the next election" are probably unstated; patron and client are *not* bound as seller and buyer.

5.2.3   Duration

A patronage relationship takes time to develop. Because such relationships are not governed by impersonal rules, each party must be sure of the other's trustworthiness (in reciprocating favors, keeping confidences) before committing him/herself. By implication, the persons involved may be long-time acquaintances, perhaps as neighbors. Casson and Nicholas (1989) argue that where social mobility is low, individuals have more repeated contact, and so consider reputations for good behavior to be more important; on the other hand, social mobility reduces trustworthiness. Once developed, a patronage relationship may continue for the lifetimes of the participants.

You cannot buy in and out of patronage relationships as easily as you change your orthodontist or management consultant. For a client to deny a justifiable request for service, or to refuse reciprocation, or to seek a new patron, may be tantamount to betrayal. The client who betrays his/her patron risks punishment and also a reputation for unreliability, which makes it all the harder to find a new patron. Similarly the patron who fails his/her clients is likely to lose them and hence lose his/her power base.

By creating the conditions for loyalty and rewarding it, patronage creates social relationships based on *mutual obligation*. This principle of mutual obligation means that each side can be confident that, in time, a favor given will be reciprocated – materially or symbolically. Hence the distribution of a particular resource may not be immediately reciprocated (except perhaps by promises of loyalty and solidarity), and builds up long-term credit with the other side (Eisenstadt and Roniger, 1981, p. 276).

5.2.4   A stream of exchanges

A patronage relationship sets up expectations of a stream of exchanges for an indefinite period.

For instance, a professor in a Thai university had a car to sell. (Mead, 1990, p. 192). She asked her maid for help and the maid took the trouble to enquire among her family and friends. Eventually she suggested that a distant cousin might be interested. The cousin, a skilled electrician, came to see the car. He could not afford to buy this model on the market; nevertheless a price was agreed. This was well below the car's value and greatly to the electrician's advantage. However, her patronage relationship with the maid gave the professor some guarantee that the sale would not be to her disadvantage.

When the professor wanted electrical repairs done to her house, her maid contacted her relation who was bound to help his family member when he could, and he did the work for a minimal charge. And when the professor's new car broke down, he lent her back the old one rent-free until it was fixed.

All three benefited. By acting as broker, the maid had strengthened her relationships with both her relation and employer, and was thus better placed to call on favors from both in the future. She had helped her cousin purchase a car at a price he could afford and also find new work – particularly when the professor recommended him on to her colleagues. The professor had found a purchaser for the car, the guarantee of a rent-free car loan when she needed it, and a handyman bound to provide reliable service.

None of these future benefits was promised at the time of the sale. However, the two existing sets of relationships (between the professor and maid, the maid and her cousin) and their shared understanding of the culture gave the three participants a reasonable guarantee that

- their relationships would continue into the future;
- favors given in the present would be reciprocated in the future.

5.2.5   Insiders and outsiders

Patronage relationships commonly extend beyond a single patron and client and may involve a host of people tapping into different sources of power and influence. Over time these linkings build into a network of social, economic, and political influence, and the patron sets him/herself up as the focus of the network. The network distinguishes between its members, and non-members or outsiders.

The network reserves for the use of its members those resources of prestige, influence, finance, information, etc., that it is able to corner. As significantly, it denies these resources to non-members. Patronage is both an *inclusion* and an *exclusion* mechanism; economic and social opportunities are channeled to the favored few and kept out of the grasp of outsiders – who may be technically more deserving.

The point is illustrated by events in a department of Kuwait University shortly after the Gulf War. The Egyptian head controlled a patronage network that was in "open conflict" with other members of the department.

> The key issues were recruitment and promotion, always the levers of patronage and power, and the head's manipulation of the committees involved.
>
> On the recruitment side, the department believed the head was delaying advertisements and appointments in order to bring in his "supporters club" during the summer. . . .
>
> Promotion was a running scandal, owing to the head's propensity for delaying the promotion of well-qualified but politically unwelcome members, while accelerating the procedures for the "supporters club."[2]

For instance, applications might be lost in the mail, "something easily arranged given the appalling state of the Kuwait Post Office this past year." One deserving candidate was informed that all his work had been lost, another that a vital part was missing.

A patronage network is self-generating in the sense that its members exploit their shared resources to increase their power. For instance, in Thailand:[3]

> "It is important to understand that Thai politics, like Thai culture, is not about policies. It is about personalities," said an MP. "It is about the class you were within military academy, about your business associates, about your friends. And it is about patronage. People want to become MPs so that they can become ministers, because ministers can make money."

And implicitly, the rewards of a ministry provide the means to reward clients and buy further influence.

5.2.6 Friendship relationships

Friendship relationships include:

(a) vertical relationships that do *not* fit the patronage model discussed above; that is, a superior and subordinate are bound in an affective relationship, and may involve the occasional exchange of resources – for instance, birthday and other presents; this exchange differs from patronage in that

- resources are not exchanged in expectations of support and loyalty, and do not commit the parties to further obligations;
- exchanges may be only very occasional;
- the relationship may be of short duration;

(b) relationships between peers; ties of mutual dependence and loyalty are horizontal;

(c) association relationships; for instance, members of the same class at school.

Friendship cliques are significant when a group exchange favors on a peer basis. Recruiting from a friendship clique can benefit the organization. For instance, a graduate manager in a firm manipulates recruitment procedures in order to bring in his/her university friends. As members of the same clique, they share similar qualifications and hence by hiring one member the firm attracts far wider recruitment among his/her educational equals.

The line between friendship involving an exchange of resources and patronage is imprecise. This last category in particular shades into patronage when members of a senior class have jobs and favors at their disposal which they channel to members of junior classes. Outsiders are effectively excluded from participating.

For instance, Tokyo University (Todai) alumni maintained such a lock on government jobs that in 1992 the cabinet was forced to declare that in future no more than 50 percent of top bureaucrats would be Todai graduates:

> Ever since the Emperor Meiji created Tokyo Imperial University a century ago, the university, and particularly its law faculty, has been the breeding ground of Japan's governmental and business leadership. Todai graduates plotted Japan's strategy in autos and computer chips. They set foreign policy and industrial policy, rising in lockstep with their "class" on rungs of the government ladder. And despite a lot of loose talk about how quickly Japan is changing, the Todai tradition seems in little danger.[4]

The control of labor resources (jobs) by a restricted social group means that persons with alternative experiences and viewpoints have no opportunity to contribute.[5] Whether such control is in itself unethical is an open question; but, like all patronage, it creates the conditions for corruption.

5.3 Patronage, Society, and Culture

Perhaps no society is entirely free of patronage influence, and examples of such relationships can be found in all cultures.

In the United States, patronage was accepted as a fact of life in Chicago city politics even before the rise to power of Richard J. Daley. But Daley perfected the system (or "Organization"), first as Chairman of Cook County Democratic Party and then as six-term Mayor (1955–76). Patronage was deeply entrenched in all aspects of city government. It moved into top gear during election years, and accusations and denials of vote rigging were a constant feature of Chicago's political life.

Recruitment to the payroll and promotions in city government and support for official programs were determined by needs to build and maintain loyalty to the Mayor and his political lieutenants. City building inspectors and other officials employed statutory sanctions to enforce, discourage, and punish any signs of disaffection. Thus patronage usurped official functions.

These days were recently recalled, in 1988, when a Chicago city official was accused of trading jobs for sexual favors.

> [A] local watchdog group that cooperated in an investigation ... characterized [his] activities as "the ultimate abuse of the patronage system."
>
> "You can't use public money to stash mistresses on the public payroll," said Terry Brunner, [the Association's executive director]. ... "We have a jaded, insensitive electorate here," said Mr Brunner, who characterized much of the public reaction as, "Is this any worse than anything else that goes on here?"
>
> "The problem," Mr Brunner added, "is that people don't see anything wrong with patronage."[6]

In the United States (as in other Anglo cultures and in most of northern Europe) patronage relationships have drastically declined in importance over the past few decades. In so far as patronage is still a factor in determining official and commercial policy, perceptions of obligation and commitments to stable interactions between patron and client are weaker.

In other cultures the official's sexual activities might only be a cause for concern if his mistresses were perceived to exert excessive influence in the administration (never an issue in this case). For instance in Latin America where macho culture is strong, political dalliances are given greater toleration.

> [I]n Venezuela, where presidential mistresses show up on society pages, the limits of their powers are openly debated... [R]ecent presidential

mistresses are said to have wielded great political power, a fact that has almost split a major political party and has led to accusations of corruption and influence peddling.[7]

A mistress of the president of the time (1991) had surplanted his wife in the presidential palace and forced her to move to a separate residence. She influenced appointments to the cabinet and the military. And close friends of hers were accused of defrauding the state of millions of dollars in an arms purchase.

Why are patronage relationships so much more significant in some cultures than others? Below, we examine the social and cultural factors within which patronage thrives.

5.3.1 The social conditions for patronage

What type of organization fosters patronage relationships? The owner of a family business who fears losing his/her skilled labor to competitors may be naturally inclined to develop personal links of obligation with them. Research conducted by Wong Siu-lun (1986) into Hong Kong cotton spinners showed them to be

> patriarchal business leaders. They conferred welfare benefits on their employees as favors, took a personal interest in their subordinates' behaviour not directly related to work, and disapproved of trade union activities ... Personalized ties with the subordinates are forged in an attempt to counter their centrifugal tendency to set up on their own and become rival competitors. For industries such as spinning and weaving which require a stable workforce to deal with regular business cycles, benevolent paternalism is also one means to retain workers. (p. 313)

Elsewhere, patronage may offer the only hope of social justice in a society where, most importantly, authority is arbitrary and weak. Other factors that give rise to patronage include the following:

- public officials are not able or not willing to protect individual rights and liberties;
- public officials abuse their powers;
- public officials are relatively inaccessible to the public – unless tea money is paid;
- wellfare services are weak or non-existent;
- opportunities for social and physical mobility are few;
- public resources are not channeled equitably.

Patronage is sometimes associated with private property, particularly in the less developed world. But this is not necessarily the case. The extent of patronage in such developed societies as Italy and Japan and elsewhere in the Asian Pacific region suggests that even when poverty is alleviated, patronage is not necessarily eroded.

Many of these conditions for patronage once existed (or still exist) in Italy. Italy was only united as a nation in 1870. Local loyalties are still very significant, and determine how decisions taken by central government are implemented at the local level – if at all. Thus (until 1993) political parties such as the dominant Christian Democratic Party really constituted a clutch of patronage factions rather than a monolithic national organization (Zuckerman, 1979).

The corruptions scandals of 1992–3 revealed that patronage was still common throughout the country, including Sicily, that part least accessible to Rome and least resourced. Feudal Sicily produced the Mafia, which originated among small landowners anxious to protect their estates from royal (and alien) authority.

When large numbers of Sicilians migrated to New York and the United States in the nineteenth century, the *padrone* or sponsor commonly advanced money for the immigrant's passage and found him work – in return for a fee. The immigrants were ripe for exploitation; most knew no English, had very little understanding of the new society, and were otherwise defenceless. The *padroni* system fostered the spread of the Mafia system.

> It thrives in situations of corruption and relative normlessness. It could not be avoided in the New World. (Lopreato, 1970, p. 130)

And the Mafia still depends upon overlapping patronage networks (or "families") to link its members.

In less developed countries today, where central government is unable to satisfy all the demands made upon its resources, the criminal boss plays a patronage role very similar to that of the Mafia chieftain. In the example below, a prominent Indian gangster enjoys patronage relationships with a range of clients – even though he lives in exile. He is credited with

> enormous clout over Indian politicians, police, customs officials, the directorate of revenue and intelligence and the income tax authorities . . . Businessmen, film producers, builders and actors regularly fly to Dubai to attend his parties or to ask him to solve problems.
>
> One oft-told tale involves a dispute of about $1 million. It was first referred to a leader of Maharashtra state. He looked through the court case and said, "I'll refer it to the *bhai* (brother) in Dubai. He'll settle it in your favor in ten minutes. Here it could take months, and I can't even guarantee it'll be settled."[8]

So in this instance, the decision-making processes exercised by a gangster patron were seen as more efficient and preferred to the state legal system – even by a senior servant of the state.

5.3.2 The cultural conditions for patronage

The examples given in this chapter indicate that patronage is usually found in collectivist cultures where power distances are high. An obvious exception is Italy. According to Hofstede's measure, Italy scores low on collectivism. This might give a fairer measure of values around Milan than in Sicily.

Nevertheless, when the revolution against patronage in politics and state enterprise got underway in 1992–3, hundreds of politicians and business leaders were under investigation in all parts of the country, in the north as much as in the south.[9] By June 1993, 800 had been arrested or were under investigation in Milan, and up to 1,700 were facing investigations elsewhere; these included powerful executives in private-sector companies (Fiat, Olivetti), and in the state sector (IRI, ENI). The head of virtually every major political party had been forced to quit, and five former prime ministers called before the magistrates.[10]

Patronage and clientelism reflect needs for vertical dependency relationships, and a tendency to distinguish insiders (members of the patronage network) and outsiders. In so far as they demonstrate a respect for loyalty to the superior, a conservative distaste for social change, and a perceived (and perhaps actual) need for protection against abstract authority, they reflect needs to avoid uncertainty.

Where the client is rewarded for his/her loyalty rather than ability, patronage within the organization reinforces one-way communication downwards; the client is anxious to say nothing that might be interpreted as challenging the patron and causing him/her to lose face (Mabry and Srisermbhok, 1985, p. 628).

Patronage relationships tend to be weaker in cultures that restrict the manager's status to the workplace; Denmark and the United Kingdom are the extreme examples (Laurent, 1983, p. 80). But they flourish in countries where his/her professional status gives the manager status in other areas of life.

5.4 The Organizational Context

Because they are informal and personal, patronage relationships usually involve the patron and client in regular personal contacts, and the generalized feelings of mutual loyalty and even affection between them are developed and maintained through face-to-face interactions. This is not an absolute condition, and Legg summarizes evidence of patronage relationships where the participants meet only occasionally (Legg, no date, pp. 10–12). But in general such dependency relationships develop where there is limited physical and social mobility and where potentially competing relationships are few; and they decrease in importance where social and economic conditions enhance opportunities for physical and social mobility.

Patronage links resemble traditional authority relationships in that a superior in one social realm (the workplace, for instance) is also superior in another (the informal patronage relationship). In this respect they differ from authority relations in the "ideal" bureaucracy, which are limited in scope and cannot normally be transferred to another context (Etzioni, 1964, pp. 50–3).

By implication, then, we should not expect to find patronage relationships closely duplicating formal relationships. They occur within a range of contexts:

- the domestic context – illustrated by the case of the Thai professor, section 5.2.4 above;
- the community; e.g., a village;
- the organizational context;
- between organizations; for instance, between a state bureaucracy and a company in the private sector.

And as we would expect (given the lack of formal restrictions), they bridge these contexts. Ong describes recruitment patterns in a small Malaysian town; access to coveted government jobs and in large factories is controlled by older permanent workers who serve as patrons (Ong, 1987). Because they have their own reputations and careers to protect, they select those candidates whose performance will rebound to their (the patrons') credit, and screen out those who are undesirable. Thus relationships within a village determine participation and relationships within a state bureaucracy.

5.4.1 Patronage networks and formal systems

Table 5.1 distinguishes patronage networks from formal systems.

Individuals may relate to each other in both arrangements. The organizational superior and subordinate may be linked in a patronage network; but not always. When formal and patronage roles do correspond, the reporting and controlling functions of the formal structure are reinforced.

In practice, the pulls of informal loyalty may be stronger, and this has

Table 5.1 Patronage networks vs formal systems

	Patronage networks	Formal systems
Scope of influence	Unrestricted	Restricted by task/ role specifications
Source of influence	Control of resources	Rules
Seniority/juniority determined by	Status, ability to control resources	Bureaucratic criteria
Purpose	To serve the needs of members of the patronage network	To serve the needs of the organization
Relations to other members of the organization determined by	Membership or not of the patronage network; in- and out-groups	Organizational structure
Decision to reward/ sanction determined by	Needs to reciprocate, and for future exchange; face-to-face relationship	Performance of proscribed tasks; rank; line of command
Typical mode of communication	Relatively greater face-to-face interaction, between patron and clients	Relatively greater use of written memos, between ranks

the effect of confusing lines of command. In the introductory case, the chairman's nominal subordinate was excluded from the relationship linking chairman and general manager. This rendered him powerless in a social situation in which patronage rather than organizational norms applied – the chairman's recuperation home.

When the formal superior and the patron of a network of clients are different persons, and when these two persons are in conflict, the loyalties of subordinates are divided. The greater the disparity in patronage network and formal structure, the greater the dangers for the organization, and in particular when patronage links are strong.

5.4.2 Government-business patronage

Organizations are linked in formal relationships when a business empire consists of a flagship company and a number of subsidiaries. Organizations are linked informally by patronage when

- the entrepreneur plays the role of client to a powerful patron in politics or the government bureaucracy;
- individuals in different organizations are linked by patronage ties.

The first of these links is considered in this section, the second in section 5.4.3.

The political/bureaucratic patron

- steers government contracts towards his/her client entrepreneur;
- secures government funding;
- provides inside information about government policy, future opportunities and threats;
- supports legislation favorable to the entrepreneur and opposes unfavorable legislation;
- gives protection against other arms of the bureaucracy attempting to implement legislation which threatens the entrepreneur's interests;
- gives protection against business competitors; helps the entrepreneur secure a monopoly position;
- acts as a consultant and middleman.

The client reciprocates by

- making straightforward payments – perhaps disguised as "consultancy fees;"
- giving favorable stock options;
- paying election expenses (in cases when the patron is an elected politician);
- demonstrating loyalty and respect. For instance, the patron is invited as guest of honour to family celebrations.

Such a relationship is particularly significant in societies undergoing rapid economic and social transformation, where

- massive development programs offer unusual opportunities for personal enrichment;
- concepts of collective responsibility by state officials are weak;
- systems for disciplining state officials are weak;
- codes governing the conduct of state officials and their relationships with business people are inadequate or unenforced;
- monopolies, and a lack of competition, are tolerated.

In the Philippines before 1986, "crony capitalists" were public-sector businessmen who benefited enormously from their patronage relationships with the then President, Ferdinand Marcos. For instance, Lucio Tan made a fortune as head of the Allied Banking Corporation, and Rudolfo Cuenca as head of Construction and Development Corp. of the

Phillipines. These and similar crony capitalists did particularly well during the martial law period (Kunio, 1988, pp. 71–2).

When practiced on a large scale, business patronage negatively affects the economy. Competition and growth is restricted, and consumers are forced to pay monopoly prices. Despite their immediate profitability, clients may be wary of investing in long-term domestic projects. In Indonesia, for example, some of the most successful Indonesian-Chinese entrepreneurs have moved their surplus capital out of the country, fearful of incurring massive losses should their patrons fall from power (Robinson, 1986, p. 310). Thus business patronage significantly damages the development of the manufacturing sector.

A 1992 magazine article on the business activities of Indonesian President Suharto's children commented that

> Suharto is coming under increasing criticism for allowing [them] to roost in the commanding heights of the economy. . . . The more preferential treatment [they] receive, the more they need the protection of their father. The bigger their businesses become, the more difficult it is to ensure their interests are not harmed after the president steps down or dies.
>
> The spread of Suharto-linked businesses carries a political risk. Some political analysts . . . fear that the activities are draining legitimacy from the nation's leadership. A weakening of the president's authority could make a peaceful transition of power more difficult . . .[11]

This means that the entrepreneur may benefit greatly from a patronage link to a powerful politician in the short term, but is at risk in the long term.

Irwan (1989) compared Indonesia to two neighbors.

> South Korea's manufacturing sector has been successful due, among other factors, to the non-existence of business patronage, and the strong and persistent class struggle which is the source of increased domestic demand. Thailand lies somewhere between Indonesia and South Korea. (pp. 429–30)

But the case of South Korea may be more complex than Irwan portrayed it. A 1992 *Business Week* article traced how the country's top nine family business groups, including Sunkyong, Dongbang Yuryang, Poongsan, and Hyundai, were linked by marriage to two presidents, two prime ministers, top ministers, and influential members of Parliament.[12]

5.4.3   Patronage linking organizations

Individuals in organizations may be linked by patronage ties, for instance between a purchasing manager in Company A and sales manager in Company B. The sales manager studies his "patron's" tastes and interests, and finds ways to satisfy them. The purchasing manager reciprocates by directing orders to Company B.

Relationships must be built slowly and carefully. A Thai manager was assigned by his company to develop informal links with a Thai Board of Investment (BOI) officer, who was empowered to award raw material import licenses.

> It is widely known that BOI has a long list of promoted companies to handle and [its staff are overloaded]. One officer has to take care of about 50 companies. As a result, without a personal relationship with the officer who is in charge of your project, you would be always at the bottom of the list when seeking permission in any matter. Time is money so everyone tries to get his documentation approved as fast as possible. . . . The ways to create a personal relationship are firstly to find friends who used to be this officer's [class mate at school or university, or] to find someone who knows him and introduce you . . . In my case I was introduced to BOI people by a member of a consulting company . . . We visited BOI almost every day to follow up the case and try to establish a personal connection. . . . One surprising thing was that our [German] President used to learn Thai from a BOI staff member in Frankfurt and this relationship was always referred to . . .

When dealing with BOI, he took care to avoid offering a straight bribe or any favor "against the law. It would be considered as corruption." But his company's relations with the Customs Department were assigned to a shipping company whose staff were known to have good relations with customs officers and to use bribery.

> I cannot remember how much "tea money" we paid. We did not know who received the money but we were asked to pay through the shipping agency, otherwise our shipment would be pending at the Customs warehouse.

This case demonstrates how complex and multi-layered patronage-building can become. None of the alternatives considered or implemented for building the desired relationships was created "cold." Each was designed to exploit some previous social connection, bridging different contexts; school and university friends, friends of friends, a connection made by a consultant, a connection made by the Company President, a long-term arrangement between the shipping agency and the Customs Department. And when he dealt with his BOI officer this Thai manager took along his assistant so if I leave the company [the assistant] is still the link with him. [And if the assistant leaves too] he takes these experiences and personal relationships to his new job.

Thus the manager does his client assistant a favor which he expects to be reciprocated with devoted and loyal service, both now and in the future should they be working for different companies.

In this case the relationship is transferable – given the condition that BOI officer (patron) and the assistant (new client) have formed an acquaintance while the manager (old client) was still in office. If the BOI officer wished he could also transfer the relationship by bringing to meetings that subordinate whom he has selected as his successor as patron. But he might prefer to delay in committing his subordinate to the relationship until it proved particularly rewarding.

Many patronage relationships cannot be transferred. In his study of patronage in Central Luzon, the Philippines, Wolters noted that the relationships were normally very durable and continuous, but tended to break down as soon as either the landlord patron or tenant client changed (Wolters, 1983, p. 110).

5.5 Building Modern Organizations in Patronage Cultures

The cross-cultural manager posted to a multinational branch in a patronage culture has the task of sustaining and building a modern organization in a context where at least some workplace values are in fundamental opposition to those he/she represents.

In pre-modern organizations (such as traditional farms), mental qualities are likely to be less in demand than are physical qualities. But a patronage network can seldom guarantee the supply of persons with the technical and intellectual qualifications needed to operate a modern organization. And it seems to be in the nature of things that no client was ever overqualified for a patronage job.

Developing countries that have only recently established central public-sector organizations often have serious difficulties in developing impersonal criteria for recruitment and promotion, and in moving away from traditional patronage systems. For instance, patronage, or *sifarish*, is basic to social and political life in Pakistan. As a general rule, political leaders are also tribal or clan leaders, and when they achieve power, are expected to find employment for their clansman – who helped them in winning their positions. During Miss Benezir Bhutto's tenure as Prime

Minister (1988–9), a Placement Bureau was established with the function of securing positions for clients of her elite.

The Bureau managed to place 26,000 people

> by sending lists of those to be employed to the heads of nationalised industries, banks and government departments. . . . The head of one of the nationalised commercial banks is said to have refused to find jobs for 400 people on a Bhutto list. He has been removed.
>
> *Sifarish* did the government little harm among the voters, but the scale of it was a big reason for Miss Bhutto's sacking. . . . Neither the civil service nor the army likes to see newcomers, often incompetent, jumping on to the promotional ladder; and both were infuriated by Miss Bhutto's casual attitude to the systems and procedures that govern their worlds.[13]

In a society which lacks formal welfare institutions, patronage serves as a means of channeling social resources. The problems of trying to abolish patronage when the formal institutions are not yet in place have been demonstrated in Brazil. A reforming politician, Tasso Jereissati, made clear on his election as Governor of Ceará province that he intended to dismantle the traditional patronage system.[14] All personal favors were banned, and relatives and friends were warned that they could not expect jobs in his administration. He encountered significant opposition from within his community.

> "The Governor is trying to administer the state like a business, and that won't work," [a critic], who is now a Senator, said recently, referring to cuts in the bureaucracy. "He is forgetting the social side of things." . . .
>
> Even among bureaucrats who have survived the shrinking of the state apparatus from 150,000 to 114,000 employees, there is resistance, not least of all because the Governor has declared that 91,000 of the workers were hired "irregularly" and that in the coming months they will have to take examinations to test their competence.

The depth of opposition shows that in this society at this stage in its economic development, patronage relationships were still widely regarded as a legitimate means by which to allocate employment. And a further example comes from the Philippines.

As Commissioner of Immigration, Mrs Miriam Defensor Santiago worked hard to bring about fundamental change in her department, and in so doing, encountered significant opposition. Death threats began arriving at an average of three a day. She was attacked by powerful politicians with criminal links, and by members of her own staff, who stood to lose fortunes in bribes.

Many of the officials with whom she is doing battle may not feel they are doing anything so very wrong. ... She spoke of the Filipino value of *pakikisama*, "the art and skill of getting along with others," that puts a premium on compromise and avoidance of confrontation.

"This is an authentic Philippine value in some areas," she said. "But its mischief and nuisance value is so high that it simply cannot be accommodated in the legal structure we have copied from the West."[15]

5.5.1 The risk to bureaucracies in less developed societies

The cross-cultural manager may have to work or negotiate with public-sector organizations in societies where patronage is significant. He/she needs to be aware of the pressures that constrain the activities of the bureaucrats. Often, they are caught by the contradictions that arise between traditional and modern bureaucratic values.

The patronage network is primarily concerned with advancing the interests of its members, to the exclusion of non-members. The modern organization has rational ends (profit in the private sector, efficient administration in the public sector), designed to serve the interests of the organization as a whole and its backers (stock holders, the "public interest"). These aims need not necessarily be in conflict – for instance, when efficiency within their limited context of activities promises to secure rewards for network members. But when there is a conflict, the patronage network is in essence an organizational parasite.

The logic of bureaucracy dictates that *all* recruitments and promotions should be determined by impersonal criteria. The notion of structure presupposes that relationships (between superior, subordinate, and peers) can be contrasted in terms of authority and power. And the individual bureaucrat's capacities are described (precisely, in terms of the organization's needs) by his/her job description – which, in turn, reflects his/her qualifications, themselves measurable and hence able to be contrasted.

When unqualified clients are appointed, the bureaucracy suffers in two ways. First, these client placeholders are more or less unable to perform the tasks allotted them – which reflects upon their bureaucratic superiors in practice, not upon their patrons. Second, the professional identities of all other members are called into question. And the imbalance in power particularly affects those with nominally greater authority than the client placeholder but less than the patron. Again, the introductory case is illustrative; the Chairman's relationship with the General Manager undermines the authority of the middleman, the Vice-Chairman.

But where bureaucratic institutions and procedures are rooted, for instance where

- central government demonstrates a capacity for impartial and strong government;
- public officials are able and willing to protect individual rights and liberties;
- public officials do not abuse their power;
- public officials are relatively accessible to the public – and freely so;
- welfare services are effective;
- a significant proportion of society are above subsistence levels;
- opportunities for social and physical mobility are common;
- public resources are channeled equitably;

bureaucratic organization is valued and patronage systems gradually lose their hold.

Reeves (1990) quotes evidence from Egypt that shows how rules for recruitment and promotion, when implemented fairly, undermine the old patronage networks. Previously, a government officer experienced little difficulty in finding a government appointment for a relative or *baladivat* (from the same village or town) by creating a new post or job description. But central authority has grown strong enough to ensure that general rules are kept, and it is no longer easy to appoint an applicant obviously less well qualified than others. He explains:

> The more heavily bureaucracy has weighed on society, the more patron-client dependency has given way to friendship cliques and similar horizontal arrangements for promoting mutual aid. . . . Moreover, new political formulas of whatever stripe – socialism, parliamentary government, laissez-faire economy, Islamic fundamentalism – have a better "fit" with the impersonal norms associated with bureaucracy and a rationalized legal system. (p. 185)

"Friendship cliques and similar horizontal arrangements" are often no less effective than patronage relationships in barring the qualified outsider. However, they may be much less damaging to the organization – and even beneficial, as was suggested in section 5.2.1.

5.6 The "Outsider" Manager and Informal Relationships

Adjustment problems may arise for the cross-cultural manager who comes from a culture in which informal power arrangements are suspect. Where bureaucratic systems of organization are most fully developed and accepted, relationships which appear to pose a threat to bureaucratic norms can create serious anxieties.

Except in certain specialized fields – for instance, the arts – the term "patronage" has negative connotations in Anglo cultures – as the Chicago story in section 5.3 suggests.

The Anglo manager's suspicion of patronage is conditioned by his/her culture and professional training. Very few Western management schools attempt to explain the phenomenon, and even less, to investigate circumstances under which patronage satisfies the moral norms of the cultural context.

The Anglo cross-cultural manager is conditioned not to "see" patronage within the organization. He/she either overlooks its existence or characterizes it as inherently corrupt. But ethnocentric responses should be avoided. The outsider's first task is to understand how patronage works within the organization and effects relationships among members. And second, see who benefits and why patronage relationships promise greater security, satisfaction, and rewards than formal relationships. (It may be that you need to rethink your formal structures.) The advantages of eliminating patronage influences may have to be weighed against possible loss of morale, damage to the organizational culture, and weakened vertical linkages – at least in the short term.

Deep-rooted patronage networks within an organization often reflect insecurity and fear on the part of its members in response to bureaucratic structures that they experience as arbitrary and impersonal. Where this is the case, the cross-cultural manager might need to start by modifying these structures.

5.6.1 Taking action

How does the cross-cultural manager relate to a patronage network within the other-culture organization? The alternatives would seem to include:

- join the network;
- disband the network;
- tolerate the network.

In a culture where mobility is traditionally restricted, the cross-cultural manager in post for only two or three years is no more than a short-term visitor. He/she is unlikely to break into a patronage network. Patronage relationships are based upon trust between patron and client and a perception of mutual dependence over the long-term. Where the level of trust is low, or where one of the participants feels unable to commit him/herself to a long-term dependency relationship with the other, the relationship does not take root.

Some Japanese multinationals with branches in Asian Pacific countries are trying to overcome the difficulty of forming informal power relationships within other cultures in a way that ingeniously exploits their own cultural values of loyalty to the firm and lifetime employment.

They post new graduates to their local branches, enrol them in management-related post-graduate courses in universities, and in language schools to learn the native language, then keep them at the branches for several years more. These graduates thus become country-experts, with all-important class contacts among the future elites. Even when they return to Japan, they maintain these classroom links, and are excellently positioned to manage future relations with these countries.

Few Western companies would find it easy to follow this path. Rooted in far more individualistic cultures, they cannot assume lifetime loyalty by their young managers and cannot guarantee lifetime employment. Even if prepared to plan its human-resource requirements so far ahead, the company would flinch from making this training commitment to a prospective cross-cultural manager with every likelihood of his/her being poached by a competitor.

Whether the patronage network should be disbanded (for instance, by dispersing its members to other departments) or tolerated must depend in part on the effects it has. When patronage encourages corruption, it must be uprooted; when benign, it might be tolerated. Patronage serves a useful purpose when it provides members of a bureaucratic organization with opportunities to form relationships more "natural" and "warmer" than those prescribed by authority.

5.6.2 Changing the manager's attitudes

How can a traditional organization escape from its patronage climate and develop rational bureaucratic criteria, and how can the traditional manager learn the new ways?

The organization is transformed when

- an impersonal rule system is accepted;
- bureaucratic procedures and systems in recruiting, promoting, etc. are accepted;
- rules governing formal relationships between peers, superiors and subordinates are accepted;
- rules for rewarding members are accepted; they are fairly rewarded and do not have to sell their influence;
- fair disciplinary rules are accepted;
- rules governing the conduct of employees are accepted;
- a culture of collective responsibility is developed.

But in practice, radical change within the organization may depend upon changes within the wider context. These changes include the following.

- *Environmental change* The political and business climate rewards favors bureaucratic efficiency. The moral and social climate turns against patronage.
- *Opportunities for geographical, social and occupational mobility* Increased opportunities mean that the employee is no longer so dependent upon the favor of a single employer or patron.
- *Educational and professional opportunities* The better trained the workforce, the wider its opportunities for mobility.
- *Increased capital investment, including foreign investment* Investments by large companies, including multinationals, make new demands for skilled labor and new opportunities for an educated workforce.

What new interpersonal skills are demanded from the manager? Boisot (1986) analyses change processes within the People's Republic of China; he warns that the traditional manager may find the development of a "market transactional style very hard going" (p. 169). Nevertheless, acquisition of the following is recommended:

- an ability to analyse problems in such a way that procedures for resolving them are specified;
- an ability to communicate effectively with key decision makers;
- a change of attitudes towards information, from regarding the possession of information as an expression of power to the transmission and sharing of information as an expression of power;
- a change from belief in the absolute efficacy of hierarchical control to recognizing the power of modern management processes, which involve efficient use of communication.

5.7 Implications for the Manager

How important are informal and patronage relationships within your own culture and in some other culture that you know? Make comparisons between:

- a typical organization that you know well in *your own culture*;
- a typical organization that you know well in *some other culture*.

1. What cultural features explain the significance and functions of patronage relationships within each organization? Take into account such cultural, social, and economic features as:

- typical power distances;
- typical individualism/collectivism;
- typical needs to avoid uncertainty and fears of outsiders;
- high/low-context features;
- the authority exercised by national political and administrative institutions;
- the quality of public officials;
- the existence of welfare services and public resources;
- degrees of private poverty/wealth;
- opportunities for social and physical mobility.

2. Within each organization, identify and analyse a patronage network;

- Who is involved, as

   (a) patron?
   (b) client(s)?

- What patterns of obligation can you identify?
- What resources are exchanged between the patron and his/her clients?
- How do the members of the network benefit?
- Supposing some member of the network fails to reciprocate a favor, how is such behavior typically sanctioned?
- In what respects does the organization as a whole benefit from the activities of this patronage network? (For instance, consider motivation, loyalty, speed of communication, etc.)
- In what respects does the organization suffer from the activities of this network?

3. Compare your answers for the two organizations. How do you explain differences?

4. Evaluate the effects of patronage relationships in each of the two organizations;

- Are their effects generally positive or negative?
- If negative, should patronage influence be weakened?
- If so, how?

5.8 Summary

This chapter has examined informal structures, in particular patronage relationships. It has shown how these affect the organization and has examined the problems they set the cross-cultural manager.

Patronage networks are always likely to compromise official structures and systems. But for the individuals involved, patronage may offer the only means of securing protection and competitive advantage. Before condemning patronage out of hand, the cross-cultural manager needs to understand it as a social and economic phenomenon.

Section 5.2 discussed *informal relationships and patronage*. Formal and informal, and patronage and friendship relationships, were distinguished. Patronage was studied in detail. Patronage relationships impose control and distribute a stream of resources on a reciprocal basis between the patron (senior) and client (junior). The relationship involves the expression of mutual obligation over a lengthy period of time – perhaps the participants' lifetimes. Section 5.3 saw how *social* and *cultural* conditions influence the development of *patronage* relationships – which can occur in all societies.

Section 5.4 examined the contexts within which such relationships occur, focusing on the *organizational context* when patron and client belong to the same, or different, organizations. Section 5.5 dealt with the impact of *patronage* on developing countries, and why public-sector *bureaucracies* are so much at risk in traditional *patronage cultures*. Section 5.6 examined the problems of the cross-cultural *manager* who transfers to another-culture organization whose *informal* systems differ from those with which he/she is familiar. The *outsider* cannot take for granted that informal and formal structures match, and that the organizational chart accurately maps lines of real influence.

5.9 Exercise

This exercise asks you to analyze informal power and patronage relationships. Answer the questions in groups. If necessary refer to the analytical techniques discussed in chapter 2.

1. Analyse informal power relationships within an organization that you know well, in your own culture.

    *   Who exercises informal power?
    *   From what do they derive they power?
    *   How do they maintain their power?
    *   How far do informal power structures coincide with formal structures (as denoted by the organization chart)?
    *   Where they do not coincide, how is the organization affected?
    *   How far do these informal power relationships correspond to patronage relationships? How far do the power-holders act as patrons? What patterns of obligation can you identify? What

resources are exchanged between the patron and his/her clients? Supposing some member of the network fails to reciprocate a favor, how is such behavior typically sanctioned?

2. If information is available, analyse informal power relationships within an organization in some other culture, answering the same questions.
3. If you can complete 2, compare your answers to 1 and 2. How far do cultural differences explain differences in the importance and functioning of these power relationships?
4. Present your answers to the class.

Notes

1. Marie Colvin, "Gadaffi goes back on his promise to reveal IRA deals," *Sunday Times*, May 10, 1992.
2. Ralph Berry, "Long war in the Gulf," *The Times Higher Education Supplement*, June 26, 1992.
3. Roger Matthews, "Poll will be test for democracy in Thai power system," *Financial Times*, May 21, 1988.
4. David E. Sanger, "Tokyo seeks to loosen old school ties," *International Herald Tribune*, March 7–8, 1992.
5. The process by which a social group maximizes its own advantages and excluding outsiders is termed "social closure" by Weber (1968, p. 342).
6. Dirk Johnson, "Chicago unmoved by a sex scandal," *New York Times*, May 4, 1988.
7. Douglas Farrah, "Venezuela and its dangerous liaisons," *International Herald Tribune*, July 30, 1991.
8. "Bombay's riotous mobsters," *Asiaweek*, November 22, 1991.
9. "Signorina Guillotine," *The Economist*, April 3–9, 1993.
10. Alan Cowell, "In Italy, corruption scandal recasts the political map," *International Herald Tribune*, June 9, 1993.
11. Adam Schwarz, "All is relative," *Far Eastern Economic Review*, 30 April, 1992, pp. 54, 56.
12. Laxmi Nakarmi, "Paralysis in South Korea," *Business Week*, June 1, 1992.
13. "Between the dock and the hustings," *The Economist*, September 8, 1990.
14. Alan Riding, "Maverick tilts at lords of patronage," *New York Times*, May 4 1988.
15. Seth Mydans, "'Culture of corruption' draws fire day by day," *New York Times*, May 26, 1988. Lynch (1970) defines *pakikisama* as the "lauded practice of yielding to the will of the leader or majority so as to make the group decision unanimous." See also De Leon (1987).

6

Organizational Culture

6.1 Introduction

In South Korea, a pathologist in the National Institute of Scientific Investigation was asked to examine the corpse of a student who had died while undergoing police questioning about his political connections. Dr Hwang submitted a routine report concluding that the young man had been tortured. The report was taken up by a journalist friend, and to his surprise, published.

> The atmosphere at the Institute grew instantly hostile . . . "I had to resign," he said. "Under the circumstances that exist in Korea, I would not have been able to work any longer in that place. I caused my superiors to lose face, and, according to the ethics of our society, one cannot stay in the job after that. . . . It disturbs me that I disrupted the normal processes of the organization and I feel guilty about it," he said. "I would assume now that every intellectual Korean would criticize me because I didn't do the right thing as an organization man. . . . I'm not interested in being a hero. Frankly, I think I may be a fool."[1]

Inadvertently, Dr Hwang enraged the informal norms of his culture and organization and was forced to pay the price. This case illustrates the following points which are developed in the course of this chapter:

- Members of an organization commonly have a strong sense of how they and their colleagues should properly behave.
- This "organizational culture" may reflect values in the wider context of the national culture. Hofstede's (1984a) data show South Korea to be a typical personnel bureaucracy, with strong needs to avoid anxiety and large power distances. Dr Hwang's description of his colleagues' attitudes seems to fit this model.

This chapter develops these points. It distinguishes where necessary between national culture and organizational culture, and shows that the term "culture" has different connotations in these different contexts. The chapter is organized as follows:

6.2 Organizational Culture and National Culture

The term "organizational culture" is used with a wide range of meanings in management literature; for instance, Schein (1987) lists six of the most common, and adds his own (p. 6). This multiplicity need not be confusing, so long as the writer or manager using the term chooses the definition that best suits his/her purpose, and then makes clear to others what this definition is and why it has been selected.

So this is the meaning used here. The term "organizational culture" refers to the sum of perceptions that develop within an organization.

This is general enough to include both perceptions that develop through the employees" own experience and perceptions deliberately manipulated by top management; the chapter deals with both. These organizational perceptions include organizational values, beliefs and attitudes. They are defined as follows:

- *organizational beliefs*   conscious certainty that something exists, or is good, in the organization;
- *organizational attitudes*   conscious stances about how things are, or ought to be, in the organization; these are expressed in rituals, mission statements, etc.;
- *organizational values*   are preconscious assumptions about "how things ought to be" in the organization, and are acquired there.

Values lie deepest. In reporting research made of 20 different organizations in Denmark and the Netherlands, Hofstede et al. (1990) represented the organizational climate like an onion, composed of successive "skins"; an external skin of symbols, then heroes, then rituals. And at the core lie values in the sense of broad, nonspecific feelings of good and evil, beautiful and ugly, normal and abnormal, rational and irrational – feelings that are often unconscious and rarely discussable, that cannot be observed as such but are manifested in alternatives of behavior.

And because they are preconscious, values are enduring and not so easily accessible to change. In this respect, they bear some resemblance to values acquired through the national culture.

6.2.1 Organizational culture as distinct from national culture

The organizational culture

- provides the individual member with a sense of identity;
- provides a source of commitment to an organizational reality bigger than him/herself;
- acts as a framework for interpreting reality, and thus for moulding behaviour.

In these respects the concepts of organizational culture and national culture cannot be significantly distinguished. Hofstede's (1984a) definition of culture can be applied broadly to both:

the collective programming of the mind which distinguishes the members of one human group from another. ... Culture, in this sense, includes systems of values; and values are among the building blocks of culture. (p. 21)

And in chapter 1, section 1.5.3, the following implications were drawn:

- a culture is particular to one group and not others;
- it is learned, and is not innate;
- it is passed down from one generation to the next;
- it influences the behavior of group members in uniform and predictable ways;
- it includes systems of values.

This definition applies to the organizational culture in so far as:

- every organization has its own culture, and no two are ever quite the same;
- members of the organization have to learn its culture;
- when top management decides that the employees' organizational values should be changed, new beliefs and attitudes are taught. In addition, workplace values are passed on from experienced to novice

employees – which may or may not correspond to the values that top managament wishes to instill.

The concept of national culture applies less closely in the fourth instance – influencing behavior of members. In one respect, of course, the influence of organizational culture is crucial; members of an organization who cannot adjust their perceptions and behavior to its prevailing culture are likely to quit at an early stage, or be dismissed. But the extent to which members are influenced by its culture varies much. Where top management are able to build a strong and positive culture which also reflects the national culture, their behavior may indeed be predictable. But in other conditions, not.

The most significant disparity occurs in the notions of national cultural values and organizational values, and for this reason the concepts of national and organizational cultures have to be distinguished. National cultural values are learned so early in life that the individual is generally unaware of his/her cultural conditioning. However, organizational values are learned much later, in the workplace, and are more likely to be assimilated at a conscious level.

6.2.2 Organizational values

This leads to the question, are organizational values ever so powerful an influence on behavior as national culture? The point is significant; it has bearings on the development of an organizational culture in a multinational subsidiary, and specifically when top management attempts to replicate headquarters' values in another national setting.

If the behavior of subsidiary employees can be primarily influenced by values in their organizational culture, than top management has cause to invest in moulding it, perhaps by replicating the organizational culture of headquarters. But if national culture is always of greater influence, then headquarters systems and structures may have to be modified to fit with local values.

The scholarly evidence is ambiguous. Burack (1991) believes that values in the organizational culture are

> *deeply ingrained*; they give rise to patterns of uniformity in behavioural patterns and underlying values among organizational units regardless of geographic, functional or business boundaries. (p. 89)

In similar vein, Schein (1987) regards organizational values as equivalent to national culture in influence, and represents them as a basic set of implicit assumptions about how to behave (p. 14).

Laurent (1986) queries whether this representation of culture at its most profound level is applicable to organizations; Schein and those who share his position

> may be searching for the reality of organizational culture at a deeper level than it really is. (p. 91)

And his argument implies that

- the organizational culture is unlikely to modify national cultural values;
- when national and organizational cultures come into conflict, the first is likely to override values in the second.

Ray (1986) doubts whether even the best efforts by top management have any significant effect on their employees' behavior patterns – at least, so far as American corporations are concerned.

> At this time there is no persuasive evidence ... that the manipulation of U.S. corporations' cultures really functions as a form of control. It is even less certain that its use as a management strategy is generalizable to other societies any more than other management techniques which have been espoused in the United States. (p. 295)

This problem of whether a company can effectively "export" its headquarters organizational culture is discussed in section 6.4.

Finally, Hofstede (1991) points to an essential difference:

> organizational cultures are a phenomenon *per se*, different in many respects from national cultures. An organization is a social system of a different nature than a nation; if only because the organization's members usually had a certain influence in their decision to join it, are only involved in it during working hours, and may one day leave it again. (p. 18)

In practice, the issue boils down to two questions. First, is the organizational culture strong enough to influence the values of its members? Second, how far is the individual accessible to the culture? The "job-hopper," who moves rapidly between jobs, is unlikely to be much influenced by their cultures. On the other hand, the person who stays with an organization all his/her career may indeed be significantly affected.

Aramco (the Arabian American Oil Co. in Saudi Arabia) during the 1970s represented an extreme case. Many American employees had been born in the company compound, educated in its schools, and then worked there throughout their careers. Company restaurants, clubs, and cinemas catered for social needs, and many employees only rarely left the compound. Other than following tertiary-level education and taking

Table 6.1 National culture vs organizational culture

National culture	Organizational culture
Perceptions .... *Level 1* (higher consciousness) .... Perceptions	
Beliefs: conscious certainty that something exists, or is good	*Organizational beliefs:* conscious certainty that something exists, or is good, in the organization
Attitudes: conscious stances about how things are, or ought to be	*Organizational attitudes:* conscious stances about how things are, or ought to be, in the organization
Perceptions .... *Level 2* (intermediary) .... Perceptions	
	Organizational values: assumptions about how things ought to be. Learnt in the organization
Perceptions .... *Level 3* (lower preconsciousness) .... Perceptions	
Values: assumptions about how things ought to be. Learnt from birth	

vacations in the United States, they were accessible to few cultural influences other than those expressed by Aramco.

This book follows the line that in most cases, national culture is predominant as an influence – always allowing for extreme cases. You may acquire (and shed) a series of organizational cultures in the course of your working life. But there is no shedding your national culture.

6.2.3 Modeling organizational beliefs, attitudes, and values

Table 6.1 represents how the elements involved in national culture and organizational culture are differentiated in this chapter.

Figure 6.1 is more schematic, and maps how the elements of national and organizational cultures influence each other. Values in the national culture are held preconsciously, and are fundamental. They influence

- beliefs and attitudes in the national culture;
- beliefs and attitudes in the organizational culture;
- values in the organizational culture.

Figure 6.1   How the elements of national and organizational culture influence each other.

Values specific to the organizational culture are also influenced by

- beliefs and attitudes specific to the organization;
- beliefs and attitudes common to the wider culture.

These values are pictured at a higher level than cultural values, and are held at an intermediary level of consciousness.

National cultural values are represented as the preeminently active element; directly or indirectly they influence all other elements of the model and are themselves influenced only by the general national cultural context (early learning, cultural history, etc.) This cultural context may include experential influences on beliefs and attitudes when these are acquired sufficiently early in life or are sufficiently radical as to modify the national culture. But in practice, such influences likely to affect organizational beliefs and attitudes are probably acquired too late in life to have much significance to values.

When the company wishes to modify its employees' organizational values, it rearranges their experiences inside the organization. It may attempt to change perceptions of the external environment. For instance, Asahi Brewery mobilized 600 people from all departments in a sales campaign. This had the effect of making employees more conscious of their consumers (Kono, 1990, p. 17). But this is unlikely to affect perceptions of the national culture at any great depth.

6.2.4 Strong/weak, positive/negative organizational cultures

The organizational culture is *strong* when

- it is cohesive; group members share the same values, beliefs and attitudes;
- communication is easy; members can easily communicate between themselves;
- members depend upon each other in order to meet individual needs.

A strong culture is shown by the uniformity in members' organizational values. Where management fails to impose a uniform system of perceptions on employees, individual differences in beliefs and attitudes are more marked. But organizational constraints are not the only factor; as we know, national culture appears to be the greater determinant of uniformity or individuality. And we should expect to find greater uniformity within the workplace where collectivist tendencies reinforce this trait. The degree of uniformity that a particular organization's culture induces within its members can only be measured by comparing that organizational culture to others within the same national context.

The organizational culture is *positive* when its members support top management. This is more likely when:

- members perceive that they have a stake in the official outcomes of the organization; when the organization benefits, they benefit;
- profits (expressed in pay and other benefits) and losses are perceived to be shared fairly;
- demands for productivity are considered reasonable;
- official relationships are considered reasonable.

When the culture is strong and positive, relations between management and workforce are good. Communication is easy, open, and fruitful, morale is high, and productivity climbs.

The manager most fears a strong organizational culture which is negative. In such a situation, members are united in their sense of alienation from official structures, their disbelief in management messages, and their perceptions that management is not dealing with them correctly. Lightning strikes are an ever-present threat.

6.2.5 The meaning of a strong organizational culture

The organizational culture contributes most to performance and productivity when it is strong (Dennison, 1984). But this does not mean a one-to-one relationship between culture and performance. Obviously, many other factors affect performance – market demand, the activities of competitors, availability of labor and technology, and so on (Saffold, 1988). The organizational culture is only one of the many contributory factors, and investments made in developing a strong culture may be wasted when some other factor intervenes.

Job applicants are attracted to an organization that projects a homogeneous and intense culture on the labor market. Normally, many new recruits drop out within a few months or weeks of joining the firm. Perhaps they discover that after all the culture does not suit their tastes or needs, or quickly despair of making a personal impact upon an organization that seems set in its ways. Not everyone wishes to work for an organization such as Marks & Spencer, which has a strong culture where uniformity in values is keenly enforced by management. However, there always those who are searching for just these qualities in an employer. And those whose needs are met may continue in loyal service for long careers.

Managers tend to stay with the organization whose culture fits their needs. Schneider (1988) cited a human resources manager at Olivetti:

> those Italians who want autonomy go to Olivetti instead of IBM. He described the culture of Olivetti as being informal and non-structured, and as having more freedom, fewer constraints, and low discipline. (p. 239)

This has implications for a multinational that hopes to replicate the headquarters culture within a foreign subsidiary. Assuming that the headquarters culture closely reflects its national culture, then applicants most likely to be attracted, and to stay when hired, are those who identify with the national cultural context of the headquarters. For instances, a Country Y subsidiary based in Country X is most successful at recruiting those Country X citizens who admire Country Y culture. Such recruits may prove loyal employees; but when the cultures of the two countries are far apart, they make poor representatives of their own cultures, and may be out of touch with changes in local taste and the local market.

6.2.6 The organizational culture as a set of sub-cultures

The concept of a strong culture can imply a unitary set of beliefs to which all members of the organization are expected to subscribe, in the interests of greater productivity. This culture makes sense when tasks to be performed are relatively routine, and where individualist achievement is not prized.

But deliberate attempts to build such a culture may be counter-productive in an individualist culture where tasks are non-routine and innovation is at a premium. As Ray (1986) suggests, management policies to build a strong culture may reflect an appetite for control rather than any real insight into the problems of productivity. Where the tasks performed by the organization are various and include both routine and non-routine, we should

- recognize the inevitable heterogeneity of interests in a complex organization; *and*
- identify those groups in which uniformity is to be valued; *and/or*
- identify those issues over which uniformity is to be valued.

Chapter 1, section 1.3.4 warned against taking absolute cultural uniformity for granted; it is sometimes necessary to distinguish sub-cultures. The same point applies to the organization. In practice, the experiences and goals of different groups (for instance, top management, lower levels of management, shop floor employees, and staff in different functions) are unlikely to coincide at all points. In an organization comprising different role and seniority groups, the organizational culture can most likely be represented as a set of over-lapping sub-cultures.

Kono (1988) distinguishes the

- *uniform* culture: values accepted by all members; *and group* culture: each department's own culture;
- *upper* culture: the values, ways of thinking, and behavior patterns of top and middle management; *and lower* culture: the culture of the rank and file;
- *home headquarters* culture; *and overseas subsidiary's* culture. (See also Fujita, 1990.)

This way of thinking about organizational culture is attractive. It permits us to cross-cut the data in a range of ways, and to differentiate:

- core organizational perceptions that are shared by all members of the organization from those that are not shared;
- the perceptions of different groups;

- (in the case of perceptions that are not shared by all) actual conflicts in perception, and potential conflicts – where one group is positive in an organizational belief/attitude/value, and some other group is neutral;
- the perceptions of groups within different units – including headquarters and subsidiary.

It also raises new questions about the notion of culture "strength." Given the organization's environment and its goals, what type of culture should it aim for? A culture in which there is:

(a) the highest possible level of shared perceptions?
(b) diversity in perceptions around a shared core?
(c) shared perceptions within operating units and diversity between units?
(d) both great diversity and a significant lack of conflict in perceptions?
(e) significant conflict in perceptions, channeled towards creativity?

6.2.7 Shared perceptions

We might expect (a) above (emphasis on shared perceptions) to be most attractive in a national culture where needs to avoid anxiety are high. The success of Japanese companies in this respect is well known, but they do not have a monopoly on building perceptions and many Western companies have followed suit. Texas Instruments in the 1970s emphasized company loyalty, and more than 83 percent of employees participated in groups designed to improve their own productivity. IBM under Tom Watson Snr owed much of its success to company commitments to the workforce:

> Lush benefits and a no-layoffs "practice" inspired great loyalty among the company's rank and file.
> By the 1980s, however, the IBM culture had turned insular. IBMers even had their own language. Other computer makers spoke of disk drives. IBMers insisted on "hard files." Circuit boards were "planer boards." But the culture's cornerstone, the promise of a job for life, became a millstone as the organization ballooned.[2]

The other side of this coin, company loyalty to the employee, is that the company demands the same in return. The case of Stanley Adams, a British senior manager with the Swiss-based pharmeceutical company, Hoffman-La Roche, is extreme. He decided that the company was guilty of unfair trading practices, and reported his worries to the EEC Commissioner for Competition.

As he was not a Swiss national, [he] was not imbued with the values of Swiss corporate loyalty which demand loyalty to the company regardless of the cost to individuals. (Greenley 1989, p. 218)

After his disloyalty was discovered, he was arrested by the Swiss police and charged with industrial sabotage.

6.3 Changing the Organizational Culture

Changing the culture is often painful, and particularly in cases where the culture is well-established – even when this is apparently liberal. For instance, by 1993 Apple Computers

> had long been revered as a special kind of company, successfully violating many norms of corporate behavior with its blue-jeans and T-shirt culture.
>
> But the company's new chief executive, Michael Spindler, has sent what some consider his first clear signal that the new Apple, facing the realities of a slumping economy, will increasingly fit, rather than break, the mold of corporate America. . . .
>
> The question now is how his nuts-and-bolts management style will mesh with his employees' work style, an unconventional style that might be described as "nuts-and-granola."[3]

Many Japanese companies combat this problem of cultural obsolescence by deliberately changing their corporate philosophy every five years (Kono, 1990, p. 14). But the cross-cultural manager is probably wise to avoid emulating this routine unless entirely confident of

- the extent of the planned change; goals and techniques;
- control of outcomes;
- his/her understanding of the culture.

To the extent that the change process is intended to have deep-rooted effects, the outcomes are bound to be in doubt and the process can easily backfire, causing new and more serious problems than those it was designed to rectify.

In some circumstances, there may be little point in attempting any radical change. For instance:

- where members of the national culture have large needs to avoid uncertainty, changes designed to make them tolerant of high levels of ambiguity are unlikely to succeed;
- in a family company (of the South-east Asian model) attempts to introduce a participative management style are unlikely to win support

from top management; the culture is dominated by kinship and patronage values;

- the organization employs unskilled labor in a context where labor is plentiful; morale problems are easily resolved by shedding dissatisfied workers and hiring afresh; management is under no pressure to invest in changes designed to make workers feel good about their work;
- employees work at home; they are not dependent upon each other, and do not need to communicate with each other;
- the organization faces real problems (for instance, emergence of new competition), but these are not reflected in the culture, which is sound.

On the other hand, management may decide that the risk has to be taken in these situations:

- environmental conditions have changed, and existing value systems are inappropriate to the new conditions;
- the organization is acquired by a new owner, with a new agenda; for instance, a family business is taken over by a multinational;
- a new strategy is adopted; "for a strategy to be successfully implemented, it requires an appropriate culture" (O'Reilly, 1989, p. 17);
- internal conditions have changed; for instance, functional responsibilities have been reorganized;
- internal systems have deteriorated, and productivity is suffering.

6.3.1 Selecting change agents

Who is responsible for designing the change strategy and implementing it? The alternatives are:

- an outsider/outsiders;
- an insider/insiders;
- a team composing an insider/insiders and an outsider/outsiders.

External consultants may have more varied experience than insiders, and can refer to similar situations in a wide range of other organizations. Both because they are independent of the client power structure and do not have prior experience of working within the culture, they see it with fresh eyes, and can be more objective. In Anglo cultures, this objectivity is usually welcomed. If the consultants have been hired by a powerful manager, they may have greater influence than insiders.

The insiders have the advantage of knowing the organization and the background to the problem. They perhaps suffer from being too close to it, and lacking objectivity. They may have to live down past affiliations.

Obviously, these generalizations do not apply in the case of a new employee – for instance, a new chief executive or some other senior person appointed with a specific brief to change the culture. A too radical approach on his/her part may lead to damaging conflict with old-timer employees trained up in the old values.

In practice, a combination of insiders and outsiders may be optimal. The insiders will have to live within the culture as a consequence of changing it, and hence have good reason to impose breaks upon the more radical notions put forward by the external consultants. They liaise between the organization and the externals, funneling ideas and information between the two (McLean et al., 1982).

The best combination in any one situation is influenced by factors within both the national culture and the organization's past culture. Within a hierarchical organization, the change process must be championed by a person of high status. Where security is perceived to be a major issue – for instance, where Chinese business culture is significant – any suggestion that outsiders be invited to scrutinize company "secrets" may be heavily resisted. Exceptions may be made in the case of foreigners who are not linked to any competitors. For instance, in 1985 the National Fertilizer Corporation of Thailand brought in two American academics to advise on policy when all local consultants had to be disqualified by virtue of their previous professional and patronage relationships.

6.3.2 The extent of the change

When it has taken the decision to change the culture, top management may, at one extreme, push for radical change. At the other extreme, it may decide to introduce relatively minor modifications to specific aspects only (Wiener, 1988); for instance, it provides a loose framework of change within which individuals and units adjust their behavior so far as they think fit. How radical management wishes to be depends very much on its goals for the organization (for instance, to become market leader, to improve external relations, to secure long-term profitability); and how it expects the climate to contribute towards achieving those goals (Deal and Kennedy, 1982, 1988). And the relationship between organizational culture and goals is circular. A statement of goals helps create an appropriate culture when articulated in terms that attract the employees.

For instance, Japanese companies work hard to design appropriate creeds that both reflect and create their cultures. Honda emphasizes "dreams and youthfulness" – and delegates authority to young people. Nissan

changed its creed from "Distinctive Technology" to "Feel the Beat" meaning that the feeling of the consumer is respected. In this way the corporate culture changed to a consumer oriented one. After that, successful new models started to appear. (Kono, 1990, p. 14)

Individuals come and go, but the organization retains its capacity to preserve information and create maps of the world and norms of behavior (Daft and Weick, 1984, p. 285). That is, the development and survival of the organizational culture is not entirely dependent on the identities of the particular individuals who make up the organization. Hence, the relationship between culture and goals can be two-way. The culture influences the design of goals and goals change over time as the culture changes (Handy, 1976, 1985, p. 200).

In this respect, also, the organizational culture differs from the national culture. Every effective government formulates political and economic policies that reflect its perception of national interests, and these policies may even be implemented. But they will not significantly influence the culture at the level of values; as we have seen, these are inherently slow to change.

6.3.3 Building a strong, positive culture

Given a top management determined to build a strong positive culture, the questions that need to be answered include:

- what factors affect the development of the organizational culture?
- what factors are primarily responsible for the development of a strong and positive culture?
- how can these factors be fostered?

The analyses of strong and positive cultures given in section 6.2.2 indicate broad strategies for achieving these qualities.

The culture is made *stronger* by:

- creating conditions for greater cohesion;
- creating conditions for more efficient communication between members;
- organizing tasks so that members are forced to depend upon each other in at least one crucial aspect in order to satisfy their needs.

The culture is made *more positive* by

- increasing members' stake in official outcomes;
- improving systems so that gains and losses are perceived to be shared fairly;
- communicating productivity demands so that they are considered reasonable;
- structuring official relationships so that they are considered reasonable.

In short, the culture is improved by reinforcing members' good experiences of working in the organization. Top management hopes that these experiences will reflect the beliefs and attitudes that it is trying to foster among its members. It hopes that eventually these beliefs and attitudes will be taken for granted as "how things ought to be" in the organization.

6.3.4 The variable influences

However, no matter how much it may advertise the beliefs and attitudes to which it thinks its members should subscribe, no management can guarantee the organizational culture. A number of other variable factors also contribute to employees' values, over some of which management has no control. Values in the national culture provide a clear example of one such elusive factor. The full range of influences includes the following:

(a) the national culture, including values associated with working and the workplace;

(b) other environmental factors; for instance:

- the economic environment;
- market forces and marketing;
- industry factors;

(c) the organizational profile; for instance:

- history and ownership;
- size;
- technology;

(d) members' experience of formal systems:

- structures given to relationships and roles;
- management practice;
- schedules, systems, etc.;
- relationships and communications with superiors and subordinates;

(e) members' informal interactions with peers:

- norms, routines, procedures, conventions followed in the workplace;
- unofficial gossip, rituals, history;
- informal rules for surviving and getting along;

(f)   official goals, aims, philosophy, missions:

- organizational attitudes;
- organizational beliefs;
- official rituals, ceremonies, history, symbols.

6.3.5   Control of the variables

The national culture lies outside the manager's power to manipulate. Nothing that he/she does can cause members of the organization to "unlearn" this culture. However, management can exploit the power of culture by defining official goals in terms that reflect significant values and needs expressed by the culture and which are therefore likely to appeal to members.

Where management and subordinates belong to the same national culture, this process is natural and usually preconscious. But when management of a multinational corporation is planning the culture of a foreign subsidiary, a conscious effort must be made to take national cultural differences on board.

Where the organization is a significant player within its industry and a market leader,[4] employees are more likely to identify with it. And because marketing focuses on the organization's relationships with the environment and the problems of responding to the needs of customers, it plays a key part in developing the organization's sense of identity. Top management exploits the organization's relationship with its environment by selling its marketplace success to members ("We're number one").

The size of the organization and the uses made of technology affect members' relationships with each other and their superiors. By 1993 traffic conditions in Bangkok had so far deteriorated that the Thai Interior Ministry debated a proposal for permitting those of its officials who did not deal directly with the public to work from computers at home:

> officials whose work concerned finance, examination of disciplinary reports, and structures of various projects and designs might be able to take their work home on Monday and return with the finished work on Friday ... While at home, they would be subject to proper supervision to make sure that they were on duty.[5]

This indirectly threatened informal ties between employees, perhaps without subtracting from management's supervisory functions.

In general, any technology program that decreases dependencies between employees – perhaps by raising dependence upon a central data bank – can weaken the organization culture, which may be to management's advantage. In 1983 the Managing Director of Olivetti argued that information technology "is basically a technology of coordination and control of the labour force" (Preece, 1989, ch. 2).

But an information technology strategy does not necessarily disempower the workforce. In a flatter organization and where there is a strong and positive culture, technology operators are provided opportunities to enrich their working lives, by experimenting with their job specifications, roles and relationships. That is,

> the experimentation taking place on the shop floor is no more controlled from above that that taking place in the R&D lab. (Hayes and Jaikumur, 1988, p. 83)

When employees resent the conditions under which they have to earn their livings, they adopt alternative beliefs and attitudes. They develop informal procedures for short-circuiting unpopular systems and side-tracking routines. In an extreme case the energies released by this adversarial culture may be primarily directed towards subverting management's interests, towards the "disruption of production or subversion of the boss's authority and status" (Willis, 1979, p. 191). The sense of "us" against "them" in management is enhanced by rituals and myths that attack management's symbolic and real control of the workplace.

6.3.6 Controlling culture symbols

All organizational activities, including management, occur on two levels:

- substantive actions and results; making the product and selling it;
- symbolic actions.

An organization is a system of shared meanings, and individual members respond to the image of the workplace and the values that they share with each other.

Where different groups – for instance, management and workforce – respond to different sets of values, and where these values are diametrically opposed (as when an "us" and "them" mentality rules) the organization is in trouble. The importance of symbol and ritual in organizational relationships is increasingly recognized (Pfeffer, 1981). Specifically, the manager must

- reinforce and dramatize in symbolic form management central values (Deal and Kennedy, 1982, 1988);
- create a system of symbols that expresses management aspirations;
- project and interpret these symbols throughout the organization;

- create a consensus around these "official" symbols, so that conflict is dissipated and all members share the same symbols.

Management symbols, designed to foster a specific culture and to build a positive culture, include

- rituals and ceremonies; for instance, an award made to the employee of the month (Trice and Beyer, 1984);
- myths; "how we brought home the deal with Amex;"
- history; the early years, epic struggles, heroes and villains;
- language; in-house jargon that distinguishes insiders from outsider non-members.

In sum, management's capacity to control and mold the variables that influence the development of the culture within its particular organization varies widely. Management cannot influence features of the national culture, but may be able to influence how they are interpreted within the workplace. At the other end of the spectrum, considerable investment is made in creating and interpreting effective symbols. But even in this respect, success is never certain.

6.4 National and Organizational Cultures in Multinational Companies

In much of what has been said above it should be clear that plans for an organizational culture are unlikely to capture the loyalty of members if it attempts to wrench them too far from their expectations of their national culture. The values expressed by an organizational culture that is strong and positive in practice reflect both the members' feelings about the workplace, and also their national cultural values.

How widely can successful organizational cultures vary within any one national culture? The research conducted by Hofstede et al. (1990) into 20 different organizations in Denmark and the Netherlands found that membership of one organization rather than some other explained a significant share of variance in members' responses to questions probing their values. Organizational climates reflected not only the nationality, demographics of employees and managers, industry and market factors. They also reflected the structure and control systems practiced in the organization:

> organization culture differences are thus composed of other elements than those that make up national culture differences. (p. 312)

On the other hand, a brief review made by Berry et al. (1992) of the literature – including Hofstede et al. (1990) – argued that

> there is little evidence collected ... that points to major differences in values between employees of various organizations within a more or less culturally homogeneous country. Differences that have been mentioned [in their review] are not so much a matter of cultural values or meanings, but, more superficially, a matter of style. (pp. 321–2)

In themselves, these two answers to the problem are inconclusive, and we lack empirical evidence by which to decide the issue. If, as a cross-cultural manager, you accept the "strong" theory and believe that you really can create a culture that conditions your employees' behavior, regardless of other influences, then you are unlikely to accept Berry et al.'s pessimism on this score. And you are then relatively uninhibited in planning the culture of your overseas subsidiary.

But if your experience leads you to agree with Berry, then the clear implication is that organizational cultures vary little within the national context, and that national culture is the essential determinant of values and behavior within the organization. And this also means that

- the organizational culture of an existing organization reflects the national culture in strong focus;
- members of the organization will tend to resist plans to impose a culture that does not reflect their national values;
- a significant lack of correspondence between organizational and national values may lead to conflict between employees and top management.

The cross-cultural manager whose social and professional acquaintances with members of the other culture are limited to the workplace experiences their values only as they are expressed in the workplace. When the organizational culture is weak and appears to have little influence, workplace values and behaviors give a clear reflection of national values. But when the organizational culture is strong, the visiting manager cannot take for granted that what he/she observes in the workplace is typical of the wider context.

6.4.1 Headquarters and the organizational culture

In cases where the firm establishes a foreign subsidiary as a means of developing its international interests, headquarters–subsidiary tensions are almost inevitable. Headquarters has needs to control the subsidiary, and the mechanisms applied may compromise the subsidiary's needs for local responsibility. The subsidiary must attempt to represent head-quarters while still responding effectively to local market demands and labor market conditions.

Even radical differences in their organizational cultures can be toler-ated when headquarters feels little need to control the day-to-day activities of the subsidiary (so long as profit margins are satisfactory) and when staff in headquarters and the subsidiary have low needs to interact. But where each is dependent upon the other, differences in organizational cultures create the conditions for conflict.

How are differences resolved? The subsidiary hopes to develop an organizational culture within which its members also perceive interests shared with headquarters. They do not feel alienated by the headquarters culture, and when visiting there, find it easy to participate in the same value system. How successfully the multinational fosters this process depends upon:

- the development of the subsidiary at the point of acquisition;
- how the subsidiary is acquired;
- relations between headquarters and the subsidiary, and the style of control exerted by headquarters.

When the headquarters builds its foreign subsidiary from scratch, it has the best chance of fostering a culture that integrates with head-quarters values. At the opposite extreme, when a subsidiary is acquired with a history of independent management and a strong culture, members resist assimilation unless treated with great sensitivity.[6]

An atmosphere of suspicion and fear is disastrous in a cross-cultural situation where members of the acquired subsidiary interpret every ambiguity as evidence of hostility to their ethnic and cultural identity. When the acquisition is forced, the need for sensitivity in dealing with the "losing" party is all the greater. Both sides need to agree on how harmony in their cultures can be developed.

Fujita (1990) describes "fusion" processes by which Japanese com-panies attempt to create a "hybrid/problem-solving culture" when acquir-ing a foreign company. The process may be slow, and involves commitment by both parties.

> When a production engineer and a foreman resolve a problem in co-operation with workers as practiced in Japan, the process fosters organ-izational fusion; recurrences of the process will gradually give form to a new culture. (pp. 66–7)

By implication, this new culture neither replicates the Japanese head-quarters climate, nor typifies climates in the local culture.

Fusion appears to be most active in overseas plants of auto companies, normal in materials and high-tec companies, less than normal in food and pharmaceutical companies, and least successful in R & D companies, which Fujita labels "individualistic." The use of this term is not explained, but suggests that members of an organization characterized by a highly individualist culture may be most resistant to acquisition when this means accepting certain types of change in the organizational culture.

The expatriate manager's problems may stem less from conflicts between his/her own and the other national culture than from conflicts with home-based headquarters staff who are insensitive to local cultural priorities and to the problems of working within it.

6.4.2 Bureaucratic and cultural control

Jaeger (1983) distinguishes two extreme styles by which the headquarters controls its subsidiary:

- bureaucratic control;
- cultural control.

Headquarters exerts *bureaucratic control* by enforcing impersonal rules that govern the selection, recruitment, training, and rewarding of employees, and regulate the individual's behavior and output. This form of control is achieved through use of written manuals, instructions and reports. Training is restricted to teaching these manuals and specific technical competences.

Anglo multinationals tend towards this form of control – but they are not alone. In the five years after Nestlé (based in Switzerland) acquired Carnation (United States), Timm F. Crull,

> who was then Carnation's president, spoke by phone only twice to Nestlé Chairman Helmut Maucher. Called back to Vevey headquarters for only two visits each year, Crull ran Carnation with minimal interference from his new boss. "We would go months, and I wouldn't hear from him," Crull recalls.[7]

But when Nestlé began suffering in price wars with local rivals, it folded Carnation and its other United States subsidiaries into a single $7.4 billion-a-year food giant. And now Crull, who believed in centralization, found himself

> spending one week every month at Vevey. As chairman and CEO of Nestlé USA Inc., he is scrambling to reshape what had been a sprawling, inefficient organization.[8]

Cultural control is created through the use of implicit norms that induce members of the subsidiary to make a moral commitment to it. Manuals are used as training tools, but at least as much emphasis is laid on developing an awareness of the organization's norms and values, and integrating the newcomer into the shared culture. This is achieved by subjecting him/her to personal interactions with established members of staff.

The expense of imposing cultural control is heavy and in the early stages involves:

- staffing the subsidiary with large numbers of expatriates who act as role-models;
- extensive employee socialization programs;
- visits between the subsidiary and headquarters;
- company seminars;
- social events. Yeh's (1991) study of management activities in Taiwanese-based subsidiaries owned by Japanese and United States firms discovered that activities such as dining and drinking together, picnics, group travel, and group sports were organized far more frequently in the Japanese subsidiaries.

In time, the culture of the subsidiary resembles that of headquarters. According to Jaeger (1983), cultural control is typically applied by Japanese multinationals (although many, and perhaps most, do not follow this mode); the alternative discussed by Neghandi and Baliga (1979) is to treat local employees in a manner similar to the way they are treated by local companies.

Subsidiaries of bureaucratic control companies are freer to do business in accordance with local practice and have greater flexibility to adapt to local laws and cultural norms. But control by memo from a distance does not win loyalty in a collectivist culture where personal relationships between superior and subordinates are all-important. Cultural control companies aim to induce headquarter values at a much deeper cultural and psychological level.

When headquarters controls the technology and expertise, a heavy headquarters input may be necessary in order to guarantee effective use – and protect their intellectual rights. The relationship between control of technology and climate is demonstrated by its negative – an unusual case in which Japanese companies did *not* have the technical know-how, and as a result were unable to exercise culture control. In 1989 and 1990 Sony and Matsushita took over two leading Hollywood film producers, Columbia Pictures and MCA. Sony sent only one Japanese manager to Columbia and Matsushita left MCA's management team in place, sending only a few Japanese staff and not to the studio.

Both Japanese multinationals' policies

> towards the entertainment business [are] being driven by the same simple
> point: the parent company's obvious ignorance. When Japanese firms
> operate factories abroad, they act as teachers, bringing in their superior
> manufacturing methods. In the entertainment business it is different. The
> Americans are teachers and the Japanese are the students.
> . . . Sony and Matsushita have concluded that, if they are to stay in
> entertainment, they have to do things the American way. That means no
> penny pinching, and giving the American managers a free hand. . . . it is
> an uncomfortable formula for Japanese bosses accustomed to being in
> control.[9]

One problem in exercising cultural control may be that it widens the
divide between subsidiary employees, who are loyal to organizational
norms, and other persons in the community, who respond primarily to
values in the national culture. Jaeger (1983) argues that it creates a con-
traculture or deviant group within the host country:

> whose norms are in conflict with the surrounding society. This can ultim-
> ately result in frustration, anxiety, and resentment among the members of
> the subsidiary, harming both the firm and the host country (p. 102)

Neghandi (1987, p. 273) describes research showing that, whether
practicing cultural control or following local models, Japanese companies often have greater problems in attracting, retaining and motivating
all levels of employees than do their main competitors. (See also Gan,
1988.)

The national culture indirectly affects the choice of control style. The
greater the level of anxiety at headquarters, the greater its demand that
headquarters values are accepted at a deep psychological level. Where a
cultural control style seems most likely to win this acceptance, it is appropriate. But needs for control of proprietory technology, and industry
and the other environmental factors, also have to be taken into account.

6.5 Implications for the Manager

Answer questions 1–4 for

- an organization that you know well in *your own* culture; *and*
- an organization that you know well in *some other* culture.

Answer questions 5–6 for a *multinational headquarters* and *subsidiary* that
you know well.

1. In each organization, look for evidence that

   - values in the national culture are a more significant influence on behavior in the organization than is the organizational culture;
   - organizational culture is a more significant influence on behavior in the organization than are values in the national culture.

2. For each organization, decide whether its culture is

   (a) *strong* or *weak*;
   (b) *positive* or *negative*.

   - What factors make it strong/weak?
   - What factors make in positive/negative?
   - How might it be made stronger?
   - How might it be made more positive?
   - In general, how can it be improved?

3. For each organization, decide how values are influenced by the following factors:

   (a) the national culture, including values associated with working and the workplace;
   (b) other environmental factors;
   (c) the history and ownership of the organization;
   (d) size and staffing of the organization;
   (e) technology employed in the organization;
   (f) members' experience of formal systems;
   (g) members' informal interactions with peers;
   (h) norms, routines, gossip in the workplace;
   (i) official rituals, ceremonies and symbols;
   (j) official goals;
   (k) organizational beliefs;
   (l) organizational attitudes.

   - How can these factors be manipulated in order to improve the culture?

4. In each organization, what sub-cultures can you discern? How similar or dissimilar are the values accepted by the following groups?

   (a) top management;
   (b) middle management;
   (c) junior management;
   (d) shop floor;
   (e) different functional groups;

(f) different plants/subsidiaries;
(g) headquarters staff, expatriate staff, local staff in overseas subsidaries.

- How does the organization benefit from these similarities? From the dissimilarities?
- How far does the organization suffer from the similarities? From the dissimilarities?
- How can these sub-cultures be changed to the advantage of the organization?

5. In the case of the multinational you have chosen, how does headquarters control values and behavior in the subsidiary? By policies of

(a) bureaucratic control?
(b) cultural control?

- What problems arise from implementing this control policy?
- How might these problems be resolved by

    (a) implementing the policy more efficiently?
    (b) modifying the policy and moving towards more/less cultural control?

6. In the case of the multinational subsidiary, what factors influence its culture?

- In what respects does the subsidiary's culture reflect

    (a) values in headquarters culture?
    (b) values in the local national culture?

- In what respects is the subsidiary culture similar to the cultures of locally owned firms (in a comparable industry, or comparable size)?
- In what respects are the cultures of the subsidiary and these locally owned firms dissimilar?

6.6 Summary

This chapter has discussed the concept of organization culture.

Section 6.2 dealt with the problems of distinguishing the *organizational culture* and *national culture*. The section went on to model organizational beliefs, attitudes, and values. Strong and weak, positive and negative, organizational cultures were distinguished.

Section 6.3 dealt with the issue of how top management can set about *changing the organizational culture*. Top management makes a significant impact by influencing its employees' organizational values. Section 6.4 discussed problems for the *multinational* when trying to build a *culture* in a foreign subsidiary. The company has difficulties winning locals to its cause if it attempts to build a subsidiary culture that reflects only the national culture of headquarters, and denies the legitimacy of the local national culture. The difficulties will be particularly severe if the subsidiary has been recently acquired and had a strong organizational culture, reflecting the local national culture, before acquisition. Two functions of bureaucratic and cultural control were discussed.

6.7 Exercise

Comment on this case.[10] *Analyse the problems and suggest solutions.*

Five years ago, Luigi Feraro, established an electronics company in Singapore. He continues to be Chief Executive Officer. The national identities of the current management team and their tenures are listed:

General Manager	Swiss	4 months
Finance Manager	British	19 months
Production Manager	Italian	32 months
Marketing Manager	Singaporean	15 months
Personnel Manager	Singaporean	13 months
Administration Manager	Singaporean	12 months
Engineering Manager	Taiwanese	28 months
R & D Manager	Singaporean	33 months
Transportation Manager	Malaysian	46 months

The company started with a staff of three – Feraro and two Singaporean business friends, Hervey Tan and Michael Swee. But after a series of bitter rows, the two Singaporeans left.

Feraro says:

> They left to start their own business together. In some product lines we are directly competing. Even so, I have to admit that I owe them a lot. They were hard workers. Whatever I told them, they got on and did. Usually I couldn't have done better myself. Another thing I learned from them was the value of internationalism in a country like this. It was their idea. When we make a new staff appointment, the first question we ask is how can the applicant help make this a more international firm.

However, the team has found it difficult to work together successfully. There has been considerable turnover in management personnel.

Meetings are not successful. The Western staff tend to contribute far more than the Asian staff, but even they experience difficulties in communicating among themselves.

Feraro complains

> I've tried to inspire them, to give them my enthusiasm. I set them off in the direction I want them to take, but they never seem to take off. I encourage them to take initiatives but frankly, they usually come up with ideas that are impractical. When that happens, it's always up to me to straighten them out. And although each one of them could be good on his – or her – own, they can't work as a team.

In an attempt to generate a stronger culture, Feraro asked his Finance Manager to arrange a series of social events for the top management team and their spouses/significant others.

The first event involved dinner on a luxury cruiser, touring around the island. Two senior French managers, visiting from a Brussels company with which Feraro hoped to do business, were invited.

By the end of the evening, the Europeans were seated in a group down one end of the deck, and the Asians down the other.

Notes

1. Clyde Haberman, "How a pathologist reshaped Seoul's politics," *New York Times*, May 4, 1988.
2. Geoff Lewis, "One fresh face at IBM may not be enough," *Business Week*, April 12, 1993.
3. John Markoff, "At Apple, nuts and bolts versus granola," *International Herald Tribune*, July 10–11, 1993.
4. For instance, Gordon (1991) argues that the culture is strongly influenced by the characteristics of the industry within which the organization operates. Three classes of industry-driven culture elements are identified; competitive environment, customer requirements, and societal expectations.
5. "Interior Ministry ponders 'home work,'" *Bangkok Post*, July 26, 1993. (Reported also in *Thai Rat*, Bangkok, July 25, 1993.)
6. For discussion of processes of adaptation and organizational acculturation, see Nahavandi and Malekzadeh (1988).
7. Amy Barrett and Zachary Schiller, "At Carnation, Nestlé makes the very best . . . cutbacks," *Business Week*, March 22, 1993.
8. Ibid.
9. "Hooked by Hollywood," *The Economist*, September 21, 1991.
10. This case was suggested by material produced by Professor Fredric Swierczek.

Part III

Culture and Relationships

7

Cross-Cultural Management Communication

7.1 Introduction

A newspaper story describes the problems of a Japanese executive returning home after working in the United States and acquiring American communication habits:

> In New York Mr Kashima did a lot of business on the telephone. In Japan, he must personally visit people in order to conduct any important business – "so they can see my eyes."

> When he returns from meetings, he has to write his employer a full report. Because only top managers are allocated personal secretaries, he types this himself.

> Below the surface, he says, things get even more complicated. "Suppose I want to propose something new," he says. "In Japan, the first thing I should do is take a colleague from the office to the nightclub and talk around the theme – without mentioning my idea directly. Only after my office colleague and I understand each other would I go to my superior and propose the idea. But when I first returned from the U.S., I tended to go straight ahead with my ideas."[1]

But when problems developed he reverted to normal Japanese style. A number of points arise:

- Culture influences communication priorities. This Japanese manager has to build good will among his peers before taking an idea to a superior. In the United States the manager feels less restricted by needs to avoid conflict and to establish peer consensus.

- For instance, culture influences communicative style. In this case, culture determines whether direct or indirect communication is acceptable in different situations. In Japan, the manager feels constrained to introduce his idea indirectly, first establishing a general understanding. In the United States, "blunt" direct expression is often preferred.
- Culture is reflected in non-verbal behavior. The need to make eye contact reflects the importance of face-to-face contact in Japanese business negotiations – to be expected in a high-context culture. But in the low-context United States, the lesser importance of face-to-face contact means that more business can be done by telephone.
- Non-cultural factors also influence communicative priorities. The lack of secretaries for Japanese middle managers means that Mr Kashima must write his own reports.

This chapter discusses the relationship between culture, organization, and communication systems. Problems of communicating between international joint ventures and their parent companies, and between headquarters and subsidiary, are dealt with in chapters 13 and 14.

The chapter has the following sections:

7.2 Appropriate Communication across Cultures
7.3 One-Way Communication
7.4 Two-Way Communication
7.5 A Transactional Model
7.6 Implications for the Manager
7.7 Summary
7.8 Exercise

7.2 Appropriate Communication across Cultures

Perhaps all cultures carry stereotypes about the ideal mode of communication. Communicative difficulties arise when members of a culture group impose their stereotypes on some other culture, and refuse to make concessions when either producing messages or interpreting messages sent to them.

For example, Americans often pride themselves on their "blunt" and "direct" communicative style – despite the capacity shown by many American politicians for calculated ambiguity. And they do not have a monopoly on bluntness, as this story about Gulf War military briefings suggests.

> Most foreign correspondents covering the war . . . say British officers speak with more style, frankness, and are more polite about saying "No."
>
> American spokesmen are criticized for using too much military jargon and giving too little information. . . .
>
> "Being told 'No' really gets people's backs up," [an American radio correspondent] said.
>
> "The British are much more frank, direct and polite especially in explaining why they can't tell you something. . . . PR officers should realize that they can lose people when they talk tech – Joe public does not understand."[2]

However, directness is not equally effective in all cultural contexts. In much of the Asian Pacific region, for instance, over-directness is disliked because it seems likely to ferment conflict, as this example shows:

> Australians have reached the conclusion that "G'day mate, how's it going," followed by a hearty slap on the back, is no way to do business in Asia.
>
> The blunt greeting has in the past been an endearing formula for winning contracts in many parts of the world.
>
> But in Asia, it can be as insulting as a slap in the face.[3]

Such a greeting would be unacceptable in Indonesia, for instance, where physical contact with a stranger is avoided.

The Japanese stringently avoid using language forms likely to cause offence (in circumstances where this might rebound to their disadvantage) and involve the other person in loss of face. Imai (1975) notes 16 ways of avoiding saying "no." Here is an example.

> Take "Eii doryoku shimasu," which means "We shall make efforts," and seems straightforward enough. When a Cabinet member says it, most of his listeners in the Parliament know that he intends to do nothing.
>
> The same goes for a minister who announces that he will accomplish something "kakyuteki sumiyaka," or "with the greatest expedition possible." Be assured, Japanese say, that that is a call for tortoise-like action. . . .
>
> [One former Cabinet member commented] that "[a]ny civilized language is ambiguous because in human relationships you cannot be terribly blunt."[4]

When this style reflects a high-context culture, it may present no problems in understanding to cultural insiders who play by the same rules. However, they can lead to cross-cultural confusion with, for instance, the low-context Anglo.

Anglo: "Can I interest you in our plastics range?"
Japanese: "I shall give it careful consideration."

The Japanese means a negative response to the offer, which is intended to discourage further discussion. The Anglo who interprets it as a indication of positive interest and who pushes ahead with his sales pitch is likely to meet embarrassment and eventual silence. This damages not only present but also future business possibilities.

7.2.1 Appropriacy

A management message is efficient in so far as the person for whom it is intended is persuaded of the addressor's credibility and trustworthiness, and (where applicable) to comply with his/her wishes (Shelby, 1986). A message is more likely to be persuasive and to achieve its purpose when it is appropriate, and the audience recognizes this fact. When planning a communication, this means selecting the best option for each of these parameters:

- *who* will communicate;
- *to whom* – the appropriate person or persons to whom the message should be communicated; the addressee, or audience;
- *what* – appropriate content of the message;
- *how* – appropriate medium for communicating the message;
- *when* – appropriate time for communicating the message;
- *where* – appropriate location for communicating the message.

In other words, a message loses credibility when it is communicated

- by an inappropriate addressor;   *and/or*
- to an inappropriate addressee;   *and/or*
- with an inappropriate content;   *and/or*
- by an inappropriate medium;   *and/or*
- at an inappropriate time;   *and/or*
- in an inappropriate location.

Each option for an appropriate message takes into account the option selected for each of these parameters, the purpose of the message, and the relevant environmental parameters.

The environmental factors that determine appropriacy include:

- economic and market conditions;
- industry type;
- organizational structure;
- national culture.

7.2.2 The addressor

In general, the selection of any one of the six parameters influences selection of each of the other five. For instance, the selection of *who* gives the message is influenced by (and influences) selection of audience and their needs, the selection of content, and occasion.

When making an annual report to stockholders in a formal meeting, the company CEO may restrict his/her own remarks to general reporting and strategic issues. He/she refers detailed questions on financial issues to the finance director. This does not mean that the CEO does not have this information, but that in this setting, it is considered appropriate that other senior officers should be seen to be involved, and that specialist concerns should be addressed by specialists.

Seldom, anywhere, is bad news welcomed, and the manager may prefer to delegate the responsibility for communicating it to a lesser official. This tendency is strong in cultures where giving bad news involves loss of face. In Japan in 1990,

> [a] group of Japanese pundits were discussing on television where they thought the stockmarket was heading. The strange part of it was that, like drug dealers, rape victims or mafiosi turned government witnesses, the pundits' faces were fuzzed out. The social significance, however, was crystal clear: no one in group-think Japan wants the dishonor of being associated with a declining market.
>
> Such extraordinary behavior explains the part-embarrassment, part-shame felt by so many individuals and so many companies at losing money in the stockmarket.[5]

7.2.3 The addressee

A message sent to the wrong person may fail as a communication, even when parameters of content, medium, time, situation, and reason are satisfied. And you cannot take for granted that the norms governing addressor–addressee relationships in your culture apply elsewhere.

Suppose that you are an assistant marketing manager in a US firm that typifies Hofstede's model of the market bureaucracy (discussed in chapter 4, section 4.5.3). In developing a new project, you decide that you need advice from the production department, and find it convenient and acceptable to communicate directly with your counterpart, the assistant production manager. However, if you were working within a typical French (full bureaucracy) firm, you might be making a serious mistake if you failed to route your communication through your boss, the marketing manager, and his, the production manager.

7.2.4 Content

The subject of the communication may be described in terms of the information communicated; but the choice of information is restricted. In general, information is given for a purpose, usually to persuade. Suppose that a badly dressed man approaches me in the street and says, "I am poor and hungry. My wife is sick and my children don't have any shoes for walking to school." Given the information and the context, I interpret it as a persuasive utterance designed to elicit a hand-out. But if he were to say, "I am rich and happy. The wife and kids are all healthy," and I am unable to attach a purpose to his giving me this information, I conclude that his behavior is irrational.

That is, you fail to fully grasp the content if you

- do not understand the context of the information;
- do not understand why the information is being conveyed;

almost as much as if you fail to understand the lexical meaning of the words used.

This has cross-cultural implications. The significance of an item of business information is determined by its context, which may include situational, economic, political, and cultural factors. Business deals often go wrong because one side does not understand why certain information is being given, or requested, and because its informational priorities do not correspond to those of the other side.

For instance, Western companies have experienced problems in planning joint ventures with organizations in the People's Republic of China because the two sides' perceptions of what information is needed do not coincide. Westerners commonly complain about the lack of "hard" data and of coordinated information systems (Beamish and Wang, 1989). In practice, this often indicates a lack of correspondence in Western capitalist and Chinese Communist perceptions of what data is "hard," significant, and persuasive. It may be the case that, in their terms, the Chinese *are* supplying persuasive information. (On the other hand, it might simply indicate a lack of interest in playing Anglo information "games" when a line of other Western firms are competing for the same business.)

So a message is persuasive when the addressor selects information that the addressee perceives as relevant – in terms of his/her situational and cultural values. This information must be presented at the appropriate level of explicitness; and important points should be appropriately highlighted – so far as possible, in terms of the expectations of the other culture (Haworth and Savage, 1989).

Even when the information is relevant, an excess creates information overload. Research shows that as more information is provided, it has declining effect (Eagly, 1974). And the addressee predisposed to argue with or reject the information assimilates even less, and is less likely to respond to the message (Insko et al., 1976). So effective communication takes into account the quantity of information that the receiver can be expected to digest and act upon.

How does this affect the cross-cultural manager? When sender and receiver come from different cultures, they have different perceptions of what information is significant and relevant. Hence they follow different criteria in selecting and sequencing information. In general, the cross-cultural manager builds far more repetitions and paraphrase into a message than when communicating in a mono-cultural context.

When communicating with a stranger from another culture for the first time, the experienced communicator spells out his/her message in more detail than would be normal with a member of his/her own culture. This helps make his/her communicative purpose clear, and also helps identify shared values and experiences.

7.2.5 Medium

The manager has access to a wide range of media when selecting the appropriate form for communicating his/her message. He can use speech (in formal or informal meetings, by telephone, etc.), text (in letters, reports, memos, etc.), pictorial forms (Mead, 1990, ch. 5). These can be used in combinations; for instance, a report used as input to a large-group meeting in which points are illustrated with video.

The skilled manager selects the appropriate mode for communicating with members of his/her own culture group with a minimum of difficulty. This selection process is influenced by such non-cultural factors as

- the number and identities of the audience;
- the complexity and importance of the message; feedback needs;
- the message function; its routine or original quality;
- distance;
- expense;
- the need for accuracy and legal considerations;
- the availability of communications technology.

But cultural factors also play a part, and you cannot jump to the conclusion that the same factors that influence your perception of the appropriate medium are significant for the other culture. In other words, you need to consider the cultural implications of your selection before committing yourself.

For instance, the Anglo manager relies relatively heavily on memos when communicating within the organization. But in a culture where personal relationships (between peers, levels on the hierarchy) are of paramount importance, the apparent advantages of efficient communication are delusory. The memo suggests coldness, aloofness, and a deliberate distancing from the other person, and achieves far less than a personal meeting – despite the greater investment in time that this entails.

A Thai financial analyst reports that

> I have to write memos (call reports) to the boss after I meet customers. Memos are important for investment bankers. [But] talking with colleagues and superiors about what I do is easier. I can express my feeling to them. . . . By talking like this, we can know by his face. From memos, we cannot know his real feeling.

That is, a written mode is select d only when absolutely necessary – in this case, to record completed business. But the Thai does not use a memo when, for instance, suggesting a new policy. In this case he/she prefers speech, or at least takes the opportunity to discuss the point before recording it on paper. The low-context American manager might reverse the process, first writing the memo in order to establish legal ownership of the idea, then proceeding to discussion.

But even when a mode has been selected that meets both instrumental and cultural criteria, it may still fail to persuade its intended audience if the style is inappropriate.

7.2.6 Time

The appropriacy of communication is also influenced by time. Hall and Whyte's (1961) analysis of four aspects of time shows how perceptions vary in different cultures.

Schedule time Refers to the time by when a job should be completed. Anglo cultures place a premium on a job being finished by the appointed time. Less urgency is attached to schedule time in cultures that show greater pessimism about completing plans as formulated.

Discussion time Refers to the length of time that should be spent in discussing business. Anglo cultures tend to censor discussion that is not focused as "time wasting" – even when this is building the relationship between the participants.

Acquaintance time Determines how long you need to know the other person before he/she will do business with you. This varies across cultures. In a low-context culture such as the United States, acquaintance time is often cut back to a single meeting, and your business card – which says more about your identity as an employee of a particular organization than about your personality – may be considered an adequate credential.

But in high-context cultures, where relationships between individuals are long-lasting and significant, and where insiders and outsiders are distinguished, you may need to invest considerable time in creating a relationship.

If you are not acquainted, you need to find a third person or institution, known to both parties, to make a proper introduction and to vouch for your integrity. For instance, in Japan the non-Japanese might seek the help of JETRO – the Japanese External Trade Organization.

Appointment time Deals with the issue of punctuality. If you are kept waiting an hour for an appointment with an Anglo businessperson you are probably right to feel that an apology and explanation is in order. But in Latin American or Arabic cultures, punctuality is not valued similarly, and you should not assume that you have been deliberately insulted or that your business is discounted.

In the Anglo cultures, the manager may be up to five minutes late for an appointment without feeling it necessary to apologize. But Swedes are more particular; an appointment for ten o'clock often means ten on the dot.

7.2.7 Location

The locational parameter determines:

- where business is appropriately communicated; for instance, in the United States, you can talk business at most social events, but often not in Southern Italy, where business entertaining is not popular;
- what sort of business is communicated in different locations;
- the symbolic meaning that the choice of location imparts to the communication.

Where the individual works, the access or lack of it that this affords other people, and how the space is furnished, communicate messages of power and status. These may vary across cultures.

In American companies the CEO typically occupies a top-floor office (often on a corner), distancing him/her from the workforce, and aides compete for an office nearby. But the manager of a Federal Express subsidiary in Mexico

1. (Addressor) A decided what to communicate > . . . .
. . . .
. . > 2. (Addressor) A encodes a message > . . . .
. . . .
. . > 3. (Addressor) A transmits the message > . . . .
. . . .
. . > 4. (Addressee) B decodes the message > . . . .
. . . .
. . > 5. (Addressee) B acknowledges and/or acts upon the message.

Figure 7.1 Communicative process between addressor and addressee.

managed to keep closer tabs on delivery workers by converting a plush conference room next to his office into an employee cafeteria. "In Mexico, people will work harder for you if they can see you, if work becomes a personal thing between you and them," says Mr Duenas. Federal Express's rate of late delivery has fallen to less than 1 percent.[6]

In a Japanese office, manager and subordinates often share the same room and the manager perhaps only uses a personal office in order to meet honored guests.

7.3 One-Way Communication

Figure 7.1 is a simple model of a communicative process between the Addressor, A, and Addressee, B.

This model implies the following.

- The communicative process is linear. The activities of deciding to communicate, formulating the message, transmitting, (etc.), occur within the same sequence each time the process is followed, and each must be completed before the next begins.
- The process is one-way in direction. Participant B makes no substantive verbal contribution to the communication (beyond, perhaps, acknowledging and/or acting upon the message in Stage 5).
- The message given to B is straightforward, and does not need clarification. B does not need to respond. When the message directs the performance of some task, the task is

Routine B has performed the task before, and does not need further instructions; for example,

A: "Can I have a photocopy of this brochure, please." *And/or*

Simple Even if B is new to the task or the organization, he/she can easily infer what activity has to be performed from contextual clues; for example,

A: [pointing at a broom] "Could you give the floor a quick brush please."
And/or

Close-ended There can be only one successful outcome to the activity. In the examples above, a photocopy is made, the floor is brushed.
And/or

Urgent As in the case of fire-fighting.

- Any non-verbal signaling that occurs will not significantly affect the meaning of the message.

When these conditions apply, two-way communication may be inappropriate.

This pattern of interaction may be observed in all cultural settings. But when

- it is repeated on a regular basis
- A regularly takes the role of Sender
- A is superior and B is subordinate

it is likely that power distances are high, and that the power relationship between A and B is constant. And it also occurs when needs to avoid uncertainty are high. B is inhibited from initiating an interaction, or from making any significant verbal contribution (for instance, commenting, querying, posing an alternative).

7.3.1 How one-way communication may reflect the culture

Where power distances are large, the superior's rights to delegate are associated with social and political authority. When the superior uses his/her authority in ways perceived as legitimate, members of the group in general perceive it in their interests to preserve his/her authority. Hence the subordinate makes little feedback; comments and suggestions are often interpreted as a challenge to superior authority. Even a request for clarification may suggest that the superior has failed to explain adequately the first time, and thus be interpreted as criticism.

When members place a priority on preserving social harmony, they avoid communicative situations in which disagreement is overt. Expressions of conflict are repressed. In practice this means that subordinates avoid making negative or unwelcomed contributions which may be interpreted as disagreeing with the superior. And this often means keeping as silent as possible. When decision-making is associated with senior rank, any attempt to involve subordinates in the process may threaten social norms and be resisted.

Table 7.1 Preference for one-way communication

Preference for sending *one-way communications*	*Preference for receiving* *one-way communications*
1. (showing most preference) India	1. (showing most preference) India
2. United Kingdom	2. Denmark
3. Denmark	3. United Kingdom
4. United States	4. Belgium
5=. Belgium	5. Norway
5=. Italy	6=. Italy
7. Norway	6=. United States

Source: Barrett and Frank (1969).

7.3.2 Preferences for one-way communication

If you try to impose this communication pattern upon your subordinates where it is inappropriate, you may be perceived to impose greater power distances upon them. But at least in so far as written modes are concerned, it cannot be assumed that one-way communication is favored only where power distances are large. For instance, Hofstede's analysis shows the United Kingdom, Denmark, and Norway to be among the dozen countries with the smallest power distances. Yet table 7.1 shows that research by Barrett and Frank (1969) ranks them high in terms of their managers' preferences for sending and receiving one-way communications over two-way communications; (see also Gibson and Hodgetts, 1991).

What this research does *not* tell us about are the circumstances under which a written mode may be more acceptable in different cultures. For instance, we might expect different values attached to the memo when it is used to

- report on a routine activity; e.g., a sale;
- report on a special project;
- plan future activity;
- propose an initiative.

In some Anglo cultures the prejudice has grown up that one-way communication is inherently "bad" and inefficient. This is not so. Whether or not a communication pattern is efficient depends entirely upon its appropriacy, given factors that include the task and the participants. For instance, fire-fighters and military personnel are trained to accept orders with a minimum of feedback because the urgency of their task does not permit extensive two-way debates on correct procedure.

But even in these extreme situations, the underlying cultural norms may significantly influence the communication process. A magazine article (written during the Cold War) describes a unit of the United States army trained to model Russian battle strategy and to provide combat training for regular US forces. The fictitious "Russians" replicate genuine Russian behavior as closely as possible:

> Talk on the radio, for example, flows in only one direction – down from the commander. American units, on the other hand, have many more people talking, which can add to confusion during a battle.[7]

7.3.3 Interpreting ambiguity

Where power distances are large, subordinates are wary of asking for clarification of ambiguous utterances lest this involve the superior in loss of face (by implying that he/she communicated inadequately the first time) and so work to make sure that they interpret correctly. They observe his/her behavior, and predict appropriate responses in part on the basis of past experience. In turn, the considerate superior tries to avoid ambiguity and unpredictability. But where power distances are small, a failure to make a correct interpretation

- costs less in terms of face;
- can be easily repaired by asking for clarification.

This difference creates cross-cultural problems, for instance when the Japanese is sent to manage his company's subsidiary in the United States. Local employees appear less competent than are his Japanese employees in interpreting his directions, and spend more time in debating instructions. The employees also suffer; in their terms, his dislike for discussing work assignments seems like arrogance and aloofness.

The point is illustrated by the following dialogue. The CEO and his Assistant belong to a culture in which power distances are large and the subordinate Assistant invests energy in identifying and serving his/her superior's needs. They are situated in the office.

CEO: I don't have any quarterly figures from the warehousing department.

Assistant: Yes sir. [Calls the warehousing department and requests that the figures be submitted].

The Assistant's perception of the distance in their social relationship means that he interprets any utterance by the CEO as a directive, and where this interpretation is appropriate, tries to fulfil it.

The information given by the CEO is restricted by what the Assistant already knows. When speaking to a visitor he might feel called upon to spell out additional information presupposed by his message.

> CEO: Our company has a large warehousing department which usually issues quarterly inflow and outflow figures. These are sent to me in my role as CEO. But for some reason which I do not understand, I haven't received them this quarter.

But in the context of a meeting with his Assistant, he does not need to recapitulate this old, shared, information, which would be redundant.

Now consider this second dialogue, also in the office. When the CEO and Assistant come from a narrow power distance culture, in which the Assistant spends much less in intuiting and trying to anticipate his/her superior's needs, responses to the same utterance might include the following (Sinclair, 1980):

> CEO: I don't have any quarterly figures from the warehousing department.
> Assistant: (a) I see. [*Takes no action*]
> (b) Late again, are they.
> (c) Do you want me to call them?
> (d) I'll call for them now. [*Calls*]

Response

(a) provides a minimal acknowledgement;
(b) makes a comment;
(c) asks whether the CEO intends his utterance as a directive; requests clarification of the purpose;
(d) interprets the utterance as a directive.

The range of alternatives available shows that where power distances are low, the CEO's utterance cannot be interpreted only as a directive requesting activity.

7.3.4 Communicating upwards where power distances are high

A question arises; in a culture and organization where power distances are large, how does the subordinate convey criticism back up the line to the boss – in so far as this is permitted at all? The Japanese manage this process by institutionalizing after-hours eating and drinking. Japanese culture is relatively tolerant of drunkenness, and once in the bar subordinates may express opinions that would not be tolerated back in the office. Hence, communication between the same superior and subordinate appropriate when one set of temporal and locational factors apply (after working hours, in the bar) is entirely inappropriate when another set apply (during working hours, in the office).

Elsewhere, a message might be sent anonymously or passed out of the organization to a third party who mediates its re-entry at the appropriate level. For instance, a subordinate talks to a cousin who passes the complaint on to a friend of the superior.

In some high-context cultures where the foreigner never becomes entirely assimilated into social structures, he/she may serve as a conduit to convey messages between ranks that would otherwise be unacceptable. His/her equivocal status also provides opportunities for informal communication that might otherwise not arise. An American manager working in a Thai company gives examples:

> Exchanging gossip with someone's secretary or driver can often be much more informative than going directly to a top executive, as he may feel uncomfortable expressing dissatisfaction directly . . . Likewise, most of the Thai executives in my firm use my secretary to convey messages to me or ask my feelings about something rather than communicating with me, even though their English may be better than my secretary's. . . . If she gets it wrong, [that is] her mistake, not theirs.

The example of Japanese salarymen in their after-working-hours bar example shows how otherwise inappropriate messages may be legitimated by changing temporal and locational parameters. In contrast, this Thai case shows the same result achieved by channeling messages through a local intermediary with low formal status (the Thai secretary) and a social outsider with high formal status (the foreign manager). That is, the parameter of addressee is differently expressed.

7.4 Two-Way Communication

Two-way communication involves the addressee in making significant verbal contributions to the interaction (see figure 7.2).

Like the one-way model discussed in section 7.3, this two-way model is linear, and describes the interactional process as a series of similar moves taking place in real time. It implies that only one person at a time contributes, either when initiating or after decoding the other person's completed message. Hence it is useful for describing communication transmitted by an appropriate written mode:

1. (Addressor) A decides what to communicate > . . . .
. . . .
. . > 2. (Addressor) A encodes a message > . . . .
. . . .
. . > 3. (Addressor) A transmits the message > . . . .
. . . .
. . > 4. (Addressee) B decodes the message > . . . .
. . . .
. . > 5. (Addressee/Addressor) B decides what to communicate in feedback > . . . .
. . . .
. . > 6. (Addressee/Addressor) B encodes a message > . . . .
. . . .
. . > 7. (Addressee/Addressor) B transmits a message > . . . .
. . . .
. . > 8. (Addressee/Addressor) A decodes the message > . . . .
. . . .
. . > 9. (Addressee/Addressor) A/B acknowledges and/or acts upon the message, or
returns to Stage 1.

Figure 7.2   Two-way communication model.

> Interaction through an electronics or paper medium (e.g., letters, memor-
> andums, or computer terminals) separates the communicators and often
> structures communication as a process of message exchange. A sends a
> message to B, then must wait for B to follow up with a reply. (Daniels and
> Spiker, 1991, p. 45)

When modeling typical patterns of spoken communication in a face-
to-face mode, it illuminates aspects of the interpersonal relationship
between A and B. B's contribution in Stage 7 expresses feedback to A's
in Stage 3; it may also serve to elicit feedback from A.[8] Feedback responses express a range of functions, which include:

- responding to a question:
- requesting clarification of a previous utterance;
- adding information;
- making a query;
- suggesting an alternative;
- giving support.

Applying Hofstede's (1984a) model we can infer that power distances
are small when, as a matter of course,

- the subordinate feels free to take the role of A, and to initiate communications;
- A and B are peers, and peers are uninhibited in asking each other
  for help, giving advice, etc.

The previous section suggested that predominantly one-way communication from superior to subordinate betokens routine, and/or urgent, and/or simple, and/or close-ended tasks. When all ranks need to initiate two-way communications on vertical and horizontal axes, the reverse conditions may apply. That is, tasks are

- *non-routine* The company is continually readjusting to a changing market and short-run demands;   *and/or*
- *complex* Individuals are new to the task, or need help from a variety of sources in order to complete the task; the possibilities of misunderstanding are great, and must be avoided;   *and/or*
- *open-ended* A number of outcomes may resolve the issue; for instance, there may be no one way of designing a new product that will fit market demand;   *and/or*
- *not urgent.*

When these conditions apply, one-way communication is inappropriate.

7.4.1 Changing from one-way to two-way communication

Why should superior and subordinate change from one- to two-way patterns as the regular form of communication between them? In general, people only adopt new behaviors when the old ones are no longer appropriate or efficient. Here are some of the examples of factors that influence the change:

- the company moves into new markets, and employees are needed to perform a wider range of short-run tasks;
- employees are needed to perform more complex tasks, and implementation procedures must be negotiated with supervisors;
- new technologies modify needs for supervision;
- employees are given open-ended tasks to perform; for instance, the company "pulls down" management planning activities in an effort to enrich their jobs and motivate them;
- the company enters an alliance (a joint-venture agreement, for example) with a second company in which two-way communication patterns are usual.

Thus the forces that compel the company to develop new products, adopt new technologies, and new structures, indirectly influence communication patterns.

The apparent advantages of two-way communication may not be immediately apparent within a large-power-distance culture which associates superior understanding and rights to control with superior members of the organization. Woodworth and Nelson (1980) explain why an attempt by United States consultants to introduce participative management styles to a Puerto Rican factory resulted in an exodus of hourly-paid workers:

> Queried by researchers as to their reasons for exiting, the employees said it was apparent that their supervisors did not know what they were doing anymore, for they kept enquiring what their employees thought. Therefore the obvious conclusion was that the company must be in trouble and would soon fold. (p. 63)

This communication process failed because the supervisors assumed, falsely, that workers shared with management the same management values; specifically, a belief in the advantages of employee participation.

7.4.2 Communication patterns and managerial roles

A move towards greater two-way communication, and greater participation by the employees in decision-making processes, affects not only the subordinate. For instance, assume a situation in which tasks are routine, simple, and close-ended; and a culture where

- needs to avoid uncertainty are large;
- power distances are large;
- conflict between ranks is feared, and avoided.

In this context, the manager performs such roles as:

- leading and acting as figurehead;
- providing information and opinions;
- initiating and directing operations;
- supervising operations;
- peace-keeping; developing group harmony.

However, assume that the situation changes. The company enters new markets, and tasks performed by the subordinate are increasingly non-routine, complex, and open-ended. The manager is increasingly pushed to become more participative, and hence to modify his/her traditional communicative style. This means adopting a communicative style appropriate to the new task as facilitator, to negotiate with and between a wide range of groups. In time and slowly, new patterns of communication within the workplace will feed back to wider society, and hence will modify norms within the national culture.

Mintzberg (1975) describes the ten essential roles performed by an American manager in a typical United States organization:

- *interpersonal roles*: the manager as figurehead, leader, liaison;
- *informational roles*: the manager as monitor, disseminator, spokesman;
- *decisional roles*: the manager as entrepreneur, disturbance handler, resource allocator, negotiator.

This model reflects an American manager's need to participate in a range of very different communicative situations within an organic structure, where two-way patterns are the norm. The manager needs the skill to recognize and adjust to continually shifting relationships within a relatively open organization, which is itself continually adjusting to new forces within the competitive environment.

7.4.3 Style of address

Where power distances are large and one-way communication more readily tolerated, relationships and hence styles of address are more easily predicted. The usual expectation of the Japanese is that everyone calls everyone else by last name plus "-san" (Mr, Mrs, Ms, etc.), or title (for instance, "-sensi," teacher; "- kacho," section chief). In South Korea, your rank at work has significance generally in society, and so the award of a new title that impresses your acquaintances may be highly motivating.

> A new title is another coveted reward. "In Korea," a business consultant noted, "You are manager Kim, director Kim, both on the job and off. Even your neighbors will call you manager Kim." In part, job titles are used in this way to simplify personal identification because the majority of the populace is named Lee, Kim, Park, or Choi. Titles are also a badge of status in a country more important than financial remuneration.[9]

The individual's title is known to a wide range of people in Laurent's cultures where "managers play an important role in society" and enjoy social status as a result of their professional activities (1983). France and Italy are examples.

In the United States, sub-cultural groups (and in particular recent immigrant groups) may try to maintain their traditional styles of address. In the mainstream culture, titles are ascribed less importance and even members of the same profession may be uncertain as to what title is appropriate. A newspaper story describes the Chief Justice's annoyance at being addressed as "Justice" or "Judge" rather than "Chief Justice."

Chief Justice Rehnquist may be particularly prickly on the subject, but he is not alone. The issue of how properly to address Justices, judges, former Justices, and former judges is much discussed, with majority and dissenting opinions alike.[10]

In a small power distance culture, the correct style of address is determined by a complex interrelationship of factors. It must express the correct degrees of formality/informality and personal distance/closeness, and how these should be appropriately expressed within the social and situational context of the communication.

In languages which offer a choice, relationships measured in terms of distance or closeness are also signaled by choice of pronoun. Whether you use singular or plural form to address an individual is determined by his/her sex, age, superiority/inferiority to yourself, and the closeness or distance of the relationship (Brown and Gilman, 1960). In French the singular form *tu* is intimate; when addressing even one other person with whom you are not on intimate terms, use the polite form, plural *vous*. Equivalents in Spanish are *usted* and *tu*, and in German *sie* and *du*. Many oriental languages have even more complex systems. Japanese has fourteen synonyms for "you," and the appropriate choice depends on the other person's sex, age, occupation, social and professional status.

7.4.4 Speech style

The greater the power distances and the greater the need for social distance and formality, the more appropriate is a formal communicative style. But where you wish to narrow the distance between you or to reflect small power distances, an informal style may be better (Drake and Moburg, 1986). Informal styles in English tend to be

- grammatically simple;
- abbreviated; for instance, "if anyone asks I'm in the lab" as against the full form and non-abbreviated "if anyone asks for me please tell them I will be in the laboratory";
- casual; features typifying a casual style and not appropriate to formal situations include:

  - slurring, running words together, lack of pausing;
  - overuse of intensifiers; "very," "basically," etc.;
  - empty modifiers; "kinda/kind of," "sorta/sort of," etc.;
  - empty adjectives; "cute," "super," "neat."

Using an informal style risks confusing a non-native speaker of the language who may understand imperfectly. Selection of both grammar and vocabulary must be geared towards the other person's competence. A word may have different connotations in different cultures. Anglo negotiators see no disgrace in actively searching for a "compromise" – which does not imply they they intend to "compromise" their values; but in Iranian terms, the concepts are less easily separated and a request for a "compromise" implies an invitation to sell-out basic principles.

Such differences occur even within one language. The Briton resolves to "table a motion" when he puts a motion before a meeting for discussion; the American interprets this to mean that the motion is delayed. By "I'm quite pleased that you've decided to join us," the American means that he is "very pleased;" but the Briton interpets this as only "fairly pleased."

7.4.5 Listening

Two-way spoken communication is made more efficient by careful listening to what the other person is saying. This is important when, for instance, you are the superior and the subordinate

- does not speak your language as a first language;
- is stressed by two-way communication with a superior.

If you interrupt and reply without thinking about what he/she has just said, your subordinate very quickly decides that giving feedback is more trouble than it is worth. So develop listening habits of:

- listening for the whole message;
- listening for what has *not* been said; what are the unspoken cultural priorities that underpin the message?
- asking questions to check your understanding; if necessary, paraphrase your understanding of his/her message;
- thinking before replying.

Particularly at the beginning of a relationship, when you are using your language and before you fully evaluate the other person's competence in using it, make it easier for him/her to communicate with you by your

- speaking slowly and carefully;
- avoiding unnecessary jargon, slang, and complex words;
- avoiding complex grammar;
- explaining difficult ideas more than once, and asking checking questions as you go along to make sure that you are being understood.

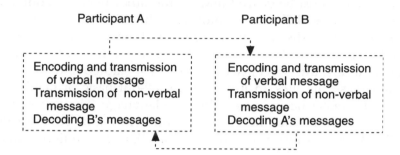

Figure 7.3 Transactional model.
(*Source*: adapted from Wenburg and Wilmot, 1973)

7.5   A transactional model

A transactional model emphasizes the importance of the personal relationship in verbal communication. Figure 7.3 adapts the model proposed by Wenburg and Wilmot (1973).

This model shows both participants involved in sending and receiving (encoding and decoding) messages at the same time. This differs significantly from the linear two-way interactional model described in section 7.4. It recognizes that we are often making decisions about sending a message and its content *during* the other participant's contribution, and not merely on its completion. And so planning your next contribution is influenced by what is he/she is communicating to you. That is, each person simultaneously creates and decodes communication cues; each influences and is influenced by the other (Wilmot, 1975).

7.5.1   Non-verbal signaling

The interactional model takes into account the importance of non-verbal messages. These messages are transmitted while the participant is both speaking and silent, and are continuous (see Hall, 1960). This is a non-linear process, which the two-way model discussed above cannot account for.

Many non-verbal signals have different meanings in different cultures, and culture groups interpret such signals differently. The following are discussed briefly;

- stance;
- gesture;
- eye movement;
- voice quality.

Stance How and where you position yourself in relation to the other person. Here is an example that shows how stance conveys messages, albeit involuntarily. An Englishman and an Egyptian met at a reception to discuss a proposed business deal. Each unconsciously adopted the posture which his culture associates with good manners. Egyptians value proximity and the opportunities to assess the other person's sincerity, and tend to stand face to face, at perhaps only 18 inches from each other. But when conversing with strangers, Anglos are used to standing at a distance of about four feet apart, often at right angles to each other. In this case, the Englishman responded to the Egyptian's proximity by moving away and to one side. The Egyptian reacted by moving closer in front of him. The Englishman moved again. This pattern continued throughout the evening.

The Egyptian came away from the receptian sensing that the Englishman was distant and untrustworthy, and the Englishman felt the Egyptian to be pushy. So each interpreted the other's stance negatively, but was probably not consciously able to rationalize his/her own sense of disquiet. The opportunities for doing business, that would have benefited both, were not pursued.

Gesture How you use your hands, head, shoulders, etc. to reflect and reinforce verbal messages, or to substitute for verbal messages.

In some cultures it is acceptable to make physical contact with another person, for instance in a greeting. Anglos typically shake hands, but should not assume that this habit is universally appreciated. For instance, in Malaysia,

> Prime Minister Mahathir Mohamad has ordered Malaysian women serving the government overseas to shake hands with foreigners at official functions after receiving reports that Muslims were not doing so. . . .
> "Some Muslim women both married and single feel it wrong to touch the bodies particularly of men who are not their relatives," a senior government official said, adding: "This is, however, the minority view."[11]

On the other hand, Anglo males usually resist embracing in public, which is normal in Latin cultures. In Latin America a kiss on both cheeks is accompanied by placing a hand on the other person's shoulder and is known as the *abrazzo*. In Asian cultures, almost any form of physical contact is avoided. In India and some South-east Asian cultures members greet each other by placing their hands together and making a slight bow (see chapter 2, section 2.4.1). The Japanese and Koreans bow in greeting, and the depth of the bow indicates the degree of respect shown.

Eye movement Length of gaze, maintaining eye contact, dilation, blinking. Some cultures ascribe great importance to feelings communicated by the eyes. The Egyptian prefers to stand close to the other person in conversation in order to "read" his/her eyes. In both Arab and Indian cultures a subordinate averts his/her gaze when communicating with a superior. The Anglo manager has been conditioned to expect some eye contact, and is likely to interpret this behavior as evasiveness. The traditional Indian woman avoids looking into the eyes of a man to whom she is not related.

Voice quality Different cultures associate different communicative meanings to such qualities of the human voice as:

- voice quality;
- tempo;
- pitch variation;
- volume.

Cultures respond differently to variations in voice quality. For instance, a wide pitch-range may be expected among males in some societies (in West Africa, for instance), but be considered effeminate elsewhere. And writing about a Japanese woman politician, a magazine commented:

> Miss Doi has a firm manner, more European in tone than Japanese. She speaks unhurriedly and fluently in a low-pitched voice. Most Japanese women consider it polite to pitch their voices high.[12]

An American manager commented that he never flew Japan Air Lines because the voices of female Japanese flight announcers made him too nervous.

> They sound too whispery and feminine. They don't sound serious enough. I can't believe they're in control. I know that they don't fly the planes but they ought to sound as though they could.

7.5.2 Non-verbal signaling and the cross-cultural manager

During all your transactions with a member of the other culture, you are making non-verbal signals that convey meaning in your own culture, but may convey no meaning in his/her culture, or a very different meaning. Many of these signals are involuntary.

This means

- being sensitive to the non-verbal signals, and recognizing that they are significant;
- recognizing that signals made in some other culture may have a significance different to what they would in your own culture;
- recognizing that your signals may be interpreted other than you intend or expect in some other culture.

In general, high-context cultures place greater importance on non-verbal signaling, and their members may depend very heavily upon such messages when communicating.

7.5.3 Non-verbal meaning and dress

Non-verbal meaning is also carried by dress. Your choice of dress has symbolic meaning, and indicates your perceptions of the occasion, the degree of formality, and your relationship with other people there. Dress codes are common in all societies, and these are sometimes endorsed by law. For instance, in India, a politician was banned entry to the prestigious Gymkhana Club on the grounds that he was "improperly dressed" when he was wearing the dhoti (a rectangle of white cloth draped into a loose pantaloon).

> The dhoti is the garment of choice among many male villagers. Politicians often wear it as a symbol of Indian nationalism and oneness with the people. . . . The Gymkhana Club dress code allows a wide latitude . . . but no dhotis.
> [And so the MP] raised the matter in parliament, which has no dress code. His party leader . . . said such rules were outdated. Another MP denounced them as a violation of human rights, and socialist firebrand George Fernandes called for a protest outside the club if the rules were not changed. . . . [P]rotestors gathered outside the club shouting slogans like "brown Englishmen, quit India."[13]

The implication for the cross-cultural manager is to check on what sort of dress is considered appropriate in the office, at a board meeting, at a range of more or less formal social functions.

7.6 Implications for the Manager

Communication norms within the organization are determined by

- cultural values;
- task variables;
- situational variables.

This section asks you to compare norms within a typical organization in *your own culture*, and a typical (and similar) organization in *the other culture*.

1. Practice using the system of situational categories (section 7.2.1) to plan appropriate messages in both organizations.

    - Assume messages designed to achieve the same purpose in both organizations. (For example, consider messages used to communicate good news, such as a promotion; a reprimand; a query for technical information; a directive; a policy change.) What differences occur in:

        (a) selection of appropriate addressor?
        (b) selection of appropriate addressee?
        (c) selection of appropriate content?
        (d) selection of appropriate medium/style?
        (e) selection of appropriate time?
        (f) selection of appropriate location?

    - What cultural and other factors explain these differences?

2. How typical are two-way communication patterns between superior and subordinate in the two organizations?

    - How far do these factors explain why two-way communication patterns *are/are not* selected?

        (a) task characteristics;
        (b) other situational characteristics.
        (c) culture.

3. When communicating functions of

    (a) giving instructions;
    (b) negotiating a deal;
    (c) evaluating performance;
    (d) motivating;
    (e) making a suggestion;

    - what vocabulary words and grammatical forms do you commonly use in *your own culture* that might be ambiguous to members of the *other culture*?
    - what words and forms do you commonly use that might be ambiguous?
    - what alternatives might you use that are less ambiguous and will not cause offence?

4. How far does Mintzberg's list of ten roles describe your activities in *your-own-culture* organization?

   (a) *interpersonal roles*: the manager as figurehead, leader, liaison;
   (b) *informational roles*: the manager as monitor, disseminator, spokesman;
   (c) *decisional roles*: the manager as entrepreneur, disturbance handler, resource allocator, negotiator.

   - How far does this list describe the activities of an equivalent manager in *the-other-culture* organization?
   - How far can differences be explained by

     (a) cultural factors?
     (b) organizational factors?
     (c) other situational factors?

5. What differences between the two organizations do you observe in levels of formality/informality, and emotional distance/closeness between superior and subordinate? Between peers?

   - How do differences reflect

     (c) cultural differences?
     (d) organizational factors?
     (e) other situational factors?

6. Identify non-verbal signals used in *the-other-culture* organization that strike you as unlikely to be used in *your-own-culture* organization. Find examples of signals conveyed by:

   (a) stance;
   (b) gesture;
   (c) eye movement;
   (d) voice quality;

   - identify their meanings.

7.7 Summary

This chapter has briefly reviewed those aspects of management communication that most concern the cross-cultural manager. Section 7.2 dealt with the notion of *communicative appropriacy* in different *cultural* contexts. A set of situational categories was discussed and illustrated; addressor, addressee, content, medium, time, location. Because the selected expression made of any one category influences the appropriacy of other selections, the set is formally systematic.

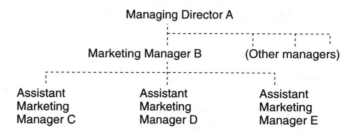

Figure 7.4   Acme organizational chart.

The next three sections focused on three communication models, all of which have something of value to contribute. Section 7.3 showed how communication can be modeled as a one-way process. Where *one-way communication* patterns are typical, they reflect the participants' perceptions of task, relationship, and culture. Section 7.4 saw how *two-way communication* involves the addressee in making substantive contributions to the interaction. This pattern reflects a different relationship between participants, and leads to a wider discussion of managerial roles and style.

The one- and two-way models are both linear; this mode of representation offers descriptive strengths, and also weaknesses. The non-linear *transactional model*, examined in section 7.5, can account for influences on planning a spoken message simultaneous with some other message being transmitted. Particular emphasis was given to non-verbal signaling.

7.8   Exercise

This exercise examines how the cultural context influences

* *what information is communicated;*
* *the choice of person to whom it is communicated;*
* *how it is communicated.*

You work for a small engineering company, Acme. The organizational chart includes the details shown in figure 7.4.

You are Assistant Marketing Manager C. You have been with Acme for six months. Your relations with D and E are neutral, neither particularly good nor bad. B is also a newcomer, appointed to this position nine months ago.

1. *Situation*

   In your own time, you recently attended a trade exhibition at which Acme was not represented. (Acme publicizes its product range by other means.) You were very interested by the display made by a competitor, and believe that it offered lessons which Acme could usefully apply. This would not involve any serious modifications to your current marketing strategy.

   Acme is in a culture where:

   i.   power distances are large;
   ii. relationships are collectivist;
   iii. needs to avoid uncertainty are large.

   Question A

   To *whom* should you communicate your ideas?

   i.   No one. Only express your opinions if these are requested.
   ii.   Inform B of your experience, but make no proposals unless these are requested.
   iii. Inform A of your experience, but make no proposals unless these are requested.
   iv.   Inform B, making proposals.
   v.   Inform A, making proposals.
   vi.   Discuss your experiences with D and E; then all three of you inform B, making proposals.
   vii. Discuss your experiences with D and E; then all three of you inform A, making proposals.
   viii. Any other alternative.

   Question B

   And depending on your choice of i–viii, how should you communicate?

   (a) by memo;
   (b) in a full written report;
   (c) in a casual conversation, face-to-face;
   (d) in a casual conversation, by telephone;
   (e) in a formal meeting;
   (f) any other alternative.

2. *Situation*

   As for 1, *except* that Acme is in a culture where

   i.   power distances are small;
   ii. relationships are individualist;
   iii. needs to avoid uncertainty are small.

Question A
To whom should you communicate your ideas?
As for 1, i–viii.

Question B
And depending on your choice of i–viii, how should you communicate?
As for 1(a)–(f).

3. *Situation*
    It is apparent to you, as a recent recruit, that the workload in the marketing department is ridiculously heavy. Too much time is being spent on unnecessary paper work and the opportunities for creative marketing are seriously restricted. All staff at your level and at subordinate levels are demoralized.
    Acme is in a culture where:

    i.   power distances are large;
    ii. relationships are collectivist;
    iii. needs to avoid uncertainty are large.

    Question A
    To whom should you communicate your ideas?

    As for 1, i–viii.

    Question B
    And depending on your choice of i-viii, how should you communicate?
    As for 1(a)–(f).

4. *Situation*
    As for 3, except that Acme is in a culture where:

    i.   power distances are small;
    ii. relationships are individualist;
    iii. needs to avoid uncertainty are small.

    Question A
    To whom should you communicate your ideas?
    As for 1, i–viii.

    Question B
    And depending on your choice of i–viii, how should you communicate?
    As for 1(a)–(f).

Notes

1. E. S. Browning, "Unhappy returns," *Wall Street Journal*, May 6, 1986.
2. Reuter, "British stealing show from US counterparts at war briefings," *Bangkok Post*, February 11, 1991.
3. Brian Timms (Reuter), "'G'day mate' not working in Asia," *The Nation* (Bangkok), January 5, 1989.
4. Clyde Haberman, "Some Japanese (one) urge plain speaking," *The New York Times*, March 27, 1988.
5. "Lucky but useless" (survey: Japanese finance), The Economist, December 8, 1990.
6. Matt Moffett, "Culture shock: moving to Mexico," *Asian Wall Street Journal*, September 24, 1992.
7. J. Robbins, "America's Red Army," *The New York Times Magazine*, April 17, 1988.
8. In communications theory, the term "feedback" is applied variously. Discourse analysts may use it in a precise technical sense to refer to an element of discourse structure; see, for instance, Coulthard (1977, 1991). Feedback can also refer to the manager's practice of collecting data and reporting; see London, Wohlers, and Gallagher (1990).
9. Robert P. Kearney, "A unique management style," in "South Korea: a country report," *World Executive's Digest*, July 1992.
10. David Margolick, "Here comes the Chief Justice (please don't call him Judge)," *The New York Times*, April 26, 1991.
11. AFP, "KL order to women" *The Nation* (Bangkok), August 14, 1992.
12. "All aboard the Doi express," *The Economist*, July 22, 1989.
13. Hamish McDonald, "Empire rules," *Far Eastern Economic Review*, October 10, 1991.

8

Motivating across Cultures

8.1 Introduction

The Malaysian branch of an international non-government organization (NGO) rewarded the most productive members of its local staff by sending them abroad for further training and then promoting them on return. But after they were promoted, they never quite fulfilled their earlier promise. Top management wondered why not.

Research showed that local staff valued their cohesion as a group and distrusted those who raised themselves to higher management levels, composed mostly of Western expatriates. They were content with their expatriate superiors, but did not like taking directions from compatriates who had raised themselves to superior status and were perceived to be disloyal to their group. Local staff who accepted promotions found themselves estranged from their old colleagues and unable or unwilling to communicate as equals with their new expatriate colleagues.

The rewards of further training abroad were valued as opportunities for personal gratification (travel, shopping), as indicators of merit and for the symbolic status they conferred, but not as steps towards promotion. Hence those trainees who were sent abroad tended to under-achieve in their training. This under-achievement insulated them against unwelcomed promotion; but the organization's staff development budget allocation was largely wasted.

In sum then this case illustrates:

- the importance of finding motivators that reflect values held within the culture;
- the danger of assuming that a motivator in one culture will have the same effect in some other culture.

This chapter deals with the problems of motivating members of another culture, and thus changing their work attitudes and behavior. It has the following sections:

8.2   Identifying Needs

Your design of motivators is most likely to succeed when it

- reflects real needs;
- takes account of environmental practicalities – for instance, your capacity to deliver.

This section focuses on problems of reflecting real needs.

Identifying real needs is not an automatic process. In practice, many motivational programs fail because their designers think that they can depend upon intuitions rather than bother with informed analysis.

Almost all the research suggests that people need more from their work than their pay packets, and value interesting work. Work is central in most people's lives, and this seems to be true across cultures. A study by the MOW International Research Team (1986) showed that between 65 percent and 95 percent of employees in Belgium, Britain, Israel, the Netherlands, Japan, Germany, and the United States stated that they would continue working even if they had enough money to live comfortably for the rest of their lives.

Similarly, Nicholson and West's (1988) survey of 2,300 members of the British Institute of Management shows that although managers aged 25 to 40 are switching jobs on average every 3 years, money and high position are not their prime motives for making the change. These factors are well down a list of 17, below a quest for challenge, recognition, learning opportunities, and creativity.

And research conducted in the United States in 1946, 1981, and 1986 by Kovach (1987) showed similar results among industrial employees – ranging from unskilled blue-collar workers to skilled white-collar workers.

Table 8.1 Ten "job reward" factors, 1986

1.	Interesting work	(6)
2.	Full appreciation of work done	(1)
3.	Feeling of being in on things	(2)
4.	Job security	(4)
5.	Good wages	(5)
6.	Promotion and growth in organization	(7)
7.	Good working conditions	(9)
8.	Personal loyalty to employees	(8)
9.	Tactful discipline	(10)
10.	Sympathetic help with personal problems	(3)

Source: Kovach (1987)

In 1986, ten "job reward" factors were ranked as ahown in table 8.1. 1946 rankings are given in parenthesis – and at most points, priorities had not changed significantly.

Why should interesting work rather than wages be accounted most important? Kovach's figures show that among the lowest paid employees (under $12,000 in 1986), good wages are indeed ranked as most important. But good wages is ranked at increasingly less important among better paid groups, and among the best paid (earning over $25,000) good wages has slipped to tenth, and interesting work is ranked first.

Can we infer

- first, that employees value most such rewards as they require to fulfil their basic requirements?
- second, that employees value least such rewards as they have already obtained?

Kovach's figures present some evidence for both these statements. The lowest paid would appear to have most need for good wages, and therefore to value them most; this supposition is supported by data that shows good wages also valued most by the youngest group of employees surveyed.

> The under 30 group chose good wages, job security, and promotion and growth as their first three choices. This could indicate that these new workers have not yet fulfilled their basic needs according to Maslow. When the under 30 group is compared with other groups, it is interesting to note that the 31–40 group still place job security high on their hierarchy of values but that this basic need becomes less important as one moves up through the age groups. (Kovach, 1987, p. 62)

But if this logic is carried through, we are forced to suppose that the best paid value interest in their work above all other factors because

Table 8.2 Supervisors' rankings of job rewards

1. Good wages
2. Job security
3. Promotion and growth in organization
4. Good working conditions
5. Interesting work
6. Personal loyalty to employers
7. Tactful discipline
8. Full appreciation of work down
9. Sympathetic help with personal problems
10. Feeling of being in on things

Source: Kovach (1987)

their work currently provides very little interest, and less than does the work of the poorer paid; and this is questionable. In practice, white-collar work is least defined and self-contained, and offers the most alternatives for self-expression.

8.2.1 Supervisors' assessments of employee needs

Kovach (1987) also reported on rankings made by these employees' direct supervisors (see table 8.2). The supervisors were asked to order job rewards as they believed that their employees would rank them. Supervisors' assumptions about employees' values changed very little over the years.

A comparison between this ranking and employees' rankings for themselves demonstrates that supervisors often have inaccurate perceptions of what motivated their subordinates. (Similar discrepancies between management perceptions and self-reported needs are found by Gluskinos, 1970.)

The first issue that arises is that the United States manager appears to have only mixed optimistic and pessimistic views about human nature, and has no great hopes that his/her subordinates will be primarily motivated by their work. This pessimism is reflected in England's (1986) study showing that on a four-point scale, United States managers scored only 2.9 in response to the proposition "Every person in society should be entitled to interesting and meaningful work." In contrast, Japanese managers scored 3.1 and Germans 3.5.

Deciding what goes into the pay packet is the responsibility of top management, not line supervisors. And so it seems that supervisors nominate as most significant those motivators (good wages and job security) for which they have least responsibility for providing, and the absence of which reflects least on their own performances. The rewards listed as most valued by the employees (interesting work; full appreciation of work done; feeling of being in on things) require management skills in planning jobs and human-relations skills in giving feedback to performance. These skills in job planning and giving feedback are difficult to teach and those who have them may be only poorly rewarded.

Finally, the failure to correctly assess subordinate needs has implications in situations where individuals have different experiences, including cultural experiences. The data show that management can easily make mistakes in identifying the needs of their own workforce, within their own culture and with similar values. Hence we should expect even greater errors to occur when management has to analyse the needs of employees with different values and expectations.

8.3   Identifying Needs in Another Culture

Table 8.3 provides evidence for the claim that employees in different cultures have different needs from their work. In response to England's (1986) questions, "What about the nature of your working life? How important to you is it that your work life contains the following?" respondents in Germany, Japan, and the United States ranked these 11 work goals as follows:

Table 8.3   Work goals: German, Japanese, and US respondents' rankings

Work goals	Germany	Japan	USA
Interesting work	3	2	1
Good pay	1	5	2
Good interpersonal relations	4	6	7
Good job security	2	4	3
A good match between you and your job	5	1	4
A lot of autonomy	8	3	8
Opportunity to learn	9	7	5
A lot of variety	6	9	6
Convenient work hours	6	8	9
Good physical working conditions	11	10	11
Good opportunity for upgrading or promotion	10	11	10

Source: England (1986), p. 181.

However, these figures do not explain *why* employees in these different countries rank these goals differently. This question is discussed here.

8.3.1 What factors influence needs?

The individual's needs are determined by such factors as:

- heredity and early environmental factors;
- sex;
- age;
- education, and levels achieved;
- economic status;
- experience, including work experience;
- organizational culture;
- industry and sectoral factors;
- national culture.

National culture, then, is only one of several influences, and the manager needs to take the total mix into account when analysing needs and designing motivators.

In general, the greater the level of poverty, the greater the importance attached to the resources needed to sustain life. Singh and Wherry (1963) showed that in Indian companies the lower the worker's rank and income level the more importance was given to satisfying basic physiological needs. But at a later date, Jaggi's (1979) study of Indian managers discovered that experience was a significant factor. Younger managers below the age of 35 who had been brought up since Independence (1947) showed much greater needs for esteem and autonomy in their work than did their less dynamic elders, who attached greater importance to job security.

Sectorial factors are reported by Chow (1988), who distinguishes public-sector managers in Hong Kong, who most valued advancement opportunities and security for employment, and private-sector managers, who most favored advancement opportunities and opportunities for high earnings. The implication is that a motivator that works well within one sector, or one organization, may be ineffective within some other – even within the same country.

The manager has to decide which factors are significant in any one situation. For instance, Kovach's (1987) study showed that older employees over age 50 placed their priority on interesting work, while younger employees below age 30 were most concerned with good wages, and then with job security. Because such employees are also likely to be among the least well paid, economic status and experience would appear to be key. But it can also be argued that the culture has changed significantly during the lifetimes of this age group, and that this is the true explanatory variable.

Similarly, Gan (1988) discovered from analysis of Singaporean branches of banks headquartered in the Asian Pacific region (Singapore, Japan, India, and the United States) that employees of the Japanese banks expressed most dissatisfaction on all five dimensions investigated, including pay. But in practice, most Singaporean bank branches offer competitive salaries as they compete in a tight labor market. The low levels of satisfaction recorded on all dimensions in the Japanese banks seemed to reflect dissatisfaction with

> promotion on the basis of seniority – a practice widely accepted in their country of origin. However, this particular practice appears to be unacceptable to young Singaporean bank officers. . . . (p. A96)

That is, perceptions of needing more money in fact reflected dissatisfaction with the structural components to the job.

8.3.2 Applying Anglo theories

A description of values in Culture A may be quite irrelevant to Culture B. Hofstede (1980b) suggests that Sigmund Freud's psychological model accurately reflects such features of Austrian culture as high needs to avoid uncertainty and low individualism, and notes that Freudian thinking has never been successful in the United States – which differs significantly on these two dimensions. Hence, a motivational system based on values in Culture A may be ineffective in Culture B – and possibly demotivating.

Freud has had negligible influence on theories of motivation in the workplace. Almost all models have been formulated in Anglo countries, and in particular in the United States. Thus they are characterized by certain presuppositions; relatively high masculinity and a Protestant work ethic, high individualism, narrow power distances, low needs to avoid uncertainty, and high needs for continual streams of explicit information to be communicated from the context.

The cross-cultural manager has the task of discovering how far a given model can be applied outside the cultural context within which it was designed.

8.3.3 Needs in a context of cultural dislocation

Abudu (1986) sums up the problem in an analysis of work attitudes in Nigeria. Traditional culture certainly valued hard work, but the values of a craft culture do not necessarily translate into an industrial culture when new relationships between the worker and the means of production, and the employer and employee, are introduced.

> Cultural expectations relative to work in traditional Africa did not emphasize commitment, diligence and proper attitudes towards work. Consequently, the African became stereotyped as lazy, of low productivity, and unwilling to respond to economic incentives. These notions stemmed from improper appreciation of the sociocultural milieu of early African employees. The African's reluctance to accept wage employment arose from his cherished independence in agriculture, his unwillingness to sever family ties because of the security they offered, and a fear of illness and death in urban areas. (p. 34)

The practical problem boils down to discovering what work values do apply, and designing new motivators that elicit the appropriate behavior. Abudu shows that in Nigeria this presents particular difficulties. Colonial rule followed by ill-considered industrialization has created a cultural milieu that is neither entirely local nor foreign, but a "hybrid monstrosity of cultures." But the clock cannot be set back. And any attempt to apply traditional values (for instance, by focusing on small-scale rural and family-based developments) is not likely to be any more productive than treating Nigerian enterprises as though they belonged – or ought to belong – to a traditional Western economy.

Abudu poses the problem in terms of the prevailing situation. He attributes unsatisfactory attitudes towards work in contemporary Nigeria to a range of factors which include

- inequities in the reward system;
- application of criteria other than merit in determining recruitment, placement and training;
- the effects of corruption.

These factors may also be significant in other cultures and subcultures. Before the lessons can be applied in Nigeria – or elsewhere – further questions have to be answered:

- Why is the reward system perceived as inequitable, and what reward system would be regarded as equitable within this context?
- How can merit be assessed in this context?
- What behavior should be considered corrupt and discouraged in this context? How can it be discouraged? What ethical guidelines should and can be enforced?

That is, the analysis of motivational problems and proposals for solutions is bound to be culture specific and in the final resort, organization specific.

8.3.4 Designing motivators for another culture

Hofstede's (1984a) model provides a basic tool for predicting motivations in different cultural contexts. For instance, we would expect

- opportunities for individual promotion and growth to be valued more highly where the culture is individualist;
- autonomy to be valued more highly where the culture is individualist;
- opportunities to belong to a supportive group to be valued more highly where the culture is collectivist;
- job security to be valued more highly where needs to avoid uncertainty are greater;
- variety to be valued more highly where needs to avoid uncertainty are lesser;
- opportunities to cooperate with peers to be valued more highly where power distances are lesser;
- personal loyalty shown by superiors to subordinates to be valued more highly where power distances are greater;
- a service ideal to be valued more highly where the culture is feminine;
- shorter and convenient working hours to be valued more highly where the culture is feminine.

In a strongly collectivist culture, the individual who advances his/her personal interests may threaten the cohesion and shared interests of the group as a whole. Mutiso (1974) shows that in East Africa the community dominates almost all aspects of thought; hence social needs are paramount, and needs for individual achievement are deviant.[1]

That is, when individualism is sanctioned, members are not attracted by individual recognition and the opportunity to shine above others. Mann (1989) tells a story of Beijing Jeep, a joint venture between AMC and Beijing Automative Works, in which some workers willingly gave up their pay rises in order to appease the resentment of their less productive colleagues.

Rieger and Wong-Rieger (1990) suggest that

> in Thailand, the introduction of an individual merit bonus plan, which runs counter to the societal norm of group cooperation, may result in a decline rather than an increase in productivity from employees who refuse to openly compete with each other. Such a scheme might be compatible with existing cultural behaviors (as in the case of Singapore where the Chinese value individual achievement) or the organization is able to modify certain of its members' values, norms, and beliefs which come from the surrounding culture. (pp. 1–2)

Similarly, a manager from a feminine culture which places a premium on concern for others may feel impelled to award a promotion to a female employee who displays these qualities to a greater degree than her male colleague. In a highly masculine culture which values assertiveness, this affronts male dignity. Male employees are demoralized by being forced into this (to them) irregular competition for promotion and obliged to take direction from a person they perceive to be unqualified.

Where the need to avoid uncertainty is also high, females are unlikely to wish for promotion in circumstances which place them in antagonistic relationships with male colleagues and hence are demotivated from making the effort to win promotion. The cross-cultural manager who needs both to maintain the morale of his/her workforce and motivate female employees is therefore obliged to redefine their needs in terms other than promotion where this seems likely to engender conflict and insecurity.

In a full bureaucracy where needs to avoid uncertainty are high, employees might be attracted by the opportunity to earn extended job security and pension rights. But in an entrepreneurial market bureaucracy, such an opportunity might be little valued, and a job that offers chances for individual achievement working in conditions of relative autonomy might enjoy far greater success.

8.4 Maslow's Hierarchy of Needs

Although subsequent research has cast substantial doubt on Maslow's (1943) model, it continues to have a profound effect on the theory of motivation. The mechanics of the model may be debatable, but the questions it raises about application, and the function of monetary rewards, are essential.

Needs are organized on five hierarchical levels.

Level 5 and highest – self-actualization and achievement needs
Level 4 esteem needs – both self-esteem and the esteem of others
Level 3 belonging and social needs
Level 2 safety and security needs
Level 1 physiological (existence) needs

Needs at Levels 1–3 may be considered basic or "deficit" needs, to be satisfied by extrinsic outcomes that are external to the individual, such as food, money, praise from other people. Only when these basic needs are satisfied will the individual strive to satisfy the ego and self-actualizations needs at Levels 4–5. These are satisfied by intrinsic outcomes that are internal to the individual; for instance, a sense of achievement and competence springs from your own feelings of worth and cannot be donated to you by someone else.

Maslow argues that when you have satisfied needs at one level you try to satisfy your needs at the next level up. Thus a satisfied need is no longer motivating, and you satisfy needs progressively, and only satisfy a higher level need when you have satisfied those lower.

These needs are motivating when the individual engages in an activity with the expectation that by succeeding in it (achieving a successful outcome) he/she will satisfy his need. That is: assume that a man needs money in order to buy a house. He knows that if he completes his job satisfactorily he will be rewarded with that money, and hence he works to complete the job. When the effects of behavior are valued, the individual continues to repeat that behavior; and so he continues the work until his needs for money are satisfied.

This model helps explain why Kovach's (1987) better paid employees, who have satisfied their "deficit" needs on Levels 1 and 2, should place a premium on work that is interesting (section 8.3.1); and why the younger and most poorly paid, who are not yet secure in satisfying their physiological and safety needs, should most value good wages. But the fact that can be applied to one situation in the United States does not guarantee its general efficacy there, and even less so in other cultural contexts.

8.4.1 Differences across cultures

In different countries, needs are likely to vary in intensity, for a range of reasons. Huo and Steers (1993) argue that the following factors affect degrees of motivation:

- culture;
- historical events; for instance, in Japan, the end of isolation and the arrival of Commander Perry in 1853;
- economic and political structures; the role of the Communist Party in the People's Republic of China;
- geographic location; in isolated countries such as Nepal, Tibet and Afghanistan, social relations are valued more highly than in centrally located countries;
- language.

It also seems likely that across cultures, each need may be associated with different values. For instance, in a collectivist culture members derive self-actualization from contributing to the success of the in-group. But in an individualist culture this sense is derived from individual achievement; work on behalf of the group might satisfy your needs for esteem or (at a lower level again) belonging. Maslow's model does not tell us how to identify higher order needs in different cultures.

Environmental factors influence how much is needed to provide satisfaction at any one level. Buera and Glueck's (1979) study of Libyan managers discovered that their social needs were more satisfied than their (lower level) security levels. This met the authors' expectations that

> the People's Revolution would cause the security need to be paramount. Executives were being fired every day. (p. 115)

Their security needs were far higher than were those of Non-Libyan Arabs, Europeans, and Americans working in Libya, who were presumably at less risk. Similarly, Sirota and Greenwood (1971) showed that the security needs of foreign employees in the United States were higher than their social needs.

These examples suggest that particular circumstances significantly influence how the model should be applied. Nevis (1983) proposes a variation on Maslow which describes needs in the People's Republic of China. Level 4 shows how the concept of an intrinsic outcome entirely internal to the individual has been transformed:

Level 4   and highest – needs for self-actualization in the service of society
Level 3   safety and security needs
Level 2   physiological needs
Level 1   belonging (social) needs (p. 21)

Superficially, the model reflects an extraordinarily high degree of collectivism – to the point that physiological needs are subordinated to belonging needs. But we should take into account the date when this research was conducted; in 1981 the country was reeling from the effects of Maoist totalitarianism and the Cultural Revolution, and post-Maoist free-market reforms were scarcely underway.

Tung (1991) argues that Chinese industrial enterprises continue to motivate their employees by a system of rule enforcement, external rewards, and internalized motivation. But over time the emphasis has shifted between these elements, depending on the political and economic situation.

> In periods of greater political oppenness, external rewards were paramount. During times of political retrenchment, ideology and internalized motivation have assumed a greater role. (p. 342)

Nevis's (1983) model reflects a time of retrenchment, but by the end of the decade it was acceptable to preach "To be rich is glorious!" In 1993, *Time* quoted a middle-aged Beijing entrepreneur: "The only thing we believe in today is making money."[2]

Nevertheless, Nevis's variation serves two useful purposes. First, it illustrates the point that a model appropriate to one context may be inappropriate elsewhere. Second, it shows that an incentive system must be adjusted to account for changes in needs prompted by shifts in the environment.

Onedo (1991) suggests that all less developed countries share some priorities in need importance and satisfaction, and this may be a function of their stage of economic growth. His samples of Australian and Papua New Guinea managers both regard self-actualization as their most important need. But unlike the Australians, the Papua New Guineans expressed most dissatisfaction with their levels of security, and placed security needs higher than autonomy needs – which parallels results found by other studies of managers in Argentina, Chile, India, Malawi, and Kenya.

Kanungo and Wright (1983) discuss cross-cultural studies which

> have suggested that the orientations and values which managers hold with respect to job outcomes are, to a large extent, culturally determined, particularly with respect to the relative importance of intrinsic and extrinsic job outcomes. (p. 117)

Hofstede (1984b) similarly relates the issue of motivational differences to cultural differences. He argues that Maslow's "self-actualization as a presumed need is a product of an individualist society" – and that this American value cannot be held up as a model for the rest of the world.

8.5 Monetary Incentives and the Alternatives

All the evidence shows that a pay rise is not the only possible motivator of effective behavior, and often not the most valued motivator. Why, then, is so much emphasis placed upon pay rises and other financial incentives, by both employers and employees?

The simple answer must be that monetary incentives are the easiest to specify and quantify, and the easiest to negotiate. No management or workforce would find it easy to agree on a reward system posed in terms of "good interpersonal relations," "full appreciation of work done," "a feeling of being in on things," etc.

Maslow's model does not mention "money," and a superficial reading would suggest that this denies the potency of financial need as a motivator. But in practice, money can enter the equation at every level of the model. Maslow's model helps us distinguish monetary rewards as a means to an end rather than an end in itself.

Money enables you to purchase the necessities to support physiological existence, thus satisfy your needs at Level 1. And when you have consumed sufficient food, water, etc., and still have money, you can purchase secure accommodation, thus meeting your safety and security requirements at Level 2. The purchase of an expensive car and clothes to impress people, and restaurant reservations to entertain your friends, will help you satisfy your social needs at Level 3.

At Levels 4 and 5, where needs are satisfied by intrinsic outcomes, the size of your pay packet has symbolic values. It justifies your sense of self-esteem and reflects your achievement. It serves as a means of keeping score with other people (are you more or less successful?) and with yourself (have you achieved more this year than last?) In McClelland's (1965) words, the person with a high need for achievement

> works hard anyway, provided there is an opportunity of achieving something. He is interested in money rewards or profits primarily because of the feedback they give him as to how well he is doing. Money is not the incentive to effort but rather the measure of its success to the entrepreneur. (p. 65)

In 1991 the CEOs of 282 large to medium-sized industrials polled by *Fortune* magazine in the United States were paid an average of $1,700,000 per year – including base salary, long-term awards, annual incentives, benefits and perks.[3] (This compares to $725,000 in 1985.) These persons did not need so much money in order to cover their existence needs; yet perhaps any one of them would have felt seriously insulted if it were suggested that his/her salary should be reduced by, say, a million dollars. The deprivation would not be physical but psychological; his/her achievements would appear belittled.

The more materialistic the culture, the more likely the assumption that the promise of monetary rewards can motivate at all levels. Highly materialistic cultures may be defined as those in which financial wealth is valued because it enables you to consume more material goods, and the more you consume the higher your status. The less materialistic the culture, the more likely are its members to value wealth by the benefits it confers upon society (Kitch, 1967).[4]

8.5.1   Needs within collectivist cultures

Hofstede's analysis argues that the more collectivist the culture, the greater the degree to which the individual is motivated by group membership and group decisions.

For instance, in Japan the quality circle consists typically of a small group of volunteers from the same work area who meet on a regular basis in order to identify, analyse, and resolve production problems. By one calculation, nearly one-fourth of all hourly paid Japanese employees belong to quality circles (Yeager, 1980). Many of these groups meet in the members' own time, and even suggestions taken up by the company receive little financial compensation, if any (Munchus, 1983). However, Japanese successes in using quality circles to motivate employee participation does not mean that the practice will enjoy equal success wherever the culture is collectivist – or even in Japan, when the practice becomes thoroughly institutionalized.

Collectivism is also expressed by the values ascribed to financial rewards, and a motivator may be most effective when it promises obvious benefits to the group with which the manager most closely identifies. In Chinese cultures, he/she identifies not with the work group but with the family. Yau (1988) argues that when making decisions the individual Chinese takes immediate account of family interests:

> He/she is more motivated towards achieving the goal of the (extended) family or the group that he/she is affiliated with than with individualized self-fulfilment. (p. 52)

Similarly, qualitative research conducted in Saudi Arabia among male medical students showed that they expected to be paid less in their chosen profession than as business men but still preferred a medical career because it gave them the opportunity to obtain professional status and to distinguish themselves from their fathers – who were almost all in commerce (Mead, 1980). The Saudi medical student was motivated by felt needs to

- secure a sense of identity;
- enhance his reputation within the family and social circle;
- enhance his family's reputation.

8.5.2   The alternatives to a pay rise

The evidence suggests that:

- a promise of a pay rise may not be the most effective motivator;
- the alternatives to a pay rise may be at least as effective;

- within the culture, there may always be more than one motivator capable of producing the desired effect.[5]

The manager who hopes to complement monetary rewards as a means of encouraging good performance may find an effective motivator among the following:

- encouraging promotion and growth in the organization – for instance, by giving titles and responsibilities that are non-trivial; encouraging and rewarding training; encouraging and rewarding incentives;
- showing appreciation of work done – for instance, by recognition within the company, giving praise and positive feedback, and positive work appraisal;
- giving the employee a feeling of being in on things – for instance, by communicating management strategy within the organization, and inviting contributions;
- improving working conditions;
- showing personal loyalty to employees;
- using tact when disciplining; improving interpersonal relations;
- improving job security;
- giving sympathetic help with personal problems;
- improving the quality of work; making the work more interesting;
- giving variety in work – where this is desired;
- giving autonomy in work – where this is desired.

Your selection of motivator for a particular work group will be influenced by the factors listed at the head of section 8.3.1. In addition, take into account the following.

- *Consistency* Motivators and rewards must be perceived as consistent, both over time and when applied to different individuals and groups. For instance, promising to send the entire group to Paris for a vacation may be highly motivating, but will that set up expectations of a visit every year? Your failure to measure up to these expectations may be highly demotivating.
- *Cost* How will the profits resulting from successful motivation measure against the costs of putting the motivator in place? Communicating praise is often the cheapest of all options. Insincere or misplaced praise may be perceived as threatening, and an honest and empathic response may be preferred (Farson, 1963).

The organization influences the behavior of its employees by its choice and management of motivators. And in turn, the employees ought to be able to influence organizational values by responding positively to one set of motivators rather than another. In order for this selective and positive reinforcement to occur, the employees must be presented with a range of motivators, and the organization must have systems in place for monitoring the effects of using various motivators.

We now turn to research that examines the conditions under which efforts to make the work intrinsically more interesting and rewarding pay greater dividends than investing in pay rises.

8.6 Satisfaction and Motivation

This section deals with the Herzberg's two-factor theory. Herzberg (1959) developed his two-factor theory in response to evidence showing that job-satisfaction and job-dissatisfaction result from different causes (see also Herzberg, 1968). He argued that there are two types of motivational factors, "hygiene" factors and motivators. If the hygiene factors are absent, the employee will be dissatisfied; but their presence does not guarantee satisfaction.

The hygiene factors include:

- wages;
- security;
- working conditions;
- company policy and administration;
- relationships with supervisors and peers.

And the motivators include:

- intrinsic value of the work;
- achievement;
- responsibility;
- recognition.

Increasing the level of hygiene by paying better wages, improving working conditions, etc., contains levels of dissatisfaction, but they do not stimulate the will to work. A satisfied worker is not necessarily more productive, or more motivated to work harder – but satisfaction appears to correlate positively with mental health, and a more satisfied worker is less likely to quit the job.

In order to motivate positive habits and to increase production, management must provide factors that increase the intrinsic value of the work, and give the employee a sense of achievement, responsibility, and recognition. Herzberg's motivators approximate to Levels 1 and 2, self-actualization and self-esteem, on Maslow's hierarchy.

His conclusion that workers were motivated by challenge and

achievement led Herzberg to develop strategies for "enriching" job specifications, so that they offered more opportunities for challenge and achievement.

8.6.1 The job enrichment movement

The various techniques proposed by the job enrichment movement are designed to modify the employee's responsibilities in ways that increase his/her sense of worth and motivation (see Paul et al., 1969; Yorks, 1976). We deal here and in section 8.6.2 with the practical and cultural implications of

- job rotation;
- job enlargement;
- job enrichment.

Job rotation Involves planning the employee's time so that he/she performs a variety of tasks. For instance, he/she spends, say, a week working in Process A, then moves to Process B, then moves to Process C. Job rotation introduces variety to the employee's routine, and helps develop a multi-skilled workforce.

Job rotation has proved successful in a range of contexts. However, it presents a number of practical problems. First, not all jobs can be easily exchanged; a high-status specialist is unlikely to accept even a temporary move to a job perceived appropriate for someone of lower status.

Second, rotation can be expensive. An assistant marketing manager may be transferable to the accounts department only after considerable costly training. Employees are bound to make early mistakes when rotated to new tasks, and to take time in perfecting their new skills. The more (related) skills the workforce master, the greater their value in the labor market; and hence, the more the employer has to pay in order to keep their services.

Culture is also significant. Job rotation is unlikely to succeed where needs to avoid uncertainty are high, and so where resistance to change is greater and employees prefer specialist to general careers. In high-power distance cultures where status differentials between roles are significant, problems arise in identifying jobs of equivalent status between which employees may be rotated. In collectivist cultures where group membership is significant, members of Workgroup A are unlikely to welcome the temporary membership of an employee rotated from his/her normal assignments in Workgroup B. And the employee in question may perceive this "banishment" from his/her regular group to be a form of punishment.

Job enlargement   Involves reorganizing the job specification so that all the tasks required to produce one unit of work are performed by the individual. Rather than have Tasks C, D, E performed by employees P, Q, R respectively, all three tasks are made the responsibility for each of P, Q, R. In theory, the individual derives greater satisfaction from completing all tasks needed in the production process and seeing the completed unit, than from specializing in a single task.

Job enlargement is unlikely to motivate employees in a cultural context that values specialization. In a highly collectivist context where tasks have previously been associated with work groups, the cross-cultural manager can expect resistance to attempts to amalgamate groups so that all members of all groups perform all tasks.

8.6.2   Job enrichment

Jobs can be enriched in a range of ways. First, responsibilities are pulled down from above, and the employee is trained to take new responsibilities for aspects of the task, including planning and scheduling, that previously were performed by a supervisor, or by the employee only in emergencies.

Second, earlier work stages are pushed forward into the job. Third, later work stages are pulled back. That is, the employee is made responsible for upstream and downstream activities that were previously handled by other persons. Fourth, parts of the task are pushed down to a lower job classification and are performed by a lower grade of employee (whose jobs are thus enriched by these responsibilities being pulled down). Fifth, parts of the job are rearranged and reordered.

The concept of job enrichment expresses a reaction against the excessive division of labor, and the notion that maximally efficient productivity is best for the organization. All these techniques involve making the job more challenging by making it more complex, and thus imply that the new organization works best when its members are motivated by the task, not necessarily by the size of the pay packet.

Job enrichment programs that ask non-managerial employees to take non-trivial decisions about how to organize their work schedules are, in practice, asking them to participate in management. Evidence from New Zealand shows that in this egalitarian and individualist culture, there is a positive relationship between high participation and high job satisfaction (Hines, 1974).

However, this finding cannot be automatically generalized to other cultural contexts. Kono's (1990) data show that when the corporate culture is innovative, power differentials are slight and members participate, members are more highly motivated than when the culture is either bureaucratic or stagnant.

8.6.3 Applying job enrichment programs

A number of problems occur in job-enrichment programs.

- The notion that jobs should be enriched within a particular environment presupposes that employees really are best motivated by an interesting task; they may not be.
- Similarly, the notion presupposes that employees are frustrated and demotivated by the routine inherent in their present jobs; they may not be.
- Job enrichment works only when bureaucratic practices are sufficiently flexible to handle the reorganization of control and communication systems. When middle-management feel they have a stake in preserving the old system and see no advantages in the new system, they oppose it. By implication, job enrichment is most likely to work within the cultural conditions of Hofstede's (1984a) market bureaucracy and least likely in the full bureaucracy.
- job enrichment fails to have positive long-term effects when employees whose jobs are supposedly enriched do not understand the reasons for change or the changes made. If they are inadequately trained to manage the change, they react against the added complexity of their jobs. Hence a culture of open and efficient communication between management and employees is essential.
- The advantages of job enrichment are diminished or reversed because the changes have unanticipated effects elsewhere in the organization.

These problems can be overcome when the following general conditions apply:

- jobs can be enriched;
- employees aspire towards more rewarding jobs;
- employees welcome the climate of change and experimentation;
- employees are secure; they are confident that the enrichment program will not lead to enforced redundancies and sackings, and that good-faith difficulties in implementing the program will not be sanctioned.

In addition, a number of cultural conditions aid the process of job enrichment. The process is helped when:

- employees have relatively low needs to avoid anxiety, and can tolerate the ambiguities involved;
- collectivist tendencies are weak, and employees tolerate change in work-group membership;
- power distances are low, and employees tolerate ambiguity and change in lateral relationships;

- experimentation is welcomed;
- bureaucratic practices are flexible.

Where these conditions occur, the organization can be optimistic about the success of an enrichment program. Where they do not occur, the program needs to be implemented cautiously, progress at each stage being checked before the next stage is begun.

8.7 Motivated to Achieve

Working at about the same time as Herzberg, McClelland (1976) developed his theory of achievement motivation. On the bases of historical and contemporary data, he argued that the greater the motivation to achieve in a society, the greater that society's economic growth and tendency to innovate.

The next step was to apply the general theory to the individual, and to develop a profile of the achieving individual. The need for achievement can be defined as a a desire to meet and exceed performance standards, and to succeed in the face of competition. High achievers seem to have in common:

- a preference for taking moderate risks;
- a need for immediate and frequent feedback on performance;
- a preference for specific performance criteria;
- a dislike for leaving tasks incomplete;
- a sense of urgency.

Achievement motivation in the individual is measured by coding his/her thoughts, or in stories, the frequency with which he refers to competing with set criteria of excellence or exceeding previous targets.

8.7.1 Applying the profile

Despite some evidence that high achievement motivation is developed in the early years of childhood (Winterbottom, 1958), McClelland has argued that it can be taught to adults.

An experimental program developed for United States companies was subsequently applied in India (McClelland, 1965). First it was run with potential entrepreneurs in a number of small cities, then with salaried executives in Bombay. Training consisted of:

- goal setting – the goals that the individual sets are used as targets against which he/she measures his/her progress every six months for two years;

- developing a language of achievement so that the individual expresses him/herself in terms of achievement;
- developing cognitive supports; learning to think in terms that relate to achievement; among other processes, the individual learns to work through on a conscious plain those assumptions made in the culture which inhibit achievement;
- developing group support systems for emotional support. Participants from the city of Kakinanda decided to maintain their new solidarity by establishing the Kakinanda Entrepreneurs' Association.

McClelland provides figures to attest to the program's success. He then makes some general points about the value of such achievement motivation training in less developed countries, and among sub-cultures in the United States. To summarize:

- the psychological and social climate of the culture or organization – that is, the context of confidence and optimism – crucially affects needs to achieve;
- even individuals and cultural groups with low needs for achievement can be trained to develop higher achievement needs;
- for historical reasons, some cultures and sub-cultures have lower achievement needs than others.[6]

The fact that McClelland's Indian participants had taken time off from their other occupations suggests that they had already accepted the concept that they were capable of raising their achievement levels. And to the extent that their cultural climate is under-achieving (as McClelland appears to assume), they were untypical individuals. Hence, the argument that high achievement needs can be taught, contrary to prevailing cultural values, is unproven.

The notion that achievement needs can be measured and fostered is important, even if we do not yet know how to apply it within cultural contexts where Western concepts of achievement and the values of competition appeal to only a minority. As we have seen, the cross-cultural manager has particular difficulty in recognizing what needs motivate members of the other culture, and then assisting the underachiever to realize his/her potential.

No one of the theories discussed in this chapter consistently predicts how work behavior can be improved within the cultural context within which the theory was elaborated, and far less within some other culture where perceptions of need, satisfaction and achievement may have very different connotation. The cross-cultural manager is wise to keep an open mind and experiment within his/her own context with the wide range of potential satisfiers that are available.

8.8 Implications for the Manager

Compare an organization that you know well in *your own culture* with a similar organization in *some other culture.*

1. How do members of the two organizations (at the same level of seniority) rank these rewards for working?

    (a) good wages;
    (b) interesting work;
    (c) good job security;
    (d) feeling of being in on things;
    (e) opportunity to learn;
    (f) appreciation for work done;
    (g) promotion and growth in organization;
    (h) good working conditions;
    (i) personal loyalty to employees;
    (j) sympathetic help with personal problems.

    - Explain the differences.

2. Rank the rewards listed in 1 in terms of how effectively they motivate performance within the two organizations. Take into account such factors as

    (a) the target behavior required;
    (b) cost;
    (c) risk;
    (d) ease of implementation;
    (e) any other significant factors.

    - Explain any differences in the rankings.

3. What resources are available to satisfy the needs felt by members of the two organizations?

4. How might *job enrichment* programs be applied within the two organizations?

    (a) job rotation;
    (b) job enlargement;
    (c) job enrichment.

    For each organization, take into account:

    (d) the nature of the jobs to be enriched;
    (e) the employees' aspirations for enriched jobs;
    (f) factors in the national culture;

(g)   factors in the organizational culture;

(h)   the expense of planning, communicating and implementing the program.

5.   How might *achievement motivation* be increased within the two organizations? Consider the possibilities for:

(a)   developing skills in goal setting;

(b)   developing a language, and organizational culture, of achievement;

(c)   developing cognitive supports for achievement;

(d)   developing group support systems.

- How might *achievement motivation* be increased within *the-other-culture* organization?

6.   Given your answers to 1–5 above, how should the motivational policies that are applied in *your-own-culture* organization be modified for use in *the-other-culture* organization?

8.9   Summary

This chapter has dealt with the complex issue of motivation. Needs and satisfiers of those vary between different groups, including cultural groups. A need felt in one context may not be significant in another, and a successful motivator on one culture may have no effect elsewhere.

Section 8.2 dealt with the problems of *identifying needs*. The manager bases his/her selection of motivators upon analysis of employee's needs. Data produced in the United States show that needs are often wrongly identified. If managers regularly make such errors within their own culture, the likelihood of misunderstanding needs in some other culture is all the greater. Section 8.3 dealt with the general issues of *identifying needs in another culture* and of designing motivators appropriate to the needs of its members.

Section 8.4 discussed *Maslow's Hierarchy of Needs* and examined the cross-cultural implications. The manager might decide that the model should be modified in order to more accurately reflect priorities within the specific culture. Section 8.5 led on to consider the functions of *monetary incentives and the alternatives*. The values associated with monetary rewards vary in different industrial and organizational contexts, even within a single national culture. Section 8.6 described Herzberg's theory and its application in the job enrichment program. The theory suggests that the opportunity to do *satisfying* work is in itself *motivating*. Section 8.7 dealt with McClelland's *achievement motivation*.

8.10 Exercise

This exercise gives practice in designing motivators.

1. Assess the needs of managers in an organization that you know well. What motivators are effective? Add to this list:

   - status and recognition outside the organization;
   - praise in the organization's house journal;
   - opportunities to develop new skills;
   - responsibility;
   - health insurance and/or a pension scheme;
   - better facilities at the workplace.

2. From the total list, select the eight that you think might be most effective. Order these eight.
3. Decide how each motivator can be applied in order to stimulate maximum productivity from the managers.
4. Now review the hierarchies of needs modelled by Maslow and Nevis to fit the United States and the People's Republic of China (sections 8.4 and 8.4.1). Design a variant that fits your organization.
5. Check your ordering and application of motivators by relating each to a level on your hierarchy. If necessary, revise your motivators.

Notes

1. Mutiso (1974) is cited and discussed in Adler (1991).
2. Marguerite Johnson, "From bad to worse," *Time*, July 26, 1993.
3. Geoffrey Colvin, "How to pay the CEO right," *Fortune*, April 6, 1992, **125**(7).
4. This definition is discussed and applied by Kelley et al. (1986). Both the Korean and Japanese managers studied in this paper showed moderate support for the importance that materialism should play in their lives.
5. Work goals used by the Meaning of Work International Research Team and their importance across cultures are discussed by MOW International Research Team (1986). See also Harpaz (1990).
6. McClelland (1965) compares the low achievement needs of Afro-Americans to those of immigrant Greeks and Jews, and cites Rosen (1959).

9

Dispute

9.1 Introduction

A newspaper article discusses the cultural problems facing a new Israeli ambassador to the United States.

> Mr Shoval's talent for "hasbara" – the Hebrew euphemism for propaganda – is appreciated at American Jewish gatherings. But as an Israeli living here put it: "Hasbara grates on [US Secretary of State] Baker. The State Department doesn't like to be preached at."[1]

Mr Shoval ran into trouble when the State Department canceled a $400 million guarantee that the Israeli Government apparently wished to spend on housing in the occupied West bank. In response, Mr Shoval gave an on-record news-agency interview in which he referred to the issue and said "we sometimes feel we are being given the runaround."

Mr Shoval's comments on United States policy towards Israel were received with bitter denunciations. An observer noted that

> in the rough and tumble of [Israeli parliament] Knesset politics, where people scream at each other, to say that "he is giving us the runaround" is the mildest form of criticism. There was a lesson for him: when you are dealing with the boys from the country club, you have to be more polite.

This shows that criticism (among other expressions of dispute) is interpreted differently in different situations, and cultures. This chapter explores this issue. It asks how the context influences perceptions of dispute, and how contextual features determine the extent to which dispute is tolerated and even encouraged.

The chapter has the following sections:

9.2 The Meaning of Dispute in Different Cultures

People's attitudes towards a dispute depend very much upon how far it threatens their own interests. This point is illustrated by the problems that arose for Schein (1987) when he worked as a consultant to a small family-owned food company. He described it thus:

> I asked some managers whether, in their daily work, they experienced any conflicts with subordinates, peers, or superiors. ... I usually elicited an immediate and flat denial of any conflict whatsoever. This response puzzled me, since I had been called in to help figure out what to do about "severe conflicts" that members of the organization were perceiving or experiencing. (pp. 66–7)

Schein finally realized that he and his interviewees were making very different assumptions. He, on his part, was

- using the term "conflict" to refer to any degree of disagreement between two or more people;
- assuming that conflict is a normal human condition, always present to some degree.[7]

But they were

- restricting use of the term "conflict" to severe disagreements;
- assuming that conflict is bad, and reflecting badly upon managerial capacities of the person involved.

Thus very different interpretations of the notion "conflict" were made by

(a) the consultant (Schein) who is

- expert in investigating conflict;
- an outsider to the organization;
- a non-protagonist in the relationships investigated;

(b)   the managers, who were

- non-experts in investigating conflict;
- insiders to the organization;
- protagonists in the relationships investigated.

And, by implication, a third party;

(c)   the top manager responsible for hiring Schein, who was

- a non-expert in investigating conflict;
- insider to the organization;
- a non-protagonist in the relationships investigated.

These parties were all American, and their different perceptions of these particular disagreements arose not from varying commitments to the culture but from situational factors. The consultant was trained to be objective, and was neither involved in the conflicts nor stood to benefit from their outcomes. The managers, on the other hand, were involved, and perceived that their reputations suffered if they were thought unable to control conflicts. Not surprisingly, then, they invested the term with negative connotations.

In sum, the factors that influence degrees to which dispute is tolerated include the following:

- *Industrial and occupational factors* Some industries (politics, law) are more tolerant; some (public-sector organizations) may be less.
- *Organizational culture.*
- *Urgency* A military unit tolerates disputes among its members less in time of war than when off-duty, in peace.
- *Proximity* You are likely to be less tolerant when you perceive that your financial and other interests are threatened.
- *Individual psychology* Some individuals show greater tolerance than others – which may influence choice of occupation and company.
- *Culture.*

We go on to deal with culture.

9.2.1   Dispute and culture

In the Anglo cultures, a certain level of open disagreement is treated as inevitable and is tolerated. In the United States,

> it has become accepted that tension is normal, even desirable, with the thought growing that "healthy" personalities actually seek to increase tension. (Litterer, 1966)

And when well-handled, disputes can bring new energy and added value to an organization (Evans, 1992). But other cultures may be far less certain of how to manage and positively apply disagreements between members.

9.2.2 Different tolerances of dispute

Research findings show very different tolerances. Hofstede (1984a) associates attitudes towards dispute with power distance and needs to avoid uncertainty.

Large-power distance cultures

- assume that latent conflict between ranks is normal;
- assume that peers are reluctant to trust each other.

And small-power distance cultures

- value harmony between the powerful and the powerless;
- assume that peers are relatively willing to cooperate (p. 77).

Where needs to avoid uncertainty are large,

- conflict in organizations is considered highly undesirable;
- competition is emotionally disapproved of;
- there is a low readiness to compromise with opponents.

Where needs to avoid uncertainty are small,

- conflict in organizations is considered natural;
- competition between employees can be fair and right;
- there is a greater readiness to compromise with opponents (Hofstede, 1984a, p. 112).

A study by Laurent (1983) asked managers from a range of countries to respond to the statement:

> most organizations would be better off if conflict could be eliminated forever. (p. 86)

He elicited agreement from 4 percent of his Swedish respondents, from 6 percent of the Americans, 24 percent of the French, 27 percent of the Germans, and 41 percent of the Italians.

In general, a high concern with eliminating conflict was associated with the belief that the manager should be able to answer questions asked by subordinates, and that organizations should not be threatened by practices such as by-passing the boss to communicate elsewhere, or by reporting to two bosses. In such cultures, for instance, matrix structures are regarded as likely to cause disputes and are seldom implemented.

This indicates that cultures protect themselves against the negative affects of disagreement by regulating those types of behavior which seem most likely to provoke it and so most threatening.

9.2.3 What aversion to dispute means

A dispute develops in stages. At one extreme, it is latent. Participants may be aware of contradictions in their relationship, but do not let these affect their behavior. Perhaps in time the frustrations and tensions are felt but still the participants maintain superficial courtesies. At a further extreme, the relationship breaks down into verbal conflict and perhaps even violence.

Can we usefully distinguish cultures that are more or less prone to open conflict?

It cannot be assumed that, in countries where power distances, needs to avoid uncertainty, and collectivism are all large that violence is necessarily less likely to occur than elsewhere. National murder rates give one indicator, and these figures (selected from a 1991 ranking and shown in table 9.1) indicate that a collectivist culture does not guarantee passivity:[3]

Table 9.1 National murder rates, 1991

Country	1991 world ranking	Murders per 100,000 people
Colombia	5	40.5
The Philippines	7	36.9
Thailand	17	11.1
United States	33	8.4
Sweden	40	7.2
Australia	59	4.5
Libya	75	2.3
United Kingdom	82	2.0

Source: Britannica World Data, from Interpol and national crime statistics.

The individualist cultures represented here (the United States, Sweden, Australia, the United Kingdom) show lower murder rates than in the more collectivist (with the exception of Libya – a warning against ignoring local features).

Of course, figures for other forms of violence (rape, child abuse, violent robbery, etc.) might order these countries differently. And that is the point; there is little sense in making blanket generalizations about levels of violence within and between cultures. The problem, rather, is to identify how far cultural factors constrain conflict in different situations, within each culture.

Collectivists restrict expressions of open conflict first by developing a greater tolerance of latent disagreement (Johnson et al., 1990). For instance, implicit challenges are ignored or smoothed over. Second, when these techniques are unsuccessful, open conflict is sanctioned; the offender may be ostracized from the in-group. Third, communicative techniques are developed that maintain at least the appearance of harmony. Hofstede (1991) noted that in Japan

> direct confrontation of another person is considered rude and undesirable. The word "no" is seldom used, because saying no *is* a confrontation ... In the same vein, the word "yes" should not necessarily be seen as an approval but as maintenance of the communication line: "yes, I heard you" is the meaning it has in Japan.
>
> In individualist cultures, on the other hand, speaking one's mind is a virtue. ... Confrontation can be salutary; a clash of opinions is believed to lead to a higher truth. (Hofstede, 1991, p. 58)

The other side of the collectivist coin is that confrontation occurs when it carries few risks. To the extent that the other person is an outsider and open disagreement threatens neither upsetting group values and norms, nor your loss of face, the constraints are removed.

Leung's (1988) analysis supports the notion that Chinese collectivists prioritize considerations of how their behavior might affect their standing within the group. He discovered that Hong Kong Chinese were more likely to pursue conflict if the stakes involved were high and if the other disputant was from an out-group. They were more likely to pursue a conflict with an out-group disputant than were Americans.

In South-east Asia, collectivism is reflected in loyalty to the immediate group and the leader (for instance, the departmental manager). Disagreements are maintained at a latent level. But this does not necessarily apply to other groups under the same organizational umbrella – the company. The company may be only able to fully coordinate the activities of its members when it delineates a specific opponent – a competitor for the same market share. When members of competing departments have no incentive to resolve the anomolies, each refuses to risk losing face by making the first step towards a reconciliation.

9.2.4　Culture and industrial disputes

The Anglo cultures tolerate high levels of workforce-management disputes. These are complicated by disagreements within each side when both union and management negotiators have to negotiate their bargaining positions with their own constituents, whose support is always conditional.

In the United Kingdom, the 1984–5 miners' strike ended without a formal agreement and a slow drift back to work when the union leaders were unable to maintain the solid support of their members. This conflict within the National Union of Miners led to a split and the formation of a rival miners' union. Similar problems of maintaining constituent solidarity afflicted the National Coal Board. Partly as a result of this failure by both sides to negotiate a creative solution to their shared problems, the industry fell further into decline. By 1991 104 out of the 169 pits in 1985, and 114,000 jobs, had disappeared.[4]

As a rule of thumb, unions and management in the United States expect their relationship to be antagonistic, whereas in Japan they need a good reason for not maintaining harmony.

In the United States, the relationship between management and workforce is usually perceived by both sides as inherently conflictual, and their interests as contradictory. Unions strategies are typically to

- identify and intensify points of conflict;
- foster an adverserial industrial relations climate;
- create, and maintain a rift between management and the workforce;
- insist on monopoly rights to negotiate with management on behalf of the workforce, and thus pre-empt "unofficial" initiatives by either side to resolve conflicts.

But this does not mean that the union welcomes *all* conflicts. Those that appear to threaten its own monopoly position and powers are severely curtailed.

Relationships between Japanese unions and their management may not be entirely collusive, particularly in the annual Spring offensives (*shunto*) when the coming years's labor contracts are negotiated. Nevertheless, they do demonstrate a much greater emphasis on collaborating to find mutually satisfactory solutions. In part because unions are company-based rather than industry-based, the union president and top management are mutually dependent upon each other for an atmosphere of goodwill in order to carry out their responsibilities to their different constituencies. And the union president in effect acts as the company's senior executive in charge of labor relations (Hanami, 1979, p. 56).[5]

The American manager expects to resort to confrontational tactics when disputing a contract with a trade partner, and uses contracts that allow for arbitration by an agency such as the American Arbitration Association.

The Japanese, on the other hand, prefers to resolve disagreements by compromise and consensus not only within his own organization but also with other organizations, and avoids employing contractual clauses that stress rigid performance criteria. The emphasis is on flexibility in interpreting agreements. Influence to reach agreement and avoid conflict is typically mediated by third parties (Johnson et al., 1990). Sullivan et al. (1981) cite the Japan Trade Center (no date given):

> If some contractual language is necessary, a phrase like the following translation is sometimes used: "All items not found in this contract will be deliberated and decided upon in a spirit of honesty and trust." (p. 3)

Hostile takeovers of firms are deeply repugnant to the Japanese sensibility. When a United States finance company attempted to take over a Japanese high-technology concern, it was unable to find a local securities firm prepared to act as tender offer agents. (Ishizumi, 1985; 1990). The target defended itself by a variant on

> what tends to be the most common form of defense in Japan when a company is under threat: namely, to place large blocks of shares in the hands of stable shareholders, such as financial institutions or banks. Minebea's placement of bonds, although a novelty in Japan, had the same effect. (pp. 148–9)

This preference for resolving disputes by consensus rather than by confrontation is shown by the fact that less than 1 percent of the cases brought to the Japanese Commercial Arbitration Association end in binding arbitration. The Japanese avoids conflict by stressing the mutual benefits to be derived from a trusting relationship. And it follows that a Japanese company is unlikely to form a relationship with an organization that it feels unable to trust and which seems to favor conflict as a means of settling disagreements.

9.3 Argument, Competition, and Conflict

Why are disputes inevitable? Pascale (1990) expresses American values associated with "doing" when he comments:

[c]reativity and adaptation are born of tension, passion, and conflict. Contention does more than make us more creative. It makes us whole, it propels us along the journey of development. (p. 263)

That is, people need a degree of conflict in their lives because this provides opportunities for growth and self-expression, and allows them to test their performance.

The question can also be answered in terms of simple economic theory. Resources are always limited and no organization can hope to satisfy all needs of all its members all the time. For instance, changing market demands mean that staff have to be laid off or extra staff hired, fewer resources or more resources are available and in either event have to be shared differently.

What issues give rise to disagreement in the workplace, whether between individuals or groups? The range includes:

- the organizational structure; roles and responsibilities; for instance, middle management resist decentralization policies that appear to threaten their authority. Ciba-Geigy's moves to empower individuals throughout the company and to weaken departmental barriers (chapter 4, section 4.3.1) were resisted by middle management;
- resource allocations, and competition for scarce resources;
- administrative procedures and processes;
- competition for status, promotion, pay and other rewards;
- goals and priorities;
- concealed agendas;
- clashes of loyalties;
- personality differences;
- communication issues; discourse misunderstandings;
- cultural antagonisms.

9.3.1 Constructive and destructive disputes

Not all disputes are destructive. Every negotiation begins with a conflict in interests which is resolved, usually by each side surrendering some of its objectives and finishing up in better circumstances than at the onset of the process. Writing in an American context, one manager suggests that disputes are constructive when they

- bring up, rather than hide, issues over which there are differences;
- force individuals to be direct, and so accelerate problem-solving;
- attack issues rather than individuals.[6]

Handy (1976; 1985) similarly argues that workplace disputes may be productive. He distinguishes between

- argument;
- competition;
- conflict.

An *argument* between two persons (or groups) enables them to resolve differences through discussion. Assuming that the topic of the argument is properly framed, the disputants are arguing about the same thing, and information is available to resolve the issue, argument is potentially constructive and is a useful way of learning. For instance, disagreements over strategic issues may force management to clarify and modify its thinking far more effectively than formal planning procedures, in which participants are under far greater pressure to build and maintain consensus (Huff, 1988). Such positive argument, in this sense, encourages synergy. But when these conditions are not present, argument deteriorates into quarreling and name-calling.

Competition, for resources, responsibilities, power, etc.

- stimulates activity and channels energy;
- sets standards;
- sorts out the best from the field.

In free-market conditions, competition with other firms in the environment leads smaller players to develop new niches and develop new alternatives. Top management may encourage competition within the organization by giving overlapping briefs to different individuals or units.

When the firm has a technological mission, there may be real disagreements on which of competing product ideas to develop, so competing project groups are set up. In the case of IBM, teams were not allowed contact with each other. Peters (1990) reports

> "Shootouts" between the projects were to settle upon the eventual winner – which would then move to final development. (p. 11)

This appeared to be a successful strategy; but in practice, differences between alternative outputs tend to have little significance outside the organizational culture.

Competition is more likely to be beneficial when it is open, in the sense that all competitors stand to profit by developing new ideas and opportunities. It is damaging when zero-sum; that is, there can only be one winner who takes all.

Conflict arises when argument and competition is negative and uncontrolled, and by implication has undesired consequences. When real issues are involved (for instance, on allocation of resources, disagreements over principle, etc.) and the two sides are in possession of shared and reliable information, the dispute is substantive. (Falk, 1982). When it involves vague feelings, personal antipathies, and displays of emotion, or the two sides base their claims on inaccurate or contradictory information, the dispute is affective (Putnam, 1986).

Substantive and affective conflict are not always easy to distinguish. First, the participants are unlikely to admit to conflicting over a purely affective issue, even when that is the case. Second, unresolved disputes over matters of substance easily degenerate into personal clashes, and personality differences are often expressed in differences over ostensibly substantive issues.

Conflict occurs when

- the participants refuse to collaborate to find a solution;
- a superior is unwilling or unable to arbitrate;
- one or both of the participants refuse to accept the superior's arbitration;
- rules and dispute-resolution procedures are inadequate, ambiguous, or contradictory;
- communication is poor; the participants are unable to communicate essential information, or disagree on how it should be interpreted.

That is, conflict erupts when arguments and competition spin out of control and cannot be mediated. This implies that cultures showing greater tolerance of intra-organizational disagreements have greater confidence in the power of their mediators and dispute-resolution procedures to create acceptable degrees of harmony.

Even in cultures most tolerant of inter-organizational disputes, excessive conflict is feared. A technical manager at Motorola in the United States describes his response to the ferocity of competition within the company:

I was amazed when I came here. The discussions get violent – verbally, fortunately.

Two legendary protagonists are John Mitchell, Motorola's vice chairman, and Ed Staiano, the respected head of the company's cellular operations. . . .

Some of these scenes have been played out before a bemused board of directors. Mr Staiano admits to some "embarrassingly conflictive dialogues" but says that "good ideas end up surviving." Messrs. Mitchell and Staiano manage to remain friendly after the fireworks.

[The technical manager] says he himself was "uncomfortable" with such conflict as a younger manager, but now he is convinced that "out of conflict comes catharsis."[7]

On an informal or formal basis, restrictions are set and compliance imposed. When a person seems to be continually involved in fermenting conflicts, and these are perceived to cause more damage than good, he/she is treated as deviant. In American firms,

> [m]en and women of high, sometimes brilliant, achievement who stubbornly insist on having their own way, and are contemptuous of others, are the bane of bosses, subordinates, peers and colleagues. . . . In fact, top executives probably refer more managers with abrasive personalities to psychologists and psychiatrists, and human relations training programs in order to rescue them, than any other single classification of executives. (Levinson, 1976, p. 112)

9.4   Communicating Dispute

This section addresses

- failure to recognize that a dispute has arisen;
- failure to recognize the causes of a dispute.

When the cross-cultural manager misreads a dispute it can rapidly spin out of control. These are real problems because disputes are signaled differently in different cultures.

Here is an example where management interests are attacked by a symbolic action that would seem absurd in an Anglo culture but makes good sense within its actual setting. The story describes a threat to divorce by more than 1,250 Turkish road workers. They

> marched to court Tuesday to demand divorces in a bizarre twist to the country's mounting labor militancy.
> "We have to try everything to win our rights. We've already refused to shave. We've walked barefoot to work. We've reported sick together," a Yol-Is road builders union official said.
> [They] lined up under a hot sun to file for divorce on the grounds of poverty.
> "We . . . can no longer bear ourselves with honor in front of our spouses," said [the union boss].
> Turkey's 600,000 state-employed workers have staged unorthodox protests . . . because of restrictive union laws that make strikes difficult and expensive.[8]

Within the context, what is the symbolic importance of this action? From the workers' point of view, this mass demand for divorce represents an escalation of their struggle – beyond, for instance, reporting sick together. In a Turkish context, where power distances are relatively high, relationships collectivist, and family loyalties dominant, this demand for divorce on grounds of poverty is a form of self-abasement. And by implying that they have been forced to this extremity by the nigardliness of their state employer, they cause this employer loss of face – significant where the employer is expected to take a paternalistic interest in the livelihood of employees.

The social, legal and political circumstances mean that the costs of a violent expression of their rights or even going on strike are bound to be prohibitive. Given the possible benefits and the costs involved, this action promises to be a potent weapon – at least, in the eyes of these Turkish workers. Although symbolic, it is designed to shame the employer into a non-symbolic response; granting a pay rise.

In a different cultural context, for instance in an Anglo culture, where the employer is not expected to play much of a social role outside the workplace and is not responsible for the domestic relationships of his/her workforce, a mass divorce would elicit only mockery. The employer would have been far more inconvenienced by the previous demonstration of mass sickness.

9.4.1 Communicating dispute within the hierarchy

Cultures not only tolerate interorganizational disputes differently; they communicate disputes differently. Hence messages that pass without question in Culture X may be viewed as confrontational in Culture Y. And the cross-cultural manager coming from Culture X to Culture Y is in danger of

- overlooking expressions of disagreement made by Culture Y members;
- communicating messages which he/she intends as neutral but which are interpreted as confrontational by Culture Y members.

How do we characterize Cultures X and Y? To apply Hofstede's model discussed in section 9.2.1, let us assume that in Culture X

- power distances are small; that is, members value harmony between the powerful and the powerless, and as peers are relatively willing to cooperate;
- needs to avoid uncertainty are small. Members consider conflict in organizations to be natural, accept that competition between employees can be fair and right, and are more prepared to compromise;
- interests are individualist. Speaking one's mind can be a virtue and confrontation can be salutary.

But in Culture Y

- power distances are large; members assume that latent conflict between ranks is normal, and as peers are relatively unwilling to cooperate;

- needs to avoid uncertainty are large; members consider conflict in organizations to be undesirable, disapprove of competition, and are unwilling to compromise with opponents;
- interests are collectivist; any utterance that implies confrontation is considered rude and undesirable.

In a Culture Y group, the expression of disagreement with superior authority causes loss of face and a disruption of harmony, and thus attacks the interests of all. Such behavior is disapproved by authority, peer pressure, and self-discipline. And the traditional subordinate takes care to avoid any action that might

- imply disagreement or criticism;
- imply that the superior has failed to express himself adequately;
- otherwise cause his superior loss of face.

9.4.2 Thai and American dispute

Thai culture gives a moderate example of our Culture Y, and United States culture of Culture X.

Here is an example. A Thai student in a Thai business school is describing the behavior of cross-registered American students. (The school is English-medium and almost all the professors come from the United States.)

> Today in ... class, I observed that many questions [asked] by American exchange students often came out strongly and directly. To most Thai students, the questions sound very aggressive and impolite. The questions that they make are often stated in a way that [suggests that] the professor is wrong or the explanation is not good enough. ... [but] the way Thai students asked sounds [as if] they really want more information because they themselves do not understand the topic.

That is, the Thai student *avoids* behavior that has the effect of

- making an explicit or implicit challenge;
- raising an objection;
- expressing an opinion with which the superior might disagree;
- requesting clarification.

The need to avoid loss of face and confrontation also constrains the behavior of the traditional Thai boss. He/she avoids making demands that

- are over-complex or ambiguous, and require clarification, or lead to the subordinate making a mistake;

- challenge the subordinate's perceptions of the world;
- are divisive, and place the subordinate in conflict with other members of the organization.

The Culture Y/Thai response is to avoid communication that can be construed as negative or confrontational. In practice, this restricts the opportunities for argument or competition which has positive effects.

Suppose that the superior gives an opinion and his subordinate responds "I'm afraid I can't agree on all points." Within an American organization this might still be tolerated. But in the traditional Thai organization, tolerances are narrower, and the utterance is likely to be interpreted as antagonistic.

An obvious cross-cultural implication is that the American may intend as non-confrontational an utterance which the Thai perceives as offensive (Mead, 1992). But we can go further. The American expects confrontation to be expressed covertly. For instance, the subordinate makes a flat refusal to cooperate; "If you want that done, do it yourself." Hence when the Thai responds in terms that should warn a Thai superior not to push any further in this direction, the American does not recognize its intended affect. For instance:

American boss:	[gives an opinion] Is that a problem for you?
Traditional Thai employee:	[says nothing; drops his eyes]

The American pays more attention to explicit verbal behavior, and may largely ignore non-verbal signals. But the Thai's silence and downcast eyes means different things when the other person is a subordinate, peer, family member; in this context, of an interaction with a superior, the behavior implies resistance at the level of argument. But, ironically, the contextual feature of the superior's cultural identity also determines that the intended function of the behavior is not apparent.

How does the American react to this apparent lack of a response? Given his own conditioning, he may assume that

- his opinion has been accepted;
- the Thai has not been listening; the question needs to be asked again – and again, until it elicits a substantive response;
- the Thai withdraws from the conflict; his objections can be safely overlooked.

When subsequent events demonstrate that these assumptions are false, cross-cultural misunderstandings escalate.

9.5 Coping with Conflict and Finding a Resolution

Thomas (1976) models the options for resolving a dispute:[9]

Point A   Attempt to dominate; force your solution on the other side. This position is highly assertive and shows no desire to cooperate.

Point B   Collaborate to find a solution that integrates the needs of both sides. New interests are introduced, and the scale of the negotiation is increased, to the mutual advantage of both. This balances needs to assert and cooperate at a high level.

Point C   Compromise, for instance by bargaining down to a 50/50 split of resources.

Point D   Avoid conflict.

Point E   Accommodate and appease the other side. This position is highly cooperative but shows no desire to assert.

Forcing, with the hope of achieving domination, is high on the assertive axis and no attempt is made to cooperate. Hopes to reach an amicable resolution are dashed for as long as both sides force. Cooperation and compromise reflect both parties' willingness to cooperate. Evans (1992) suggests stages in reaching a cooperated agreement:

1. communicating about issues and interests;
2. exploring divergent values, expectations and assumptions;
3. understanding different perspectives;
4. reframing issues and interests, and reaching agreement.

In Anglo cultures, the posture that the disputants and other interested parties (a superior or mediator) take is influenced by such factors as the following.

- The stakes associated with the outcome. When the outcome is very important to one side, it invests more in winning.
- The urgency of finding an immediate solution. The less time there is available to negotiate a comprehensive settlement, the greater the pressure to assert power or to withdraw. When the sides cannot agree, a superior may impose a solution. When one side decides that more can be gained from preserving the relationship, it may decide to withdraw in favor of the other party on this particular issue.
- The emotional involvement of the parties involved. When one side is highly involved it feels less inclined to look for a sharing solution.

In these cultures, avoidance and appeasement appear to be strategies for only coping with the symptoms. They fail to resolve fundamental issues and may only delay eventual open conflict – as the attempts made by British politicians to appease Hitler and the German Nazis before the outbreak of war in 1939 demonstrated. But in Japan, argue Black and Mendenhall (1993), conflict avoidance and the achievement of harmony are not necessarily exclusive. Both can be the means to another end:

> [t]he end state most desired by Japanese in interpersonal relationships is a condition in which the incurrence of obligations is minimized and the flexibility in fulfilling obligations is maximized. (p. 50)

Human beings in general wish to rid themselves of feelings of social and psychological debt to other persons. But most other cultures do not go as far as the Japanese in either prescribing what obligations are incurred in different social situations, or how these obligations should be paid off. In a Japanese business negotiation, the winner incurs future obligations towards the loser, and unless these are paid off the disharmony affects not only their future relationship but also the attitudes of observers. This acts as a constraint on winning too clearly.

9.5.1 Intervention by a superior

When subordinates are in dispute, the superior has a range of options (Ware and Barnes, 1983):

- avoidance (the least assertive option); the manager ignores the dispute when

    (a) it is likely to have positive outcomes;
    (b) it is unlikely to have negative outcomes;
    (c) the disputants seem likely to reach a satisfactory outcome without outside intervention;
    (d) the superior is likely to damage his own interests by intervening; for instance, he loses face if the intervention is unsuccessful;

- imposition of a solution; (the most assertive option) – for instance, when

    (a) an outcome is urgently needed;
    (b) the dispute is likely to escalate;
    (c) the superior feels his authority threatened by the dispute continuing;

- negotiating a solution; for instance, the superior gives the disputants time in which to cool off and then initiates a process of identifying the real issues and solving the problem by redefining it; this means agreeing on the goal, then looking for alternative routes to achieve this goal;

- mediating a solution; acting as a disinterested third party – as in Japan, for instance;
- counseling the disputants, in the hope that they can resolve their difference on their own;
- separation of the disputants.

Avoidance on the one hand and attempting to impose a solution on the other are illustrated at national level by governmental responses to industrial dispute. During the 18-month-long 1984–5 coal strike in the United Kingdom, it was politically unacceptable for the government to intervene by force as a means of forcing a resolution (although police action was taken against illegal picketing and damage to property).

But in South Korea, a 1963 law decided that serious industrial disputes should be resolved by a compulsory 20-day cooling-off period, then negotiations within ten days. If no settlement was reached, a government labor committee was set up to choose a compromise plan. Violations of the law were punishable by up to two years in prison. On July 20, 1993, thousands of riot police were brought in to crush illegal strikes that had afflicted the Hyundai Motor Co for the previous five weeks.[10]

9.5.2   Culture and resolution

Across cultures, organizations vary in terms of

- perceptions of when a disagreement has reached the point at which it endangers the interests of the organization and its members; and hence their tolerances of disagreement;
- the strategies that members adopt for coping with disagreement;
- perceptions of when and how a superior must intervene.

Assertiveness is more valued in cultures that are both individualist and masculine, and there may be a feeling that conflicts should be resolved by openly fighting them out (Hofstede, 1991, p. 92). In this example, from the United States, the "fighting out" is symbolic, and perhaps intended as parody of the culture.

Southwest Airline began using a slogan "plane smart" which was already in use by Stevens Aviation Inc., an airline service business. The Stevens CEO, 38-year-old Kurt Herwald, challenged the Southwest chairman Herb Kelleher (61) to arm-wrestle for rights to use the slogan. This was eagerly taken up by Kelleher.

He rented a seedy wrestling auditorium, gave Southwest employees the morning off, dressed some as cheerleaders, brought in pro wrestlers and staged a 30-minute pep rally before the showdown.

Kelleher sent in a champion arm-wrestler in the first round, and the substitute won. Stevens sent in an employee as substitute in the second round, and she beat Kelleher to even the score. Then Herwald beat Kelleher in the final round.

"Just to show sympathy for the elderly and that there's no hard feelings, we've decided to allow Southwest Airlines to continue using our slogan," Herwald said afterward.

"Frankly, it was their slogan," Kelleher said from the stretcher that whisked him away from the match. "You could have had a substantial lawsuit."[11]

Why did the participants choose to resolve their dispute in this fashion? The apparent alternatives were to fight an expensive legal action, which Southwest was unlikely to win, or for one side to back down. The arm-wrestling solution reaped wide publicity for both companies, gave employees a morale-raising party, and masked a withdrawal while still avoiding conflict.

In Anglo cultures, the non-assertive strategies of withdrawal or smoothing are equated with an admission of defeat; the individual who habitually withdraws from conflict is likely to be scorned as a "wimp," and the manager who regularly ignores subordinates' disputes is in danger of losing their respect. Withdrawal may not be an acceptable alternative.[12] One study shows that among American managers withdrawal is the least often used means of conflict resolution, and confrontation the most often used (Burke, 1970).

But when the confrontation has taken place and achieved a result, the restoration of normal relations is demonstrated symbolically – for instance by a handshake. In the United Kingdom, resolution to an open and bitter dispute between two airlines was signaled by a visit of the loser (Sir Colin Marshall, CEO of British Airways) to the London house of the winner (Richard Branson of Virgin) for "tea and a cosy chat."[13] As it turned out, this resolution was only temporary and hostilities resumed.

In cultures where withdrawal is acceptable, an apparent withdrawal cannot always be taken at face value. It may carry a hidden message, that the "loser" is making a tactical retreat only, to make a retaliatory strike at some later date when conditions are decisively in his/her favor. The dispute, then is set within a long-term context.

Cultures that particularly avoid disputes within the in-group also need to maintain a united front to outsiders when disputes do occur. In Arab cultures, efforts will be made to resolve these by mediation (Moran, 1986). Lacey (1981) reports that before King Abdul Aziz of Saudi Arabia died, he drew together his sons Sa'ud and Faisal, who had a long history of personal disagreements. He told them,

> Join hands across my body . . . and swear that you will work together when I am gone. Swear too that, if you quarrel, you will argue in private. You must not let the world catch sight of your disagreements. (p. 318)

A dispute must be resolved as quickly as possible – perhaps by other group members imposing a solution. When a peace formula has been agreed, the participants move rapidly towards smoothing and down-playing disagreements. If one party continues trying to force its own solution and overlooks the obligations incurred in forcing the other to withdraw, the other is more likely to win sympathy and less likely to incur odium than the party that has prolonged the conflict to the apparent disadvantage of all.

Writing about Malaysian politics in 1987, a journalist explained why the Prime Minister's response to a political attack did not conform to convention, and thus seemed likely to cause him problems in the future.

> Traditionally, after a fierce fight the loser acknowledges his errors and begs forgiveness. The winner magnanimously obliges. Mahathir refused to do that. He sacked three Cabinet ministers and four deputy ministers, all of whom had opposed him in the leadership fight. That may sound proper in Western eyes, but it is an action that will cause Mahathir much trouble in the coming months. . . . A Malay saying that one should rather die than defy (tradition) is still an article of faith . . .[14]

And his opponents continued to challenge his authority for many years thereafter.

9.5.3 Avoiding conflict by exploiting ambiguity

Conflict between individuals or units is avoided when there is general agreement on abstractions but each party makes its own interpretation of specifics, and is unaware or uncaring that other parties are implementing different interpretations. Ambiguity has positive values when it

- promotes diversity within a unified structure;
- preserves essential symbols and existing impressions;
- facilitates organizational change when a previous interpretation of the unifying symbol has become inappropriate over time. For instance, a broad and flexible statement of the organizational mission

can be reinterpreted as events unfold, and avoids the clashes that occur when too narrow a statement precludes evolutionary adaptation and has to be radically revised (Eisenberg, 1984).

However, the manager runs certain risks in implementing this strategy. When planned ambiguity results in different parties taking decisions that are contradictory, the likelihood of conflict is increased rather than diminished. When the parties perceive that they have been manipulated and that the assumptions on which they have based their plans and actions are false, they are likely to respond negatively to the sudden stress (McCaskey, 1988). Should they perceive that this manipulation has been planned and deliberate, and that their interests diverge rather than converge as they had been led to accept, they may react strongly against the source of the confusion. Over time, these dangers grow.

Cultures that have high needs to avoid uncertainty in regard to roles do not welcome ambiguity in determining who has responsibilities for a task. Problems in implementing matrix structures in Latin cultures illustrate the point. But where uncertainty avoidance needs are lesser and potential disputes can be resolved by competition, the matrix creates an organizational culture that transforms potential conflicts into innovatory processes. For this reason, many Scandinavian firms have developed matrix structures as their strategic nucleus (Poulsen, 1988).

9.6 Implications for the Manager

Compare an organization that you know well in *your own culture*, and a similar organization in *some other culture*.

1. Within each of the two organizations, when is argument and competition viewed as beneficial? Reflect on specific situations, and answer these questions:

   - What types of argument and competition are encouraged, and what types discouraged? Identify examples of each type using these questions:

     (a) *Who* are the protagonists?
     (b) *What* issues are argued/competed over?
     (c) *How* are the arguments/competitions conducted?
     (d) *Where* are the arguments/competitions conducted?
     (e) *When* and for how long are the arguments/competitions conducted?

   - How far is argument encouraged?
   - How far is competition encouraged?

      (g)   between peers?

      (h)   units and departments?

- What strategies are adopted for preventing argument and competition escalating into conflict?
- What attitudes might a superior adopt towards conflict between subordinate groups or individuals?

2. Within each of the two organizations, what strategies do members typically adopt when disagreements occur, as a first response?

      (a)   forcing, attempting to dominate;

      (b)   collaboration;

      (c)   compromising and sharing;

      (d)   avoidance;

      (e)   accommodation and appeasement;

- If these initial moves fail, what new strategy may be adopted?
- How readily does a superior intervene to resolve or cope with disagreement between subordinates?
- What strategies might a superior adopt to resolve or cope with subordinate disagreement?
- By what formal and informal networks is disagreement communicated? And resolved? How significant is the use of mediators?
- What sanctions does the culture impose on persons responsible for provoking conflict?

3. How far do cultural factors explain differences between the two organizations?

- What other factors explain the differences?

9.7 Summary

This chapter has examined the meanings of disagreement within an organization, and has seen the cross-cultural implications.

Section 9.2 examined *the meaning of dispute in different cultures*. Cultures show different tolerances of disagreement. Within one culture, disagreement may be interpreted at varying levels of severity. Section 9.3 showed why *argument* and *competition* between individuals and groups is sometimes beneficial. But when they cannot be controlled, they degenerate into *conflict*, which here has negative connotations. Cultural factors influence perceptions of argument and competition.

Section 9.4 saw that the *communication* of *dispute* is often symbolic, and so may pose interpretation problems for the outsider. For instance, the cross-cultural manager is always in danger of overlooking expressions of disagreement in the other culture when these do not correspond to how disagreement is communicated in his/her own. Section 9.5 dealt with strategies for *coping with conflict and finding a resolution.* In Anglo cultures, strategies of compromise and collaboration are more likely to achieve a lasting resolution than withdrawal – but this does not necessarily apply elsewhere. Culture is a major factor in determining the choice of strategy.

9.8 Exercise

This exercise examines how culture and other contextual features influence strategies for conflict resolution.

Global Enterprises is headquartered in Darana. This case occurs in the Computer Department of the Ruritanian subsidiary, Global Enterprises (Ruritania).

One morning, Jon Kay, the star computer analyst, arrives two hours late for work. Jon has been with the Department for seven years – since the establishment of the firm – and is by far its most experienced analyst. He is respected by other members of the Department but feared for his bitter sense of humor. This is not the first time that he has been seriously late, and Paula Zed, the Computer Manager, has frequently reprimanded him for it.

This morning, Paula is absent on leave. Karl Gee, the assistant manager standing in for her, was appointed to this post two weeks ago.

Karl has been previously warned that Jon might be late by a junior clerk who saw Jon at a party last night. In a drunken rage, the analyst told everyone who would listen that Paula and Karl are "incompetent" and that he would turn up for work whenever he liked.

As soon as Jon enters, Karl begins to criticize him, loudly, in front of all other departmental members. He complains about his lateness, called him a "drunken imbecile," and says that his pay will be docked for the two hours' absence and that his performance will be negatively assessed in the next staff evaluation. (Both these actions lie outside Karl's area of responsibility.)

The conversation then goes like this:

Jon: Hey, it's not my fault I'm late, I've got flu.
Karl: You're a drunken liar.
Jon: (Waving his face in Karl's face.) And you're incompetent, you couldn't manage a sweet shop.

Karl pushes Jon away. Jon falls, and cracks a bone in his ankle.

When Paula returns to work after two days' absence, Karl insists that Jon should be fired. Jon says that he will quit his job unless Karl is fired, and demands that the firm pay him the cost of medication for his ankle and damages.

1. Given that the context is as follows, what option should Paula choose in order to resolve this conflict? What problems could arise from her choosing this best option?

Context

(a) There is currently a slump, and if Jon and Karl quit or are fired, they can expect to be unemployed for some months.
(b) Ruritanian culture is highly collectivist and power distances are large. Ruritanians have great needs to avoid uncertainty.
(c) Daranese culture is far more individualist. Power distances and needs to avoid uncertainty are small.
(d) Paula, her superior, and Karl are Daranese. Jon, and all other members of the Department are Ruritanian.
(e) Most members of the Department are sympathetic to Karl.
(f) Under Ruritanian law, the firm must pay at least 50 percent of Jon's medical costs and *unless* it is decided that he is responsible for the accident, damages of between 200 and 600 Ruris (to be negotiated).
(g) The use of alcohol is illegal in Ruritania. In Darana, it is widespread among both sexes.

Paula's options
i. Refer the dispute to her superior in Darana, on the grounds that she is personally involved (Jon publicly insulted her) and so cannot decide.
ii. Take no action, and hope that either the issue blows over or that one or the other of the disputants quits.
iii. Arrange that Jon is paid medical costs and minimal damages, and otherwise for ii.
iv. Reprimand the junior clerk for spreading gossip, and otherwise as for iii.
v. Fire Jon.
vi. Fire Karl.
vii. Fire them both.
viii. Mediate privately between Jon and Karl; if they cannot resolve their problem, then *either* for v *or* vi *or* vii.
ix. Any combination of the above, or alternative.

2. Given that the context is as follows, what option should Paula choose in order to resolve this conflict? What problems could arise from her choosing this best option?

    Context
    (a) The labor market is highly competitive, and Jon and Karl could easily find other jobs – possibly working for a competitor.
    (b) Daranese culture is highly collectivist, and power distances are large. Daranese have great needs to avoid uncertainty.
    (c) Ruritanian culture is far more individualist. Power distances and needs to avoid uncertainty are small.
    (d) Paula's superior is Daranese; all other persons are Ruritanian.
    (e) Members of the Department are divided in their opinions.
    (f) Under Ruritanian law, the firm must pay Karl's medical costs and *unless* it is decided that he is responsible for the accident, damages of between 500 and 1,000 Ruris (to be negotiated).
    (g) In Ruritania, behavior that would otherwise be socially sanctioned is often tolerated when performed under the influence of alcohol; Ruritanians consider that the individual should be punished only lightly when he/she is not fully in control of his/her faculties. In Darana, drunkenness is heavily sanctioned, whatever the circumstances.

    Paula's options
    As for 1.

3. Compare your answers to 1 and 2. How do they differ? What factors determine the difference?

Now, assume that Paula chooses option vii, and that the context as in 1 applies.

4. In groups of three, role-play a meeting to negotiate a solution.

    Student 1: play the part of Paula.
    Student 2: play the part of Karl.
    Student 3: play the part of Jon.

5. If you fail to agree on a solution, and any sanctions, Paula has the power to sack *either* Karl *or* Jon – which ever one's presence is most likely to harm future operations of the Department, given the context. Assume that, within these circumstances, neither (if fired) will benefit from alleging wrongful dismissal in a court of law.

6. Complete the negotiation within 15 minutes (or however long the instructor allows).

7. Report and explain the results of your negotiation to the class.

Notes

1. Clifford Krauss, "Israel's man, scorched once, adjusts to life in the diplomatic minefield," *New York Times*, May 10, 1991.
2. Kelly (1969) contrasts the "old view" that "conflict is by definition avoidable" with the "new view" that "conflict is inevitable." (In the adapted version, p. 131.)
3. "The New World Order: where life is cheap," *Asiaweek*, October 23, 1992. Original source: *Britannica World Order*, from Interpol and national crime statistics.
4. "King Coal's shrinking kingdom," *The Economist*, July 20, 1991.
5. This point is cited by Lincoln (1989), who compares unions in the United States and Japan.
6. Andrew S. Grove, "How to make confrontation work for you," *Fortune*, July 23, 1984.
7. G. Christian Hill and Ken Yamada, "Motorola's record shows giants can be nimble, too," *Asian Wall Street Journal*, December 10, 1992.
8. Reuters, "Unshaven Turks try a barefoot route to divorce," *Chicago Tribune*, May 17, 1989.
9. Thomas's (1976) basic model is developed and applied to multinational negotiations by Gladwin (1980). At point A, Thomas uses the term "competitive;" "forcing" has been substituted here in order to avoid confusion with the sense of "competitive" used in the previous section.
10. "Auto Union threatens strike at Hyundai," *Asian Wall Street Journal*, July 21, 1991.
11. Associated Press, "Executives settle dispute through arm-wrestling," *Bangkok Post*, March 22, 1992.
12. For instance, Pruitt (1983) notes that a withdrawal strategy is "available" to negotiators but does not find it worth discussion.
13. "Virgin's Revenge," *The Economist*, January 30, 1993.
14. M. G. G. Pilai, "Defiant PM in for trouble from Malays," *Bangkok Post*, June 19, 1987.

10

Negotiations

10.1 Introduction

Ian, a Briton, was negotiating in Jeddah with a Saudi Arabian bureau-crat, a senior hospital administrator. The deal was for specialized hospital equipment. The administrator gave every sign of being happy with the high-quality equipment offered and seemed about to settle, yet was never willing to totally commit himself. Ian was mystified. He was confident that the quality of his products and the terms asked were highly competitive. He proposed alternative schedules for payments, freight, delivery dates, and installation, but still his counterpart appeared uninterested. He began to wonder again about the Saudi's real interests in conducting the negotiation.

Then he remembered an early meeting in which he had started talking about his family background and had volunteered the information that his brother was a partner in a small bank in the City of London. And he recalled other conversations, in which the Saudi had indirectly alluded to his son's own interests in taking up a career in finance after completing his undergraduate studies. Suddenly the pieces fell into place!

Having met him a couple of times, Ian was confident of the young man's abilities, and telephoned his brother. Later that evening he suggested to the Saudi that his family in the United Kingdom would be very honored if Ahmed would care to visit them, and perhaps consider working for a spell in the family bank where his undoubted talents would be more than welcomed. The Saudi expressed his own interest in this original idea that promised to unite their families, and felt sure that his son would be happy to agree.

The contract was signed a few days later. Ahmed showed an immediate talent for banking, and introduced Ian's brother to a number of valuable connections. Everybody benefited.

This case shows the need to analyse the other person's real interests in a negotiation. It introduces the themes of developing a trusting relationship with your negotiation counterpart and the problems that arise when he/she belongs to some other culture. The chapter is organized as follows:

10.2 Preparing for an International Negotiation
10.3 Who Are They?
10.4 Why Negotiate?
10.5 How Should You Negotiate?
10.6 Implications for the Manager
10.7 Summary
10.8 Exercise

10.2 Preparing for an International Negotiation

All negotiations demand careful preparation, and this need is even greater when the other party belongs to a different nation and culture. A number of points have to be considered which are normally unimportant in domestic negotiations. Salacuse (1988) lists the following six:

- political and legal pluralism; for instance, transactions may be taxed in more than one country, and contracts may be subject to two or more legal systems;
- international monetary factors;
- the roles played by foreign governments and bureaucrats;
- instability and sudden political and economic changes – in some areas of the world;
- ideological differences;
- cultural differences (within a single culture, sub-cultural differences may be significant).

The more long-term the proposed deal, the greater the need for additional detail on the following.

Financial and economic data For instance, what national investment policies are followed? What subsidies and tax incentives are offered? How easily can you repatriate profits? What is the inflation rate? What financial security is offered your investment?

Infrastructure data One American company spent a year setting up a production deal with an East Asian company. Eventually, the CEO flew

Table 10.1 Access to telephone in six representative countries, 1992

Country	Numbers of people per telephone
United States	1.3
Hong Kong	2.0
Philippines	60.0
Vietnam	537.0
Nepal	686.0
Cambodia	790.0

in from Chicago to sign the contract. When he arrived at the East Asian headquarters, he announced that the traffic from the airport had been far worse than he had could ever have feared. If internal travel conditions were normally that bad, he did not understand how the proposed production schedule could be implemented; and so he felt unable to continue discussions. His reasoning may have been correct, but in practice he should have secured this information at a far earlier stage in the negotiations.

Similarly, you need to know about the availability, efficiency and cost of telecommunications, computer networking, and other hi-tech communications systems. For instance, access to telephones varies widely, as the 1992 figures in table 10.1 indicate.[1]

In some rapidly developing countries, where demand for telecommunications far surpasses supply, delays of several years may occur in securing a new installation;

Labor force data You need to know what skills are supplied on the labor market and at what prices; training facilities and educational structures; literacy rates; opportunities for employing groups who may not have contributed proportionately to the traditional workforce – for instance, women and minorities.

Legal data How will you be affected by legislation relating to employment? Hiring and firing? Redundancy and severance payments? Salary structures, wage rates and fringe benefits? Ownership of land, plant, technology, intellectual property? Business zoning and construction? Pollution and the environment? Ethical issues? How significant are religious codes? (In many societies, Islamic law is a major factor.)

Political data Who has power, who is contending for it, who is likely to have power in five years' time, what political beliefs do these various parties proclaim and what do they practice? How are political debates conducted? Who has trade union power, and how is it exercised?

Cultural data What values influence the design of structures and systems within the organization, and how are structures implemented? What values influence relationships with customers, suppliers, competitors, the government, others within the environment?

When preparing for a domestic negotiation, you may still need to consider such factors as zoning regulations, local laws and political factors, pools of immigrant labor. But in general, preparing for an international negotiation is bound to be more demanding – to the point that domestic and international negotiations are scarcely comparable.

In addition, you need information about the other organization. This includes:

- marketing data;
- competitors;
- alliances, trading partners;
- workforce data, labor relations;
- financial situation, including bank payment record;
- ownership and legal status;
- organizational structure and systems;
- technology;
- negotiating record;
- organizational culture.

10.2.1 Information about the negotiation

You are well prepared to the extent that you collect detailed information about the expected negotiation process. These questions are briefly examined below:

- where?
- when?
- what?

Questions arising over the identity of counterparts (who?), their reasons for negotiating (who?) and the style of negotiating (how?) are dealt with in sections 10.3, 10.4, and 10.5.

Answers must be found to the following:

Where will you negotiate? In theory, you hold the territorial advantage if you negotiate in your own premises (your headquarters, or local subsidiary); and failing that, on neutral ground (a hotel, a chamber of commerce). However, Salacuse and Rubin (1990) suggest that negotiating at their place enables you to hide from your own constituents in cases about which you would prefer the negotiation to be secret. The visit may give insights into their capacities and how they manage their operations.

When the other organization lacks capital, your visit may save their expenses (when costs incurred in travelling exceed those in hosting the negotiation) and thus express your concern and interest.

An American businessman started off running a hair-care company from his loft. Because this was an obviously unsuitable venue for dealing with clients, he always visited their offices. He comments, "*All* negotiations took place in enemy territory. If not, I would have quickly sunk!"[2]

A third alternative is that both sides conduct the negotiations from their own premises, linking by teleconferencing, videoconferencing, and fax. But this may not be advisable in a context where a personal meeting is valued. The following was written before the days of electronic conferencing, but is still valid.

> Arabs like to meet the seller. This is why it is easier to sell merchandise than a concept or a service. . . . [M]ost Arab firms have developed a reputation for being bad when it comes to correspondence. You want to do business? Then put up with long flights, heat, dust, overbooked hotels, interrupted business meetings. But meet them periodically. Do not assume that good correspondence will bring equally good results. It rarely does. . . . Drawn-out discussions, often with a good deal of digression, are the rule rather than the exception, even on relatively minor questions.[3]

When will you negotiate? If this is in some other country, when is the best time of year to negotiate? Climatic conditions may be significant if you expect negotiations to be lengthy. Check the dates of their religious and national holidays. For instance, negotiations with Muslims might be better timetabled than during the pilgrimage month of Ramadan, when strict believers fast from morn to dusk.

Is this a culture in which members are happy to continue negotiations after regular working hours and over weekends?

How much time should you allow to recover from jet lag, after arriving and before starting negotiating?

When traveling to some countries, you may need to acquire a passport visa, which may take sometime. This means that the visit can only be planned for several weeks or even months ahead. In addition, check what documentation is needed to support a visa and then entry – including health certification;

What do you need in order to negotiate abroad? If you want to use large quantities of display and other material which cannot be carried in luggage, how much time should be given for it to clear their customs department? Who will be responsible for taking delivery? Is it more convenient to have publicity and other material printed locally?

How much currency can be carried in, and what credit cards are commonly accepted?

With whom should gifts be exchanged? What gifts are appropriate and valued? What gifts can you expect to be given? This information may save embarrassment; in Japan, for instance, your hosts lose face if you reciprocate with a gift worth significantly more than that they give.

10.2.2   Sources of information

Chapter 2 lists a range of sources; at an early stage of the negotiation particular attention will be paid to

- official bodies;
- reports, etc.

And here is one further sources:

- an agent.

An agent should be able to advise on conditions within the local culture, economy, and organization. He/she has responsibilities for:

- advising on possibilities for business within the local context;
- introducing prospective business partners;
- arranging the negotiation and doing the groundwork;
- arranging official documentation in preparation for a negotiation within the local context (for instance, visas) and for implementing a contract (work permits, customs clearance, etc.);
- performing public relations and consultancy roles.

In cultures where personal relationships are particularly important in negotiating and implementing business deals, an agent cannot substitute for your personal intervention. A company that only deals through its agent may come to be distrusted. Nevertheless, his/her services are often essential in identifying likely counterparts and in making connections. An embassy, chamber of commerce, or other official bodies, should be able to advise on local agents who can be contacted.

10.3   Who Are They?

Before negotiating with another organization you need to research them. Data on their financial, marketing, and logistical profiles is needed.

What is their history of negotiating, and of implementing agreements? If negotiating a long-term alliance, information about the organizational structure, systems and climate will help you decide what sort of relationship will suit – and whether the cultures of the two organizations are well-matched for an international joint venture, for example. What history of international joint ventures, licensing agreements, (etc.), do they have?

High-context cultures place great importance on personal relationships. A member of a culture in Latin America, the Arab world, some of the Mediterranean countries and parts of Asia may focus his/her energies on developing their understanding and trust of the other person, and give less attention to the specifics of the deal.

Only when convinced of your integrity and reliability (at least so far as this specific deal is concerned) does he/she agree to settle. And perhaps relatively little time need be spent on discussion of details – terms of payment, delivery, quality and even price, details to which the Anglo business person is used to paying most attention.

This need for confidence in a counterpart is particularly strong in countries where the business person is unable to depend upon a strong and independent legal system to iron out business conflicts, and is forced to rely upon personal relationships for protection. This means that he/she will invest energy and intelligence in making an accurate reading of the other person's personality, and social and business connections.

An expatriate manager based in Ho Chi Minh City advises

> Vietnam's market has vast potential, but it takes time and effort to find solid local partners to form a joint venture, obtain and vet information, negotiate agreements and secure government approval. . . . There is a common saying among the barflies about doing business in Vietnam: "The government interprets the law for its friends, and applies the law to strangers." Vietnam is no place for strangers to do business. The foreign investment law is tailored to approve investments based on the government's view of how a company and its project will further certain economic and social objectives.[4]

The point, to spend time in getting to know and in getting to be known, applies throughout the region whether one is dealing with the public or private sector.

10.3.1 Who negotiates?

The other party's decisions about their representation at the negotiating table should also affect the composition of your team.

Choices of representation vary. Greek and Latin American top managers may prefer to maintain personal control of all aspects of the process, and so may head the team rather than delegate to a subordinate. The Mexican may be selected for his rhetorical skills. And research by Campbell et al. (1988) shows that negotiator characteristics are of major importance in negotiations between French business people; firms should consider sending representatives who are similar in background and personality to their French clients.

The identity of the other team is dealt with below in terms of

- numbers and functions;
- sex;
- age;
- rank.

Numbers and functions A single negotiator faces obvious difficulty if sent up against a team representating the full range of functions in the other organization.

When dealing with an organization in the People's Republic of China, expect a large team. This may include not only functional experts and administrators, but also representatives of local, provincial and national authorities. Similarly, a Japanese team represents a wide range of constituent groups within the organization, whose interests they have to take into consideration.

American teams often include a legal representative, and this may have adverse consequences when dealing with an Asian Pacific culture that stresses conciliation and compromise rather than conflict in business arrangements. For instance, *The Economist* magazine explains how

[c]ulture plays its part in Japan's aversion to legal recourse. A Japanese corporate lawyer says that if two companies sue each other any further business dealings between them become impossible. . . . [N]obody knows of a recent case that pitted two big Japanese companies against each other [in the courts].[5]

The attitudes held by the culture group towards courtroom litigation are also reflected in the size of the legal profession. The 1986 figures quoted in this magazine show a total of only 13,200 lawyers in Japan, or 11 per 100,000 people, compared with 655,000 or 279 per 100,000, in the United States.

The American inclusion of a lawyer may be intended to remove misunderstandings and to prevent any problems arising in the implementation phase, as much as because they mistrust the other side. Americans want to assume that their negotiation counterparts are telling the truth (Radnor, 1991). But many Asians prefer an element of ambiguity in the agreed settlement, which will be gradually dispelled in the course of implementation. (This point is developed in section 10.6.) And so it is understandable that Japanese should perceive American practice as hostile and threatening. Increasing numbers of Japanese firms are now beginning to follow this example of including lawyers in their negotiation teams – when dealing with Westerners.

Sex A team that includes women may be at an advantage in feminine cultures such as in Scandinavia, but not in a context where women are not normally accepted in business, for instance in the more traditional Arab countries.

Age An Anglo company may be mistaken in selecting a young high-flier to head a team negotiating with a Chinese or Japanese team. The Asian team is likely to be led by a senior and older person, who has high status, and who loses face if called upon to deal with a younger person as an equal. He may play little part in the detailed discussions, but take a significant "figurehead" role.

Rank The problem of matching team leaders is further complicated by the far wider currency of the title "Vice President" in United States organizations than in Japanese organizations. Whereas the United States company may have 20 or more VPs, a Japanese company of equivalent size has three or four.

The staff of one Tokyo firm were much put out to discover that a visiting American delegation were led by a "VP for computer services" – of far lesser importance than their own VPs and equivalent to a departmental manager. The visitors were kept waiting for 20 minutes outside the door until an officer of appropriate rank could be found to ceremonially welcome them in.

10.3.2 Who has authority?

The leader of the team may not be the person who makes the final decision on whether or not to settle on the negotiated terms.

A team in the People's Republic of China may have to report back to municipal, provincial and national authorities – and can use this as an excuse for delaying the final settlement, in hopes that the impatient Westerner (and in particular the American) will try to hasten the process by lowering his/her conditions (Graham and Herberger, 1983). The Chinese typically demand large quantities of technical information, and progress may be further delayed by time taken in digesting this.

A team from a market bureaucracy may also have to check with their constituents – departments not represented at the negotiation, unions, professional associations. Coming from an individualist culture, the leader perhaps resents these restrictions, and prefers to present him/herself as the person of authority. However, you risk losing face if talks take an unexpected turn and after all you are forced to check with head office. And the excuse for temporarily abdicating responsibility may be to your tactical advantage if it permits you to call time-out when a delay is to your advantage.

In all cultures, a team representing a family company may not be empowered to settle until they have consulted with stock-holding family members who are not present at the negotiation.

You can never take for granted that the person who does most of the talking has commensurate authority. The real decision-maker may be a person sitting silently in the corner and contributing nothing towards joint meetings, but who enjoys immense power behind the scenes. In the People's Republic of China the technical representatives may appear to be the most active members of the team, but the final decision is made by bureaucrats.

In some countries, delays in making the final decision arise because even members of the team are unsure as to who has authority. This problem occurs in countries once in the Soviet bloc, now working to develop their market economies, and still lacking regulatory controls. This was the experience of a United States company trying to mount a joint venture with a Hungarian corporation.

> Negotiations were "time consuming" – well over a year – "and tedious" . . . simply because there were no uniform procedures. Joint-venture laws had changed several times and have changed again since. Nobody – lawyers, officials or company managers – knew precisely what had to be done.[6]

10.4 Why Negotiate?

Assuming that it is dealing in good faith and really wants a negotiated settlement, the other party choose to negotiate because this offers them the best hopes of achieving their specific objectives, and because they trust you as a negotiation counterpart.

10.4.1 Objectives

The introductory case shows that the ostensive focus of a negotiation may not reflect the parties' real priorities. And you cannot necessarily deduce your counterpart's priorities from what is valued in your own culture. Cultural differences intensify the difficulty in identifying

- why the other party has chosen to come to negotiate;
- what they want to achieve;
- what you can offer that is likely to be valued.

Their objectives can be prioritized:

1. what they *must* achieve;
2. what they *hope* to achieve;
3. what they *would like* to achieve.

They are most concerned to achieve on level 1, and their objectives on level 3 are least essential.

How far does this list match your own objectives, in terms of what you *must* achieve, *hope* to achieve, and *would like* to achieve? This early preparation helps you identify

(a) what you are *most willing* to concede in order to achieve your essential objectives;
(b) what you are *moderately willing* to concede;
(c) what you are *least willing* to concede.

You hope for a match between 1 and (a); they most value what you are most willing to concede. For instance, their priority is that the goods should be transported by an early date (to meet a seasonal demand) and early transportation presents you with fewest problems (because the goods are already in production). The introductory case shows a negotiator able to achieve settlement because he can offer a service which is greatly desired by his counterpart but which costs him nothing – a job for his counterpart's son.

An international negotiation in which different local interests are at stake offers a wide range of opportunities for making and offering attractive concessions. These include opportunities for bartering and countertrading, which require a high degree of entrepreneurial zeal and flexibility to find and develop. A small firm may be at an advantage. In 1993, a Czech import–export service, Transakta, won a European award for its success in bartering technology for imported consumer goods. (Prizes also went to firms in Latvia and Gabon.)[7] Your capacity to capitalize upon opportunities is dependent upon your understanding of the local environment, including the national and organizational cultures.

10.4.2 The importance of trust

If you have no trust in your counterparts, then you are unlikely to enter negotiations with them, or to agree to a settlement. Trust is all important. However, it is not always clear what the notion of "trust" entails, and you may have considerable difficulty in deciding how far you can trust someone from another culture whose values differ from your own.

The more trusting both sides are of each other, the more willing they are to resolve their problems. But this does not guarantee that they enter negotiations prepared to make concessions. If they trust you but also sense that you are prepared to make major concessions and will buckle under pressure, they may make non-negotiable demands and otherwise refuse to cooperate (Pruitt and Rubin, 1986).

You trust the other side when you believe in the truthfulness of what the other party says. But this may not be enough. You also need to believe in their good intentions. This means accepting the following.

- It is in their interests to do business with you. They will negotiate in good faith. Writing about negotiations in the People's Republic of China, Pye (1982) makes clear that you cannot depend upon feelings of empathy and the other side's expressions of personal warmth. You need a clear assessment of their objectives and interests – and this means investing time in preparation.
- They will not resort to unethical behavior during the negotiation process – for instance, by tapping your communications with head office or by making announcements to the media that are intended to force your hand.
- They will respect information and opinions made in confidence and not leak these to outsiders.
- They will do their best to convince their constituents to accept any agreements that they make with you. This may be an issue when your counterpart comes from a highly individualist culture and widens the scope of the negotiation without prior consultations with other interested parties, or represents a heterogeneous organization in which the interests of different constituents are in potential conflict. Such problems are less likely when negotiating with a Japanese team, for instance. The Japanese negotiator comes to the table having already discussed with other departments in his organization the terms under which to settle, and cannot accept substantial modifications without checking back.
- They will do their best to implement your agreement.

Perhaps you feel that you can trust them – and even if you do not it might be wise to feign trust until you have a clearer picture of their real interests. But how far do they trust you? Their behavior may give you a more reliable guide to the level of trust than formal expressions of friendship, and real trust may take a long time to cultivate. For instance, Russians respond to unknown outsiders with fear and suspicion, yet this is balanced by strong loyalty to those outsiders with whom they are able

Table 10.2 Most trusting and most suspicious countries

Most trusting	United States
∨	Thailand
	Spain
	South Africa
∧	Japan
Most suspicious	Greece

Source: Harnett and Cummings (1980)

to develop personal relationships – which are essential (Rajan and Graham, 1991). Despite their reputation for driving a very hard bargain, Russians abide by the negotiated provisions of a contract – and expect the other party to do the same.

Research indicates generally that where there is high trust, negotiators are more likely to take a mutual problem-solving approach and to share information, even about their profit schedules. But where trust is low, they tend instead to depend heavily upon persuasive arguments, threats and other forms of contentious behavior (Kimmel et al., 1980).

10.4.3   The meaning of trust in different cultures

Different cultures are more or less willing to trust the other side in a negotiation, and more or less suspicious. Harnett and Cummings (1980) order six representative countries as shown in table 10.2.[8]

Hofstede's (1984a, pp. 132–3) model does nor explicitly refer to trust or suspicion of negotiating partners. Shane (1993) suggests that low degrees of interpersonal trust correlate with high-power distance; he cites Williams et al.'s (1966) study showing greater trust among workers in the United States (low-power distance) than in Peru (high-power distance), and Neghandi and Prasad's (1971) study finding low trust in Argentina, Brazil and Uruguay (all high-power distance).

Needs to avoid uncertainty also appear significant. Hofstede (1984a) associates low needs to avoid uncertainty with employee optimism about the motives behind company activities, and with a greater readiness to compromise with opponents – both of which seem to indicate trust. And his rankings for these six countries largely correlates with the Harnett and Cummings (1980) rankings (see table 10.3).

Needs for strong uncertainty avoidance also indicate "suspicion towards foreigners as managers," and "greater aggressiveness versus other nations" (Hofstede, 1984a, pp. 133, 142). Hence an outsider might expect to work harder in building trust with a Greek negotiating partner than with an American.

Table 10.3 Hofstede's rankings (Uncertainty Avoidance Index)

Lowest needs to avoid uncertainty	United States
	South Africa
	Thailand
	Spain
	Japan
Highest needs to avoid uncertainty	Greece

Source: Hofstede (1984a)

When dealing with a new market in a less developed country, it is often important to invest energy to familiarize potential customers with the company's products. Research conducted in the People's Republic of China underlined the importance of visiting potential customers, informing them of the product range, and trying to understand their needs (McGuinness et al., 1991). Representation through agents is unlikely in itself to create strong customer preferences.

10.4.4 The duration of the relationship

A lengthy duration offers obvious advantages; the businessman who counts upon a long-standing supplier has a guaranteed source, can hope for discounts, and is saved the costs of finding a new supplier.

This introduces a practical question. How far should the negotiator try to win as much as possible from a single negotiation with a new counterpart, and how far make concessions when these seem likely to build towards a continuing relationship? In one sense, these are not alternatives; ideally, he/she would like both. However, the emphasis placed on long- or short-term expectations can significantly influence perceptions of interests, and decisions about what issues should be placed on the agenda.

Business relationships of long duration can occur in Anglo countries and elsewhere in the West; Hallen et al. (1987) found examples in the United Kingdom, and also in Sweden and Germany. Nevertheless Anglo negotiators tend to focus on the advantages offered from a single deal (Bazerman et al., 1985). And a negotiation is likely to be evaluated in terms of how many immediate options are developed. For instance, Fisher and Ury (1983) regret that

> [i]n most people's minds, inventing simply is not part of the negotiating process. People see their jobs as narrowing the gap between positions, not broadening the options available. ... By looking from the outset for a single best answer, you are likely to short-circuit a wiser decision-making

process in which you select from a large number of possible answers. (p. 61)

This proposal, to create a comprehensive agenda, is not culture-free. First, it reflects a context that tolerates ambiguity, and hence risk, competition, and even conflict. These conditions occur less frequently in cultures with higher needs to avoid uncertainty, and where increased complexity entails greater anxiety. Second, in contexts in which the negotiator is committed to absentee constituents who do not tolerate his/her taking initiatives, he/she is inhibited from brainstorming the range of options available.

Third, it takes for granted the advantages of sorting out as much business as possible within a single negotiation rather than setting up a stream of restricted but related deals. However, where long-lasting relationships are valued and the negotiators expect to have to do business again on a regular basis, greater importance may be associated with finding a solution that maintains the relationship and motivates the parties to deal together in the future. That is, criteria of success or failure attach to a stream of negotiations in which trade-offs are made on a sequential basis (I gain this time, you gain next time) rather than to a single event.

Cultures with longer-term orientations towards relationships place a greater stress on achieving harmony in a negotiated settlement. (Hofstede, 1991, ch. 7). The Japanese value long-term commitments in which trust has developed (Johnson et al., 1990). Harnett and Cummings (1980, p. 144) showed Japanese and Thai bargainers working harder to achieve an even split in final profit between buyers and sellers than either European or United States bargainers. Their United States buyers achieved the largest average profits, possibly because of greater success in manipulating structural features (for instance, numbers and roles of participants, external pressures, information given).

10.4.5   Duration in cross-cultural relationships

How far can an outsider to a culture hope to develop a long-term relationship with its members, and hence to gain preference? Johnson et al.'s (1990) study of Japanese distributors of United States products indicated that even when their relationships were long-term, American suppliers enjoyed little success influencing their Japanese business partners, whether or not a third-party mediator was used. Further research is needed to show show how far the same issue arises between countries with similar cultural profiles – for instance, when one is high-context, and generally inhospitable to foreign influence.

Market factors may determine circumstances in which culture is *not* a factor. If the seller monopolizes the supply of goods or services in question, then the buyer has no choice *but* to deal with them. For instance, Japanese suppliers have monopolized many auto parts in the United States, and auto manufacturers have no alternative suppliers.

10.4.6 Business relationships in the People's Republic of China

Pye (1982) and other scholars have focused on the difficulties facing Western firms in building strong and enduring relationships with their customers in the People's Republic of China. In the initial stages, the Chinese play up notions of friendship, mutual interest, and the importance of shared trust, then appeal to these "principles" at later meetings in order to shame their counterparts into giving the best possible terms.

The McGuinness et al. (1991) study, conducted with German, Swiss, United Kingdom, Italian, Japanese, and French companies dealing with the Chinese), shows that foreign suppliers are in danger of overvaluing promises of long-term relationships, particularly when product or service quality is an issue. The Chinese most frequently evaluated relationships in a utilitarian manner that reflected the value of the package. That is, the traditional Chinese approach to relationships with suppliers appeared to be fading in significance – at least so far as those outside the Chinese system were concerned.

Many foreign firms have made the mistake of not listening closely enough to what Chinese firms ask for, and what they can offer, and have wandered into alliances that do not suit either of their long-term interests (Simon, 1990).

Other research shows that Chinese negotiators tend to compete fiercely and take a long time before finally agreeing on terms – partly because of the need to consult with other authorities within the political and administrative environment. When problems arise, they may take pains to place the blame on the foreign team – which is consistent with the general tendency of the Chinese to use shaming techniques to influence behavior (Frankenstein, 1986).

10.5 How Should You Negotiate?

The topic of *how* to negotiate is dealt with here in terms of how relationships can be developed and maintained.

This emphasis reflects the notions that negotiation is first and foremost a communications activity, and that problems arise in cross-cultural negotiations when the communication is culturally and situationally inappropriate. In Elgström's (1990) words:

> Culture influences negotiation through its effects on communication. Intercultural differences may cause misperceptions and misunderstandings. Failure to appreciate the cultural patterns of opponents is detrimental to the quality of the decision-making process. An actor's culture-bound images of self, the other actor, and the situation seem to be vital ingredients in understanding negotiating behavior. (pp. 157–8)

Like all communications, a negotiation must be appropriately structured. Graham and Herberger (1983) identify four stages to negotiations, which have varying importances in different cultures. They are:

1. non-task relationship creation;
2. task-related exchange of information;
3. persuasion;
4. concession and agreement.

Many negotiations may not pass through such a clearly defined chronology. Perhaps persuasion is significant at all stages; even when first introducing yourself, you hope to persuade the other person that you are a good person to deal with.

Clear structuring is likely to be preferred in cultures where needs to avoid uncertainty are high (Hofstede, 1989), particularly where the relationship is new and therefore stressful. But where the parties are both trying to brainstorm their way towards a more complex agenda and wider range of options, attempting to adhere to a rigid structure is counterproductive.

In low-context cultures (such as Germany and Switzerland) initial relationship creation may be passed over fairly rapidly, perhaps assuming greater significance when the deal has been signed. In high-context cultures, this is a very important function throughout the process; that is, the decision whether or not to sign may depend very largely on the capacity of the counterparts to project sympathetic and reliable personalities. As Graham and Herberger (1983) point out, in many countries

> the heart of the matter, the point of the negotiation, is not so much information and persuasion, as it is to get to know the people involved. In Brazil much time is spent in developing a strong relationship of trust before business can begin. Americans to the Brazilian way of doing business are particularly susceptible to the "wrist watch syndrome." In the United States looking at your watch almost always gets things moving along.

However, in Brazil, impatience causes apprehension, thus necessitating ever-longer periods of non-task sounding. (p. 163)

Whereas low-context cultures get quickly down to business, high-context cultures first establish the relationship, and the implication for visitors is that they should first learn about expectations regarding hospitality. One American businessman suggests that at a first meeting in Brazil you should expect to spend two hours in general discussion before even mentioning the topic of your business, and in Bolivia, three hours.

Many Anglos experience difficulties in handling this apparently undirected activity. They are uncomfortable spending time developing a relationship with a business acquaintance, particularly when this involves making general conversation. They are inclined to introduce the business interest early in the conversation and to focus on this.

Cultural priorities influence what topics should be introduced into this informal communication. Here are some examples. In Mexico you can usually ask your host about his wife and children. In Saudi Arabia, never do; he will be particularly unwilling to answer questions about pubescent daughters. In Latin America, you show your sophistication by being able to discuss the region's rich literature. A few topics have world-wide appeal – soccer for one.[9]

10.5.1 Exchanging business cards

In some cultures, the beginning of a relationship is symbolized by the exchange of business cards. In Japan and Korea, formally present cards at the beginning of every first-time meeting, first to the most important member of their team and then to other members in descending order of importance. One implication is that you need to be very well supplied with cards when making an extensive business trip in these countries. No further exchange with these persons should be made, unless you wish to present a new card giving significantly different information. By giving the same card to the same person at a later meeting, you imply that you have forgotten him/her, and this may be taken as a deliberate insult.

In these cultures, etiquette is involved in giving and receiving cards. The card should be presented with the other person's language face up – presuming that you have taken the trouble to have your cards translated into the local language. (In general, have your language printed on one side, the local language on the other. Including more than one other language on the card may be a false saving; for instance, many business people in the Middle East may be offended by being given a card printed in both Arabic and Hebrew.) Always take a few seconds reading the other person's card carefully. In Korea, an audible intake of breath – in respect for his/her title – is appropriate.

At a meeting, each person places the cards before him on the table, where they are left for several minutes and possibly for the duration.

Anglos invest far less formality in card-presentations, and may exchange them only at the end of a meeting to serve as reminders. Germans include their full academic and professional titles – and expect to be addressed by them.

10.5.2 Adapting to their cultural values

How far should you try to adapt to the other person's cultural values when negotiating? Experimental evidence suggests that Americans are more likely to be sympathetic to moderate adaptation than to either none or to substantial adaptation (Francis, 1991). But how far is this true for the culture group with whom you are dealing?

There may be strategic advantages in NOT attempting to adapt too closely to the other person's value system. One American manager with many years of Asian Pacific experience explains why:

> [I]n the beginning stages of negotiation, acting according to the expectations of the opposed negotiators helps the process considerably. This means performing to their stereotype of the American in Asia. First, everybody I do business with is well travelled, multi-lingual, and familiar with Americans. They are not readily offended or confused over cultural differences such as . . . using a knife and fork instead of chopsticks. Second, by performing to their stereotype it makes them feel knowledgeable. Their previous experiences with Americans are being tested and confirmed. . . . For them, I appear a predictable entity.

This manager speaks local languages and knows the cultures well. By down-playing his real level of experience, he has a covert advantage on business opposites who underestimate him.

10.5.3 Interpreters

A Malaysian used to dealing with Anglos always brings an interpreter to negotiations – although he speaks English fluently. When his counterpart addresses the interpreter, and when the interpreter translates into his Chinese dialect, he has twice the time to plan his answer, a second bite of the apple.

The interpreter should be properly briefed. The International Association of Conference Interpreters always tells clients that "if you are not prepared to trust an interpreter with confidential information, don't use one." The failure to provide in advance background information and specialized terminology involved in complex negotiations makes the interpreters' job all the more difficult, [the Association president] says.[11]

In addition, interpreters are most efficient when you

- speak slowly and carefully;
- explain complex ideas more than once;
- speak no more than a few sentences at a time;
- do not interrupt the interpretation.

They should be treated with respect. An interpreter who is reprimanded in front of his/her fellow nationals loses face, and is alienated. And an alientated interpreter is more likely to constitute a security risk.

But mistakes do happen. For instance, in a United States–Israeli negotiation "it goes without saying" was interpreted as equivalent to "it walks without talking;" and in a United States–Russian negotiation, "the spirit's willing but the flesh is weak" as equivalent to "the vodka is strong but the meat is undercooked." When President Carter visited Poland in 1977, he used a Polish-speaking American who rephrased Carter's "when I left the United States" as "when I abandoned the United States."

Such gaffes occur when the interpreter has less than intimate knowledge of the other language.

Speak towards your opposite number rather than the interpreter. In Japan, a British businessman was dealing with a senior executive who brought along his junior to act as interpreter.

The Briton spoke directly to the negotiator

> as if I was negotiating with him. The senior executive . . . rejected my proposal. He believed I wasn't giving him the attention he deserved, and took it as a sign of disrespect.

10.5.4 Concessions

You hope to gain disproportionately from the concessions you make. That is, you hope that the other side most value what you are most willing to concede. However, this does not mean that you should belittle your concessions; "I'm more than happy to give you X – and as a matter of fact, it is of no importance to me." This not only insults their aspirations and perhaps cause them to rethink their objectives; it also increases your difficulty in demanding significant concessions in return. And in general, link each concession with a demand; "If you will accept my X, I will agree to your Y."

Formal analytical models give help in assessing the values of various trade-offs and what values they have on the dynamics of negotiations (Raiffa, 1982). However, cultures vary in terms of when concessions are offered, and what size of concessions are offered, and formal models may be of limited assistance in evaluating a particular concession made at a specific point in the proceedings.

For instance, research by Graham (1985) suggests that Brazilians tend to demand more than either North Americans or Japanese. The Japanese ask for higher profits when making an initial offer, and are then consistent in making small concessions throughout. The Americans are more likely to make larger initial concessions. Another study shows North Americans making small concessions early in order to build the relationship and usually reciprocating concessions; Arabs making concessions throughout and almost always reciprocating; and Russians making very few and viewing concessions made by the other side as a sign of weakness. (Glenn et al., 1984).

In Mexico, allow a margin for bargaining when making a proposal; but do not overinflate your initial figure or the Mexican may feel exploited. In Germany, you can expect little elasticity in the price; negotiations tend to focus on technical details and quality (Copeland and Griggs, 1985, p. 243).

10.5.5 Implementation

In some cultures, the negotiation process effectively ends when the contract is signed; elsewhere, it may not.

In Anglo cultures the action of signing a contract symbolizes an intention to fulfill the stated terms. For instance, in the United States, the outcomes of marketing negotiations are determined primarily by events at the negotiation table (Campbell et al., 1988). And the legal advisor is included in the team in order to reduce the level of misunderstanding and conflict after signing. The business person with a reputation for constantly attempting to renegotiate contracts is not trusted.

Elsewhere, this may not be the case. The contract does not represent finality in the discussions, but rather an honest intention to do business along the lines agreed, all other things being equal and in the light of foreseeable events.

For instance, Frankenstein (1986) suggests that implementation, rather than signing the contract, is the final stage to negotiating in the People's Republic of China.

> Rather than a straightforward realization of the contract, there is a continuing process of adjustment and discussion. Sometimes, the research

suggests, the Chinese side tries to expand the scope of the agreement; they refer back to the general principles agreed at the onset of the talks and base their demands on the requirements of mutual equality and friendship. (p. 149)

And describing the same context, Pye (1982) reports the surprise felt by many of his informants

that the Chinese brought up proposals for revising what had been agreed upon, right on the heels of signing a contract. Thus although they are reportedly scrupulous in adhering to agreements, they have no inhibitions in proposing changes. (p. 78)

A United States businessman with extensive experience of negotiating with family companies in the Asian Pacific region reports

When the Chinese negotiate a contract, they never argue at the beginning, they argue when they implement it. An American contract, you argue at the beginning and keep quiet when the contract is signed.

This has implications for the specialist negotiator's responsibilities. He/she cannot assume that once a contract has been signed where such conditions apply, his/her responsibilities are at end. Rather, the negotiator needs to keep aware of all stages of implementation lest he/she is called back to the table.

A final example comes from Thailand. In 1993, the Bangkok Expressways Company Limited (BECL) completed construction of an expressway contracted (indirectly) by the Bangkok Metropolitan Authority (BMA). The project was worth US$1.08 billion. The original contract had guaranteed a toll of US$1.20, apparently to be collected by BECL. On completion, the BMA argued that political pressures forced them to demand a reduction of the toll to US$0.8; the right to collect tolls; and rebuilding of some exits and entrances that were too narrow and dangerous.

When re-negotiations got underway, a government mediator

reminded the two parties to take into consideration the public interest and asked them to continue their talks in a friendly atmosphere, bearing in mind their long term interests and the fact they have to cooperate with each other for the next 27 years.[12]

These factors were given precedence over issues of narrowly defined legality in the talks that followed.

10.6 Implications for the Manager

This section deals with issues that need preparing in advance of a cross-cultural negotiation.

1. In which of these areas do you need more data?

    - about the other country:

        (a) financial and economic situation, policy, prospects;
        (b) infrastructure;
        (c) labor force and employment;
        (d) laws and legal system;
        (e) political situation;
        (f) culture;
        (g) other;

    - about the other organization:

        (h) marketing data
        (i) competitors;
        (j) alliances, partners;.
        (k) workforce data, labor relations;
        (l) financial situation;
        (m) ownership and legal status;
        (n) organizational structure and systems;
        (o) technology;
        (p) negotiating record;
        (q) organizational climate;
        (r) other.

2. From what sources can you collect this information?

3. Given what you know of the other organization's national culture, organizational culture and history of negotiating:

    - who can you expect to be included in their team?
    - who might lead their team?
    - who, on their side, has authority to decide on a settlement?
    - who should you include in your team?

        (a) a senior and elderly member (or retired member), whose functions may be mostly ceremonial;
        (b) a person who will be responsible for implementing any settlement;
        (c) a general manager;

(d) a technical specialist;
(e) a member of an ethnic minority;
(f) a male/female;
(g) any others.

- Which of these persons should lead your team?
- how much authority to settle should be given to

(a) team leader?
(b) other members of the team?
(c) persons not present at the negotiation?

- Who else needs to be consulted before you agree to settle?

4. Assess objectives and prepare concessions.

- So far as you can, prioritize their needs from the negotiation.
- Identify concessions they might be willing to make.
- Prioritize your own needs.
- Identify and prioritize the concessions that you might be willing to make.
- Attempt to match their and your needs, their and your concessions.

5. In the two cultures, how do personal relationships between negotiators typically affect the negotiation process?

- In your culture, how important is it that you should have good personal relationships with your counterparts?
- How far do you trust them? What factors contribute towards this trust (or lack of it)?
- In their culture, how important is it that they should have good personal relationships with their counterparts?
- How far do they trust you? What factors contribute towards this trust (or lack of it)?
- What can you do in order to increase their trust in you?
- How important is it that your relationship be long-term?
- If it is important, what can you do in order to develop the relationship – without giving up your short-term interests?

6. Should a settlement be agreed, what expectations do you have that problems will arise in the implementation phase?

- What steps can you take to protect your interests during the implementation phase, and without unnecessarily damaging your personal relationship with your counterparts?

10.7   Summary

This chapter has examined how far cultural difference influences international negotiations.

Section 10.2 showed the importance of *preparing for an international negotiation*. When considering a long-term investment, the negotiator needs to take account of country-risk factors. When the negotiation will be held overseas, he/she also needs data about the specifics of the process: Where will you negotiate? When will you negotiate? What do you need in order to negotiate?

The chapter then focused on cultural factors. Section 10.3 asked *Who are they?*, and dealt with identity issues; who, in different cultures, is chosen to negotiate on behalf of the organization, and who has authority for agreeing to a settlement. Section 10.4 asked a further question: *Why should they negotiate?* It examined the problems of analysing both your own and your counterparts' needs, and the opportunities that a cross-cultural negotiation presents for designing valued concessions. The notion of trust between negotiators was discussed. Their readiness to trust is influenced by needs to avoid uncertainty.

Section 10.5 asked *How should you negotiate?*, and focused on how notions of counterpart relationships affect the process. The point was made finally that the status of a signed contract varies across cultures. In some contexts, negotiations can be expected to continue through the implementation phase of an agreement.

10.8   Exercise

Decide what went wrong in the case below, and how the conflict could have been avoided.

A major Canadian industrialist signed a property deal with a Chinese Indonesian businessman with whom he had hitherto enjoyed a long and mutually profitable association. At first, everything went well; then the Indonesian began suffering acute losses in his core business, and began withdrawing funds from the property investment in order to cover the shortfall. After a few months, the Canadian decided to take action. Tied up with other work, he sent over his legal advisor on a fact-finding mission in order to discover what had happened, and to find a basis for negotiating a compromise.

The Chinese had not previously heard of this lawyer, and first learned of his presence in the country when he received a phone call from the airport. "I am Mr X's legal advisor. He has asked me to find a solution to his problems."

The Chinese was proud of his status as an independent and successful entrepreneur. He was used to dealing only with persons of equivalent status, and was not prepared to negotiate on equal terms with a "servant." He responded by delaying, and finally refusing to meet his partner's emissary. After spending three days kicking his heels in a hotel, the lawyer returned to Toronto. The Canadian responded by taking his counterpart to court in a series of expensive actions.

Notes

1. "Vital Signs," *Asiaweek*, February 14, 1992.
2. I am grateful to Mr Robert McCann for this example.
3. Ananda Rao, "Rebuilding Arabia," *Asiaweek*, March 1, 1991. Reprinted from *Asiaweek*, May 6, 1977.
4. Michael J. Scown, "Manager's journal: barstool advice for the Vietnam investor," *Asian Wall Street Journal*, July 15, 1993.
5. "A law unto itself," *The Economist*, August 22, 1987.
6. "A bicycle made by two," *The Economist*, June 8, 1991.
7. "Insider: Don't overlook Latvia" (source: The European), *Bangkok Post*, July 19, 1993.
8. These figures from Harnett and Cummings (1980) omit the writers' rankings for two very disparate groups, "Scandinavia" consisting of Denmark and Finland, and "Central Europe" consisting of Belgium, France, Switzerland, and England.
9. "A nice one-two in the suburbs," *The Economist*, August 18, 1990.
10. I am grateful to Mr Lawnin Crawford for this observation.
11. Barry James, "Interpreting: Perils of Palaver," *International Herald Tribune*, January 11, 1991.
12. "Deputy Premier lays down the law on expressway negotiations," *Bangkok Post Weekly Review*, June 18, 1993.

Culture and Ethics

11.1 Introduction

A senior Filipino executive of an American subsidiary based in Metro Manila and an American executive from the Chicago headquarters together interviewed a Filipino seeking promotion to the position of payroll manager.

When they came to the dimension of "integrity," the interviewers asked: "Everyone has to bend or break the rules sometime. Can you give an example of when you had to do this?" The candidate had never broken any major company rules. But he confessed to once helping a colleague who had asked him to issue a letter certifying his salary at a higher level than was true, in order that he could qualify for a bank loan. He had decided that he could not easily deny his colleague, who was a close friend and undergoing difficulties. So he calculated a salary figure that included bonus and other allowances, and certified this as the basic salary.

The Filipino interviewer ranked him as acceptable on this dimension. He valued the candidate's sensitivity towards people in need, and his consideration for the harmony of the work group.

He did not consider the subterfuge to be serious. But the American did. Seeing no reason why the candidate should not have denied the request, he ranked the candidate as weak. The differences between the interviewers was only resolved when the American washed his hands of the process, insisting that the Filipino take responsibility for any problems that arose in making the promotion.

The main idea pursued in this chapter is that ethical norms vary across cultures. The cross-cultural manager cannot assume that he and counterparts from another culture share the same code, nor that his/her own is necessarily superior.

The chapter has the following sections:

11.2   Ethics

Broad ethical norms are shared around the world. The major religions all condemn murder, theft, lying, and so on. However, the practical implications are far more controversial, and sincere and ethical individuals have serious problems in agreeing on how far the prohibition on murder, for instance, includes killing

- in defence of your own life;
- a burglar breaking into your house;
- an enemy soldier in time of war;
- an enemy civilian in time of war;
- a spouse who commits adultery;
- animals, for pleasure;
- vermin and insects (killing even these forms of life is forbidden to some Buddhist sects).

Deciding between right and wrong is not easy when different ethical values are in conflict. An illustration is provided by the case of a Turkish entrepreneur, nearly 80 years old, whose empire included real estate, a packaging plant, a textile producer, and 37 shopping centers, but was originally based on brothels – of which she still owned 11:

> she commands more respect than ever for her individualist streak, her fierce loyalty to the Turkish state, her generosity toward the poor, and the fact that she paid about $9 million in income tax last year ...

"Paying taxes is an honor," she says, making a point of her respectability in at least one area. "I never considered ripping off the state."[1]

So should she be praised for her patriotism, charity, and fiscal honesty, or condemned for profiting from prostitution? If condemned, should you do business with her? The immam of the local mosque was unwilling to accept her charity.

"We have a word in Islam, haram, which means forbidden . . . Money that was earned through haram cannot be used to serve Allah." The immam nevertheless is reluctant to come down too hard on Manoykyan. His predecessor tried and was forced to retire.[2]

The immam's problem is both practical and ethical. If he accepts her money, he transgresses religious law; if he refuses it, he risks insulting her, and experience shows that she is prepared to exercise her power.

11.2.1   Changes in ethical perceptions

The problems of deciding what behavior is ethical are further complicated when values seem to change across time.

Thirty years ago, few people thought of cigarette smoking as an ethical problem. But now, the medical dangers of "passively" inhaling smoke from another person's cigarette are generally recognized, and in some societies public smoking is "politically incorrect." Does this change arise from new values attached to anti-social behavior, or from new evidence that smoking is a public health hazard?

Here are two further examples of apparent change. During the 1960s and 1970s, the Japanese became wearily used to their politicians taking pay-offs, and seemed willing to tolerate it for so long as the economy continued to grow at its previous rates. But in the early 1980s, the economy began to slow down.

In 1984, a company called Recruit Cosmos offered dozens of client politicians, civil servants, business people and others the chance to purchase preflotation shares before they were sold publicly in 1986. This was not simply an issue of insider trading – which in 1984, was not illegal in Japan. It illustrated business patronage in an extreme form. The recipients, who were able to recoup their investments at a 100 percent profit or more, were in many cases expected to perform favors for the company.

There had been little reaction to previous scandals – for instance, the Lockheed case. But on this occasion the Japanese erupted in disgust and shame. When the scandal was exposed in 1988, the public furore led to prosecutions, disgrace, at least one suicide, and the fall of the then Prime Minister – who was personally implicated. Many observers were puzzled by this reaction.

Experts agree that none of the revelations would have had such shock value if Japan's middle class had not begun to feel a bit beleagured itself . . .

The problem is that most Japanese say they do not feel rich, and Japan's success may have brought a polarization of feelings that could have far-reaching political consequences in the future. ... Thus young people starting out in Tokyo, who can no longer afford to buy a house or who have to spend hours each day commuting to work, are increasingly resentful of those who are making it big and who seem heedless to the plight of everyone else.[3]

In other words, social factors generated envy, and envy is a powerful spur to action. Whether or not these patronage relationships and the purchase of political favors were previously regarded as unethical, the decision to sanction such behavior was animated by factors within the context.

This further case suggests that forces in the external environment played some part in a society reordering its ethical priorities. In Argentina in 1991, the need to "gain international credibility ... and attract foreign investment" forced President Menem's government to investigate a string of scandals that seemed to involve even the President's family. This was a change from the past, when foreign opinion was ignored (at great expense) and

> military governments and the Peronist party concentrated so much power in the executive branch that the leaders could keep a lid on any scandal.
>
> "For so long we lived with such an absence of law or with a law so arbitrary that it did not permit one to question what was good or bad and created a perversion of perception," said Marta Sauane, a psychologist. "This is similar to the development of an individual: When you educate someone using no limits whatsoever, it is very difficult for that person to understand what are the proper norms of action."[4]

This chapter focuses on how far practical considerations of dealing with the environment influence ethical perceptions.

11.2.2 Ethics in business

Interest in business ethics has blossomed since the mid-1980s, thanks largely to a long list of scandals involving organizations and individuals across the world. They include the cases of Salomon Brothers, Drexel Burnham Lambert (United States); Banco Ambrosiano, Olivetti, Fiat (Italy); Robert Maxwell, Guinness (United Kingdom); Alan Bond (Australia); Triangle Corporation (France); Bank of Credit and Commerce International (Luxembourg and elsewhere); Carrian (Hong Kong and Malaysia); Pan-Electric (Malaysia and Singapore); Recruit, Sagawa Kyubin and Kinemaru Shin (Japan), among others.

What role can ethics play in business? Carroll (1987) suggests the following:

[m]oral management strives to be ethical in its focus on ethical norms, professional standards of conduct, motives, goals, orientation towards the law, and general operating strategy. (Carroll, 1987, p. 9)

But how should this be interpreted in practice? In abstract terms, the easy solution is to adopt the extreme view, that the manager should be committed to the letter of the code, whatever the outcome.

As one recent treatise on business ethics put it, "If in some instance it turns out that what is ethical leads to a company's demise, so be it."

Back in the real world, however, no businessman is going to sacrifice his company on the altar of such altruistic extremism.[5]

And even an extreme solution is likely to be ambiguous in practice. For instance, suppose that your company bans acceptance of gifts from customers. This appears cut and dried, but the decision to refuse a gift is not so straightforward

- when the customer is a family member;
- at a religious festival, when gifts are normally exchanged;
- when non-acceptance will be construed as a serious insult; your firm will lose the contract, and many of your colleagues will be thrown out of work;
- when your agent offers to accept the gift on your behalf, and to deduct the proceeds from his expense account.

Moral absolutism may be unrealistic, and some experts argue that ethics has no place in management, that a firm's main responsibility is to make profits, and that business is morally neutral. Carr (1968) argues that the practicing manager sometimes takes decisions that happen to coincide with ethical ideals, but

the major tests of every move in business, as in all games of strategy, are legality and profit. A man who intends to be a winner in the business game must have a game player's attitude. (p. 148)

(See also Wolfe, 1993; Drucker, 1981; Carr, 1968. For responses to Carr see Blodgett, 1968).

Nevertheless, there appear to be definite benefits in enforcing some sort of ethical framework. Many companies would prefer to take a mid-way position (reflecting, for instance, the pragmatism of Stark, 1993). They perceive that a reputation for ethical behavior is profitable; a study by Becker and Fritzsche (1987) found evidence that French, German, and United States managers overwhelmingly agreed that in the long run sound ethics was good business.

When employees are given practical codes of conduct to follow and these are applied consistently to all members of the organization, an area of moral ambiguity is removed. Morale rises, and the sense of organizational identity, "the way we do things around here," is reinforced. And when no ethical norms are applied, or are applied so wilfully that no member of the organization can predict what behavior will be punished and what rewarded, initiatives are stifled and standards slide.

The company formulates guidelines for its employees defining

- which business activities are ethical, and which are unethical; for instance, what forms of bluffing are acceptable in a negotiation? what presents may be given to business partners, and when does present-giving and acceptance constitute corruption? what information can an employer legitimately demand from a job applicant, to whom can this be communicated, and how truthful should he/she be in communicating information about the company to the applicant? (Bies and Moag, 1986);
- how managers can be persuaded to behave more ethically;
- how ethical behavior can be rewarded, and how unethical behavior can be prevented and punished.

11.2.3 Raising ethical standards

When the organization perceives that it benefits from its employees meeting specified ethical standards in their business activities, it implements ethical codes of conduct, sets up ethical ombudsmen, ethics committees and the like.

Cooke and Ryan (1988) listed United States corporations devoting resources to ethical education. These included Alcoa, Atlantic, Richfield, Chemical Bank, Cummins Engine, and McDonnell-Douglas. The strategies adopted by these and other firms include the following – discussed in McDonald and Zepp (1989):

- ethical awareness programmes;
- developing an appreciation of individual differences;
- group seminars;
- fostering internal staff associations;
- developing codes of ethics and ethical policy statements;
- establishing an ethical ombudsperson;
- establishing an ethical committee;
- reassessing performance and reward schemes so that ethical behavior is rewarded and unethical behavior is not;
- fostering an ethical corporate culture.

Carroll (1987) discusses six major capacities essential in making moral judgements:

1. moral imagination; this means becoming sensitive to ethical issues in business;
2. moral identification and ordering; this means discerning the relevance or non-relevance of moral factors in business situations;
3. moral evaluation; this includes weighing both moral and economic outcomes of a decision;
4. tolerating moral ambiguity and disagreement. By implication, this recognizes that in an individualist culture, ethical disagreements are inevitable; and, as we see in section 11.3, the cross-cultural manager needs a capacity for tolerating differences between moral codes in his/her own and the other culture;
5. integrating managerial and moral competences;
6. a sense of moral obligation; this requires developing an awareness that modern management and the free enterprise system depends on an understanding of such moral concerns as fairness, justice, due process.

Some ethicists argue that ambiguities are resolved when the manager confronts the code in which he/she was reared – whatever this may be. A laboratory study by Dolores (1976) provides empirical support for this approach. She reports that a control group of 25 students who had been trained to clarify their own values were then much better able to make decisions that were consistent with these values.

11.2.4 Ethics in the business school

Can ethical values be taught in a business school? Mulligan (1987) claimed that management research and education is traditionally empirical and mathematical, and restricted to describing the means of achieving business ends – the generation of profits. But the humanities and in particular ethics are chiefly concerned with the ends of business activity measured in terms of human fulfilment and merit. Hence an accent on ethics seemingly contradicts most other elements of the regular business school curriculum. He stressed the difficulties of designing a coherent structure for management education which integrates these two traditions.

However, many institutions and scholars were less pessimistic. By 1993, globally more than 20 dedicated research units studies the topic, and United States business schools alone were offering about 500 courses on the subject.[6]

Mahoney (1990) suggests that in business schools, material on ethics should be integrated into every course taught in the business school curriculum, rather than treated as a subject in itself – which tends to be current practice.

Whether the new discovery of ethics in business and in business schools will prevent even a single scandal is open to doubt. Schools that teach ethics include Harvard, although this had not "spared the school from embarrassing lapses in ethics by its students."[7]

11.3   Ethics across Cultures

Values in the culture are reflected not only in choices of behaviors, but also in moral qualities associated with behaviors.

In all cultures, members are likely to associate moral worth with behavior that gives a positive reflection of their cultural values. To take an example, the Sydney Lumet movie, *Twelve Angry Men*, tells a story of a juror persuading his 11 colleagues in the American jury room that the accused is not guilty, rather than guilty as they were all initially inclined to find him. The jury system reflects values of small power distance; the guilt or innocence of the accused is decided by his/her peers and not by a judge. In so far as the one man refuses to be cowered by the 11 others and finally argues them round to his point of view, the movie also uses the system to celebrate qualities of individualism. And it explicitly associates moral worth with his heroic and lonely stand for justice.

Because cultures differ, behavior considered virtuous in one may be interpreted very differently in some other. A member of a collectivist culture seeing *Twelve Angry Men* might first be surprised by the operations of the jury system, which seems to pose a challenge to the authority of the "professional," the judge. Second, he/she might query the stance of the single juror who appears to have no loyalty towards the group.

Here are further examples. Where public conflict is feared, public protest against the authorities is less likely to be tolerated. Where needs to avoid uncertainty are great, loyalty towards an employer is seen as a virtue; not so, where needs are small (Hofstede 1984a, p. 132). Where power distances are small, the use of power should be legitimate and subject to judgements about good and evil; the legitimacy of power is irrelevant where power distances are large (Hofstede 1984a, p. 94).

Chapter 1 noted that most people find it difficult to objectify their cultural values. By extension, most also find it difficult to trace how far their culture influences the interpretation they make of ethics. Further, every culture is likely to suffer ethical blind spots when evaluating behavior in some other.

This story from an American newspaper, written by an American, reflects both moral worth associated with "taking responsibility" for social problems, and optimism about the possibilities for correcting human behavior. The story takes place in Austria – where Hofstede found the smallest power distances in his 1984a sample (p. 77), and where social breakdowns are most likely to be ascribed to faults in the "system" (p. 94).

When four nursing aides in an Austrian hospital admitted killing 48 old dying patients in Europe's then largest serial murders since the Second World War, many Austrians appeared little concerned. A local psychologist commented:

> We are still like the people in the Nazi times. Austrians are not willing to face the truth. The majority are driven to suppression and denial.

And a magazine editor, Peter Rabl, explained

> There is no one in the political machine or the hospital chain of command or anywhere who will say, "It is my responsibility," . . . In our culture, there is guilt and there is punishment. But there is no responsibility.

A Vienna-based reporter describes the eagerness of hospital employees to deny any sense of catastrophe, and to treat the episode as "normal," even when media interest was at its height.

> . . . I went to see the director of the department and his secretary wanted to know why I wanted to see him . . . It was just so typically Austrian. She wanted to ignore the whole thing and go on as normal. She didn't want to admit there was any kind of crisis.[8]

In sum, the report made of the story seems to reflect an unconscious cultural bias, and a need to judge the other culture in terms of this bias.

11.3.1 Measuring ethical values across cultures

Managers typically perceive that their peers have lower ethical standards than themselves (Pitt and Abratt, 1986). Morgan's (1993) respondents characterized their own ethical behavior as higher than did their co-workers. (He also found that superiors generally rate a manager's ethics more favorably than do his/her peers and subordinates.) Hence we should not be surprised when managers from Culture X perceive managers from Culture Y to be less ethical then themselves.

Vogel (1992) argued that

> [w]hile interest in business ethics has substantially increased in a number of countries in Europe, and to a lesser extent in Japan, no other capitalist nation approaches the United States in the persistence and intensity of public concern with the morality of business conduct.
>
> The unusual visibility of issues of business ethics in the United States lies in the distinctive constitutional, legal, social, and cultural context of the American business system. Moreover the American approach to business ethics is also unique: it is more individualistic, legalistic, and universalistic than in other capitalist societies. (p. 30)

And, Vogel continues, Americans tend to be the only nation that believe that their ethical codes and procedures ought to be applied universally (p. 46).

Hofstede's (1984a) model finds that thinking "in general terms; universalism" (p. 166) is a characteristic of highly individualistic cultures, and this lends some support to the argument that culture influences perceptions of the importance of ethical codes. But a concern with codifying and disseminating ethical values does not always add up to greater ethical behavior.

Different cultures apply ethical principles differently. For instance, the Japanese pride themselves on their strict adherence to law and order. Certainly figures for street crime, theft, murder, and rape are low compared with figures provided by the United States and other Western countries. Figures produced by *The Economist* magazine in 1993 assessed the Japanese black economy (on which no tax is paid) at around 5 percent of Gross Domestic Product, less than in the United States and the United Kingdom (about 7 percent), and much less than in Greece (30 percent) and Spain (25 percent) at the top end of the scale.[9] But the same year saw Japan wracked by a number of business-political corruption cases, of which the Sagawa Kyubin and Kinemaru Shin scandals were only the most publicized.

In sum, no general ethical ranking can be made across cultures. The size of the black economy in Greece and Spain does not indicate equivalent immorality in other areas of life; 1992 figures show a murder rate of 1.8 persons per 100,000 people in Greece, 2.0 in the United Kingdom, 2.3 in Spain, 8.4 in the United States.[10] Similarly, an ethical lack in one area of business does not necessarily indicate a corresponding lack in other areas. In different cultures, the business person may apply very different standards of honesty when negotiating with a business partner and with a government tax inspector.

The problem of predicting national ethical standards is further complicated by real or perceived inter-cultural differences between sub-groups. For instance, ethical perceptions may vary between sexes. A study made of students in the United States and United Kingdom found consistently higher standards among females from both countries (Whipple and Swords, 1992.)

11.3.2 Identifying unethical behavior in the other culture

The synergistic manager avoids the trap of ethnocentricity (that is, of taking for granted the superiority of one's own ethical values and behavior); he/she recognizes that typical managers in the other culture are likely to be as scrupulous in applying their ethical norms as he/she is in applying his/her own. But a problem lies unresolved. How do you identify when members of the other culture are behaving unethically?

In Thailand, the expatriate manager of an American engineering company learned that a Japanese firm had recently introduced a product that competed with his own. The Japanese product offered less service, was of lower quality, and sold for $10,000 less at $40,000. A few days later he received a phone call from the purchasing agent of an old customer. She reminded him of this competition, made clear that she regarded his as by far the better product and then suggested that he should sell it her for only $42,000 – still $2,000 more than the Japanese price. He promised to consider the deal and rang off.

On the assumption that he could only make this and similar sales by revising the pricing strategy, he spent time in reviewing the services offered and deciding which could be eliminated, and hence reorganizing sales functions. He then phoned back to propose a compromise, but now she was clearly not interested. Only later did he realize that she was asking him for a bribe – that on completion of the sale he pay back to her the $8,000 difference between the agreed price and the $50,000 for which he would bill her company.

How could he have recognized the request? Wertheim (1965, ch. 5) proposes the test of secrecy. If your business partners pressure you to keep your transaction with them secret, it can be hypothesized that they know it to be illegal or unethical in terms of society's norms or their company rules. This test is not fool-proof; they may be hiding the deal in order not to give advantage to a competitor. But in this case it would have served the American. If he suggested taking up discussions with top management of her company, she would have had the options of requesting his silence or retreating – in either event signaling her intention and thus saving him the time and effort wasted in revising the pricing strategy.

11.3.3   Institutions and rules

The individual's private ethical standards do not correspond at all points with codes formulated by public institutions. Nevertheless, these codes give some guide as to what behavior is expected and what is sanctioned.

Ethical codes are formulated by:

- the national legal system;
- religious authorities;
- professional associations;
- organizations and their organizational cultures – for instance, by issuing ethical guidelines to members.

The significance of these institutions varies in different contexts.

Chapter 5 (section 5.3) showed that informal patronage systems develop in societies where government and legal systems are weak. Elsewhere, these central institutions play a far greater role in influencing value systems.

In Islamic countries, religious authorities have greater importance than do most corresponding authorities in the United States, for instance. Badr et al. ((1982) compared the effects of value systems in Egypt and the United States, and found evidence for a "positive relationship between an individual's personal values and his managerial decision-making." Egyptian and American business students were polled. The Egyptians ranked religious values as more important than economic, social, and political values. The Americans ranked economic above political, religious then social values.

In Egypt, Algeria, and elsewhere, fundamentalist Islamic groups are actively challenging their governments' monopolies of the right to impose and implement legal systems.

In Japan, large companies play a greater role than do either legal or religious institutions in implementing ethical codes for managers. Even when laws against unethical conduct are on the Japanese statute books, complainants may prefer to settle disputes by other means. A magazine article underlines the point in describing a case brought by Wakabayashi Real Estate (WRE) against New Japan Securities, accusing the brokerage of churning its investment.

> On paper Japan has tough securities laws. Article 58 of the relevant 1948 law, which defines churning, is modeled almost verbatim on section 10(b) of an American law of 1934. But whatever the formalities, lawsuits are rare. There is little precedent for the case brought by WRE. In the few cases that have been brought, courts have tended to rule in favor of the broker, judging that investors should have known better.[11]

The relative insignificance of formal mechanisms is indicated by figures (1987) for the numbers of lawyers; 11 for every 100,000 people, compared with 279 in the United States.[12] And Dubinsky et al. (1991) found that Japanese sales personnel gave consistently lower ratings than did their equivalents from either the United States or South Korea to the need for company policies addressing potential ethical issues. In Japanese organizations, norms are typically enforced by a culture of paternalism and trust.

In all societies, problems arise when a rapidly changing environment throws up unprecedented behavior for which existing institutions have no answers. The problems are severe in newly developing countries trying to establish institutions and regulations when these are not understood. Ignorance on the part of all concerned leave open loopholes which are exploited by the unscrupulous. For instance, in 1993 the Agriculture Bank of China (the Peoples' Republic) decided that it could not honor up to 201 letters of credit valued at more than US$10 billion, because they were fake.

> China's rapid economic growth is giving rise to staggering malfeasance as order breaks down and central control splinters. . . . "With our socialist market economy in the early stage of development, many people are still not familiar with the system that has only just started to operate and do not know the rules and regulations," the Peoples' Daily said Thursday.[13]

11.3.4 Teaching ethics across cultures

Mahoney (1990) found considerably more evidence of ethics being taught in United States business schools than in Continental European schools, and even less in Britain. Similarly, British companies may formulate ethical "mission statements," but very seldom provide a structure for revealing and disciplining unethical behavior among their employees.

Schlegelmilch (1989) compared the institutionalizing of ethical guidelines in the United States and Britain and similarly concluded that relatively few British companies had formulated ethical codes. This does not, of course, mean that British managers are less ethical in their conduct. The lack can partly be explained by cultural differences, and the relative homogeneity of British culture:

> thus the values of British managers [are] less diverse than those of US managers. This might in turn reduce the necessity to formulate ethical guidelines. Some support for this hypothesis is provided in the Schlegelmilch and Houston (1988) study which concluded, judging from the many comments received by companies without formal codes of ethics,

that an ethical culture, a distinct corporate philosophy and integrity and professionalism are deeply valued in British business and apparently can sometimes be fostered without formulating corporate codes of ethics. (p. 63)

To apply the terminology of Hall's (1976) high- and low-context cultures, British management culture appears to be higher context in this respect than is United States management culture. In the United Kingdom, ethical codes do not need to be made so explicit and are transmitted as part of the organizational climate.

11.3.5   Face and social responsibility in Asian cultures

The concept of face is defined by Goffman (1956) as

the positive social value a person effectively claims for himself by the line others assume he has taken during a particular contact.

You maintain your own face by acting in accordance with the attributes and capacities that are associated with your status. You participate appropriately within the group and behave in such a manner that the group's identity is strengthened. You lose face when you are socially embarrassed, for instance, when some other person's lack of tact is construed to challenge your authority and claims to your identity. Whereas self-esteem refers to your assessment of yourself, face denotes the perception that others within your social group have of you.

Redding and Ng (1983) make the point that although the concept of face has general application, and is not specific to Asian-Pacific peoples, it has central importance within their cultures and is a major influence on their behavior. Terms used in these cultures vary slightly in emphasis (relevant research cited by the authors):

- *omoiyari* (empathy) in Japan;
- *kibun* (interpersonal sensitivity) in Korea;
- *budi* (dignity and consideration) among the Malays;
- *krengchai* (consideration for others) in Thailand;
- *pakikisama* (social acceptance) in the Philippines;
- *lien* (good moral character) and *mien-tzu* (achieved reputation) among the Chinese.

These terms are difficult to translate into English – and given that they are expressing abstract and metaphorical notions that are particular to non-Anglo cultures, this is scarcely surprising.

However, even in translation it is clear that they all refer to behavior that meets criteria of harmony, tolerance, and solidarity. They reflect a concern with social virtue; Hofstede (1991, ch. 7) associates this quality with Confucian cultures, and counterposes it to Western concerns with truth. It is also useful to recall the connotations that his 1984a system associates with the high-power-distance and collectivist cultures:

- members are morally and emotionally dependent upon the group, and distinguish group members from outsiders;
- they achieve identity through commitment to the group;
- as subordinates, they abstain from openly disagreeing with superiors, or from behavior which might be construed as a challenge to superiors.

In other words, saving one's face and that of other group members – in particular the superior – is of central importance in these highly integrated and authoritarian cultures.

Individualist cultures associate individual guilt with the transgression of ethical standards. In collectivist cultures, members are taught to associate shame and loss of face with stepping outside the group's social norms (Benedict, 1946, 1974, examines "shame" in Japan).

The inter-relationship of face and collective productivity is illustrated by McCann's (1992) study conducted in a Thai university. A student explained her readiness to cheat in her homework thus:

> I feel that friendship means that we do good things for each other. So I help my friends with something and they help me with my homework. . . . So I must copy. If I get a bad mark I will lose face.

A Thai professor commented

> . . . cheating is universal. But you have to look at it from the students' viewpoint. They are helping each other. Sometimes it is on tests. Sometimes on homework. It doesn't matter. It is called cooperation. You just can't help it.

But in describing the same behavior, an Anglo professor ignored the social implications and evaluated it in terms of his own work ethic.

> My students are lazy, unmotivated and pay little attention to their studies. They are always copying homework off friends at the last minute because they feel that this is better than no grade at all. This is hardly education. (pp. 49–50)

In Anglo terms, it might appear that harmonious group relationships take priority over short-term concerns with operational efficiency. But in practice, the contradiction is less acute; a collectivist and high-power-distance organization is unlikely to maintain operational efficiency when group relationships are inharmonious.

When measuring ethical standards, Anglos tend to give pre-eminence to financial rather than personnel issues – as the introductory case reflects. Asian cultures, on the other hand, are often more concerned with fairly treating individuals on their merits – whether employees, colleagues, business partners, etc. This is reflected in the importance given to face. Face is gained in part by practicing the social and moral codes accepted by the group. Hence this expression of group loyalty acts as a powerful constraint on unethical behavior when this is perceived to be socially irresponsible.

11.3.6   Doing business across ethical boundaries

How does a company do business with a partner from another culture when different ethical norms apply? This problem becomes acute when your customer only agrees to sign a contract if a personal payment is made to a senior manager, for instance, or a government official expects "tea money" before he licenses a joint venture agreement.

International companies resolve the cultural and ethical problems in different ways:

- Insist on upholding the cultural norms of your own company and refuse to contenance behavior which your company considers unethical. This might seem to show a lack of respect for the cultural integrity of the hosts (Donaldson, 1985); if interpreted as an insult, it might prove expensive. (In practice, an American company may have no choice; the United States is the only nation that prevents its companies from making payments in order to secure contracts outside national borders (Vogel, 1992, p. 46).)
- Accept the cultural norms of the other culture, even when they conflict with your own; "when in Rome, do as the Romans do." But even where these are acceptable locally, it may incur penalties at home.
- Hire an agent or "fixer" to handle this aspect of your relations with local companies and authorities. Provide him/her with a budget to "grease the wheels" and do not ask close questions about how these public relations funds are spent. But ignorance of unethical practices carried out in your name may make a poor defence in law.
- Redefine unethical behavior and hence whitewash it. For instance, a payment to secure a contract is made by a legitimate consultant and billed to public relations. But, again, this falls into a morally grey area and may render you liable to prosecution.

The manager is increasingly required to follow the same ethical standards wherever employed when he/she works

- for a multinational company;
- in an industry standardized across national boundaries (to a large extent banking, for instance).

This places him/her under the obligation to ascertain the ethical code used by the employer and to ensure that counterparts understand the ethical constraints upon their dealings.

11.4 The Good Corporate Citizen

The sections above discuss ethics largely in terms of how the manager recognizes what behavior is considered unethical and sanctioned. Here we examine the notion positively, and see what the manager can do that earns social recognition.

The manager is increasingly forced to deal with operational issues that are associated with issues in the wider social environment. For instance, the development of information-based industries and the run-down of smoke-stack industries in the wealthy economies place a premium on the development of educational systems that can produce a workforce with the appropriate mental skills and discipline.

The social issues that concern a company reflect its relationship with its environment and its hopes to control this relationship. These vary between companies, industries, and countries. Kanter's (1991a) poll of senior managers around the world shows significant differences in how they rank social concerns and the responsibility that business has to tackle them.

Kanter's (1991a) figures for managers from Japan, the United States, Germany, South Korea, Hungary and Mexico show that the need for an educated workforce is ranked as most important by all as an obstacle to their organization's success (78 percent among the Americans) – except for the Japanese, who rank it second to the environment. Worries about alcohol and drugs are greatest in the United States (38 percent), and least in the two Asian countries (8 percent for the Japanese, 5 percent for the South Koreans), where drunkenness carries less social stigma. Japan has "only a small drug problem and little tolerance for narcotics use."[14] Concerns with poverty are greatest where earnings GNP is least; 41 percent among the Mexicans, 35 percent for the Hungarians. The Japanese are more concerned than other managers about environmental issues (69 percent), and the Hungarians about unemployment (37 percent).

A second set of figures given by Kanter (1991a) shows percentages of respondents who think business should take either primary responsibility or an active role in finding solutions to the named concerns. South Korean managers appear to be the most interventionist. The Japanese are the least; they show least concern to rectify problems of alcohol and drugs (only 16 percent compared with 69 percent among the Americans), city crime (13 percent compared with 58 percent among the South Koreans), unemployment (48 percent compared with 95 percent among the South Koreans), education (57 percent compared with 89 percent among the Germans). Managers in all countries are most prepared to take a major role in resolving environmental problems (97 percent among the Germans).

Subjective measures suggest that corporate concerns with national social problems and readiness to assume responsibility in resolving them are increasing over time. In a second analysis of the same study, Kanter (1991b) writes:

> The high scores given to social issues, says Ernest Mario, chief executive of Glaxo, demonstrate a maturing view of corporate responsibilities. "Though some issues – education or childcare – are clearly in the immediate or longer-term interests of business itself, a manager of 20 years ago would probably have been astounded to hear that between 60 and 80 percent of his peers believe business should take an active role in such social issues. While the survey did not ask how business could help in these areas, it highlights their sense that the agenda is much wider than it used to be." (p. 65)

This change of attitude indicates that companies are increasingly aware of their dependence upon the social environment. Customers and suppliers prefer to deal with companies that have a good record on social issues, and employees to work for them. A firm with a responsible reputation finds it easier to build a healthy organizational climate. In sum, good corporate citizenship adds up to good business.

11.4.1 Good corporate citizenship can be good business

Here are two examples to show that good corporate citizenship can be good business.

In 1992 Germany passed a law requiring its industry to collect and recycle all packaging, cans, cardboard, paper and plastics. (France and Austria later adopted slightly modified versions.) And by the end of 1993, a further law was likely to be promulgated that would force manufacturers to take back and recycle their products when used.

Many months before the expected legislation, BMW had already developed a plant capable of dismantling 25 cars a day, and saving about four-fifths of the parts for later reutilization. The head of this vehicle recycling unit said

> There is no point in trying to fight the product recycling law ... There is strong public support for recycling, and we knew this law was coming.[15]

Second, Levi-Strauss showed leadership when it developed a model program to address the problem of AIDS in the workplace. Kohl et al. (1990) reported

> The firm has initiated an on-going proactive educational and training programme which has allayed employees' fears by providing factual information, given managers clear directions about how to deal with subordinates who have AIDS or who are HIV positive, and maintained high employee morale and productivity during adverse situations. (p. 34)

In both cases, their pioneering initiatives won the companies very favorable publicity, and in the case of Levi-Strauss appear to have paid off in employee relations and productivity.

It might be argued that each chose a policy of good corporate citizenship because it had no sensible alternative (although competitors faced the same dilemmas) and because its research suggested that this was likely to be profitable, rather than through an overpowering sense of moral responsibility with possibilities of profit incidental.

Whether or not this element of opportunism renders the behavior any less ethical is a question for a moral philosopher. The point rather is that these cases both lend support to the notion that business ethics can be applied on pragmatic terms that make practical sense in a business context – the issue raised in section 11.2.2.

11.4.2 Being a good corporate citizen in the other country

In order to be accepted as a good corporate citizen in the local community, a subsidiary observes both the word and spirit of local laws in respect to

- environmental and pollution controls;
- employment of women and minorities;
- employment of local citizens and expatriates;
- personnel issues, including remuneration, pension plans, recruitment and dismissal procedures, training;

- management-union relationships;
- taxation and financial controls;
- securities and investments;
- purchase of local and foreign materials;
- purchase, lease, and location of land, buildings, plant;
- market competition;
- and all other business activities constrained by the law.

The laws and social norms governing these factors may vary radically from those at home, but this does not excuse non-compliance with local norms.

When a subsidiary fails to satisfy local norms, it is unlikely to be welcomed locally as a good corporate citizen. Contributing to community activities and local charities is not sufficient. In order to be fully accepted, the foreign guest may have to not only adhere to higher standards than are legally mandated, but to show an even better record than their locally owned competitors.

An analysis of how far Japanese auto subsidiaries abide by host United States laws concerning the employment of racial minorities concludes that American plants are significantly more likely to be located in areas with higher ratios of blacks to whites, and to employ more blacks than do equivalent Japanese subsidiaries (Cole and Deskins, 1988). A preference for minimizing contacts with blacks is also shown by the small number of minority-owned dealerships. In 1987 blacks owned just eight of the nearly 5,000 Japanese car dealerships in the country, while Ford had 170 "minority dealerships" (3.4 percent of the total) and GM had 204 (2 percent).

The foreign-owned subsidiary is always more likely to come under inspection than is the locally owned firm. It can least afford the bad public relations that come from bad citizenship and should aim to at least equal the best local standards.

11.5 Implications for the Manager

Compare an organization that you know well in *your own culture* with a similar organization in *some other culture*.

1. In each of the two organizations, how far are ethical standards made explicit?

2. In each of the two organizations, what ethical guidelines are set to regulate members' activities, when working and when at leisure?

    (a) Who, within the organization, sets guidelines?
    (b) How are these guidelines communicated to members?

(c) How is ethical behavior rewarded (even when this is to the short-term disadvantage of the organization?) How is unethical behavior sanctioned?

(d) How ambiguous are the guidelines?

(e) How consistently are they applied to different ranks?

3. In each of the two organizations, how are ethical guidelines taught to members?

(a) What formal techniques are used (e.g., seminars, discussion groups)?

(b) What methodologies are used?

(c) How important is the organizational culture in transmitting ethical standards?

4. In each of the two cultures, how far do these institutions influence ethical standards within the organization? For each, answer on a five-point scale:

(a) the national legal system
5 (*greatly*) ... 4 ... 3 ... 2 ... 1 (*not at all*)

(b) religious authorities
5 (*greatly*) ... 4 ... 3 ... 2 ... 1 (*not at all*)

(c) professional associations
5 (*greatly*) ... 4 ... 3 ... 2 ... 1 (*not at all*)

(d) academic institutions, including business schools
5 (*greatly*) ... 4 ... 3 ... 2 ... 1 (*not at all*)

5. Review your answers for questions 1–4 above. Compare the answers you gave for the organization in your culture, and the organization in the other culture. Then decide on the following.

• What ethical differences could a manager from your culture organization expect to find when working in the other culture organization?

• What ethical differences could a manager from the other culture organization expect to find when working in your culture organization?

• What ethical problems might arise for managers from these two organizations when negotiating together?

11.6 Summary

This chapter has dealt with the problems of ethical decision-making within modern organizations, and the cross-cultural implications.

Section 11.2 discussed arguments that *ethics* can and should be taught in organizations and business schools. A growing number of observers believe that an emphasis on ethical standards makes good business; it increases employee morale, builds the organizational culture, and projects a positive image to employees and the environment.

Section 11.3 dealt with *ethics across cultures.* The cross-cultural manager needs to be sensitive to differences in ethical beliefs, the authority of various institutions to set guidelines, and sanctions imposed on unethical behavior. Differences between cultures cannot be taken to imply ethical inferiority in one or the other. Section 11.4 discussed the notion of the good corporate citizen, and saw how business in different countries perceives its responsibility for social issues. Because countries have different cultural systems, their organizations give different emphases to the notion of corporate responsibility.

11.7 Exercise

This exercise shows the problems of making ethical decisions in ambiguous situations.

The exercise is done by students in pairs, A and B. The results are more interesting when A and B come from different cultures.

1. Together, A and B read the following cases, and answer the questions that follow.

    You approach your travel agent and ask for details of a packaged holiday to Ruritania. You are most impressed by the color brochures and details of the facilities. The price is Fr15,000.

    (a) The travel agent neglects to tell you that all travel agents have reduced their prices for Ruritania this year (the same holiday would have cost 15 percent more last year). He refers to "our new, cheap price." Is his behavior ethical?

    (b) As in (a), but the travel agent also neglects to tell you that his competitors are selling the same holiday for Fr14,400. Is his behavior ethical?

    (c) As in (b); but he also tells you that "you can shop around, but I think you'll be lucky to get a cheaper deal anywhere else." Is his behavior ethical?

    (d) As in (b); but he also tells you that "none of my competitors can sell you this holiday at a cheaper price." Is his behavior ethical?

    (e) As in (d); but a subsequent investigation reveals that the travel agent honestly does not know that his competitors are selling the same holiday at a cheaper price. Does this affect your answer to (d)?

(f) As in (d); but a subsequent investigation reveals that the competitors are making similar claims about their holidays to Darana, that theirs are cheaper than those offered by *your* travel agent. (They are not; they are more expensive.) Does this affect your answer to (d)?

• How far do you agree on your answers? What factors, including culture, explain any disagreements?

2. *Separately*, A and B read the following cases, and answer the questions that follow.

Manager A is interviewing a candidate B for a job in his/her company. Labor market demand for B's unusual combination of skills is much higher than supply. B is not the only person who has these skills, but is the only one to show a definite interest in the job. A knows that the firm's competitors would pay B at least A$22,000 per month. A is very keen to persuade B to take up your offer at a salary of A$20,000.

• Separately, A and B decide answers to the following.

(g) A tells B: "You are not the only person with these skills, and I can't keep the vacancy open for ever. I urge you to make up your mind quickly." Is A's behavior ethical?

(h) Instead A tells B: "You are not the only person with these skills, and I can't keep the vacancy open for long. I must have your answer by noon tomorrow." Is A's behavior ethical?

(i) As (g), but A adds: "If you applied to our competitors, you'd be lucky to get an offer of more than A$18,000." Is A's behavior ethical?

(j) As (g), but A adds: "If you apply to our competitors, you won't get an offer of more than A$18,000." Is A's behavior ethical?

• A and B come together. Compare your answers. How far do you agree? What factors, including culture, explain any disagreements?

Notes

1. James M. Dorsey, "Diversified Turkish madam seeks respect for her broad holdings," Asian Wall Street Journal, July 21, 1993.
2. Ibid.

3. Steven R. Weisman, "Japan's Days of Scandal," New York Times, April 15, 1989.

4. Nathaniel C. Nash, "This is a far cry from the days of Evita," International Herald Tribune, August 8, 1991.

5. "Management focus: how to be ethical, and still come top," The Economist, June 5, 1993.

6. Ibid.

7. John A. Byrne, "Harvard B-School," Business Week, July 19, 1993.

8. Joseph A. Reaves, "Killings in hospital stir Nazi nightmares," Chicago Tribune, April 16, 1989.

9. "Ghostbusters," The Economist, August 14, 1993.

10. "The New World Order: Murder, Inc.," Asiaweek, October 23, 1992.

11. "The case of the churned account," The Economist, August 3, 1991.

12. "A law unto itself," The Economist, August 22, 1987.

13. "More Cracks in China System," International Herald Tribune, June 25, 1993.

14. Andrew Pollack, "Scandalized in Japan: a flamboyant publisher's rumored cocaine connection," International Herald Tribune, August 31, 1993. "The amount of cocaine seized in arrests [in Japan] was a bit less than 50 pounds (23 kilograms) in 1991. In the United States, . . . the amount that year was 120 tons, or roughly 5,000 times as much as in Japan, according to United Nations figures." But since 1991 the numbers of arrests on cocaine charges have been growing steadily in Japan – 110 in 1991, 133 in 1992.

15. Ferdinand Protzman, "Germany to close recycling loop," International Herald Tribune, July 6, 1993.

Part IV

Culture and Organizational Policy

Family Companies

12.1 Introduction

In 1954 George E. Johnson borrowed $250 to develop a product that would help blacks to straighten their hair other than using the traditional and sometimes dangerous method involving chemicals and a heated comb. The new company originally consisted of George, his wife Joan, and his brother.

In 1961 Johnson Products' relaxer was modified and marketed to the women's market. The company was a huge success. In 1971 a limited public stock offering made it the first black-owned family business to trade on the American Stock Exchange. Four years later, sales hit $37.6 million.

But by the 1980s, problems had set in and sales were falling. Rivals, such as Clairol, Alberto-Culver, and Revlon (who had earlier made a bid) were taking market share. Distribution problems were matched by problems of a sales force that was failing to make sales.

By 1988 the company had suffered three losses in the previous four fiscal years. George responded by making his eldest son, Eric, chief operating officer and president. Eric began a process of reorganization and an acquisition from M&M Products Co., that proved highly profitable a few years later. But these developments were not able to resolve problems within the family. The next year, the Johnsons divorced. George left the company, settling half of his stock on Joan, who took over as chairman.

> Because she already was voting trustee for the shares owned by their four children, this would give her voting power over her husband. Another choice was to sell the company and settle, but Mr Johnson was determined to keep the company in family hands.[1]

Family friction increased when the youngest daughter, Joanie, joined the company, in a midlevel job rather than the senior position that she had apparently been promised by her father. Eventually, Mrs Johnson fired her son, and increasingly turned for advice to a non-family member hired as chief financial officer. Thomas P. Polke,

> who is white, has sparked some resentment at the company. He has hired another former Arthur Andersen colleague ... as director of operations. ... "Some employees don't think (the white executives) have the respect for it being an African-American company," says a former employee.[2]

In 1993 Mrs Johnson, the company's CEO and controlling stockholder, had decided to sell out to Ivax Corp., a Miami company, for about $67 million in stock. This decision was taken in the face of opposition from George Johnson, who had always vowed to keep the company within the black community.

This case illustrates two aspects of the family company discussed in this chapter, the business problems that arise from family conflict, and the problem of employing expertise from outside the family – and here, from outside the culture group.

The chapter sees how far the priorities of family companies are influenced by values in the cultural environment. This topic is important to the international business person because

- in the course of his/her career, he/she is likely to deal at some point with a family owned business;
- it cannot be assumed that the priorities of a family business in his/ her home culture apply in a family business elsewhere;
- family company values often correspond to values held more generally in the business community. In South-east Asia, understanding the principles of Chinese family employment keys understanding to even public-sector organizations.

The chapter concentrates on two types; family companies as they are organized in the Anglo cultures – and in particular the United States – and as they are organized where Chinese values predominate, in the Asian Pacific region and particularly South-east Asia. The comparison is made in order to demonstrate how the values of an organization may reflect values in its local environment. It is *not* argued that either model is superior to the other. The United States model can operate just as efficiently in the United States as the Chinese model can in South-east Asia.

The chapter is organized as follows:

12.2   The United States Model

Tax and succession issues apart,[3] the "family business" is accorded relatively little specialist interest in United States business literature, and is more often treated as a sub-category of the "small-business."

Even as a sub-category of the small-business, the family business is viewed with considerable suspicion. The title of Bork's (1986) text sums up the prevailing attitude, *Family Business, Risky Business.* The "risks" are perceived to arise from overlapping family and company responsibilities (Levinson, 1971); it is still generally suspected that "when family and business are interrelated, a less effective business enterprise generally results" (Donnelley, 1964, p. 55). A book reviewer commented on the final decline of the Bingham family – owners of the *Louisville Courier and Journal* – that

> these were people who personalized their professional dealings and professionalized their personal relationships. Towards the end, they were communicating via memo – with copies to other relatives. Maybe there is something to be said for impersonal corporate management after all.[4]

Section 12.3 points out that South-east Asian attitudes towards the family company are very different. By employing children and other relatives the South-east Asian entrepreneur may feel that he/she has protected rather than jeopardized company interests. The employment of relatives may be the preferred alternative. The success of South-east Asian economies in the final decades of the twentieth century indicates that the notion of "family business" needs to be contextualized, and that knee-jerk responses are inappropriate. For instance, the concept of nepotism (defined by the dictionary as giving employment and other favors by a person in authority to his relatives) does not carry negative connotations in all cultures.

12.2.1   Ownership and occupation

The United States literature warns against employing family members unless they can offer exceptional skills. Bork (1986), for instance, advises that

- they must have appropriate work experience and fully meet the requirements for the position in order to apply;
- if hired, they should be treated the same as anyone else would be in that position;
- if possible, they should not participate in the hiring of other family members;
- whenever possible, they should not directly supervise other family members;
- they should be paid fair market salaries for jobs performed;
- job performances alone should determine their advancement, salary reviews, or termination (p. 144).

The message underlying these prescriptions is that impersonal rather than affective factors should determine employment policy. That is, the fact that Joe Soap is your son-in-law, or even your son, is no reason to hire him *unless* and *until* he is properly qualified; and rather, your relationship may be a good reason for *not* employing him. This message makes good sense in contexts where

- rational bureaucratic criteria are respected in making appointments and promotions;
- "nepotism" has negative connotations. The entrepreneur should guard against making any appointments that appear to make family members privileged.

However, warnings against family employment do *not* make sense where opposite conditions apply; that is, in contexts where

- rational bureaucratic criteria are not applied in appointing and promoting family members;
- the entrepreneur is expected to provide employment to family members, and family members are expected to join the family company as a matter of priority.

Such conditions apply in Chinese-influenced business cultures, and the Anglo doing a joint venture with a South-east Asian family company must expect them.

12.2.2 Non-family directors

Similarly, the United States literature proposes that the board of directors be at least supplemented by respected professionals who are outsiders and without allegiance to any particular family member. Brandt (1982) cautions against appointing a board of directors [that] consists solely or primarily of insiders – company officers, their spouses, and friends. Legal matters aside, the operating purpose of a board is to aid, abet, challenge, and replace as necessary the chief executive officer (CEO) of the enterprise in pursuit of the stockholders' expressed interests. . . . If the CEO/entrepreneur is open to seasoned advice . . . , he or she is unlikely to get it – or at least anything very powerful – from insiders. (p. 6)

This proposal reflects a cultural context in which professional conflict within the organization is tolerated – and even welcomed. And in similar vein, Danco (1981) specifies what responsibilities should be allocated to non-family directors of the United States family business:

- reviewing and authorizing corporate and financial strategy;
- establishing policies and plans to implement these strategies;
- creating good corporate controls;
- reviewing and approving employee and community relations.

Taken together, these recommendations assume that

- (family) ownership and (outsider) management issues can be effectively distinguished;
- conflicts within the board are inevitable; for as long as it is rooted in professional (rather than personal) differences, and can be objectivized, a measure of conflict is desirable;
- family members are probably not able to be objective about their professional and personal feelings; non-family professionals are more capable of supplying effective leadership;
- non-family are at least as trustworthy as family members; legal mechanisms give the entrepreneur protection against dishonest or incompetent outsiders.

12.2.3 The theory and the practice

These writers give advice which is relevant to the Anglo business culture, but is not always followed in practice.

Some family businesses, for instance the United Kingdom glass manufacturers, Pilkington, set down criteria for family participation. In order to be employed, the family member must show that he/she can perform the function better than an outsider. But if a family member and an outsider are equally qualified, the former is preferred.

The Hong Kong-based conglomerate, Jardine Matheson, exemplifies a firm in which a family retains control through minority ownership. Keswick family stockholdings amount to much less than 50 percent, but all other holdings are dissipated.

The non-family professional is not always trusted. An American manager was hired to run a small family business in Minneapolis. The firm manufactured and sold school furniture. The original owner had died several years before and hed left it in the hands of his wife as President; their son was still too inexperienced to take control. At first, non-family manager enjoyed a good relationship with the family, and the business began to grow. But after about 15 months she noticed that communications, once open, were ever more guarded. Decisions were increasingly guided by secret interests and made without her knowledge. One day an old client had their credit withdrawn, against her advice. Shocked and surprised, she felt that she had been given no alternative but to resign.

In retrospect she understood that she had begun to learn too much for the family's comfort about its confidential dealings, and hence was perceived as a threat. She later discovered that her two predecessors had resigned after similar time periods for the same reason. This process of rapid hirings and firings of expert outsiders inhibited growth and maintained profit margins at near stagnation point. Nevertheless, the family preferred this policy to risking an outsider learning their secrets. And this state would continue until the son was considered able to take over executive responsibility.

This reluctance to give authority to non-family managers has negatively affected family companies elsewhere in the Anglo world. In the United Kingdom, it is one of the main causes of failure, and why only 24 percent of family businesses reach a second generation, and a mere 14 percent survive to the third:

> [s]ons take over even though outside expertise may be needed; and then they stay for too long. Many of today's old family firms have been given a new lease of life at some point in their history by injecting fresh talent from outside: at the turn of the century Samuel Courtauld transformed his family mourning-crêpe business into a synthetics empire after bringing in two outsiders who developed viscose rayon.[5]

A virulent distrust of outsiders may seem more typical of a Chinese than Anglo company. But there is a significant difference. In the Minneapolis case, the non-family manager came into the company with reasonable expectations that she would be given a free hand to run operations so that they produced a profit. That is, the widow's behavior was unusual in that business context. In South-east Asia, no outsider could realistically hold such optimistic hopes.

12.3 The Chinese Model

Whereas the United States model stresses impersonal bureaucratic procedures (discussed in chapter 4, section 4.5), and tries to reduce the affective nature of family relationships, the Chinese family company magnifies and applies them.

This section examines the success of the Chinese family company within its context.

It is a mistake to assume that only the Chinese entrepreneur makes money in South-east Asia. The early successes of Arabs, Sikhs, Gujaratis, and then the Western and Japanese colonialists should not be ignored. Clad (1989, 1991) reminds us of

> non-Chinese Filipinos, [who] often become dazzlingly successful in the US or Australia ... Ask any Indonesian about the Sumatrans from the Padang west coast, or the Buginese from Sulawesi; see if the Penang Malays have not won a proud niche in the commercial history of their island. (p. 162)

The overseas Chinese contribute less than 50 percent of the population in all South-east Asian countries except Singapore, where (according to Limlingan, 1987) they make up 72 percent. Kunio (1988, pp. 39–40) cites two estimates, of 6 percent and 5.6 percent for the region as a whole. Precise figures are difficult to come by, in part because of intermarriage – probably highest in Thailand and lowest in Malaysia and Brunei.

In addition, the Chinese diaspora extends elsewhere in Australasia, North America (estimated at 1.8 million), Latin America (1 million), Europe (0.6 million) and Africa (0.1 million).[6]

Despite their minority status, Chinese business techniques and culture have had a disproportionate effect on the South-east Asian region. Clad (1989, 1991) estimates that the Chinese in Indonesia (2.5 percent) probably control over 60 percent of wholesale and 75 percent of all retail businesses. Another estimate credits them with control of 17 of Indonesia's 25 biggest business groups.[7] And their importance has not been restricted to the purely economic arena. The Chinese model of the family business has been a major influence on the development of family businesses throughout the region.

Two cultural factors help explain this influence:

- Chinese culture places a priority on family loyalty and needs. The organizational culture of a Chinese family company closely reflects Chinese cultural values and the traditional teachings of Confucius.
- Chinese culture is situation-oriented and pragmatic (Hsu, 1963).

These factors influence strategy and performance. The Chinese depend upon world-wide family and business links both for information and as havens for investment.

The company is based on the immediate family. Business is conducted first with extended family members, then with members of the village, clan, then ethnic group. A Hainanese typically prefers to deal with some other Hainanese, a Teochew with a Teochew.

For instance, an entrepreneur employs his eldest son in the family shop in Hong Kong. He trades gems with his brothers and a cousin in Los Angeles and Singapore, and buys property from a clan member on Vancouver. He sends his younger sons to study in Canada and Australia, where they seek residence and set up their own companies; and a daughter is sent to work for a cousin in Amsterdam. Eventually, these children will be brought back to work in the flagship company or will establish their own networks of family influence.

The wider the network, the easier it is for family members to move their capital around the world to

- wherever promises the greatest safety;
- wherever promises the highest profit.

The rapidity and ease of these transactions is enhanced by the increasing availability of telecommunications. So far as the Chinese family networks are concerned, national barriers are often unimportant.

However, the footloose quality of Chinese capital investment also has a negative aspect which does not promise well for the long-term development of the region. Asian stockmarkets are subject to wild fluctuations (often on the basis of only vague rumor), and these reflect the markets' immaturity and relative undercapitalization. Kunio (1988) gives qualitative measures of Chinese capital as against private indigenous and foreign capital in the region. He rates Chinese involvement in light industry as dominant; banking as substantial/dominant; import–export trade, machinery, property development as substantial; metals and petrochemicals as minor; oil exploration as zero (pp. 50–1). There is also a concentration in hotels, and gambling where legal.

Many of these industries call for skills in correctly estimating price, place, and time, and making rapid responses to market pressures. They are accessible on a short-term basis, and entry and exit may be rapid. When restricted to family members, the senior management team may be small. In general, Chinese family companies are not involved in long-term heavy industrial projects in which these features are inappropriate.

Finally, the short-term attitude of much South-east Asian small business is shown by the extent of product piracy. The range of consumer items that are routinely faked include designer clothing, watches, computer software, books, videos, music cassettes; Clad (1989, 1991) estimated the annual number of cassettes pirated in Indonesia as between 30 and 40 million. By the early 1990s, some of these countries were beginning to clean up their acts – Singapore and Thailand for instance. However, the small-business sector is still able to exert considerable pressure on legislators. Hesitation in signing intellectual property agreements, and refusing to enforce them adequately, obviously brings short-term advantages. But the lack of safeguards frightens off major investments from developed-country manufacturers, and so places potential local partners at a long-term disadvantage.

12.3.1 Immigrant communities

The immigrant Chinese do not constitute a single uniform group. The interests and practices of the communities vary widely, and each may consist of a range of Chinese sub-communities. For instance, one analysis of the Chinese in Malaysia distinguished the following language groups (and failed to distinguish Mandarin); Hokkien (34.2 percent), Hakka (22.1 percent), Cantonese (19.8 percent), Teochew (12.4 percent), Hainanese (4.7 percent), Kwongsai (2.5 percent), Hockchiu (1.8 percent), Henghua (0.5 percent), Hockchia (0.3 percent), others (1.7 percent) (Omar, 1979). However, they are joined by more than separates them, and each local community can be sensibly described primarily in relation to the non-Chinese community.

In Malaysia, Indonesia and Brunei, government policy and social attitudes of the majority Malays have inhibited Chinese assimilation with the host community. A report by Chee et al. (1979) on the situation in Malaysia identified "government indifference" as a major impediment to the development of small business (p. 128). This indifference seems to be inspired both by a preference for large business conglomerations, and also by the New Economic Policy of discriminating against Chinese in favor of Malays; 70 percent of the small businesses polled were Chinese, 23 percent Malay, and 7 percent Indian and other.

Elsewhere – in Thailand and the Philippines – Chinese and other families have intermarried and borrowed from each others' cultures with relative ease. And to the cultural outsider the Chinese may not be easily identifiable. In Thailand, many of the great empires were founded by Chinese immigrants who started at the bottom of society and took Thai names.

> Take Chuan Ratanarak. Born in Southern China in 1920, he first came to Thailand with his family at the age of six. At the end of the second world war he was working as a docker in Bangkok's harbor. . . . Today he con-

trols the Bank of Ayudhya, Thailand's fifth-largest bank, and Siam City Cement, the country's second-largest cement producer.[8]

The values of the Hong Kong Chinese are not entirely typical of the overseas communities. For one thing, most of the immigrants originally stemmed from elsewhere – poorer provinces from further south. But Wong (1986) does go some way to explaining the proliferation of family businesses and the significance of relations with family and non-family members.

> The norm on self-employment was vividly expressed by a small Hong Kong industrialist who reportedly said that "a Shanghainese at 40 who has not yet made himself owner of a firm is a failure, a good-for-nothing." [note] Such a preference is not confined to the small industrialists. The cotton-spinners who are large employers also hold a similar view. Nearly two thirds of those I interviewed chose the option of becoming the owner-manager of a small firm rather than the senior executive of a large corporation if both alternatives were available to them early in their career.[9]
> (p. 311)

Because employees are always likely to leave in order to strike out on their own and hence compete, or to move to join an existing competitor, they can never be entirely trusted.

12.3.2 Employing family members

The distrust of non-family members and their exclusion from senior positions in the family business is mirrored by the relative trust given to family members. (This trust is never total; South-east Asian business enterprises can become so complex that not even the heir is permitted to understand the true picture. Hence the entrepreneur protects himself against over-ambitious offspring.)

Typically, the entrepreneur starts a company and staffs senior management posts with relatives. The constraints of family authority and loyalty are thus replicated in the business. Family relationships determine how control is imposed, conflicts resolved and messages communicated. Non-family members are ruthlessly excluded from positions of responsibility. Why, after all, should Mr Tan (in figure 12.1) place trust in Wong, Chung, and Oi and promote them to the board, when each has other loyalties, to his/her own clan and family?

In this context, where family members are employed precisely because they *are* family (and therefore owe loyalty) the concept of "nepotism," carrying negative connotations, does not apply.

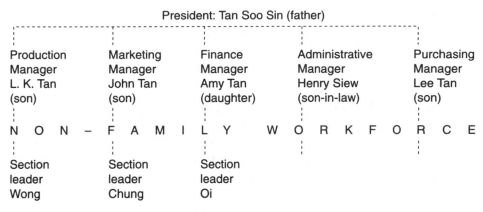

Figure 12.1 Employment of family members.

The company is organized on a strongly vertical basis below top management levels, and very little information is communicated between functions; Wong, Chung and Oi scarcely know each other. At the level of functional management, information is communicated quickly – far more quickly than in an American equivalent. John Tan and Lee Tan are unmarried and live in their father's house; L. K. Tan and his wife, and Amy and her husband Henry Siew, occupy houses in the same compound. And it is usual that all members of the family eat their dinner together. Hence decision-making is fast, and each of the managers has sufficient understanding of the others' functions to contribute useful suggestions.

In extreme instances, this dependence on family to fill responsible posts imposes an absolute limit on the size of the company; the entrepreneur prefers not to expand his/her company rather than to employ non-family members. In this respect, a culture favoring tight family loyalty is a disability rather than an asset.

12.3.3 Family roles and responsibilities

Mr Tan's company is far from fitting the bureaucratic mode of family company described in section 12.2, the United States model. The work relationships of family members may be even less structured, as the example below demonstrates.

In Thailand, a family owned and ran a highly profitable autodealership and a hardware shop. Father and Mother were Co-Presidents. Other responsibilities were nominally thus:

Eldest Son	General Manager
Second Son	Shop Manager
Third Son	Sales Manager
Eldest Daughter	After-Sales Service Manager
Second Son's Fiancée	Showroom Supervisor

In practice, Father (an ex-soldier) left decision-making to Mother, and together they devoted more attention to the shop than the dealership. Eldest Son appeared most interested in using the company assets as collateral for his own real estate and other ventures. Second Son deferred to his parents in the shop. Third Son contributed nothing. Eldest Daughter did no After-Sales work, and instead shared responsibility for sales with her fiancé.

Eldest Daughter's Fiancé had no formal involvement but was given informal responsibilities for sales on the birth of her daughter. Previously a Jaguar employee and then for several years the family's own salesman, he demonstrated energy and talent. The Second Son's Fiancée did the accounting. Between them, these two contributed most of the hard work and creative talent to the family enterprises. But they were not full family members, and were never entirely trusted. So far as possible they were ignored and their contributions belittled.[10]

When kinship relationships are good, the flexibility offered by family employment can give the company an advantage. Shared perceptions and experiences, and opportunities for informal meetings outside the workplace, help make communication fast and efficient. But if conflict erupts between family members, this mutual dependency becomes a major liability.

A discrepancy between nominal role and actual responsibility may lead to difficulties for the outsider who has to deal with the family company. In the case above, an outsider who wished to deal with someone responsible for sales and who approached Third Son would be disappointed. He would need instead to speak to Eldest Daughter and her untitled fiancé.

The frustrations are likely to be particularly acute for the Anglo outsider who has learned from his/her own culture to expect a close correspondence between role and responsibility. Here is a second example.

A New Zealand team was negotiating in Kuala Lumpur, trying to set up a deal with a Chinese family business in Malaysia. The President of the company, first son of the late founder and British-educated, impressed his visitors with his obvious sincerity and determination to reach a settlement. After three days, an informal agreement was reached and the young man announced that after sorting out a few last details, he would sign the deal, probably within 24 hours. The New Zealanders congratulated themselves on so rapidly concluding. But

[f]or the next two days thgy heard no more from the president, and telephone calls failed to reach him. Then a younger brother appeared. He greatly regretted that no deal could be made. Their widowed mother had refused her eldest son permission to sign. The New Zealanders had neither seen nor heard of the lady before. They discovered that although she held no office in the company, her family authority translated into absolute rights of veto over the company's business. (Mead, 1990, p. 166)

The person with ultimate responsibility did not appear at all on the organizational chart. An insider to the culture might have expected this to be the case. Discreet inquiries within local business circles would have warned him/her of the old lady's existence and importance, and perhaps indicated how she could be expected to respond to the proposed deal, and how her opposition might be overcome. But the outsider does not have such easy access to this "unofficial" information – and the cultural outsider expecting to deal with a bureaucratic structuring of roles and responsibilities is placed at an additional disadvantage.

12.3.4 Training family members

The importance of family companies and the spectacular successes that some achieve should not blind us to the fact that many others fail. The reasons for failure are various:

- lack of government support;
- undercapitalization and a lack of access to formal finance;
- failure to build or join trade associations;
- failure to identify niche opportunities;
- operating in an industry where competition is excessive;
- low levels of profitability;
- low levels of investment in technology and low levels of technological competence (Kunio, 1988);
- family problems;
- excessive conservatism;
- lack of technological and managerial expertise.

This last problem is dealt with here. It is seen how training helps resolve problems arising from a lack of expertise. The following case is illustrative.

Founded 70 years ago in Singapore, Shen Ping Produce (disguised name) had always specialized in exporting and importing food items. Then, in the early 1980s, Mr Shen decided that the company needed a computerized warehousing system.

His eldest son, Lee, was about to complete his MBA studies, but on his father's urging registered for an additional course in MIS systems. The course finished, he reported to his father; the market offered nothing that exactly matched their needs. "Then you'll have to design one yourself," Mr Shen replied.

Lee joined a new course which taught him what he needed to know about program design, and wrote the specialized package. The family experimented; it precisely matched their needs.

The news of this success soon leaked out, and a number of other small businessmen indicated that they would be happy to purchase such a package. After some thought, Mr Shen instructed his daughter, Amy, to study a course in software production and marketing. He then established a new company.

Shen Ping Software was soon profitable, and quickly attracted the attention of a United States computer manufacturer looking for an energetic local partner. It was agreed that the second son, John, should be trained in computer assembly technology and factory management skills back in Los Angeles. On his return, an assembly plant was started.

Thus the far-sighted entrepreneur identifies future skill needs, and arranges for training him/herself or other family members to meet these needs. This case shows a family company that could respond rapidly to market needs because sufficient family members were capable of taking relevant training and applying their new skills. In the absence of such personnel, the company could only have met market demands by delegating essential responsibilities to outsiders – probably an unpalatable option, given the context.

The dependence on family resources poses a problem for the family company. First, company growth is restricted by numbers of family members when only they can be trusted with essential responsibilities. Second, development is curtailed if the entrepreneur lacks the foresight to identify training needs, or identifies the wrong training needs, or is unable to count upon family members capable of taking the training. Autocratic domination of the company means that creative contributions and initiatives from junior levels are stifled. Third, when no new ideas are bubbling up from below, the entrepreneur is forced to become even more dependent on his/her own capacity for innovation. Perhaps he/she should seek his own further training; but this return to student status might expose him to ridicule and loss of face, and hence be unacceptable.

Problems occur when family and professional hierarchies do not correspond, and a junior member of the family possesses qualifications that outrank those of his/her seniors. The alternative of spinning off the gifted junior with his/her own company or department is not always available.

Terpstra and David (1985) relate the case of an Indian family business which started joint venture negotiations with an American company. The American company sent over an organizational specialist who proposed a much tighter organizational chart and the promotion of a young family member above two of his older cousins. He possessed an MBA; they did not. The Indian entrepreneur was faced with the alternatives of

- calling off the negotiations and thus preventing conflict between different generations in the family;
- refusing to make the promotion and so scuttling the negotiations;
- making the promotion and so saving the negotiations but at the cost of family and company unity.

12.3.5 Outsiders in the family company

Chinese family businesses may be entrepreneurial in penetrating new markets, but in some economic contexts their human-resources policies may be deeply conservative.

When unskilled labor is cheap, it may be grossly exploited in low technology and labor-intensive industries. Women may be preferred to men on the grounds that there are less likely to make trouble (Ong, 1987, describes examples in Malaysia) and in the worst cases, under-aged children are used. Elsewhere in the world, the International Labor Organization (ILO) estimates that about one million Indian children under the age of 14 are working in bonded conditions, in such industries as carpet-weaving, brick manufacture and quarrying.[11]

But when specialized and skilled labor is required, and is in short supply, a different situation prevails. Considerable energy may go into developing ties of loyalty with the workforce, and patronage relations are fostered. The subordinate shows deference and avoids making utterances that might be interpreted as challenging the superior; in practice, this means that most communications are one-way. In return, he/she is protected. Often, the unmarried employee lives with the family – which also permits the family to check on his/her acquaintances.

Throughout the region, relationships with favored servants tend to be paternalistic. This advice, given by an Indonesian on the treatment of house servants, typifies the attitude. Indonesians

> do not employ a *pembantu* (housemaid), but rather, absorb [her] into the family. The idea is to extend a sense of gentle welcome to cushion any uneasy feeling of possible "exploitation." . . .
>
> "Maids should never be mistreated. But they should also not be made your equal.
>
> "Otherwise, they will start climbing over your head, and that's where the problems come," says one Indonesian. . .

The maid may sit with her employer to watch TV, but she is expected to know that her place is on the floor.

She may use the telephone but she should not make long private calls.[12]

The valued non-family employee is both patronized and distrusted because it is feared that he/she may

- be poached by a competitor;
- leave to set up business on his/her own, and so become a competitor;
- supply confidential information to a competitor;
- supply confidential information to the authorities.

What counts as confidential information? The categories include:

- accounting and financial data;
- customer and supplier lists;
- process secrets.

This respect for confidential information and fear of losing it is often realistic, and the non-family employee may be rightly distrusted; family loyalty, that binds the company management, also gives him/her a prior commitment to his/her own family.

The Swiss general manager of a European company operating in Bangkok mistakenly allowed his Thai personal assistant to become too well acquainted with business dealings that broke Thai law. When he caviled at her pay demand, she threatened to reveal his activities. He dared not release her and trebled her salary within a year.

The distrust that Chinese family companies typically show for their environment needs to be seen in context. The Asian Pacific region is experiencing economic growth and social change equivalent to that of the United Kingdom and Northern Europe during the Industrial Revolution, but greatly compressed into a few decades. The region's contemporary problems of bad working conditions, child labor, infrastructure breakdown, corruption, and incompetence by central government all have their nineteenth-century parallels. The reluctance of the Chinese business owner to take the environment for granted is understandable.[13]

But the paranoia sometimes reaches proportions that strike the cultural outsider as self-defeating. A family confectionery business in Bangkok was known throughout the city for the quality of its produce. Unfortunately, only the owner, who cooked, knew the secret recipes; and she refused to divulge them, even to her daughter. As she moved into her eighties, the family waited in fear for her death, and the end of their prosperity. And indeed, she took her secrets to her grave.

12.3.6 Relations with the environment

The suspicion of outsiders extends to investors, who will expect to see the books. Similarly, seeking government funding or making a public share offering both involve filing financial statements, to which official bodies (including the tax department) and competitors have access. This attitude seems to reflect a traditional Chinese distrust for government; for much of the nineteenth and twentieth centures before the Communist takeover, central authority was weak, arbitrary, and unable to protect the individual against marauding neighbors. The effect is that many small companies are undercapitalized and never reach their potential growth.

The entrepreneur's distrust of central authority includes the judiciary (which has relatively low status in these countries). Should he fall into legal difficulties with company employees, he prefers to settle matters himself than call on lawyers, who can perhaps be bribed. He has greater leverage over family members – who share his fear of washing dirty family linen in the lawcourts – and employs them in preference to outsiders.

Western business scholars regularly recommend that small businesses form associations that boost their common interests – for instance,

> a communal organization under which the small firm looks for other small firms to associate with and to build a more permanent, mutually constructive network of joint support and resource sharing. (Sengenberger, 1988, p. 258)

And in immature economies, firms have all the greater need to develop efficient and flexible linkages (Schmitz, 1990).

Businesses elsewhere in the developing world have indeed managed such linkages – one study describes the success of Egyptian furniture manufacturers in building interrelationships where each performs one or two specialist operations to a semi-finished product, then moves it down the chain (Mead, 1982).

But in South-east Asia, small businesses commonly find it next to impossible to overcome their mutual suspicions, even when it would appear in their interests to collaborate. Chee (1990) shows Malaysia boasting 20,000 small businesses but only one small-business association, with two staff and an annual budget of US$6,100. And in Bali, Indonesia, of a total of 12,577 small-businessmen registered in 1982, only about 1,000 belonged to the local association, KADIN.

These figures contrast with the interest shown in Japan and South Korea. In Japan, almost 50 percent of small businesses participated in the nearly 40,000 associations; in South Korea, one association alone boasted a membership of 16,000. Chinese influence may be only indirect in these cultures, but as in South-east Asia some family companies achieve massive growth. The Hyundai, Daewoo, Lucky-Goldstar, Sunkyong and Samsung groups are all family-owned. Samsung is South Korea's leading producer of electronics, food products, pharmaceuticals and paper. Founded as a trading company in 1938, its early structure was heavily influenced by Japanese models.

In South-east Asia, the antipathy towards association cannot be explained entirely in terms of relations with non-Chinese authorities, even when (as in the case of Malaysia) the lack of representation by institutions in central government suggests indifference or even opposition to the small entrepreneur's interests (Clapham, 1985). A similar lack of horizontal linkages has been noted in the People's Republic of China. In Zhejiang province, for instance, the number of small businesses grew from 29,941 to 47,058 between 1981 and 1986 (Wu, 1991). But problems in forming business cartels for both research and manufacturing mean that efforts to encourage specialization are generally unsuccessful.

12.4 Culture and the Family Company

Hall's (1976) model of low-context cultures, of which the United States is typical, suggests that the American family companies are influenced by these aspects of the national culture:

(a) Relationships between individuals (even family members) are relatively flexible.
(b) Particularly when senior managers do not share family membership, they lack (in relative terms) a shared body of experience and opinion. Energy spent in making meaning explicit slows the communication process.
(c) Insiders and outsiders are less tightly distinguished. Values associated with family loyalty are weak, and tolerance of outsiders (as employees and as competitors) means that

- family members have no great incentive to hang together in response to outside threats;
- associations with other small-businesses are welcomed.

(d) Impersonal and rational bureaucratic norms may be applied in order to prevent problems arising from family conflict.
(e) Low power distances mean that employees and non-family members are relatively unconstrained in approaching family members with suggestions, problems, etc.

Behavior in South-east Asian family companies is influenced by these aspects of Chinese culture (high-context).

(a)   Relationships, whether or not amicable, and whether with family members or outsiders, may be long-lived.

(b)   Collectivist loyalty is expected between family members. Family members are brought up to share the same experiences and opinions. Because it is based on a shared view of the world, communication in routine situations is fast and efficient.

(c)   Insiders and outsiders are tightly distinguished. The family depends upon the loyalty and cohesion of its members in order to combat threats posed by government, competitors, disloyal non-family employees. Family loyalty is offset by distrust of the environment.

(d)   Family and patronage loyalties, rather than bureaucratic norms, determine relationships between company members.

(e)   Power distances are high and hierarchical levels are distinguished:

- the entrepreneur;
- family/management;
- non-family/work-force.

Subordinate loyalty and obedience is valued; but initiatives originate at top levels only. The company may be highly flexible in entering new markets but is conservative in management structure and style.

12.4.1   Family-business culture and national-business culture

In the Anglo cultures, rational bureaucratic norms dominate most management theory and influence notions of how all organizations, including the family business, should be run. In practice, the organizational and family cultures may significantly qualify this model, and in extreme cases where individuals are employed in the family business for all their working lives, the organizational culture may at least equal the national culture as an influence on behavior. One large Anglo family business based in East Asia is reputed to give priority to the male applicant with family connections however distant, success at sport, a reputation for womanizing, and at least one major blunder to his credit.

The introductory case gives an example where the rational bureaucratic model clashes with the organizational culture. The original entrepreneur fought to keep Johnson Products as a family business in the black community; one of the white managers commented on its eventual sale that although the company employed blacks and served a black market, it was public and was perceived by its investors as simply an investment – without regard to race. "This is really a mainstream company," he says.[14]

In small South-east Asian firms, the dominance of family values is seldom in doubt. Even a public-sector organization may be dominated by family values of loyalty and obligation.

The Chinese family company has a direct impact upon the economy. The values associated with entrepreneurship mean that gifted young managers may often prefer to strike out on their own than to work for large corporations or the public sector.

Within the family company the entrepreneur cannot take the loyalty of non-family employees for granted, and this constrains human resource policies;

- needs for security mean that supervision is close;
- communication is mostly one-way and top-down; where power distances are great, contributions from the shop-floor are perceived to challenge the entrepreneur's control of information;
- formal obedience by employees is expected and enforced;
- training is given to subordinates only when this does not challenge superiors' prerogatives to expert knowledge.

Because family-company values determine business values throughout the culture, these features also influence policy in large private and public-sector organizations.

12.4.2 Succession problems

The influence of different national cultures on family company values is illustrated by how Anglo and Chinese companies deal with succession issues.

In the United States, where consecutive second third and later marriages are not uncommon, the question of who is in the family (and therefore entitled to the benefits of ownership) is significant (Dyer, 1986, p. 88). Changes in the status of spouses, children and in-laws affect the company culture, who makes decisions and how decisions are made. Succession may not be smooth, and legal advice may be needed to resolve a range of issues. For instance, on the departure of the controlling owner:

- Who succeeds as controlling owner? How is this succession decided?
- What is the status of minority family owners?
- What rights and obligations does the new controlling owner have to his/her predecessor's management policies, including human resource policies?

- What rights does the previous controlling owner, for as long as alive, have to interfere in day-to-day operations?

These issues are always likely to be more acute to the extent that marriage relationships are unstable. And they help explain why the recruitment of non-family members both to management and to the board in preference to family members is often the preferred solution to the possibility of organizational instability in the United States.

In South-east Asian cultures, there is a greater degree of consensus across society on the status and responsibilities of spouses, children and in-laws. But this does not mean that fewer difficulties arise from family relationships. Suppose that the founder has both a legal wife and a number of minor wives (or concubines), and that each of these has given birth to a number of sons; and that each son goes on to acquire his own menage. This situation is by no means uncommon,[15] and can spark violent conflict, particularly when succession issues arise.

As values associated with family loyalty are eroded by the decline of collectivist values and growth of individualism, the damage inflicted by such conflicts is all the harder to control. Matters are made worse when successors prove less capable and more conservative than the founder, or prove unable to adjust to a new environment.

Of course, such problems are by no means restricted to South-east Asia. In Britain in 1992, family management in the long-lived show manufacturers C. & J. Clark got caught up in serious dynastic conflict.[16] In Italy in 1993, economic circumstances and in some cases accusations of corruption forced many of the great Italian family companies to give up a measure of their financial and managerial controls; Fiat (the Agnelli family), Olivetti (De Benedetti), Ferruzzi Finanziaria (Ferruzzi), Pirelli (Pirelli), Fininvest (Berlusconi).[17]

12.4.3 Resolving problems in the two models

Section 12.2 examined some of the lessons that American management texts teach owners of small and family businesses. In sum, they argue that many typical problems can be avoided if kinship and business responsibilities are uncoupled and impersonal bureaucratic standards are applied. And when conflicts between family members present serious difficulties, top management should turn for help to outside authority – for instance, to legal services.

These solutions are inappropriate in South-east Asia, given what features in the local culture influence business in the region. Employing non-family members in top management, or taking the company public, are still not acceptable alternatives for many families.

So how does the founder protect his/her company against the effects of family estrangement? One solution is to complicate the structure of a large empire, and then separate areas of responsibility, so that no subordinate can ever build up a full picture of organizational interests and strategy. But while this may protect the entrepreneur against rebellion during his/her lifetime, it does not necessarily secure the integrity of the empire when the next generation takes power.

A second answer is to diversify family interests across a number of companies so that a failure in one inflicts minimal damage on the others.

For instance, the eldest child is trained to take over the flagship company, and a group of other companies are registered to which the other children are sent to manage. Each might be given a controlling share of his/her company and some share of all others. These other businesses may be engaged in complementary industries. The owner of a construction company sets up for his children companies dealing in cement, timber, paint, interior design, and so on. Hence the group's business activities benefit from good sibling relationships while being less susceptible to family conflict. And if one child fails to make a success of a company, no one else need suffer unduly.

Over time, the employment of outsiders in high-level positions will grow as

- the company is forced to diversify into increasingly more specialized and high-tech operations in order to survive;
- more technological skills are required, and skills are required at higher levels;
- the family is unable to supply sufficient numbers of persons with these skills or capable of being trained to the appropriate levels;
- legal services are better trusted as means of protecting the company against unfair competition.

These countries are experiencing a growing mobility of professional labor. A professional middle class is growing, and a middle-class employee is far less likely than his/her parents to spend a career within one company or occupation. In practice, we can probably expect to see increasing numbers of professional outsiders employed by family companies in short-term consultancy positions.

12.5 Implications for the Manager

What values determine policy within family companies that you know? Make comparisons betweeen:

- a small family company typical of *your own culture*;
- a small family company typical of *some other culture* that you know.

1. In each of the two companies,

   - are family members employed?

     (a) If you answer *yes*, in what positions are they employed?
     (b) What criteria are used in appointing and promoting family members?

   - What conflicts arise between family members in the company?

     (c) What factors cause these conflicts?

   - How do family relationships affect communication and decision-making processes?
   - What conflicts arise between family and non-family members in the company?

     (d) What factors cause these conflicts?

   - At what levels are non-family employed?

     (e) on the board of directors;
     (f) in managerial capacities;
     (g) in professional and technical capacities.

   - Does the company belong to a small-business association?

     (h) How does the company benefit from its membership?
     (i) How is this association supported by the public sector and government? By the private sector?

2. What environmental factors explain your answers above? In each of the two companies,

   - how is the company structure and culture influenced by the following?

     (a) national culture/sub-culture;
     (b) industry values;
     (c) size of the company;
     (d) governmental and legal factors;
     (e) economic and social factors.

3. Compare your analyses of *your-own-culture* company and *the-other-culture* company.

   - What significant differences do you observe?
   - How do you explain these differences?

12.6   Summary

This chapter has dealt with family companies. It focused on two extreme types, the family company within an Anglo culture – specifically the United States – and the Chinese family company in South-east Asia.

Section 12.2 examined the *United States model*. The risks of confusing family and professional relationships in management give rise to considerable anxieties, and in practice the company may be "family" in so far as it is family owned rather than family worked. Section 12.3 discussed *the Chinese model*, which heavily influences business culture throughout South-east Asia. In important respects, company values are diametrically opposed to the ideals of the United States model. His/her collectivist values mean that the entrepreneur relies heavily upon family labor and loyalty in response to an environment which is perceived to be essentially antagonistic. Family members are employed in senior management, and non-family placed in positions where they offer least threat.

Section 12.4 compared *cultural* influences on the Anglo/United States and South-east Asian/Chinese *family companies*. The relationships between the family business models and dominant business models were compared.

12.7   Exercise

This exercise shows how industrial and cultural factors affect the systems implemented in the family company.

1. *Family company A* makes paper cups for the fast-food industry. The cups are cut from sheets of pre-printed card and glued. When this company is based in

    (a)   the United States,
    (b)   Hong Kong,

    what are the implications for

    •   recruitment policies?
    •   training policies?
    •   control in the workplace?
    •   relations with the environment?

2. *Family company B* makes laser technology, used in the manufacture of medical technology. When this company is based in

    (a)   the United States,
    (b)   Hong Kong,

what are the implications for

- recruitment policies?
- training policies?
- control in the workplace?
- relations with the environment?

Notes

1. Brett Pulley, "Sale of Johnson Products splits family," *Wall Street Journal*, August 4, 1993. The case is summarized from this source.
2. Ibid.
3. E.g., see Lasser Tax Institute (1989). Succession issues are discussed by Barnes and Hershon (1976).
4. Troy Segal, "In this old Kentucky home, a viper's nest," *Business Week*, April 11, 1988. Segal reviews Chandler (1988) and Brenner (1988).
5. "Splits, and survival," *The Economist*, October 31, 1992.
6. "The overseas Chinese: a driving force," *The Economist*, July 18, 1992.
7. Ibid.
8. "Empires in the east," *The Economist*, January 26, 1991.
9. Wong (1986) quotes from King et al. (1975, p. 34).
10. I am grateful to Duncan McCargo for this case.
11. Hamish McDonald, "Boys of bondage," *Far Eastern Economic Review*, July 9, 1992. Similar conditions exist elsewhere in the world. A team from the Anti-Slavery Society investigating reports of exploitation in the Moroccan carpet industry "found that children aged from five upwards were permanently employed, some for up to 12 hours a day and often in very bad conditions. They noted that the children were not directly employed by the factory owners, but worked for an intermediary . . . who was herself paid on a piecework basis by the factory owner. . . . [Hence] the factory owners could, if the law was not enforced, avoid all contact with their workers." Anti-Slavery Society, 1985).
12. Yang Razail Kassim, "Domestic help in Indonesia: the good, the bad and the indispensable," *Straits Times* (Singapore), June 16, 1989.
13. I am grateful to Michael Forrer for this point.
14. Pulley, "Sale of Johnson Products splits family," op. cit., n. 1.
15. "Empires in the east," op. cit., n. 8.
16. "Splits, and survival," op. cit., n. 5.
17. John Rossant, "Decline, Italian style," *Business Week*, August 2, 1993.

13

International Joint Ventures

13.1 Introduction

An international joint venture established on a 50–50 ownership basis by Gillette and a municipal company in Shenyang, north-eastern China, succeeded despite many difficulties.

> Gillette paid particular attention to workers' productivity, says [the former general manager, a Gillette employee], and many complained about the increased work load. Some quit, others were even sacked, a novel practice in China. Those who stayed were compensated with wages 25 percent–50 percent higher than at local enterprises. The Chinese deference to age was a problem: old workers would not listen to young managers. "You have to get rid of either the manager or the workers," remarks [the general manager]. And sacking someone involves lengthy dialogue with local authorities. Says he: "You have to give a good reason and they try to talk you out of it."[1]

The expatriate CEO of an international joint venture faces problems of leading and motivating a workforce and dealing with an environment when local values do not correspond to his own or his organization's values. In the case above, the problems are acute because

- the cultural, commercial, economic (etc.) environments of the two participating "parents" to the international joint venture (the United States and the People's Republic of China) differ widely. Staff of the parents attached different values to productivity, rewards, job security, basis of seniority (age and political affiliations as against qualifications);

- the organizational cultures of the two parents (a highly competitive private-sector manufacturer; an organization in a public sector characterized by a heavy emphasis on central planning) differ widely;
- the human resource strategies followed by the two parents differ widely.

This chapter deals with the problems and benefits that arise when companies form alliances in international joint ventures. Cultural differences influence planning for the venture and operations in so far as they are reflected in different perceptions of goals, strategy, human resource policy, opportunities and threats, constraints on implementation, structural relationships, priorities in communicating.

The chapter is organized as follows:

13.2 Alliances and International Joint Ventures
13.3 Success and Failure in IJVs
13.4 Human Resource Policies in IJVs
13.5 Cultural Differences between the Parents
13.6 Communicating between the Parents and the IJV
13.7 Implications for the Manager
13.8 Summary
13.9 Exercise

13.2 Alliances and International Joint Ventures

A firm proposing to expand outside its national boundaries can choose between a wide range of options:

- establishing an international joint venture;
- creating a wholly owned subsidiary;
- acquiring an on-going company and establishing it as a wholly owned subsidiary;
- signing a licensing contract with a local company;
- a distribution and sales agreeement;
- a technology agreement;
- a research agreement;
- a product development and servicing agreement;
- a management agreement;
- a turnkey agreement (that is, contracting to construct and/or deliver a "ready to operate" system, plant, etc.).

These different forms of alliance sometimes involve very complex forms of organization; for instance, a simple research agreement involves one party conducting research for the other in return for a fee, but a collaborative research program demands that both contribute researchers and facilities to work in coordination.

This book is chiefly concerned with the first three alternatives – that is, with the international joint venture and the management of foreign subsidiaries. This chapter focuses on international joint ventures, henceforth IJVs. The next chapter deals with staffing and controlling a foreign subsidiary.

Many definitions are given of the IJV. Here is a slight adaptation of that made by Shenkar and Zeira (1987).

- The IJV is created by the investments of two or more parent firms.
- It is a separate legal organizational entity, and belongs entirely to neither/none of its parents.
- It is jointly controlled by its parents.
- These parents are legally independent of each other.
- The headquarters of at least one parent is located outside the country in which the IJV operates.

13.2.1   The increasing popularity of IJVs

Up until the early 1970s, United States business was set resolutely against IJV agreements; shared ownership meant sharing profits, and most significantly, sharing control. But since then the mood has changed. For instance, General Motors owned 100 percent of equity in its six overseas subsidiaries; by 1975, 6 of its 40 subsidiaries were jointly owned, and by one 1989 estimate, 12 out of GM's new foreign subsidiaries had been IJVs (Gomes-Casseres, 1989).

Taking the United States in general, IJVs replaced the wholly owned subsidiary as the most widespread form of American investment overseas. It seems probable that between 1981 and 1990, more joint venture agreements were announced than in all previous years in total (Anderson, 1990).

Even in less developed countries, more and more firms are trying to increase their influence abroad by signing joint venture agreements with appropriate partners. Over the past two decades national governments increasingly recognize that IJV agreements bring social and economic benefits that extend beyond the limits of the involved organizations. This process was demonstrated throughout the 1980s by a global tendency to jettison outmoded restrictions that limited foreign ownership to less than 50 percent, and to liberalize their legislation concerning foreign control of equity.

Fukuyama (1991) argues that the less developed countries were persuaded to take this step by the examples of the Asian economies, whose dynamic growth confounded dependency theory and neo-Marxist arguments for protectionism against the developed world.

> [T]he most successful sectors within Asian economies have tended to be those permitting the greatest degree of competition in domestic markets and integration into international ones. . . . What Asia's postwar economic miracle demonstrates is that capitalism is a path toward economic development that is potentially available to all countries. No underdeveloped country in the Third World is disadvantaged simply because it began the growth process later than Europe, nor are the established industrial powers capable of blocking the development of a latecomer, provided that country plays by the rules of economic liberalism. (pp. 102–3)

The most significant changes between 1977 to 1982 occurred in Mexico, Nigeria, India, and South Korea (Contractor, 1990). These countries drastically revised their regulations on equity ownership by overseas parents, and benefited enormously.

Companies from the developed countries have also tended to rethink their demands for majority ownership. In some circumstances, minority ownership offers opportunities that a larger holding does not. A study of United States joint ventures in the People's Republic of China suggests that the greater the involvement of the local parent in the venture, the greater its commitment to the venture, and the less the risks to the foreign parent (Shan, 1991).

However, there may be other factors that inhibit the company accepting less that 51 percent. Franko's (1989) analysis of ownership patterns throughout the 1970s showed that although United States parent companies were in general much happier to take a minority interest, they insisted on a majority interest (or established a wholly owned subsidiary) in situations where they had proprietary technological or marketing strengths that they were unwilling to trust to their partner's control.

Although moves to liberalize ownership policies have generally been successful, they do not guarantee the success of individual IJV projects. One early study of 1,812 international joint ventures found that 464 were subsequently taken over by the multinational parent (Vaupel and Curhan, 1969). Franko's (1971) study of 1,100 showed that 182 became wholly owned subsidiaries of the American parent, 84 were dissolved, and 48 changed control (see also Franko 1974). Other estimations put the number of successes at only 30 to 50 percent, or even as few as 20 percent.[2]

Clearly, entering an IJV entails considerable risk. This leads us to a number of questions:

- Why enter an IJV?
- For what reasons other than short-term financial gain might a company enter an IJV?
- For what reasons might a company be inhibited from entering an IJV?

And section 13.3 deals with factors that influence the success or failure of an IJV.

13.2.2 Why enter an IJV?

The obvious reason for entering a joint venture is that it promises to make money. But evidence suggests that other forms of alliance may be more profitable.

Contractor and Lorange (1988) demonstrated from cost/benefit analysis that this cooperative mode is only preferred to go-it-alone alternatives when the incremental benefit of the former over the latter is greater than the other partner's share of the profits. Kent's (1991) longitudinal analysis of deals made by the seven major oil companies (British, Dutch, and five United States) showed that joint ventures produced significantly lower gross yields than did non-joint ventures. Similarly, a study of ventures by 10 large Dutch companies led Douma (1991) to conclude that their joint venture and minority interests were less successful than acquiring an on-going business with 100 percent ownership.

The acquisition of the wholly owned subsidiary was most likely to succeed when the growth was by

- related diversification; diversifying into a related field;
- vertical integration; acquiring an up-stream business.

For horizontal expansion on these bases, the success rates of domestic and foreign acquisitions were the same.

But the continuing fashion for IJVs demonstrates that these facts are not of overpowering significance when companies plan their foreign commitments. How, then, can we explain the failure of so many top managements to be convinced by what might appear an obvious case against the IJV?

One reason is that there is no general agreement on how such "objective" financial data should be analysed. Because figures for market share, sales levels, and profitability, are likely to be perceived and interpreted differently by the parents and the IJV management, they have to be treated with caution. Using Canadian data, Geringer and Hebert (1991) argue that these objective measures of IJV stability do not appear to be any more reliable than subjective assessments of overall satisfaction.

Added to this uncertainty about how short-term financial data should be interpreted are a wide range of long-term factors; and they often add up to a convincing case for entering an IJV.

13.2.3 Long-term reasons for entering an IJV Agreement

Reasons other than the predicted financial outcomes include:

- Opportunities to create greater market power by combining resources with some other company, and thus create economies of scale.
- Opportunities to reduce risk by sharing risk. Costs of investment and production are shared.
- Opportunities to enter new markets. Establishing an IJV is probably more appropriate than a wholly owned subsidiary when the firm seeks to expand its capabilities into new areas.
- Opportunities to acquire information and technology. These justify the firm forming an IJV agreement when the planned venture will operate outside its core activities, or when the firm is technologically weak – as is the case for many firms in lesser developed economies. But they offer no inducements to the firm that is a technological leader, and when the planned IJV will involve core activities. Here are examples:

> The French electronics group Thomson thrived in the Thomson/Thorn/JVC video-recorder alliance because its aim was the same as JVC's – to learn. Thorn decided to drop out. Ford learned management lessons from Mazda, which had five times fewer finance and control managers.[3]

- Opportunities to cooperate and to avoid competition, which might incur greater costs than are incurred by agreeing to the IJV. The IJV is an alliance that restricts your own capacity for independent action, but also restricts that of your partner – who might otherwise be a dangerous opponent.
- Opportunities to regain a competitive edge. Rover linked up with Honda, and Chrysler with Mitsubishi as strategies designed to win back market share.
- Opportunities to secure experience and training. Both parents benefit from opportunities to secure experience and training. The foreign parent is able to expose its staff to expatriate work conditions.

- The foreign parent wishes to meet the host government's requirements for doing business in the country. For instance, a foreign company is only permitted to establish a subsidiary if ownership is shared with a local company.
- The foreign parent wishes to export products into a protectionist local market. The IJV provides the essential channels.
- The foreign parent wishes to invest in local enterprise; to secure supplies of material and labor which are unavailable in the headquarters country, or available only at greater expense.
- The local parent wishes to generate hard (convertible) currency profits. Rosten reports that in the then Soviet Union before 1991, an international joint venture enabled the foreign partner to earn and withdraw hard currency profits (Rosten, 1991). Such opportunities were not so easily available to the Soviet-based subsidiaries of multinationals.
- The local parent expects IJV activity to generate up-stream and downstream industries. For instance, the development of an IJV pulp mill encourages local entrepreneurs to increase logging facilities, and to invest in paper manufacture.
- The local government hopes to encourage foreign investment. Only very rarely does a government veto a planned IJV involving a local firm, and operating in its national territory. However, the foreign investor may be expected to take only minority ownership, and fulfil stringent conditions regarding employment of locals, technology transfer, purchase of local materials, etc.

This list of factors distinguishes points of concern to the local and overseas parents. Even when they agree on the IJV project goals and strategies for implementing these goals, the parents are almost certain to have different reasons for deciding to make the investment. These differences cause them to evaluate project activity from different perspectives. For instance, the foreign parent may have a long-term strategic interest in penetrating the local market whereas its local partner focuses on raising its own manufacturing capacities.

13.2.4 Reasons for not entering an IJV agreement

The conditions under which the company decides *not* to enter an IJV (and instead chooses one of the alternatives listed in 13.2) include the following:

- net benefits are predicted as less than some alternative arrangement – for instance, operating through a wholly owned subsidiary (Contractor and Lorange, 1988);

- the risk of conflict with the other company is unacceptably high;
- the company fears losing control of its own technologies;
- it fears losing control of marketing data;
- it fears losing control of key human resource assets;
- ownership and other conditions imposed by the other company or government are unacceptable (Neghandi, 1987);
- the company is already market leader in this locality, and its primary need is to exploit an existing competitive advantage; in this situation, establishing a wholly owned subsidiary is the better alternative (Gomes-Casseres, 1989);
- the company cannot afford the capital and other investments;
- the company does not have an entrepreneurial culture;
- the overseas company believes that the country of operations is politically and/or economically unstable; country risk is too great;
- the overseas company lacks experience and knowledge of the country of operations;
- market conditions are highly volatile. Some other arrangement (licensing, for instance) gives greater flexibility.

13.3 Success and Failure in IJVs

This section surveys a range of factors that influence the chances of IJV success or failure. It does not deal with cultural factors, which are discussed in section 13.4.

The major determinant of success is the choice of partner (Geringer, 1991). The company looks for a partner whose strengths meet the primary goals of the planned venture, and whose characteristics make the best possible match with its own.

13.3.1 Trust

The two partners, and the managers representing them in planning and implementing the venture, must trust and respect each other. A lack of trust can be fatal. Distrust arises from the factors listed (see also Lorange and Roos, 1991):

- communications problems, on both personal and organizational levels; different priorities are applied in communicating (see section 13.6);
- personal differences, explained and rationalized in terms of climate and culture;
- lack of internal support; top managements agree enthusiastically to the IJV without marketing it to their employees; subordinate levels

fail to understand the goals of this "foreign adventure" or to sympathize with it;

- local employees of an IJV distrusting the operations of the foreign parent when it is stronger, and screening information from employees of that parent;
- conflicts caused by implementation of human resource and technology transfer policies – discussed in section 13.4;
- one parent rethinking its goals for the project, perhaps in line with a general reformulation of strategy, appointment of a new CEO, etc.;
- in the original planning, inadequate delineation of responsibilities held by the two parents when implementing the project; it is not clear who is supposed to do what, using what resources, by when;
- a strategic mismatch and perceptions of competing long-term interests which only become evident as the project develops; the initial analysis of strengths, weaknesses, opportunities and threats was inadequate.

The parents must be respected – as must the independent status of the project itself. In summarizing his typology of Japanese IJVs in the United States, Tyebjee (1988) comments that

> [i]n joint ventures by procreation, the critical issue seems to be the willingness of the partners, who tend to hold equal power, to respect the status of each other. The parents in these joint ventures tend to engage in skirmishes over issues which are largely a matter of face. It is critical in these joint ventures that the chief executive officer of the venture not have a bias in allegiance to one parent over another. The CEO must manage more than the venture, he or she must also manage the relationship between the parents. (p. 85)

The problems involved in balancing the interests of the project and its parents cannot be underestimated. When the parents share ownership on a 50–50 basis, the potential for deadlock between them is at its greatest, and so are the pressures on the CEO.

Parents trust each other when each shows its determination to meet its resource commitments. The implementation of human resource commitments are discussed in section 13.4.

13.3.2 Similar business interests

The parents must have similar business interests and belong to similar or complementary sectors. An IJV between a multinational petroleum company and a local paint manufacturer to start a business manufacturing industrial polymers may serve both their interests. Both can contribute skills and information, develop synergetic working relationships, and benefit from their cooperation. But it would make superficially little sense for the petroleum company to set up its polymer business in partnership with a hotel chain. There are almost no opportunities for synergy. The hotel chain can contribute little to the project (other, perhaps, than capital), and the petroleum company is forced to invest by far the larger share of professional expertise in R&D, manufacture, and marketing.

Companies in the same industry form alliances when they hope to benefit from discrepancies in technology, systems, markets, etc. By 1993, joint ventures parented by the Swiss food firm Nestlé included alliances with Coca Cola (canned coffee and tea drinks), General Mills (cereals), and two companies in the People's Republic of China (a coffee and creamer plant, an infant formula and milk powder plant).[4]

13.3.3   Common/complementary goals

The venture is more likely to succeed when the parents share common goals for the IJV and have complementary long-term strategic goals for themselves. If both parents hope to develop an international market, the signs are promising. But if one parent is only concerned with developing products that serve its home market, their strategic objectives conflict.

13.3.4   Compatibility in size

The size of the parents is significant when one uses its greater resources to dominate the project and to twist it to serve its own ends and these are in conflict with the interests of the smaller parent. If the petroleum company (in the example above) has the capacity to channel the project into manufacturing paints that compete with those produced by its partner the paint manufacturer, the latter stands to lose rather than gain from the association.

13.3.5   Compatibility in timescale

The parents must share the same timescale. If both are able to invest five years' development costs, the project is set fair. In a journal interview, David Hollingsworth (1988), CEO of Hercules, explains that when his company is looking for a partner, it

> should feel comfortable with our way of doing business. It should have the same time horizon that we do. . . . [Partners have] got to be compatible from both a personality and cultural standpoint and should have the same time horizon for what they hope to accomplish with the venture. (pp. 14–15)

Timescales conflict when, for instance, one parent must earn profits within two years and the other is prepared to wait ten years. Different timescales reflect different business interests and strategies; and often, different temporal orientations – and these reflect culture. According to Hofstede (1991, p. 166) Korea, Japan, and the Confucian cultures (but excepting the Philippines) normally take a long-term orientation towards projects, and the Anglo cultures take relatively short-term orientations.

An appropriate framework may be incremental; the parents use an initial limited alliance in order to test the possibilities for a greater commitment. In 1990, the two European automakers Renault and Volvo established a cross-shareholdings agreement. In 1993, they decided to form a joint strategic and product-planning department. This was intended as a step towards a possible merger.[5]

13.3.6 Environmental factors

Environmental factors that influence the success or failure of the IJV include:

- political factors, both international and local;
- economic conditions and industry conditions;
- market conditions, including demand and supply factors, markets for materials and labor, competition;
- conditions in the natural environment;
- availability of technology;
- culture.

This environment is bound to change. In retrospect it might seem that your company should not have formed an IJV at that particular point in time – or should not have gone into business with that particular partner. Or perhaps the decision and choice is triumphantly vindicated. The two parents and the project itself each are differently constrained by the environment; for instance, the two parents, in different countries, operate under different political and economic constraints.

Uncertainty and change in the environment may be an argument for focusing on only short-term alliances with highly specific goals. In 1990, Sanofi (owned by Elf Aquitaine) and Sterling Drug (owned by Eastman Kodak) created a project to share each other's distribution networks and create a combined research and development operation.[6]

13.3.7 Agreement on decision-making processes

The chances of success are greatly improved when the parents agree on decision-making procedures, and these are made explicit.

Perhaps ideally, the IJV management makes all decisions on day-to-day operations by itself with a minumum of interference by the parents, who should be concerned only with long-term strategic issues. But it practice, this is unlikely to occur.

Each parent hopes to exercise as much control over operations as is necessary to protect its interests and achieve its strategic goals. The critical issue is to achieve the necessary level of control while still maintaining as light a touch as possible over the administration (Geringer and Hebert, 1989). The parent that focuses on introducing systems and structures in order to protect its perceived interests is in danger of altogether stifling the opportunities for synergetic creativity and cooperation with its partner.

Parents agree on the *balance* of management responsibilities. Both parents attempting to dominate day-to-day decision-making is a sure recipe for disaster. Each parent takes responsibilities in those areas in which it is the stronger. For instance, an American manager working in a Swiss–United States joint venture reports that

> [the IJV] has been fortunate that [the Swiss parent] ... has assumed a subordinate role and that [the American parent] has been willing and capable of fulfilling the dominant role. The effect on [the IJV] is that all ordering, invoicing, inventory, distribution, tax obligations, and financial reporting is done through [the American parent] systems. The [Swiss parent] influence comes mainly from product-oriented issues.

The parent implements the scope of control allotted it making senior appointments to those functions that correspond with its interests. The factors which determine which parent contributes top management include the following.

- *The goals of the IJV* Lyons (1991) discusses evidence that the essential structure of the project is determined by its goals – and in particular goals in regard to securing market access or technological capability. An IJV primarily dedicated to marketing might be headed by a marketer.
- *Which parent makes the greater technological inputs (and owns brand names and patent rights)* The technological parent also tends to be that with majority equity ownership (Blodgett, 1991). And it naturally wishes to protect its property by placing its own staff in positions which give the most guarantee of security.

  When the parents represent more and less developed national economies, the company from the developed economy is most likely to be the technological parent. Conflicts arise when it appears to overvalue its techological inputs, and to demand too great a scope of control on the basis of inputs that the other parent regards as derivative or outmoded.

- *Which parent makes the greater skills and knowledge inputs* for instance, marketing expertise. In theory, the local parent from a less developed economy balances the foreign parent's technological inputs with local market expertise. But over time, its knowledge and control of local marketing channels is increasingly weakened. The foreign parent makes its own contacts and establishes its own data sources.
- *Which parent makes the greater capital inputs.*
- *Availability of top management talent in the two parents and in external labor pools.*

When the IJV is based in the national territory of the weaker parent, issues of national pride arise. The local government may demand that its nationals are placed in controlling roles, or the parent's own top management feel that they cannot be seen to be taking a subordinate position, and are not prepared to settle for only ceremonial and symbolic roles.

13.4 Human Resource Policies in IJVs

An important success factor is that employees of the venture are agreed in their

- interpretations of the project's goals;
- interests in the project;
- expectations of project outcomes;
- perceptions of how their participation will affect their long-term career prospects.

When there is significant disagreement over these factors, conflict becomes more likely. This section sees why.

Chapter 1 showed that possibilities of conflict are reduced when all members of the work group are drawn from a single culture. That is, all IJV staff are drawn from a single labor pool; they might be borrowed from the local parent for the duration of the project, and on its termination will return to this parent. Their cultural values correspond, they have related interests, and share experiences and values of the same organizational culture.

However, this situation is unlikely, given the importance that both parents attach to the venture, and to influencing operations, and hence in placing their staff in functions essential to headquarters interests.

Hence, the IJV most probably recruits from more than one labor pools. IJV staff recruited may include all of the following:

- employees temporarily transferred by the local parent;
- employees temporarily transferred by the foreign parent;
- local nationals contracted for the life of the project;
- nationals of the foreign-parent country contracted for the life of the project;
- nationals of third countries contracted for the life of the project.

These employees may also be differentiated at organizational levels (top/middle/junior managerial staff, non-managerial staff, professional, etc.), all of which may be drawn from these categories above.

A heterogeneous labor force offer opportunities for synergy. But the wider the recruitment pool, the greater also are the potential conflicts. Their different backgrounds are reflected in their loyalty to the IJV.

In the event of a conflict between project and parents, those employees tranferred from a parent (to which they expect to return on project termination) are more likely to place its interests above those of the project. They may create unofficial matrix structures, reporting to managers in both the project and their parent. They may be committed to obstructing project activities which appear likely to harm the parent's interests. Hence their loyalty to the project is always qualified.

Professional staff contracted for the life of a short-term venture have less interest in relations between the parents and with the project (unless, perhaps, they hope to be taken on by one of the parent on project termination). Their loyalties to the project are influenced by the prospects it offers for gaining experience and credentials that can earn them further contracts. They interpret the venture objectives in terms of their future career needs.

The different interests of transferred and contracted employees always threatens to bring them into conflict. At worst, contradictory loyalties are complicated by professional, hierarchical, and cultural differences. They bring different organizational values, and, when they belong to different nationalities, different cultural values. These differences affect

- their relations with each other and with project management;
- their needs for and expectations of formal structures and systems;
- their needs for and expectations of project culture.

13.4.1 Designing human resource strategies

How staffing agreements are implemented crucially affects relations between transferred and contracted staff, and between the parents.

When one parent witholds its best staff and throws on to the other the onus for contributing expertise, relations between individual project members and the parents quickly sour. This may occur in a project between a protected public-sector parent and a private-sector parent, when the former exploits the project as a means of relieving itself of "deadwood" and trouble-makers, or of securing prestigious postings for technically unqualified employees. For instance, the CEO of the parent appoints his unqualified son-in-law to a directorship in the IJV.

When parents come from different sectors, and their different experiences are compounded by different national economic factors, the imbalance may be significant. In general, managers working in a developed and complex modern economy have acquired a greater range of skills than managers in poorer, less developed economies, and bring greater expertise to the IJV.

The introductory story provides an example. A similar case is shown by Nepal at the end of the 1970s (Pradhan, 1978). Most corporations were public and most managers appointed to them had come from the civil service; and so they were without experience of commerce, and international competition. They did not possess the skills to negotiate with Western entrepreneurs and to implement agreements. The same problem occurred when communism broke down in Eastern Europe and the then Soviet Union in 1989–91, and these countries started trying to develop capitalist modes of production. Corporations lacked managers who understood the basic marketing and accounting concepts that are routinely taught in free-market economies but not in the planned economies.

A local, weaker parent may have decided to participate in the project with the clear objective of securing a transfer of technology from its stronger partner, and training for its managers and technical staff. They are employed by the project as trainees or "shadows" of their more experienced colleagues from the stronger parent. This arrangement may work well, so long as all parties (the parents and the IJV management)

- have agreed to it;
- have planned how the technology transfer and training activities should be implemented;
- are satisfied with the implementation process.

But this use of local staff in trainee roles is unlikely to be motivating when the local parent managers are significantly older (in a culture that respects age – as in the case of the Chinese community in the introductory case), or consider themselves adequately trained, or have no motivation to acquire training. The latter category includes staff from the public sector whose jobs are guaranteed, and protected from competitive forces.

13.4.2 Motivating transferred and externally recruited employees

Here we simplify the list of possible labor sources and deal with

- employees transferred by the local parent;
- employees transferred by the foreign parent;
- employees contracted for the life of the project, by either parent or by the IJV.

Transferred staff are more likely to be motivated when they are given a free choice of whether or not to join the IJV, and recognize that it is in their career and professional interests to do so. There may be particular factors that make IJV employment attractive. For instance, before the collapse of the Soviet Union, IJV employment offered the Soviet citizen an opportunity to travel abroad, and access to foreign currency – otherwise very difficult to come by (Rosten, 1991); and this is likely to be the case elsewhere that a national government restricts the free movement of its nationals.

The needs of employees transferred from the foreign parent are dealt with in chapter 16 which deals with strategies for selecting and motivating expatriates. Employees transferred from the parent headquartered in the country are in continual touch with their parent and have few problems keeping abreast of events in their parent. To this extent they may be better off than are their colleagues transferred from the foreign parent – despite developments in electronic communications.

The question then arises: how far should the parents and/or IJV invest in similar motivators, training, facilities, etc., for those staff contracted for the life of the project, who have primary loyalty to the IJV rather than to either parent? And how far can it afford not to?

Staff contracted for the life of the IJV project from outside the parents become dissatisfied if the allocation of rewards and services seems to discriminate against them in favor of transferred employees. Zeira and Harari's (1977) analysis of multinational subsidiaries located in the United States, Japan, Western Europe, and Israel found that third-country managers showed low levels of loyalty in part because of their conviction that headquarters regarded them as second-class citizens.

13.5 Cultural differences between the parents

The chances of IJV success are influenced by the atmosphere of trust generated between managers in the parents and IJV. But how is the necessary trust and understanding developed? Even before the key IJV agreement is signed,

- senior managers of the two parents are recruited to policy groups in which they work jointly on planning;
- professional staff exchange non-critical technological and business data (Dobkin, 1988);
- staff who will be lent to the project are brought together in social events.

Such ground work is essential. But it does not guarantee success, and the problems may be acute when the parents come from very different national and/or organizational cultures.

For instance, when talks designed to lead to a strategic alliance between Mitsubishi of Japan and Daimler-Benz of Germany broke down,

> [a]nalysts say the match has been strained from the beginning because the companies have fundamentally different structures.
>
> Daimler-Benz, a much smaller company than Mitsubishi, has traditionally had a closeknit management structure that has tended to set out clear strategic goals and forge ahead. Mitsubishi, an amorphous conglomerate of several large companies, has moved much more cautiously with internal factions often disagreeing over broader policy, analysts said.[7]

The companies were apparently unable to overcome differences in their

- strategies;
- organizational structures;
- organizational cultures.

And, in so far as their structures and organizational cultures reflected their national cultures, national cultural differences.

13.5.1 IJV cooperation between national cultures

Managers transferred from the two parents are better able to work together when their national cultures are "compatible." The cultural values of the managers transferred by the parents and recruited by the IJV affect their capacity to agree on common ground at all stages of IJV development, from planning the project to final assessment.

Cultural factors influence the likelihood of different groups of managers agreeing upon a range of factors. These factors include the following.

- *Structural priorities* and the design of structures designed to promote or restrict participation in decision-making and management, on both a vertical basis between different levels and a horizontal basis between different functions.

For instance, very different expectations are held by managers from a culture where needs to avoid uncertainty and power distances are small (in Hofstede's (1984a) terms, a market bureaucracy) and from a culture where the opposite features apply (a full bureaucracy). The former are used to obtaining information from sources across the organization and to taking initiatives. The latter have far greater needs to observe the hierarchy, and are more likely to refer anomolies to a direct superior (Killing, 1982).

- *Management style*   A study of Canadian IJVs in South-east Asia (that is, where the cultural contexts of the potential partners were widely dissimular) discovered that the most significant management problems were "incompatibility of management style" and "incompatibility of partners' objectives" (Hung, 1991).
- *Systems for communicating*   between the IJV and its parents, and within the IJV, and communications priorities (see section 13.6).
- *Systems for motivating, rewarding, punishing*   What behavior should be rewarded, and what punished?
- *Relations*   between different managerial and non-managerial levels, professionals and generalists, men and women, age groups.
- *Management plans*   for the organizational culture.
- *Temporal priorities*   whether a decision should be delayed for superior confirmation, or made and implemented immediately, in order to take advantage of present conditions.
- *Perceptions of needs for change.*
- *Assessments of IJV success and failure; project evaluation, both on-going and on termination*   Geringer and Hebert's (1991) study of IJVs involving Canadian, United States, and parents located outside North America found "correlation between a parent's satisfaction with IJV performance and the perception by its partner and the IJV general manager of this parent's satisfaction" was stronger when the IJV involved parents with similar national cultures (p. 253).

The structural priorities should be spelled out in the negotiation stages, and reflect the interests of that parent taking day-to-day responsibilities for running the IJV. But how the structures are interpreted and implemented can only be determined over time.

13.5.2   Significant points of similarity in national cultures

It is sometimes argued that ventures formed by parents of similar cultures necessarily stand a better chance of success than do ventures between dissimilar cultures. But such generalizations are too loose, and overlook the facts that no two cultures correspond at all points, and that otherwise very similar cultures may vary widely in some respects – as Hofstede's (1984a) data show. For instance, the cultures of Finland and Switzerland have similar needs to avoid uncertainty (ranked 19 and 20= respectively) and similar power distances (34 and 37), but Finland is far the more feminine (7 and 46=).

Hofstede (1985) hypothesizes that synergy between organizations takes place when cultures are balanced around the masculine and feminine mean and are close on the "organizational" dimensions of power distance and uncertainty avoidance (pp. 355–6). He cites the examples of British and Dutch cultures (more masculine, more feminine; otherwise similar). He suggests that most problems will be experienced by cultures that differ on the organizational dimensions. Hence, a typical company in a full-bureaucracy culture (for instance France, or Belgium) could expect greater problems cooperating with a company in a personnel-bureaucracy culture (Denmark, New Zealand, United Kingdom) than with a company from, say, Korea or Salvador. These two cultures are very close to France and Belgium in terms of both power distance and needs to avoid uncertainty, although they are in other and apparently less significant respects far apart.

13.5.3 How the IJV affects the parent organizational cultures

Parenting an IJV project may sometimes significantly influence the culture of the parent headquarters by creating a new spirit of "internationalism." This is *advantageous* when

- headquarters staff benefit from an inflow of new ideas and technologies;
- perceptions of the market environment, and opportunities and threats, are broadened.

It may be *disadvantageous* when

- the inflow of new personnel and outflow of established personnel impairs internal cohesion; the sense of shared "togetherness" is lost; a previously strong culture is weakened;
- staff respond adversely to the new challenges. They feel pressured by responsibilities outside their previous experience; champions of the new IJV project are isolated.

Planning for and operating the IJV may also influences structures and systems in the parent headquarters. In order to respond efficiently to problems and opportunities arising from parenting the IJV project, headquarters streamlines and reorganizes its structures.

Siddall et al.'s (1992) case study of British Petroleum's response to its international commitments shows how London headquarters was forced to

- reduce paperwork;
- adopt new matrix structures.
- flatten hierarchies;
- break down boundaries between units;
- rethink roles of and relationships between headquarters and foreign units.

In summarizing what has been achieved, the writers note that

[c]hanges in personnel are accommodated easily because roles and accountabilities are attached to jobs not individuals, and networks provide consistency and stability. The short-circuiting of hierarchies for the purpose of improving decisions ensures that power is applied where it is needed. (p. 45)

This shows the influence of international commitments in forcing the company to decentralize, and develop structures in which ease of access to units and individuals with expertise and information is treated as an organizational priority. Staff positions are reduced and structural interdependencies simplified.

13.6 Communicating between the Parents and the IJV

Success in planning and implementing an IJV agreement depends to a large extent upon success in communicating. Communications are extensive, and occur

- between the parents;
- between each parent and the IJV;
- within the IJV;
- between the parents or IJV and the environment; audiences within the environment include stockholders, analysts, the media, consumers, unions, trade associations, regulative and legislative bodies.

Communication is optimal when it is selective. This means, first, that the parties concerned must avoid

- under-communication;
- over-communication.

IJV development is set back when vital information is not transmitted. This includes technology. A project may fail when a parent is over-restrictive in providing technical data to the venture through fear that these will be give that other parent a commercial advantage. (In practice, the parent is very unlikely to ever employ its most up-to-date technology and best scientists on an IJV.)

Administrating the IJV is equally hampered when the various participants over-communicate, and communications are not prioritized. In many projects, quantity of information flow is achieved at the expense of quality. The more messages that flow in, the less easily can the executive identify and act decisively upon those that matter. And the process is expensive; both direct and indirect (time, energy) communication costs are incurred.

Too often, IJVs respond to problems with and between the parents by simply increasing the degree of communication. When a parent feels a strong need to exercise control, managers are deluged by memos, reports, newsletters in an ever-increasing flow. But if the essential difficulties are not addressed, this communication is likely to worsen rather than resolve them. A situation like this demands effective analysis and diagnosis, which can perhaps be achieved by relatively economic use of communication systems.

13.6.1   A communications plan

A communications plan makes clear

- *who* (in each parent, the IJV) has responsibilities for communicating with *whom* (in each parent, the IJV, the environment), given decisions about what content should be communicated, or is needed;
- *what* content should be communicated by whom (in each parent, the IJV) to whom (in each parent, the IJV, the environment);
- *how* content should be communicated; what medium is appropriate; what level of technical detail is appropriate;
- *when* content should be communicated.

Parents whose cultures differ in terms of needs to avoid uncertainty are likely to adopt different approaches to the environment. And even when they correspond, the importance of regulating communications with the environment needs underlining (Higgins and Diffenbach, 1989). Unregulated communications create bad feeling. For instance, the director of the IJV organizes a press conference in order to announce a success; and the day before the planned date, the CEO of the local parent issues the news at his own conference, thus implying that his company is chiefly responsible.

13.7 Implications for the manager

In your experience, how far do cultural values affect the planning and implementation of IJVs? How much importance do they have as against other factors? Base your answers on any knowledge you may have of a current or terminated IJV project.

1. Why did each person prefer to go into IJV partnership than to form some other sort of alliance?

   - What other alternatives were possible?
   - Why was each rejected?

2. What reasons did the parents have for agreeing to go into IJV partnership, during the initial planning?

   - What advantages and disadvantaged did an IJV partnership appear to offer the local parent?
   - What advantages and disadvantages did an IJV partnership appear to offer the foreign parent?

3. Why did the IJV project succeed, or fail?

   - What factors contributed towards the success or failure of the IJV partnership, from the local parent's point of view?
   - What factors contributed towards the success or failure of the IJV partnership, from the foreign parent's point of view?
   - Given your answers to 2, how far were these success/failure factors taken into account during the initial planning?

4. How far were cultural simularities and dissimularities a factor in determining the successes and failures of the IJV partnership? From the point of view of the local parent? The overseas parent?

   - What cultural simularities proved advantageous? Why?
   - What cultural simularities proved disadvantageous? Why?
   - What cultural dissimilarities proved advantageous? Why?
   - What cultural dissimularities proved disadvantageous? Why?

5. How did the human resources policy contribute towards success or failure?

   - Consider these groups:

(a)   employees transferred from the local parent, and
(b)   employees transferred from the foreign parent, and
(c)   employees recruited from the external labor market?

How far did they cooperate, how far compete creatively, and how far come into conflict?

- In what ways did the following factors contribute towards co-operation/competition/conflict?

(d)   in the case of (a) and (b) above, loyalty towards a parent;
(e)   professional and functional factors;
(f)   factors associated with the climates of the parents;
(g)   factors associated with the structures and systems of the parents;
(h)   factors associated with the transference of technology and skills between the parents and the IJV;
(i)   national cultural factors;
(j)   organizational cultural factors;
(k)   any other factors.

6.   Were communications between the parents, and between parents and the IJV, adequate or inadequate? Why?

13.8 Summary

This chapter has examined factors that influence the planning and implemention of an IJV.

Section 13.2 briefly considered the alternative *alliances* available to the firm looking to develop its international interests, and focused on *international joint ventures*. It dealt with the increasing popularity of IJVs as the preferred option. Section 13.3 went on to deal with factors affecting *success and failure*. The importance of choosing, and then learning to trust, the right partner, was emphasized. The section concluded by examining factors that affect how the two parents balance their interests in decision-making responsibilities.

Section 13.4 discussed *human resource policies*. Success or failure in the IJV is heavily influenced by relations between the persons who participate in the project team, their loyalties to the parents and to the project.

Section 13.5 drew together points on the importance of *culture*. The cultural attributes of each parent determines its preference in formal structures and systems, organizational culture, and other factors. Cultural factors also influence what criteria are applied in systems designed to facilitate *communicating between the parents and the IJV* (section 13.6).

13.9 Exercise

This exercise practices identifying opportunities and problems in cultural difference.

A British consulting group, Development Management Trust (DMT), and the Eastern University of Saudi Arabia (EUSA) have signed an agreement to set up a two-year technical staff training project based in EUSA. The project will be overseen by two executive directors, the London-based chairman of DMT and the EUSA Dean of Engineering, a Saudi national. The project is staffed by the following personnel, all males:

Manager	British national, responsible for day-to-day activities and reporting to the two executive directors: DMT permanent staff. Native English speaker. Good Arabic.
Assistant Manager	Saudi national: contracted by EUSA for the life of the project. Native Arabic speaker. Poor English
5 R&D Specialists	1 British national: DMT permanenent staff. 1 Jamaican and 1 United States national, both contracted by the project, both native English speakers with no Arabic. 2 Egyptian nationals, both EUSA permanent staff, both native Arabic speakers, with poor to intermediate English.
Media Specialist	Jordanian national: DMT permanent staff. Native Arabic speaker. Fluent English.
Media Assistant	Saudi national, contracted by the project. Native Arabic speaker. Intermediate English.
3 Secretaries	Palestinians: EUSA permanent staff. Native Arabic speakers. Intermediate – good English.

What opportunities and problems do you foresee?

Notes

1. "Smooth shave in a 'small' market," *Asiaweek*, January 18, 1991.
2. Roy Eales, "Partners for richer or for poorer," *Independent on Sunday*, March 18, 1990.
3. Ibid.
4. John Templeman et al., "Nestlé: a giant in a hurry," *Business Week*, March 22, 1993.

5. "Two carmakers move closer," *International Herald Tribune*, June 30, 1993.
6. "Business: managing in an age of anxiety," *The Economist*, January 19, 1991.
7. Richard E. Smith, "Daimler-Mitsubishi divorce?," *International Herald Tribune*, March 7, 1991.

14

Headquarters and Subsidiary

14.1 Introduction

Ford were employing 900 persons in their Thai subsidiary before its collapse in 1975. The failure was not to be explained by Thailand's investment and development policies, which were generous – as the history of other multinationals with Thai operations shows. A contemporary newspaper commented that

> [Ford's] departure seems to be based on internal factors. It is well known that Ford has been plagued with chronic management problems. Observers of the industry have indicated that Ford did not adjust itself soon enough to the Thai system, and there was an internal lack of communication and that no close feeling developed between the various parties involved in the enterprise.[1]

Ford's success could not be guaranteed by its initial high productivity, generous remunerations policy, modern plant, competitive pricing, and efficient dealer network. The problems, that proved fatal, arose from the company's attempting to foist onto the local market a vehicle that did not meet local demands.

Ford had sold the Fiera successfully in the Philippines – 6,900 models during its first year – and took for granted that all Asian markets were alike. Executives had not noted that the burgeoning Thai middle class was prepared to pay for a technically more sophisticated vehicle (Smith, 1982).

Why did the company not make greater efforts to analyse and understand the market, and why were its decision-makers so insensitive to local conditions? The policy was coordinated and implemented by 14 foreign experts, superimposed on the existing, indigenous management structure of Ford Thailand. And Smith argues that the failure stemmed from their lack of local experience, and refusal to make up for this lack (Smith, 1982).

> Company policy formulated in Dearborn did not have sufficient inbuilt flexibility to deal with local exigencies, even to the extent of orders for local parts having to be routed through America and Australia. In general, the Western team, without corporate guidance, made little attempt to adapt to its new . . . culture and no one made any attempt to learn Thai. Also, through largely living together with other team members and their families, a compound mentality developed . . . This life style with little involvement with the local culture further reduced the possibilities for frank and constructive communication with established Thai staff. (p. 12)

This case demonstrates the problems that can arise when subsidiary management is expatriate and too far removed from the values and realities of life. Management listened only to headquarters and appeared neither willing nor able to represent local needs. Local employees were unable to build relationships by which to break through this impasse.

This introduces questions regarding the relationship between headquarters and subsidiary management, the function of headquarters control, the balance between expatriate and local hirings in subsidiary management, and communication systems within the multinational.

These themes are all explored below. The chapter has the following sections:

14.2   The Subsidiary and the Host Society
14.3   Staffing the Multinational Subsidiary
14.4   Relations between Headquarters and the Subsidiary
14.5   Developing the Multinational
14.6   Implications for the Manager
14.7   Summary
14.8   Exercise

14.2   The Subsidiary and the Host Society

The multinational is loosely understood as a company with operations conducted in subsidiaries and associated companies throughout the world. A United Nations publication (UNECOSOC, 1978) defines multinationals as enterprises which own or control production or service facilities outside the country in which they are based. Such enterprises are not always incorporated or private; they can also be co-operatives or state owned entities. (p. 158)[2]

14.2.1 Location

When the multinational decides on a policy of foreign expansion, it chooses a country, and a location within that country, on the basis of such factors as

- market conditions; demand; availability and costs of materials;
- proximity to markets;
- production factors and labor conditions; costs and skills;
- communications and other infrastructure systems; utilities;
- economic and financial conditions, including taxes, government subsidies, ease of repatriating earnings, tariffs;
- perceptions of the culture.
- country risk, including political risk.

When the country offers positive characteristics, it attracts a wide range of companies, perhaps from a range of industries. Otherwise, the country (or region) experiences the greatest difficulty in finding any external investment at all. Schellekens (1991) listed the following to explain why many companies chose not to invest in much of Africa:

- the lack of an attractive investment climate;
- debt problems and slowdown of growth;
- negative perceptions of the culture;
- the gap between demand and supply of management talent;
- "lack of skills, knowledge and attitudes among senior executives in the government, parastatal and private sector . . . on how to deal with the relatively new phenomenon of foreign investment."

The last three points indicate that market and financial factors are not the issues that need to be considered. Qualities associated with human resources and communication between the company and the host society are of fundamental importance.

14.2.2 The welcoming host

Most countries welcome multinational investment and offer inducements in order to attract it. Typical inducements include tax concessions and rebates during early operations, incentives to settle in a less developed area of the country, advice on labor and other markets, protection against expropriation and guarantees of non-discriminatory application of laws (Jain and Puri, 1981, p. 61).

The welcome is always conditional, and some companies may be very quickly turned away. These include those with a bad international record, or with no willingness to commit substantially, or that seem likely to threaten the country's growth or defence (such as a defence-oriented firm) or to attack a powerful local monopoly. In addition, the company is expected to

- make local investments and/or take local partners;
- employ local management;
- transfer technologies;
- help develop local markets;
- provide employment and training for nationals.

Local conditions determine the structure of the agreement; for instance, authorities in the People's Republic of China are more likely to assist joint venture agreements, particularly when they transfer technology and training (Woodward and Liu, 1993). (But this should not blind us to the fact that despite developments, Chinese manufacturing is essentially labor-intensive.)

14.2.3 The welcome turns sour

Attitudes held by both the host society and the investing company are liable to change, sometimes for a range of reasons. An example is provided by the "Look East" campaign, initiated in 1981 by the Malaysian government.

The campaign was designed to break the continuing pattern of Western investment and influence, particularly by firms headquartered in Britain, the ex-colonial power. This new attitude of independence was illustrated by the 1982 "dawn raid" on the London Stock Exchange by which the government acquired a majority holding in Sime Darby, South-east Asia's then largest multinational. Government departments were instructed to avoid business with British firms unless absolutely necessary, and instead to prioritize investments from Japan and Korea.

It was hoped that Malaysians would learn their work habits and industrial discipline. Among both the Malay and Muslim majority and Chinese community this policy was regarded with suspicion, and the Prime Minister, Mahathir Mohamad, quickly had to make a public statement denying that the policy was aimed at importing East Asian (and non-Islamic) cultural values.

In return for agreements to transfer technology and train Malay engineers and workers, Japanese and Korean firms were awarded development contracts (often at the expense of local Chinese firms). They were given generous tax concesssions. Visa-abolition and double-taxation agreements were signed with Tokyo.

But the policy was not a success. Cultural antagonisms were never overcome. The East Asian companies were soon criticized for their aggressive attitudes towards their local employees. Cases were reported of Korean supervisors physically assaulting their Malay subordinates. Only second-level technologies were being transferred, and engineers returned from supposed training in East Asia complaining that they had been treated as a source of cheap manual labor. The Koreans and Japanese were correspondingly unenthusiastic about their counterparts. One Japanese university survey showed

> managers giving Malaysians an approval rating of just 19 percent while in the "care taken in work" category, they gave Malaysians a 5 percent approval rating. Not one Japanese manager gave Malaysian workers a good rating in response to a question probing assessment of "ability to adapt to changing situations". (Clad, 1989, p. 63)

Nor did the policy show the expected economic returns. Long-term investment was patchy, and the trade gap with Japan widened each year; a Malaysian $1.7 billion deficit reached M$3.6 billion in 1985 (Clad, 1989, p. 62). The policy was gradually abandoned. By the end of the decade, British, American, and other Western organizations had regained much of their former influence.

A multinational subsidiary falls out of favor with the host government when it fails, or apparently fails, to honor its original commitments. In practice, the original documentation may be insufficiently spelled out, and the two parties have different perceptions of what was intended (Root, 1972).

For instance:

- The subsidiary has failed to provide sufficient equity participation by locals. In their analysis of what caused conflict between multinationals and developing-country hosts, Neghandi and Baliga (1979) found that issues of control (below) and then equity accounted for more than half of the total issues (see also Neghandi, 1987, p. 36). IBM's then policy of 100 percent ownership of its foreign subsidiaries led the company into conflict with the governments of Nigeria and India. The company would not agree to equity participation, and in 1977 pulled out of India. But as other multinationals have learned the lesson, that majority ownership does not guarantee strength nor minority ownership weakness, local equity participation has receded as an issue.

- The subsidiary has failed to employ local managers in senior positions.
- The subsidiary has failed to respect national laws or labor practice; Marett (1984) examined complaints that Japanese subsidiaries in the United States have unfairly resisted unionism.
- The subsidiary has improperly transferred payments.

Second, the subsidiary may have failed to behave as a good corporate citizen. Perhaps it has

- failed to employ, train and develop local staff;
- built up a monopoly position that allows it to extract excessive profits and fees (Mason, 1974);
- by stifling local competition, restricted the development of local industry; this accusation was made against Coca Cola by Indian authorities when they took the decision to close the Indian subsidiary.
- unfairly exported profits to its headquarters country rather than investing them locally;
- polluted the environment;
- diverted local investment, hiring talented locals away from local companies, exhausting local resources;
- exerted unfair influence in local politics and legislation;
- exerted a negative effect upon local culture.

Third, the subsidiary becomes unwelcome because its interests and objectives and those of the government have diverged since entry was originally requested and granted (Akhter and Choudhry, 1993).

In practice, some degree of divergence is inevitable and reflects dynamism and change in both the business and political fields. But divergence presents a danger when there is no balancing convergence and when the political situation is unstable – for instance, when an election or revolution brings a new government to power with very different political and economic agenda to those of its predecessor.

14.2.4 Guarding against political risk

The worse that relations grow, the greater the political risk that the government takes action to seriously constrain the subsidiary's activities (Simon, 1982). For instance, it is subjected to such constraints as discriminatory taxation, import and export controls, bad payments, legal disputes, industrial disputes, and unfair competition from the local public sector. The worst case is that its assets are expropriated and it is forced to withdraw altogether.

Macro risks arise when nearly all foreign holdings in the host society are adversely affected by circumstances; for instance, the revolutionary expropriations that occurred in Iran in 1979–80 (Kennedy, 1991, p. 2). Micro risks affect one or a few firms selected for punishment – as was the case of Occidental and Belco in Peru, 1985.

The company lessens the dangers of political risk by, first, making a systematic analysis of the economic and political realities when first considering the location. The services of specialist country experts – political scientists and economists – provide a necessary corrective to journalism. Newspapers and television focus on dramatic and often discontinuous events such as violent coups, and tend to overlook gradual shifts in the environment which may be of far greater long-term significance – either positively or negatively.

When established in the country, the company

- implements routines to gather information about cultural and political movement;
- maintains positive relationships with a wide variety of nationals, representing a range of business, social, and political interests;
- is receptive to changes in host political and economic priorities, and looks for ways to accommodate these;
- is receptive to the local culture as reflected both within and outside the company; the introductory case indicates the dangers of an expatriate management team isolating itself from the host culture;
- adopts a flexible attitude towards local product markets;
- decentralizes decision-making in order that the voice of local management is adequately represented and heard.

14.3 Staffing the Subsidiary

When the company operates in different countries, it typically employs from their different labor markets. Legal systems permitting, a multinational might entirely staff its overseas subsidiary with employees posted from the country of its headquarters, but this degree of expatriation is expensive and most unlikely other than in a very small expatriate operation which can afford to discount the value of expertise about the local environment.

When persons from different cultures are employed within a single unit, the company faces human resource problems of reconciling their attitudes towards work, management, and each other. This section focuses on issues of senior staffing of the subsidiary. It looks at the conditions under which the multinational might appoint a manager expatriated from headquarters and when it might appoint a local manager.

A third alternative is to appoint a national of a third country. It is sufficient to note that third country nationals are employed when

- they have particular technical and managerials skills not on offer from the other two sources;
- their skills are relatively cheap;
- the company wishes to establish an international culture not typical to the countries of either headquarters or subsidiary; it employs a range of third-country nationals in order to create as wide a mix as possible.

14.3.1   Local and expatriate staffing

United States and European multinationals typically employ more local managers and far fewer expatriated staff in their foreign subsidiaries than do Japanese multinationals. This is substantiated by Tung (1982).

Tung presents research showing that in the United States, European multinationals staff their subsidiaries at senior levels with parent country nationals (PCNs) in 29 percent of cases, host country nationals (HCNs) in 67 percent, third-country nationals (TCNs) in 4 percent; Japanese multinationals staff senior levels with PCNs in 83 percent of cases, and HCNs in 17 percent.

In Western Europe, United States multinationals staff senior levels with 33 percent PCNs, 60 percent HCNs, 7 percent TCNs; European multinationals staff with 38 percent PCNs, 62 percent HCNs; Japanese multinationals staff with 77 percent PCNs, 23 percent HCNs.

In Latin/South America, United States multinationals staff senior levels with 44 percent PCNs, 47 percent HCNs, 9 percent TCNs; European multinationals staff with 78 percent PCNs, 16 percent HCNs, 5 percent HCNs; Japanese multinationals staff with 83 percent PCNs, 17 percent HCNs.

In the Far East, United States multinationals staff senior levels with 55 percent PCNs, 38 percent HCNs, 7 percent TCNs; European multinationals staff with 85 percent PCNs, 15 percent HCNs; Japanese multinationals staff with 65 percent PCNs, 35 percent HCNs.

These figures, figures for other regions (Canada, Middle/Near East, Eastern Europe, Africa) and for other managerial levels (middle, lower) indicate that in general, the Japanese still tended to post greater numbers of managers from headquarters; the Europeans rank second place and the Americans least.

How far culture is a factor in determining that, for instance, Japanese need most immediate control of their overseas holdings and Americans least, is taken up in section 14.4.1.

We are immediately concerned with other variables that can influence policy in regards to the subsidiary.

Kobrin (1988) argued on the basis of these figures that the United States retreat from subsidiary management had gone too far; headquarters control was bound to suffer, and the reduction in expatriate staffing had serious strategic implications.

> First, if most employees are local then there are precious few who either have an encompassing knowledge of the worldwide organization or identify with it and its objectives. Second, in many diversified [multinationals], personnel are a critical instrument of headquarter's strategic control and the virtual elimination of expatriates affects control adversely. Last, at least in American firms, managers have gained their international expertise on the job through overseas assignments in one or more countries. (p. 64)

Significant cutbacks in opportunities to manage overseas subsidiaries means that more Americans will spend more of their careers restricted to home branches. This means that fewer Americans will develop the competences necessary to manage multinational corporations.

Whether or not a reduced expatriate presence weakens headquarters control of the subsidiary, to the detriment of the company, raises questions about

- the style of control that is most beneficial to headquarters and to the subsidiary;
- the advantages and disadvantages of developing local managers as opposed to expatriating headquarters staff.

There can be no absolutely right or wrong figure for expatriate staffing levels. Environmental features determine what is the best staffing mix for each company. The advantages and disadvantages of expatriate and local staffing demonstrate how these features interact.

14.3.2 The advantages and disadvantages of expatriate staffing

What are the advantages and disadvantages of employing more headquarters staff to manage the foreign subsidiary? The *advantages* are:

- Opportunities to impose headquarters control are greater.
- The headquarters organizational culture can be more easily seeded in the subsidiary.
- Headquarters staff are given expatriate experience, and headquarters in internationalized.

- Headquarters controls (and checks on) local managerial and technical skills.
- When it expatriates its own technical staff, headquarters is best able to protect its proprietory technology; and, perhaps more significantly, can guarantee headquarters operating and maintenance standards.
- Closer links can be made with other local subsidiaries, also managed by headquarters staff. Group communication is stronger. This is important when the multinational is implementing a centralized global strategy.
- Communications between headquarters and subsidiary is better with a manager who is a "known quantity;" Tung (1982) found that among Japanese companies, "the most important reason for staffing with parent-country nationals and the relative frequency with which the reason was cited was that the parent-country national was the best person for the job" (p. 75).
- Headquarters is better able to control operations at critical times; for instance, in a start-up, when the subsidiary is ailing.

The *disadvantages* are:

- Local staff get fewer opportunities to manage.
- Political risk may be increased when expatriate managers lack understanding of and sympathy with host needs.
- Expatriate managers take time to develop local connections.
- Expatriate managers have less experience of and sensitivity to local markets.
- Expatriate managers may not know the local language and have less experience of dealing with local staff.
- Greater costs are involved in expatriating and recompensing headquarters staff, particularly when local labor is cheap. For example, Zenoff (1971) calculated that the initial expenses involved in transferring a United States middle manager and his wife and two children (under 12 years of age) from New York to Geneva, Switzerland, amounted to 95 percent of his annual salary (pp. 269–70).
- Acculturation training may have to be provided.
- Disparities in rewards (when expatriates are paid at a higher rate and/or receive relocation and overseas allowances) create ill-feelings among local staff.

Similarly, there are advantages and disadvantages in employing local staff to manage the foreign subsidiary. The *advantages* are:

- The multinational is "internationalized," particularly if subsidiary managers are rotated back to headquarters.

- The subsidiary has greater opportunities for independent control.
- Local managers are developed, and get opportunities to manage. (But this is not to the company's advantage in situations where more experienced local managers are quickly poached by competitors, or leave to set up their own companies.)
- Local managers have better local connections.
- Local managers have greater experience of local markets.
- Local managers are more sensitive to the behavior of local staff.
- When a local manager deals with government officials, political risk may be reduced.
- Expatriation costs are avoided.
- The problems and costs in acculturation training are reduced.
- Ill-feelings arising from disparities in expatriate and local rewards are avoided.

The *disadvantages* are:

- Headquarters control is weakened.
- The subsidiary is more likely to develop an organizational culture at variance to that of the headquarters (but this is not necessarily a problem).
- Headquarters staff get fewer opportunities for expatriate work, and headquarters organizational culture continues to be parochial.
- Headquarters is less sensitized to subsidiary conditions and needs.
- Headquarters has less check on levels of technical and managerial expertise.
- The security of proprietory technology may be at risk; and headquarters technical staff have less guarantee that their operating and maintenance standards are respected.
- When local managers have little experience working at headquarters and other subsidiaries, links and communication between subsidiaries are harder to create.
- Headquarters staff have less personal experience of the local manager. Communication is weaker.

14.3.3 Determining staffing policy

This section summarizes the main issues raised above.

When a multinational controls a range of foreign holdings, staffing policies are likely to differ according to environmental factors. The factors that lead the multinational to vary policy across its subsidiaries, and which influence the decision as to whether to expatriate a headquarters manager or to hire (or promote) a local.

- *Industry factors* Banking procedures, for instance, are highly standardized, and experiences acquired in one branch can be readily applied elsewhere (Boyacigiller, 1970). But a company involved in labor-intensive and relatively low-skilled work (such as textile manufacture) would be wise to employ a manager who spoke the local language.

  A business that depends on the rapid movement of capital and resources on a global basis needs global experience, and the national identity of a particular candidate is of lesser importance than whether he/she can offer this experience. But retail trade practices are more localized, and experiences of managing a department store in Dallas may be of limited value when managing a store in Seoul.

- *Markets* What marketing expertise is needed to manage successfully? If the subsidiary serves mostly local markets, a local manager may be preferred. But if the subsidiary serves international markets, and is closely integrated with other subsidiaries, a headquarters manager may be preferred.

- *Technology* If the use of new technology in the subsidiary presents security worries, headquarters may insist on expatriating technical staff. Standards of operating and maintaining complex technology may also be issues.

- *Age and condition of the subsidiary* In its early production phase, when innovating and growing through diversification, or when ailing, a subsidiary needs greater infusions of headquarters talent and more direct control. Local managers may take precedence when markets are mature and production processes are standardized, or when headquarters is following a deliberate policy of transnational development.

- *Criteria for internal promotion* Are local staff available and qualified to take the post in question?

- *Local national policies on staffing levels in foreign-based multinationals* For instance, some countries enforce legislation that rations the number of expatriate employees in terms of expatriate equity interest or total equity.

- *Criteria for headquarters promotion* If headquarters staff perceive an overseas assignment as a block to promotion, they resist expatriation. But if the company shows that foreign experience is valued and necessary for promotion, and if a posting is well compensated, expatriation may be welcomed.

- *Labor market factors, and the availability of managerial and technical expertise* If the local labor market cannot offer required skills, expatriate postings are made. But when these skills are available, the expenses involved in expatriate postings can be avoided. In some countries the subsidiary serves as a training facility, and multinationals constantly lose local staff who wish to join local companies or to set up on their own.

Issues of recruiting and training local managers are dealt with in sections 14.3.4–14.3.7 below.

- *Culture* When the national culture of the headquarters is more ethnocentric, and nationals dislike exposure to other culture, headquarters staff may resist taking an expatriate assignment. When headquarters needs to avoid uncertainty are high, headquarters is more likely to need the security that comes from high degrees of control. Culture is discussed in section 14.4.1.
- *Communication* How do needs for more or less complex/routine communications between headquarters and the subsidiary affect choice of audience/communicator in the subsidiary?
Communication is discussed in section 14.4.2.

14.3.4 Recruiting local managers

Factors that influence the multinational's success in recruiting managers from local labour markets include:

- *Labor supply* Opportunities to secure staff at the necessary levels of managerial and technical competence.
- *Language factors* The multinational may need to appoint a manager who can communicate easily with headquarters. Does the labor market supply these competent communicators? (But it may be a mistake to employ simply on the basis of how well an individual speaks the headquarters language. A capacity to communicate and manage within the local context is probably the main criterion.)
- *Remuneration (etc.) offered*, in competition with other organizations.
- *Other rewards offered* e.g., status attached to working for any multinational, and this particular multinational.
- *Cultural factors* Distance between the local culture and the national culture of the multinational; perceptions of the multinational's national culture.

Locals who choose to work for the subsidiary are predisposed to adapt to the values that it expresses. (Those who cannot make the adjustment will soon quit.)

Recruitment becomes a problem when the multinational applies criteria and techniques that are appropriate in the home national culture of the headquarters but are inappropriate within the local culture. For instance, it

- searches inappropriate labor pools;
- applies inappropriate search techniques; newspaper advertisements may generate a satisfactory applicant pool in one context, but in some other context be ineffective;
- applies inappropriate selection techniques; a personality test designed for one culture may be inaccurate elsewhere;
- applies inappropriate criteria; for instance, priority is given to managerial behavior that suits the headquarters culture but not the subsidiary culture.

14.3.5 Changes in the labor force

Societies that have only recently emerged from traditional systems of social organization and lack legislation enforcing equal opportunities in employment may include minorities that were previously excluded from the labor force. When barriers to education are crumbling faster than barriers to employment in local organizations, those members of such minority groups that gain access to education may offer the multinational employer excellent recruitment opportunities. This applies in the cases of ethnic minorities, and women.

In Japan (Hofstede's (1984a) most masculine culture) strong prejudices have traditionally barred women from employment in managerial positions. In 1988 a magazine reported

> [a] recent survey of 1,000 large Japanese companies showed that only 150 of them have any women at all at "kacho" (section-chief) level. Fewer than 20 of the 1,000 companies have women in positions above that level.[3]

But increasing numbers of university-educated women are coming onto the labor force. Frustrated by their failure to find sufficiently challenging employment in Japanese companies, they are easily attracted by Western companies in which sexist discrimination is less. A 1988 newspaper reports

> although nearly three quarters of Japanese women are university-educated, only one in four works after graduation.
> And prospects are dismal for the working women. . . . Thus, more egalitarian U.S. companies are appealing.
> International Business Machines Corp. cites a Japanese study showing that for the past four years, IBM has been Japanese female students' first or second choice of employer, Japanese or foreign. "We think the reason is that there is no discrimination," says an IBM spokeswoman. Last year, 24 percent of IBM Japan's new hires were female, compared with about 35 percent in the U.S.[4]

Lansing and Ready (1988) suggest:

> any job that is technology-directed and requires little contact with Japanese customers would be a very suitable opportunity for a prospective female manager. Other examples would be language schools, entertainment firms, brokerage houses, airlines, and shipping firms. . . .
>
> Once the initial hire has been accomplished, individual firms would have to devise means of maintaining their employees and advancing their career objectives. Training firms are needed internally for women to develop managerial talent. . . . Cultural norms in Japan have precluded women from the opportunity to advance vertically in the organization. (p. 125)

The relative shortage of Japanese males, who have cultural reasons for preferring not to work for foreign firms (which cannot offer such strong guarantees of long-term and life employment) provide a further reason why non-Japanese multinationals recruit women.

Similar opportunities for expatriate companies to hire educated and motivated women exist elsewhere. In Spain, government figures show that the number of women seeking jobs jumped fivefold, to 2.8 million, from 1978 to 1988. But men were still filling two out of every three jobs.[5] By the mid-1980s in Saudi Arabia, few women were educated above primary school levels and a handful found jobs outside the home. By 1989, 100,000 were in higher education and over 60,000 are in the labor force. They still constituted a small fraction of the total labor force (estimated between 2.5 to 3.5 million), but their number was growing.

> Miss al-Mosly, who is . . . married and uses her maiden name, has defied many customs, going to a boarding school in Lebanon at 4 and studying engineering, then coming back to find a job at Aramco nearly 21 years ago. She runs a department of 186 people, including 50 Saudi men who report to her.
>
> "When I first came to Aramco there were only three Saudi women working here," she said. . . . "Now we have 80."[6]

A failure to employ significant numbers of women and minorities is often excused by industry and educational factors, and this is generally the case – including in the West. 1993 data provided by the ten largest weapons-makers in the United States showed that of the 2,612 executives listed as senior management, women made up 5.3 percent, and minorities 4.8 percent. It was explained

> few women or members of minorities study either engineering or the technology used to build arms and so few are qualified to rise into management.[7]

14.3.6 Keeping local managers

Headquarters develops the loyalty and efficiency of local managers by

- showing that it trusts their judgement, particularly about local conditions. Subsidiary managers (whether or not local nationals) are more likely to be satisfied with global decision-making by headquarters when they feel that their views are listened to (Kim and Mauborgne, 1993). The strategic process must be consistent and fair.
- appraising and promoting them by criteria that recognize both their contributions to the global organization and their local expertise;
- giving them responsibilities appropriate to their level in the multinational;
- compensating them at the same rates as their headquarters equivalents; providing appropriate perks;
- providing appropriate training; giving equivalent consideration to both locals and expatriates when training budgets are designed;
- having personnel officers devote equivalent time to both locals and expatriates when planning their careers.

Policies that discriminate unfairly against local managers in favor of their expatriate colleagues are to be avoided. When local staff perceive that expatriate headquarters staff are rewarded at higher rates for the same work, or – worse still – lower performance, morale and communication problems arise. In consequence, opportunities to benefit from cultural diversity are lost, and expatriates become isolated from their local colleagues and the society – which inhibits their opportunities to develop understanding of the local culture.

14.3.7 Local priorities in training

The training that the company provides for local staff is determined by

- *Technical and professional needs – the tasks that they must perform*   Vicere and Freeman (1990) identified the following as the five most prevalent in-company executive program topics – in the United States:
  1.   leadership/motivation/communication;
  2.   general management;
  3=. human resource management;
  3=. organizational change and development;
  5.   corporate/business strategy development.

  But this ordering reflects United States culture, and some of these topics may have other relevance in other contexts – for instance, where the manager is expected to be a professional at least as much as a facilitator.

- *In-company and external facilities for training.*
- *Value-added by training.*
- *Attitudes towards and opportunities for job rotation as a training option*
  Vicere and Freeman (1990) found that job rotation was easily the
  most frequently used technique for in-company executive development – in the United States. Chapter 8, section 8.6.1 pointed out that
  job-rotation is less attractive where needs to avoid uncertainty are
  large.
- *Labor market considerations* The more that staff are trained, the easier
  they can sell their expertise on the labor market. In order to keep
  them, the company may need to increase remuneration.

The multinational brings local managers to headquarters in order to
develop their international experience and expose them to other aspects
of the company's work. This training process needs to be carefully
handled. Perlmutter and Heenan (1974) warned that it should not be
company policy to turn local managers into headquarters clones. In the
United States

> this kind of ethnocentrism produces a tendency for U.S. companies to
> accept those who will acculturate and become "more American than the
> Americans." A most surprising development is to see a non-American come
> to headquarters with the reputation of knowing Europe, become alien-
> ated from Europe, and accept proposals that reflect the ethnocentric ori-
> entation of headquarters. (p. 126)

Intensive training of local managers in headquarters values carries the
risk that they learn to over-identify entirely with headquarters, and lose
their understanding of local values and hence their local power bases.
The best local manager understands headquarters policy and the multinational nature of the organization. He/she also reports knowledgeably
on local circumstances. And when the task invites an innovative rather
than routine solution and the conditions for synergy are present, he/she
represents local values and experiences.

Operations suffer when local management is prone to what Professor
F. Gerard Adams has called "Affiliate's Disease". The victim of Affiliate's
Disease shows uncritical acceptance of headquarters policy, whatever
this may be and however distant from local realities. This results in the
subsidiary giving inadequate feedback to headquarters policy and on
local realities when these do not fit with headquarters perceptions. The
effects of excessive respect are worsened when the culture of the subsidiary
rewards large power distances, and when language differences make
open communication difficult. Headquarters can overcome Affiliate's
Disease by showing that informed disagreement is not punished and

may be rewarded, and that local feedback is more welcomed than is uncritical acceptance.

14.4 Relations between Headquarters and the Subsidiary

Hari Bedi reports that a survey of banking chief executives in Asia showed headquarters policies to be a major factors inhibiting growth of business; most corporations, he suggests, interpret globalization

> like North Korea's "yuilsasang" (ideological monotholithism) or the vision of all hearts beating as one.[8]

Rather, successful globalization needs to wed an international outlook with the needs of local autonomy. Certain functions (such as finance) need to be headquarters-based; others are better decentralized.

Relationships between headquarters and subsidiary are determined in part by market factors. When the company sells different technologies in different national markets, the subsidiary needs the freedom to respond as rapidly as possible to local needs, and acts as a technology-focused profit centers. Asea-Brown Boveri is an example. When a company such as Coca Cola sells the same global product across a range of markets, the opportunity to make economies of scale pushes the company towards centralization.

Needs to control are also influenced by culture.

14.4.1 Culture and control

This topic was first introduced in chapter 6, section 6.4, where we examined techniques by which the multinational attempts to control the organizational culture of its subsidiary.

In general, the larger the needs to avoid uncertainty in the headquarters culture, the greater the need for close control of the subordinate. This helps explain the greater expatriate staffing of Japanese subsidiaries than of either European or United States subsidiaries (section 14.3.1).

Applying Hofstede's (1984a) system, Rosenzweig and Singh (1991) develop a number of hypotheses, including these:

- The cultural similarity of a multinational subsidiary to other firms in the host country will be positively related to the tolerance for uncertainty in the parent country culture.

- Reliance on formal mechanisms of control will be positively related to the distance between the national cultures of headquarters and subsidiary (pp. 350–1).

In other words, it is argued that when the company culture has low needs for uncertainty avoidance and members are tolerant of ambiguity, top management is more likely to permit the subsidiary to respond to the local environment in its own way. When headquarters allows the subsidiary its freedom to develop in response to local conditions, the subsidiary develops management and market priorities that express local priorities rather than headquarters-culture priorities. And it will tend to respond in much the same way as do locally owned companies. But when the headquarters national culture expresses high needs to avoid uncertainty, a higher level of control is imposed on the subsidiary.

The subsidiary is always at risk of headquarters ignoring local needs in favor of global policies, to the extent that local cultural traits are ignored and differences between the national cultures of the headquarters and subsidiary contries are overlooked (Lawrence and Lorsch, 1967). This places a premium on efficient communication between headquarters and subsidiary.

14.4.2 Communications between headquarters and subsidiary

As the multinational company develops and grows, efficient integration between headquarters and subsidiaries becomes increasingly important. Inputs and outputs have to be cross-supplied. Market information needs to be circulated. And when subsidiary managers are local appointments with perhaps little experience of working together at headquarters, efficient communication helps break down cultural barriers.

Chapter 7 showed how culture influences communication priorities between individuals. The same points apply to communication priorities between headquarters and subsidiary.

Quick, efficient and accurate communication becomes a greater priority when

- the information being communicated is highly complex and non-routine;
- there is a high need for trust-based relationships;
- there is a high need for similarity in backgrounds and experiences;
- information (including feelings and emotions) cannot be verbalized.

Bartmess and Cerny (1993) point out that given such needs, the location of subsidiary in relation to headquarters is important; greater proximity facilitates greater movement of staff between the two, and the required level of interaction. These needs have similar implications for posting expatriates in preferance to hiring locals, and for training locals so that they can interact at the required levels.

The problems are made worse in a wide-ranging multinational, when the headquarters and subsidiary managers have to communicate not only with each other but with a range of other subsidiaries. A range of strategies help the company overcome this problem:

- Appointing subsidiary managers who have similar backgrounds and expertise.
- Reducing the complexity of information communicated.
- Using information technologies that have horizontal capabilities. They control and integrate information across departmental and organizational boundaries (Boynton, 1993, p. 63).

    But it is a mistake to overestimate the capabilities of technology, as Bartmess and Cerny (1993) point out. "In reality, electronic mail, facsimile, and telephone communications work well only after initial relationships have been established. Even then they cannot support the rich, constant nature of the communication required [in some relationships]" (pp. 94–5).
- Using standardized message formats.

As an example of this last point, Royal Dutch Shell institutionalized a strategic planning system across its subsidiaries. This ensures a standardization in all strategic plans, which in turn has a considerable impact on the ease with which local strategic issues can be communicated internationally.

Nevertheless, when headquarters and subsidiary managers represent different cultures, there are bound to be differences in what they perceive as significant information needing to be communicated. Hulbert and Brand (1980) describe research into interpersonal communications conducted within multinational corporations. They found that

> American subsidiaries had far heavier reporting requirements than their Japanese or European counterparts. . . . Marketing managers in American companies estimated that they devoted 20 percent of their time to collecting, collating and interpreting information requested by the head office. . . . In contrast, their counterparts in European companies spent 10 percent of their time in such duties, and in Japanese firms, only 8 percent. (p. 93)

This implies different expectations of communications systems interlinking headquarters and subsidiaries, and different perceptions of communication priorities.

Headquarters uses its subsidiary as a listening post, to collect intelligence about the local environment, local markets, the activities of competitors, etc. Such data may have no relevance to current operations, but helps headquarters consider its options for further expansion. Subsidiary managers may be happy to take on this role so long as they can be given some credible explanation as to why the request has been made, and whteher the data are then used. They become frustrated when they have spent long hours amassing information and are given no indication as to whether or not it meets headquarters' aims in making the original request.

14.5 Developing the Multinational

Bartlett and Ghoshal (1989) distinguish between multinational, global, international, and transnational companies (see also Wille, 1989):

- The headquarters of the *multinational* company decides financial policy but otherwise permits subsidiaries considerable autonomy in determining management style and responding to local product needs and markets. Examples include Unilever and Philips.
- The *global* company, exemplified by such Japanese firms as Kao and NEC, centralize their strategic, managerial, and marketing policies. Cost advantages are achieved through economies of scale and global-scale operations. The need for efficiency and economies of scale means that products are developed that exploit needs felt across the range of countries. Specific local needs tend to be ignored.
- Headquarters of the *international* company retains considerable control over the subsidiary's management systems and marketing policy, but less so than in the global company. Products and technologies are developed for the home market, extended to other countries with similar market characteristics, then diffused elsewhere; and the developmental sequence is decided on the basis of managing the product life-cycle as efficiently and flexibly as possible (Bartlett and Ghoshal, 1987).
- The *transnational* company evolved in the 1980s in response to environmental forces and simultaneous demands for global efficiency, national responsiveness, and worldwide learning. The transnational model combines features of multinational, global, and international models; for instance, a product is designed to be globally competitive, and is differentiated and adapted by local subsidiaries to meet their local market demands. Some resources are centralized at headquarters, while others, including managerial talent, are distributed among subsidiaries and integrated between them through strong interdependencies.

The transnational company evolves through learning, and then adapting the experiences of its various component parts. For instance, the writers point to the Swedish telecommunications giant, Ericsson, as a transnational organization that has succeeded in managing across national frontiers, retaining local flexibility while achieving international integration. Ericsson has developed

- an interdependence of resources and responsibilities among organizational units;
- a set of strong cross-unit integrating devices; and
- a strong corporate identification and a well-developed worldwide management perspective (Bartlett and Ghoshal, 1988).

A company achieves this interdependence between its component units by encouraging them to share not only flows of parts, finished goods, and capital, but also locally acquired skills and knowledge. And the capacity to develop markets on a transnational basis depends upon development of managers able to cope worldwide and integrated operations rather than centralized operations.

A magazine reports on Matsushita's policy to use headquarters visits as a training tool – but with a twist; the visits are primarily intended to educate headquarters' staff, not the visitors:

> Foreign managers have long been flown to Japan to learn the ropes – how to organize factories, exchange business cards, get drunk with their colleagues. Now Matsushita is taking a bolder step. It plans to import 100 foreign managers a year from overseas subsidiaries into its Japanese offices and factories. Naturally, they will learn a lot while they are there. But the real aim is to shock Matsushita's rather provincial Japanese managers into learning how to deal with foreign colleagues and issues. . . .
> . . . Neither they nor their Japanese colleagues will use interpreters; they are supposed to communicate in English.[9]

Besides fulfilling its functions of educating each side into the needs and management styles of the other, this policy should help a wider range of headquarters staff develop personal and professional links with subsidiary managers, and give these subsidiary managers the confidence that their experiences will find an audience at headquarters.

14.5.1 Human resource management in the new company

The human resource function acquires major importance in building the transnational. The responsibilities involved require the services of a unit of skilled professionals, with organizational status appropriate to the contributions they make.

In their study of human resource management within United States multinationals (applying the term in a general sense) Miller et al. (1986) discovered that:

> there was not a direct correlation between the power and prestige of the senior human resource executives and the involvement of the function, and in some cases the human resource executive was involved in the strategic planning process while similar status was not enjoyed by the human resource management function.

The new company cannot afford to restrict influence in the function to a single top manager. An increasing range of skills and experiences are required. A function that initiates proposals for change, and goes beyond responding to iniatives taken elsewhere in the organization, offers a corresponding range of career opportunities.

Human resource managers can expect to participate more fully in top-management decision-making. As the business environment evolves, so greater value will be placed on the capacity to identify environmental shifts and to interpret these in terms of labor demand and supply. The human resource manager will take on functions of developing new models of transnational roles and responsibilities. He/she will need to recruit and select staff who possess

- wide professional skills, and an understanding of the other functional areas represented across the world-wide organization;
- a capacity to develop good personal relationships across the organization;
- excellent communication skills;
- a capacity to think flexibly in terms of inter-unit linkages across the organization;
- a capacity to learn from and apply experiences;
- a sensitivity to cultural differences;
- a reputation for integrity.

14.5.2 National culture and the transnational

The transnational is built on the interactions of its component parts. By implication, then, the transnational will increasingly recruit potential top-level managers from all its subsidiaries, and not restrict itself to the labor markets of the headquarters nation. The subsidiary manager who has the confidence to project and represent his/her own cultural values in dealings with managers from other subordinates and customers will be valued more highly than the globalized, de-culturalized manager who represents only the headquarters culture.

The manager with low needs to avoid uncertainty is better able to handle the ambiguities involved in transnational management. He/she must be able to communicate widely, willing to listen to and learn from others, and be able to take decisions in the absence of superior supervision. This implies a tolerance for low power distances. The manager cannot afford to be bound by collectivist in-group/out-group thinking when these restrict his/her capacity to interact with other subsidiaries on an equal basis.

14.6   Implications for the Manager

1. What relations does your subsidiary have with its local environment?

    - How does the subsidiary contribute to local social and economic development?
    - On what grounds is your company's presence celebrated or resented within the host society?
    - How far do cultural differences contribute to any local resentment?
    - How can this resentment be overcome?

2. What staffing policies does your organization apply in staffing its foreign subsidiaries?

    - In what respects is policy uniform across all subsidiaries?
    - In what respects is policy differentiated, to take account of differences within subsidiaries, their local contexts and markets?
    - In what respects do cultural factors influence policy differences in different subsidiaries?

3. In each of the subsidiaries that you know best,

    - has the number of expatriate postings increased or decreased over the past ten years (relative to the number of subsidiary employees)?
    - has the number of local managerial appointments increased or decreased over the past ten years?
    - what factors explain any change in staffing levels?
    - how far do local cultural factors contribute towards feelings of resentment at expatriate postings? towards acceptance of expatriate postings?
    - how far do these feelings of resentment or acceptance influence staffing policy?

4. What factors influence current levels of expatriate and local staffing in your subsidiaries?

   - What are the advantages in maintaining expatriate staffing at current levels? What are the disadvantages?
   - What advantages and disadvantages would arise from increasing current levels of expatriate staffing?
   - What are the advantages in maintaining local staffing at current levels? What are the disadvantages?
   - What advantages and disadvantages would arise from increasing current levels of local staffing?

5. How committed do local staff feel to the multinational?

   - What factors (including cultural factors) encourage feelings of commitment or resentment among local staff?
   - What policies can the company adopt that will lessen any resentments and increase commitment?

6. What factors contribute to the multinational's success and/or failure in recruiting good local staff at different levels?

   - In what respects are criteria and techniques applied in recruitment and selection appropriate to the local culture?
   - Are there any possible pools of labor (including ethnic minorities and women) that you are currently underutilizing?

7. What factors influence the degree of control exercised by headquarters?

   - What factors influence the degree of freedom permitted the subsidiary to take local initiatives and conduct business without reference to headquarters?
   - How does headquarters culture influence headquarters needs to control?
   - How does subsidiary culture influence needs for autonomy?

14.7 Summary

This chapter has examined aspects of subsidiary staffing and management.

Section 14.2 focused on relations between *the subsidiary and the host society*. Most countries welcome foreign investment – so long as the multinational fulfils its commitments and respects host requirements. The conditions under which the welcome turns sour and political risk becomes a factor were discussed.

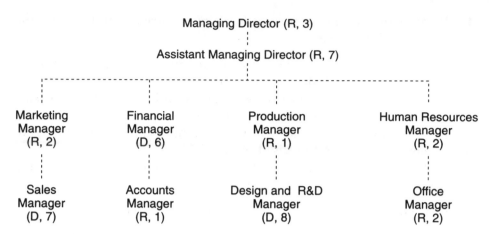

Figure 14.1 Management structure of Upanattem Universal.

Section 14.3 dealt with issues of *staffing the multinational subsidiary*, and the advantages and disadvantages of maintaining high expatriate staffing levels, and staffing top posts with locals. In practice, the optimal balance is decided by a complex interrelationship of needs, constraints, opportunities, and environmental factors.

Section 14.4 discussed *relations between headquarters and the subsidiary*. The style of relations influences staffing decisions, the development of the organizational climate in the subsidiary, and communications between headquarters and subsidiary. Section 14.5 built on this theme of control and dealt with *developments in the multinational*. A taxonomy of company–subsidiary relationships was examined, emphasis being laid on the emergence of the transnational company.

14.8 Exercise

This exercise asks you to decide on staffing policy (whether to employ expatriates or locals) in a range of situations. Students should work it in pairs.

Upanattem Universal (UU) is a multinational company headquartered in Ruritania. It develops and manufactures a complete range of children's products, from baby foods and toys, to clothing. UU has a subsidiary in Darana, Upanattem Darana. UD employs 500 people, and management is structured as follows. In figure 14.1 R indicates that the post is currently held by a Ruritanian expatriate, and D by a Daranese. The numeral indicates the number of years that person has been in post.

The costs involved in maintaining current expatriate staffing levels in UD are increasing, and some board members have queried human resource policies in the subsidiary. You and your partner have been brought in as external consultants to advise on the human resource implications of the following sets of factors.

Each of (a)–(d) lists three factors. Decide how each factor might affect the decision to employ expatriates or locals, then for the set, decide who should be repatriated, promoted, or continued, and on criteria for recruitment for posts left empty.

Assume that all staff have been performing satisfactorily. Any expatriate staff recalled to headquarters will be promoted. Any local staff that are replaced will be moved to a prestigious joint venture project. No one's career will suffer.

(a)   i.   Members of Ruritanian culture have low needs to avoid uncertainty.
     ii.   Local market conditions are stable; UD dominates the local market, and has no significant competitors.
     iii.   The Daranese economy is underdeveloped; trained managerial and technical staff are in short supply.

(b)   i.   Members of Ruritanian culture have high needs to avoid uncertainty.
     ii.   Local market conditions are volatile; until now, UD has dominated the local market, but now a major foreign multinational is competing energetically for market share.
     iii.   UU would benefit from greater communication and transfer of resources between UU and subsidiaries in other countries.

(c)   i.   Relations between expatriate and local staff members are distant, and communication within UD is poor.
     ii.   Communication between UD and headquarters is good.
     iii.   The Daranese economy is developed; there is no shortage of trained managerial and technical staff.

(d)   i.   Current UU policies reward headquarters staff who take expatriate assignments.
     ii.   New Daranese laws offer valuable tax incentives to multinationals that employ nationals in management positions; if UD replaces one of its current expatriates with a national, it will receive a 10 percent tax break, if two, a 20 percent tax break, and so on.
     iii.   Members of Ruritanian culture have high needs to avoid uncertainty.

Now assume a different situation. The same organizational chart applies (as in Figure 14.1) but UU only acquired the subsidiary two years ago from a local competitor. *All* Daranese managers have occupied their current posts for five years or more, and *all* expatriate Ruritanians have been in post for no more than two years.

(e) i. Daranese culture is highly individualist; more feminine than masculine; power distances are narrow. Daranese have high needs to avoid uncertainty and do not like travelling outside the country.

ii. Ruritanian culture is moderately collectivist; more masculine than feminine; power distances are high; needs to avoid uncertainty are high.

iii. All Daranese staff resent control from headquarters.

iv. Relations between Daranese and Ruritanian staff are poor.

v. UD's local managers are highly skilled and ambitious, but have little experience of working in headquarters and other subsidiaries.

vi. UD's current product range sells poorly outside Darana.

vii. Headquarters wishes to move towards transnational operations.

Notes

1. *Financial Post*, September 27, 1975, Thailand. This story is cited and discussed in Smith (1982).
2. See also the useful discussion of the term in Hoogvelt et al. (1987).
3. "Japanese women," *The Economist*, May 14, 1988.
4. Amanda Bennett, "Managing: Japanese women as hidden resource," *Wall Street Journal*, June 10, 1988.
5. Alan Riding, "In Spain, women to the fore! At last!," *New York Times*, May 30, 1989
6. Youssef M.Ibrahim, "Women in Saudi Arabia win some quiet battles," *New York Times*, April 26, 1989.
7. Calvin Sims, "Dire times for diversity in the weapons industry," *International Herald Tribune*, June 10, 1993.
8. Hari Bedi, "Management: the global neighbourhood," *Asiaweek*, February 19, 1988.
9. "The glamour of gaijins," *The Economist*, September 21, 1991.

15

Cross-Cultural Staffing Policies

15.1 Introduction

John worked for a multinational chemical company. One evening, he arrived home with the news that he was being posted as local manager to poor Central American Country X. The appointment was being made at short notice because of recent policy changes. No one doubted John's technical qualifications for the job. He was scheduled to be at his post within the month.

The company had not consulted his wife, Mary, about the decision. But she felt that she could not object to a move which would enhance his career. She gave up her own job, took their two young children out of their school and arranged to go with him.

At post, Mary discovered that as a dependent spouse she could not obtain a work permit. When John left for work in the morning, she took the children to their new school, communicated with a domestic servant who spoke no English (and her Spanish was elementary), and shopped in the market.

Otherwise she had little to do, and was bored and depressed. Her social circle was restricted to the wives of her husband's expatriate colleagues. She knew that she was drinking too much. She was aware that her depression worried John and made it harder for him to perform well at work. In the evenings their social life was limited to business functions, where typically she was excluded from the main topic of conversation – the company.

Their marital disputes were becoming more acrimonious, and all members of the family were suffering. Within the year, John resigned his appointment.

This story is not untypical. It shows how success in an expatriate posting can depend on far more than possession of technical qualifications. The chapter examines causes of managerial failure in foreign assignments and policies by which these problems can be avoided and overcome. It is organized in the following sections:

15.2 Success and Failure in Expatriate Postings

Most expatriate assignments succeed, and both the company and the manager benefit from the experience. But this is not always the case. Often the manager is unable to perform effectively, and so is fired or recalled.

Estimates of failures vary very widely. A survey of research findings made by Black, Mendenhall, and Oddou (1991) shows that between 16 and 40 percent of United States expatriate postings fail. Caudron (1992) cited a consultant's figures for United States failure at 36 percent in Tokyo subsidiaries and 18 percent in London – which makes the point that environmental factors have to be taken into account. Tung (1987) surveyed United States, West European, and Japanese multinationals and found that over 50 percent of the United States companies had failure rates of 10–20 percent, and 7 percent had failure rates of 30 percent. This study defined failure as the manager's inability to perform effectively in a foreign country, leading to his/her firing or recall home.

Failure rates among European and Japanese companies were lower. 59 percent of the Europeans recalled 5 percent of their overseas employees and only 3 percent recalled 11–15 percent; 76 percent of the Japanese had failure rates of below 5 percent.

The costs of failure are heavy. Caudron (1992) cited an estimate of between $250,000 to $1 million, depending on the employee's salary, location, and whether a family transfer was involved. In 1989 the average costs of maintaining a United States manager in an overseas post were estimated at about $300,000 per year.[1] A review by Mendenhall, Dunbar, and Oddou (1987) costed each premature return at between $50,000 and $150,000 to the firm (p. 341). In addition, approximately 30 to 50 percent of United States expatriates, whose compensation packages average $250,000 per year, stay at their expatriate postings when they are considered ineffective or marginally effective by their firms (Copeland and Griggs, 1985). And there are personal costs. The individual suffers a loss of self-esteem, prestige, opportunities for promotion and possibly his/her job. All these factors can spell further, indirect, costs for the firm.

Why are so many assignments unsuccessful? Managerial and technical competence may not be a major issue. Lanier (1979) showed that less than one-third of premature returns arose from work-specific reasons; cultural adaptation processes mainly determined the expatriate's success or failure.

Tung (1987) lists causes of expatriate failure in United States multinationals, in descending order of importance (p. 117):

1. inability of the manager's spouse to adjust to a different physical or cultural environment;
2. the manager's inability to adapt to a different physical or cultural environment;
3. other family-related problems;
4. the manager's personality or emotional immaturity;
5. the manager's inability to cope with the responsibilities posed by overseas work;
6. the manager's lack of technical competence;
7. the manager's lack of motivation to work overseas.

Tung derived her listing from questionnaires completed by multinational managements, and the factors reflect a management perspective. These factors show obvious weaknesses in selection procedures; why were companies sending overseas so many persons suffering personality and motivational problems, who lacked the will to adjust?

But management perspectives do not necessarily reflect the experiences of the returned manager and his/her spouse. For instance, they might cite lack of training and preparation as significant.

The point that leaps out is failure to adjust by the manager's spouse. This has most influence upon the manager's own adjustment and performance. This issue of spouse adjustment is now examined in greater detail.

15.2.1 Spouse adjustment

Black and Stephens (1989) conducted empirical research into the perceptions of expatriate United States managers and their spouses. They discovered that

- her adjustment is highly correlated to that of her husband, the expatriate manager;
- the spouse is more likely to adjust when she feels positive about the overseas assignment.

Where the second condition *does* apply, the company can seldom take any credit. For the Black and Stephens study also showed that

> only 30 percent of the firms sought the spouse's opinion concerning the international assignment. Also, over 90 percent of the firms in this study offered no predeparture training for spouses. Over 90 percent of the firms did not offer job finding assistance for spouses even though approximately 50 percent of the spouses worked prior to the international assignment. (p. 541)

The more the spouse is in early agreement with the assignment, the more he/she engages in self-initiated departure culture preparation and training, and this seems to increase the desire to succeed (Black and Gregerson, 1991a).

Black and Stephens (1989) conducted their research in Japan, Korea, Taiwan, and Hong Kong because, on Hofstede's dimensions of power distance and individualism-collectivism, these cultures appeared quite different from, and nearly opposite to, United States culture. But in practice, cultural proximity may be only one of several determinants. Here are some other factors that influence the spouse's ease of adjustment:

- the size of the expatriate national community, which affects opportunities for cultural and social support;
- relationships between the local community and the expatriate community;
- distance between the home and host country economies;
- opportunities to work.

A spouse who has qualifications and wishes to work is frustrated when circumstances in the new setting prevent this.

It may be that female employment is culturally unacceptable – as in most sectors of the Saudi Arabian economy. It may be that the government enforces legislation restricting the employment of dependants in order to safeguard opportunities for its national workforce.

This inability to work becomes a major source of discontent when the spouse comes from an Anglo culture where it is taken for granted that both marriage partners are free to take jobs so far as family commitments allow. But this will not bring similar problems to the expatriate spouse whose culture similarly restricts opportunities for employment – for the spouse of a Pakistani expatriate in Saudi Arabia, for instance.

That is, a local culture factor that creates problems for members of Expatriate Community X may be a matter of indifference to members of Expatriate Community Y.

15.2.2 Culture as a determinant of success or failure

The manager needs to be aware of cultural factors when predicting expatriate success or failure.

This point is demonstrated by comparing Tung's (1987) list first to factors that impose stress on Japanese managers expatriate in the United States (and which restrict the numbers of good Japanese employees willing to take United States postings); and second, to factors listed for British expatriates.

The factors for Japanese managers include:

- insecurities resulting from being cut off from their *dokikai*, or fraternity of co-workers;
- concern over their wives' social isolation;
- concern over their children's educational opportunities on return home;
- lack of support from relatives and friends;
- cultural dislocation;
- frustration with their United States subordinates.[2]

The institution of the *dokikai* belongs firmly within Japanese culture, and reflects the importance of the work group and the prevalence of long-term employment within the same organization, side by side with the same persons. It has no equivalent within the United States, where mobility of labor is far greater and where employees usually lack any sense of identity with their contemporaries. The importance of this factor for the Japanese (and not for the United States manager) is determined by home cultural factors rather than the culture of posting – except in cases where there is a large and stable Japanese community, for instance in Frankfurt, Germany.

The Japanese managers' worries over their children's educational opportunities on return home reflects both the importance that school and school friendships have in Japan as socializing mechanisms, and perceptions that standards in United States schools are lower. Hence, both home cultural and local cultural factors are significant here. Educational concerns do not show up as an independent factor in Tung's list for United States managers, possibly because expatriate English-language school education is relatively well established worldwide.

Among the reasons why the Japanese manager is frustrated with his United States subordinates must be included cultural differences in communication style. A *Newsweek* story reports that

> Americans, a Japanese boss [managing a US branch] often feels, need more supervision than their Japanese counterparts, who try to intuit their superior's desire.[3]

Japanese culture has a high-context, and superior and subordinate develop a shared communicative code. Because power distances are relatively large, the subordinate works to interpret his/her role implicitly from careful observation of the superior's needs. But United States culture values direct speech; the subordinate is unskilled in taking implicit supervision, and may be unwilling to act unless given explicit instructions.

The Japanese managers' concern over their wives' social isolation and lack of support from relatives and friends parallels the effects of his spouse's problems in adjusting, and other family related problems on the United States manager. And Hamill's (1989) study of expatriate policies in British multinationals similarly reports that family-related problems are the most common:

- family-related problems, including an inability of dependants to adjust;
- inadequate selection/recruitment criteria; criteria stress technical skills rather than cultural empathy;
- inadequate pre-post briefing;
- poorly designed compensation packages;
- lack of advanced planning for re-entry;
- remoteness from headquarters and ensuing loss of seniority (p. 24).

The research discussed in this section underlines the general significance of family-related issues – although the specifics may vary between cultures.

15.2.3 Organizational criteria in evaluating success and failure

Problems in comparing causes of expatriate success across cultures are complicated by disagreements over:

- the attributes of success and failure;
- the conditions under which success and failure is measured.

American multinationals regularly make overseas postings of two years or less. European and Japanese companies tend to keep their staff in overseas postings for longer – in the case of Japan, one survey showed an average of 4.67 years.[4] These figures reflect "average tenures" – the average numbers of years that employees have been with their present employer. 1989–91 figures showed average tenure ranging from 6.7 years in the United States to 10.9 years in Japan, with tenures in the various European countries between the two.[5]

Why is the American manager posted for a relatively short period? One explanation is that, given the nature of their control mechanisms, many Western companies perceive greater value in rotating the high-flier between a series of overseas posts rather than keeping him/her in a single post. The longer he/she stays in an assignment, the greater the risk of he/she "going native," and, in the eyes of the parent, identifying too strongly with local norms (Brooke and Remmers, 1970). But this policy has a negative side; the short-term manager has little time to learn how the behavior of local managers is determined by their culture, and to make predictions based on such experience.

This means that if the American manager makes early mistakes, he/she is in danger of being withdrawn before he/she and his/her family have had a proper chance to adjust. In general, American firms are less successful in handling low-level executive failures than are Japanese firms – although better when the failure is serious (Sullivan and Snodgrass, 1991).

Selmer's (1987) study of top Swedish managers working in Swedish subsidiaries in Singapore found considerable shortcomings in their understanding of their local middle-managers' values and concerns. Selmer concludes

> Considering that the average time of managerial experience in Singapore among the Swedish managers is three years, the existing policy of many Swedish multinational companies to rotate foreign assignments every three or four years is questionable. More often than not, Swedish managers assume duties in a foreign country without systematic briefings on the local work situation by previous managers. (p. 87)

But even if they wish to extend expatriate postings, many European and United States multinationals experience difficulties in persuading their managers to make the commitment. Anxieties over promotion prospects and job retention at home powerfully motivate the individual to plan for short-term goals and then seek a home posting. The problem is less acute for Japanese companies that foster a culture of long-term employment security and can count on employee loyalty – although the traditional dislike for changing jobs may be eroding.

Any evaluation of an overseas assignment should take its duration into account. An organization that demands that its expatriates perform at their headquarters standards from the day they step off the plane has unrealistic expectations. One international manager suggests that

> the very smart guy may be able to adjust in six months. Most people take at least a year.

And these estimates may be far too optimistic, given one calculation that a full cycle of culture shock, from the initial excitement of first arriving to full adjustment, can last up to 50 months. (The cycle is discussed in section 15.4.1.)

15.2.4 Headquarters and local criteria of success

The manager's performance in the expatriate post may meet requirements set by headquarters, but fail to meet the needs of the local subsidiary. In other words, the French manager who performs well in Paris may not perform well when expatriate in Tokyo, even if he is displaying the same behaviors.

This point has been demonstrated by a study that Black and Porter (1991) made of United States expatriate managers in Hong Kong. The study concluded that their sample performed similarly to an equivalent sample in the United States. But while their behaviors were positive in terms of criteria set for home-based United States managers, they did not lead to successful performance in Hong Kong, and did not match the behaviors of successful local Hong Kong Chinese managers.

Multinationals that normally prioritize headquarters interests in controlling their subsidiaries are likely to prioritize their staffing policies when selecting the expatriate manager. Zeira and Banai (1985) showed that senior managers in the multinational headquarters may believe that their selection procedures were valid for subsidiaries when these procedures actually fail to meet the subsidiaries' perceived needs. That is, headquarters and subsidiary disagree on the characteristics desired in an expatriate manager.

The implication is that the expatriate manager may fail because the local situation and needs have not been sufficiently taken into account when he/she was appointed. Not only does he/she fail to meet local criteria of success, but his/her appointment causes irritation within the subsidiary. This irritation becomes acute when local staff perceive that one of their number could perform the job at least as competently as the expatriate.

A misselection of this nature seems to indicate a breakdown in communications between headquarters and the subsidiary. Headquarters has failed to take subsidiary needs into account, or the subsidiary has failed to communicate these needs and the capacities of its local staff to satisfy them. Perhaps only when both parties are fully satisfied that no local manager can be bound who meets the agreed criteria should a headquarters manager be appointed (Torbiörn, 1985).

15.2.5 Prejudice against selecting women

Many companies hobble their chances of selecting the best candidate for an overseas assignment by unnecessarily restricting the candidate pool. They do not seriously consider posting their women managers.

Adler (1987) comments on figures showing that 3.3 percent of United States and 1.3 percent of Canadian expatriate managers were women (see also Adler, 1984). She presents qualitative data relating to Pacific basin postings which challenge conventional myths that

- women do not want to be international managers;
- foreigners' prejudices against women renders them ineffective.

In practice, many women managers would welcome the chance of taking an expatriate post; and the problems that women expatriates suffer more often arise from dealings with their home companies rather than with their Asian clients.

Nevertheless, most American companies appear prejudiced against selecting women for international assignments, even though they may lack evidence to support their positions. A newspaper reports a survey conducted by a New York consulting firm. Of the United States companies polled,

> 80 percent said there were disadvantages to sending women overseas.
> "Clients refuse to do business with female representatives," one company [said]. Another explained: "The desired expatriate is a thirtyish married man with preschool-age children. This is to project our image as a conservative institution with good moral fiber. . . . Many of our potential female expatriates are single, and a swinging single is not the right image."[6]

In practice, the great majority of expatriate managers are male. Perhaps more dependent husbands are following their manager wives to expatriate postings than was the case a few years ago, but the picture is changing only very slowly.

15.3 The Solutions

Both headquarters and subsidiary benefit when the expatriate manager is maximally effective. It is therefore in both their interests that they coordinate their systems to make his assignment a success.

This section deals with the following systems:

- selection;
- setting criteria for success;
- establishing career development paths;
- giving support at post.

Training is dealt with in the next chapter.

15.3.1 Selection

Specifications of the ideal selection reflect organizational needs; specifically

- long-term strategic concerns (Miller et al., 1986);
- headquarters' needs and interests;
- the local subsidiary's needs and interests. The subsidiary operates in a unique environment; thus, no one staffing policy can hope to meet the needs of different subsidiaries (Boyacigiller, 1990).

Given these specifications, the selectors interpret them in terms of the available individuals. This entails recognizing that perhaps no candidate will meet the specifications at all points.

The selection process takes account of the psychological, mental and emotional capacities of the manager (and dependents) to adjust and work effectively in the new setting (Mendenhall and Oddou, 1985). In detail, he/she is most likely to succeed in the following situations.

- He/she and dependent family members actively desire to adjust to living in the local culture.
- He/she and dependents have sufficient emotional maturity to deal with the new situation, and can tolerate ambiguity and uncertainty; they are well adjusted, and have the ability to utilize psychological supports as a meanings of retreating when cross-cultural conditions become over-stressful.
- He/she and dependents are adaptable (Heller, 1980). This means being willing to learn from experience and adaptable to change, able to integrate with others, confident, flexible, sensitive to differences in culture. The ideal expatriate manager is able to evaluate local behavior in terms of local culture rather than merely his/her own, and ever

on the look out for opportunities offered by difference – "geocentric" rather than "ethonocentric."

- He/she and dependents have skills in social relations and communications. They are willing and eager to communicate with locals, and have the ability to develop long-lasting friendships with locals. The manager works well in culturally diverse groups.
- He/she and dependents are non-judgemental and non-evaluative in their reactions to the other culture.
- He/she has technical and managerial expertise. The manager is competent to cope with novel technical and managerial problems, that occur within the new environment and not at home.
- He/she perceives expatriate experience as essential for career growth.
- He/she is confident of the support of the company while at post. The subsidiary attempts to respond to his/her needs. Naumann (1993) found that both job/task and organizational characteristics are significantly related to both intrinsic and extrinsic job satisfaction.

There must be agreement by all parties, including spouse, on the terms of

- the posting;
- compensation;
- (so far as possible) the manager's responsibilities on re-entry to headquarters.

Companies can go some way to resolving family-related problems by involving the spouse in the proposal to relocate as early as possible. This means, first, securing his/her opinion concerning the planned assignment. And second, he/she is given training that builds up interest in the assignment and new environment, and gives preparation in living there.

The manager and his/her family grow in confidence when they succeed in an expatriate assignment. But does this mean that the organization should treat the seasoned expatriate family as a special case when selecting a manager for some other overseas post? On the one hand, the organization values overseas experience (and should develop structures for debriefing its repatriates and applying their experiences). On the other hand, reserving the plum postings only to veterans severely restricts the development of new cross-cultural talent.

The value of prior experience is debatable. A successful mission in West Africa may not equip the manager for work in Japan. One study suggests that managers who have previous experience living abroad (particularly in the country of assignment) are more likely to adjust (Church, 1982). Elsewhere it is suggested that length of time in previous postings does not seem to be a factor; that is, a longer time spent abroad does not necessarily facilitate adjustment (Torbiörn, 1982). And Black

(1988) finds a lack of any significant relationship between previous expatriate work experience and general adjustment and interacting with locals, and no relationship between role novelty and work adjustment. He suggests that many aspects of expatriate work are either not generalizable to other locales, or that his sample of managers lacked the capacity to make such generalizations.

United States companies still tend to place most emphasis on technical experience and skills when selecting from candidates for expatriate posts (Moran, Stahl, and Boyer Inc., 1987). Tung's (1987) list suggests that technical inadequacy is a comparatively unusual cause of failure. This might indicate either that, to this extent, the selection process works and United States companies are successful in weeding out technical incompetents; or it might mean that the companies are using inappropriate criteria.

15.3.2 Setting criteria for success

The organization formulates criteria for success, and communicates these to the manager and dependents. These criteria are

- realistic;
- specific;

It is made clear what performance is expected, how it will be evaluated, and the inputs that headquarters and subordinate will make to evaluation. The criteria that are applied take into account

- the duration of the posting and of the adjustment period;
- role novelty: the difference between the manager's previous role and the new role; Pinder and Schroeder (1987) found that the greater the novelty, the longer the adjustment time;
- the freedom given the manager to define his/her own role;
- the interests of headquarters, and the interests of the subsidiary;
- headquarters policy in regard to expatriate postings at the subsidiary;
- the local culture; the perceived difficulty of adjusting to this particular cultural context;
- local business conditions, and the demands these make on the manager;
- characteristics of the subsidiary, and organizational and technological differences between it and the manager's previous posts.

15.3.3 Establishing career development paths

The manager adjusts more quickly to the expatriate posting when he/ she is first of all sure of the length of the posting. Uncertainty about duration disrupts personal, domestic, and career plans, and is a major cause of expatriate demoralization.

Second, he/she must be confident of career security on repatriation. Persons responsible within headquarters (for instance, the personnel director) help the manager plan his/her career path on repatriation before he/she takes up the post.

Some United States companies, such as Honeywell Inc. and Minnesota Mining & Manufacturing Co., give the expatriate a written guarantee that on return he/she will come back to an equal or better job at home after successfully completing the expatriate posting.[7]

Ideally, an expatriate assignment should guarantee enhanced promotion chances on repatriation. The organization that recognizes overseas experience in deciding promotions rotates its high-fliers to posts abroad, and makes clear that refusal to take a post may diminish promotion chances.

When the manager returns to the home country on home leave, he/she is given the opportunity to update and revise his/her career plans with headquarters staff.

Some organizations support their expatriate staff by appointing headquarters "shepherds" or mentors, who are responsible for

- protecting his/her professional and career interests in headquarters;
- keeping the expatriate up to date with headquarters changes and developments including policy changes;
- ensuring that all agreements reached between the expatriate and headquarters are honored;
- ensuring that repatriation training is provided, as agreed;
- reintroducing him/her to the headquarters on repatriation; Minnesota Mining and Manufacturing Co. assigns each expatriate a "re-entry sponsor."[8]

The organization has the task of "matching" the protégé with a suitable mentor (Wright and Werther, 1991). The mentor is usually the older, and can give advice and help based on seasoned judgement.

In addition, the organization can establish and coordinate support systems between repatriated and expatriate staff (Mendenhall, Dunbar, and Oddou, 1987). This "network" provides information on the day-to-day affairs (and gossip) of headquarters, and helps the expatriates avoid feeling "out of sight, out of mind." When the communication is two-way, repatriates are continually updated on activities in the overseas post – which may be very necessary, should they be reassigned, sent back on consultancies and inspection tours, or sent to negotiate new contracts. Also, the organizational newsletter, and announcements that provide information to home staff should be distributed to all expatriates.

When the employee feels protected at home, he/she is more easily committed to the expatriate assignment, and so more motivated to succeed.

15.3.4 Support at post

In addition to professional support, headquarters tries to provide cultural and other support. This includes providing support in the foreign post.

Given the importance of spouse adjustment and the failure of most companies to respond to this, support should mean finding spouse employment on a full- or part-time basis. But, as one expert points out,

> [g]iving dinner parties or cocktail receptions for visiting company executives does not count as satisfying work.
>
> Corporations should consider establishing part-time jobs and research contracts. In cases where a wife would like to upgrade her skills through local or correspondent studies, the company should foot the bill. Corporations could also emulate those governments and universities that have instituted preferential employment policies for spouses. In Beijing, this means that almost all Western embassies are staffed by embassy spouses.[9]

The company is also involved in

- locating and subsidizing appropriate housing;
- helping the manager find suitable educational facilities for his/her children, whether in the overseas location or at home; when the manager chooses to have his/her children educated at home, the wise company appoints an "uncle"/"aunt" who is responsible for their welfare in the event of an emergency;
- helping arranging and subsidizing regular home leave;
- helping the manager and his/her family find suitable medical facilities;
- providing cultural support; for instance, assisting the expatriate family keep abreast of cultural and current events in the home country (in some locations, the embassy representing the headquarters country may take responsibilities for giving such support to its locally employed nationals);
- organizing support groups for newcomers;
- organizing social events; e.g., film shows, national day celebrations, sports clubs and events;
- organizing training in the language and culture. The manager and dependants can expect to suffer some degree of culture shock on arrival at post. This may be trivial, but may not; and the subsidiary needs to have available facilities for counselling. The topic is developed in the next section.

15.4 Culture Shock

Culture shock may seriously unsettle the overseas visitor, as this story demonstrates.

> Paris is hell for the Japanese. It gives them what one Japanese psychiatrist described as the "Paris syndrome," which includes hallucinations, depression, paranoia and shocks to the nervous system.
>
> "French people tend to be moody," said Hiroaki Ota . . . "They can be very kind one moment and very mean the next." Mr Ota, based in Paris since 1984, treats fellow Japanese in Europe who are suffering from culture shock.
>
> "Japanese are shocked by these kinds of attitutide changes as they are used to more predictable people in their native country," he said.[10]

A bad case of culture-shock during the cross-cultural manager's first few months in post may radically influence his/her attitudes towards the new culture. If not trained to recognize and overcome it, he/she may be significantly less productive than at home.

Culture shock is a natural and healthy way of reacting to a new set of cultural perceptions. It may be defined as a sense of psychological disorientation that most people suffer when they move into a culture that is different from their own.

The outsider manager cannot resort to cues that are automatically employed when creating relationships, reacting to other people's behavior, and deciding how to behave in his/her own culture. Insiders' perceptions of reality and their priorities differ from his/her own. Compare this to the experience of first driving through a city that you have previously known well from walking. Familiar landmarks now seem less important, and you are forced to evaluate prominent features from a subtly different perspective.

Chapter 7 showed that successful communication depends on each participant understanding what the other takes for granted, and what has to be signaled as new and unusual information. The outsider cannot assume this body of shared experience, and does not know how to

- greet people;
- converse appropriately with superiors, peers and subordinates;
- offer, receive or refuse invitations;
- give and ask for opinions;
- express agreement and disagreement;
- etc.

Your failures to communicate these and other functions are deeply disturbing.

This sense of disorientation may not be any less when the new culture is superficially like your own. Slight differences are profoundly shocking when you expect everything to be the same.

An Indian was posted by his Chicago company to a project in Thailand. On his way from the airport he observed the crowds in the Bangkok streets, the vendors and the articles they sold, and the food stalls; all this reminded him of Delhi and he decided that he already felt quite at home. On his first evening he decided to try a local restaurant. But when he walked through the door, a sense of panic overcame him. He did not know whether to find his own table or wait to be seated as in the United States. He picked up the menu and discovered that he could not read a single word. He fled back to his international hotel and did not leave it again for the next two days.

You become aware of cultural dislocation when first encountering behavior that does not occur in your culture, or behavior that occurs, but with some other meaning in your culture. You may be equally shaken by the non-occurrence of expected behavior; for instance, the Anglo takes for granted that disagreement is sometimes expressed explicitly. The lack of such explicit negation in Japan can be very disconcerting.

15.4.1   The symptoms of culture shock

Culture shock is cumulative, and arises from a series of small incidents, but the awareness of shock may hit you suddenly. It can have pleasant effects similar to alcohol – a sense of unreality. But it is usually associated with unpleasant effects:

- *A sense of tension and frustration*   Your energy levels seem low and you cannot make decisions as quickly as usual.

- *A sense of alienation*   You feel homesickness, and antagonism towards locals and their culture. You refuse to learn or use their language, and you mix socially only with members of your own culture;

- *A need to be alone*   You resort to solitary activities, including drinking.

- *Depression.*

The culture shock cycle has four stages (see Torbiörn, 1982):

1. *Honeymoon*   You start your overseas assignment with a sense of excitement. The new and unusual is welcomed. At first it is amusing not to understand or be understood, and then a sense of frustration sets in.
2. *Irritability and hostility*   Your initial enthusiasm is exhausted, and you begin to notice that differences are greater than your first superficial

assessment indicated. More and less serious problems cannot be distinguished; all cultural differences seem to create problems on the same level. You doubt your abilities to communicate.

In his analysis of United States managers expatriate in Japan, Black (1988) reports that most experienced the low points in their adjustment processes approximately six months after arriving.

3. *Gradual adjustment* You begin to overcome your sense of isolation and to work out behavioral rules for the new culture. More and less serious problems are distinguished, and the less serious ones overcome.

4. *Full adjustment and adaptation* You recover your sense of psychological orientation, and function and communicate successfully in the new culture.

A literature review by Black and Mendenhall (1991a) suggests that the entire cycle from the honeymoon to full adjustment can last up to 50 months.

Unfortunately, you are likely to experience more than one cycle of culture shock, and Kohls (1984) is among those who think the second cycle is more extreme. When you have passed through the first cycle, it is unwise to be overconfident; an unexpected incident may plunge you again into a state of uncertainty, and this is particularly damaging to your self-esteem if you think that you have already learnt all you need to know about the new culture. You need to keep in mind that you will never finish learning.

15.4.2 Overcoming culture shock

The manager probably cannot avoid some culture shock, but can train him/herself to overcome the worst effects:

- Expect to experience culture shock. It is a natural reaction to novelty among emotionally mature people. Treating culture shock as a pathology or sign of mental imbalance is likely to create far worse problems.
- Understand why it occurs and learn the symptoms.
- Accept your need to learn about living in the new culture. Cultural adjustment is best seen as being involved in a learning process, and social learning theory provides a theoretical framework within which this adjustment can be made (Black and Mendenhall, 1991a).
- Discover as much as you can about the new country, its culture and history. Start this learning before you arrive.
- Do not restrict yourself to members of your own culture. The cultural insulation that they provide may be comforting in the first days, but

merely delays the adaptation that sooner or later you will have to make.

- Break into the local culture by using its members as informants. Find members who are happy to answer your questions about their culture.
- Keep an open mind on the new culture. Neither condemn it out of hand (and certainly not on the basis of your experiences in the airport), nor praise it excessively. What seems rational and irrational? Look for evidence that shows why apparently irrational behavior may be only non-rational in your terms, and try to think yourself into the local culture so that the non-rational appears rational.
- Check what communicative forms are appropriate. Ask informants from the local culture and experienced outsiders from your own culture. Who should be addressed by first name? Who by title? How are invitations made, accepted, and refused? How are opinions expressed? Agreement and disagreement? What do members of the culture mean when they say "Yes, maybe"? "Tomorrow"?

Immigrant communities cope with culture shock by recreating aspects of their home cultures. For instance, in Florida, USA:

> The roadside is dotted with large plastic union jacks, which mark out "British pubs," like the "Dog and Duck," the "Rover's Return" and the "Fox and Hounds." [In 1992 there were] 74 such pubs operating in Florida – the most visible sign of a British invasion which has added as many as 100,000 people to the population of the state in just over a decade. Rodney Forton, editor of the *Florida Brit* and manager of the Brit Centre in Kissimmee, reckons there are now 150,000 British citizens living in Florida.[11]

Elsewhere, many immigrants may not bother to learn the language of their new country – and when their community is large enough, may have no need to.

Experienced travelers develop their own routines for coping with the worst effects. One manager prepares himself by examining maps of the new city he expects to visit, then spends the first days walking the streets in order to turn his theoretical understanding into practical experience. Examine your own reactions to culture shock, and adapt the techniques above to meet your own needs.

A "coping" response may be sufficient for the expatriate who is sufficiently protected by members of his/her own culture, or spends only a short time in the new culture. But it does not resolve adjustment problems for the long-term visitor who has personal and professional needs to become involved in the host society. The cross-cultural manager who finds himself the sole representative of his/her country, or among a small group only, cannot depend on cultural supports. Unless prepared to accommodate the host culture, learn about it and make friends of its members, he/she is condemned to loneliness.

15.5 Repatriation

Even when the expatriate is confident of returning to a safe job at headquarters, repatriation is difficult. "Reverse culture shock" can be an unexpected and painful experience (Austin, 1986). The repatriate may need to adjust to:

- *Reduced financial benefits* Expatriate inducements including cost-of-living allowances are no longer forthcoming. This may represent a decline in his/her living standards.
- *Less power* The entrepreneurial individual who has enjoyed seniority in a small joint venture project or a foreign subsidiary finds it difficult to fit back into a headquarters post which is more routine and offers fewer opportunities for initiative.
- *Job alienation* A sense of being out of touch with technological innovations and organizational changes, including personnel moves.

  One international manager complained "When I walked into the office the first day back, I couldn't see anyone I knew. All the old faces had gone. It was like starting out again."
- *Increased cost-of-living expenses* Expenses are relatively fewer when the overseas posting is in a less developed country.
- *Poorer housing* Most companies subsidize housing in the expatriate location.
- *Less domestic help* Domestic help is easily hired and relatively cheap in many less developed countries.
- *A different pace of social life* In countries where expatriates are few, cross-cultural managers and their families often lead intense social lives, mixing with the same small group of fellow nationals and locals who speak their language. At home, social activity may be less focused.

  School children leave the friends they have made in their expatriate schools and have to fit back into home schools where they may know no one.
- *Communicating the expatriates experience to colleagues, friends and family at home.*

A study by Black and Gregerson (1991b) found that expatriates returning to the United States had the greatest trouble when they

- were relatively younger;
- had been abroad relatively longer;
- were returning to poorer housing conditions;
- were returning to somewhat ambiguous jobs.

Returning expatriates with opposite profiles faced least trouble.

This study suggests how the company can help the manager and spouse overcome reverse culture shock. The authors suggest that

- postings be shortened (but the manager may need to be in the overseas post for a considerable time in order to become fully effective);
- expatriate housing packages be reduced (but generous packages may be necessary in order to attract managers overseas);
- make job descriptions more focused (but this requires improved better strategic human resource planning by headquarters).

In addition the company can help the returned employee and his family overcome readjustment problems by

- planning career development paths for return to headquarters (this point has been dealt with in section 15.3.3, above);
- fully briefing the employee on the new post before and after returning;
- updating the employee on technological and organizational changes; properly introducing him/her to personnel who have joined the company since he/she left for the expatriate post;
- briefing the employee and spouse on current events, and economic and cultural changes in the home country;
- introducing the employee and spouse to support groups of other employees and their families who have recently returned from expatriate assignments;
- debriefing the employee and spouse on work and living conditions in the other country. This point is taken up below.

15.5.1　Debriefing

A sympathetic debriefing helps the returned expatriate and his/her spouse overcome the worst effects of reverse culture shock on re-entry to the home culture. The manager who expects to be debriefed on home leave and repatriation, and who knows that the debriefing output will serve useful functions, is made aware that his/her experiences are valued. This manager is more likely to be motivated while at post.

Debriefing serves organizational interests in other respects. Many companies possess potentially invaluable sources of information in the form of their members' expatriate experiences, but which are never properly utilized because no attempt has been made to debrief repatriates and make the output available within the organization.

A successful debriefing elicits information in a range of areas, which include

- the expatriate post; performance requirements, constraints opportunities, conditions of service, etc.;
- the foreign organization; structure, systems, policies, history, etc.; its needs and interests, and where these coincide with and diverge from the needs and interests of headquarters;
- the industrial context; market trends, competitor behavior, opportunities and threats;
- the national political and economic context;
- the cultural context; constraints and opportunities;
- living conditions.

This information is used in building a data bank on the subsidiary and its context. The data are used in

- analysing the subsidiary's needs and interests, to be applied in selecting future candidates for this expatriate post;
- briefing and training a successor to the post; briefing and training his/her spouse;
- briefing other employees who will take up postings in the same subsidiary or country;
- briefing negotiators who will deal with the same company or with other organizations in the country;
- designing training priorities; preparing training materials;
- reviewing headquarters policy in regard to the subsidiary;
- planning strategy within the local environment.

15.5.2 Repatriated Japanese

American managers are not alone in suffering reverse culture shock. Japanese companies are increasingly experiencing problems in reintegrating the employees back from United States postings who have become used to more individualist lifestyles. The numbers of persons involved has grown rapidly; between 1976 and 1986 the numbers of Japanese registered with their government as temporary residents abroad increased from 153,000 to 230,000 – a 50 percent rise.[12]

Japanese companies have faced a range of problems:

- returning managers are bored by the relative lack of challenge offered in headquarters;

- women, perhaps treated as special overseas, are frustrated by having to return to the background;
- those children who have been expatriated with their families in individualist cultures where directness is prized, find it hard to fit back into Japanese schools.

The *Wall Street Journal* describes some solutions adopted.

> To deal with the problem, the government has set up some programs for returning students in Japan and some all-Japanese private schools abroad. Returning women have established mothers' groups to counsel children – and to occupy the mothers' own time.
>
> Japanese companies have counseling programs for returning employees and, in rare cases, for families as well. So many returning employees were quitting NEC Corp. a few years ago, for example, that it set up a "big brother" program to keep employees abroad in touch with the home office.[13]

15.6 Implications for the Manager

Review the policies followed by your organization in making expatriate postings, and their outcomes.

1. What are the attributes of success and failure in expatriate postings?

   - How does the organization measure success and failure? – what criteria are set for success by headquarters?
   - What criteria are set for success by the subsidiary?
   - How does headquarters explain success and failure?
   - How does the subsidiary explain success and failure?
   - How do successful and unsuccessful managers explain their performance?

2. Are the organization's criteria appropriate? If not, how might they be revised?

   - Given existing criteria, what personality and professional types are most likely to succeed in expatriate postings?
   - Given your revised criteria and your answers to question 1, what personality and professional types would be most likely to succeed in expatriate postings?

3. How important is the failure of the manager's spouse to adjust as a cause of the manager's failure?

   - How does the organization involve the spouse in the decision to take the assignment?

- What briefing and training does the spouse receive before departure?
- What briefing and training does the spouse receive on arrival at post?
- How could the organization play a greater part in

   (a) finding employment for the spouse?
   (b) supporting the spouse at post?

4. How often are women selected for expatriate postings?

- What risks are associated with sending women on expatriate postings?
- Given changes within the environments of international business, are these assumptions of risk still realistic?
- How might the organization benefit by sending more women?

5. How important are headquarters criteria in the selection process?

- How much attention is paid to the subsidary's needs and interests in the selection process?
- Should greater attention be paid to the subsidiary's needs and interests? If so, how can these best be accommodated?

6. What support does the organization give expatriate managers in planning their career paths?

- How might this career pathing be improved?
- How would improved career pathing affect

   (a) the individual manager?
   (b) the manager's dependants?
   (c) the subsidiary?
   (d) headquarters?

7. What cultural and other support does the organization give expatriate managers, their spouses and other dependants at post?

- What welfare assistance is given?
- What cultural support is given?
- How does the organization help the manager and his/her dependants overcome the effects of culture shock?
- How might this support be improved?

8. How are managers and their spouses debriefed on their return to headquarters?

- What functions are debriefing outputs currently serving?
- How might debriefing processes be improved?
- What other functions mights debriefing outputs serve?

9. What problems do managers and their spouses typically experience on repatriation and when returning to headquarters?

- What support does headquarters give repatriated managers and their spouses?
- How might this support be improved?

15.7 Summary

This chapter has examined expatriate postings, and has seen what the organization and the individual can do in order to overcome the difficulties and optimize the conditions for success.

Section 15.2 looked at reasons for *success and failure in expatriate postings*. The spouse's ability to adjust plays a major part in determining the outcomes of an expatriate assignment. A motivated spouse is of great value to the manager, and hence the organization. Failure by the organization to include the spouse in the selection process and then train him/her appears to be factors contributing towards failure in the assignment. Section 15.3 discussed *solutions* and examined selection processes, criteria for success and failure, the importance of establishing career development paths and giving support to managers and their dependants at post.

Section 15.4 dealt with *culture shock*. This is often a cause of failure in the first few months; the syndrome, and techniques for overcoming the worst effects, were examined. Section 15.5 dealt with the problems of *repatriation*, and with the manager's re-entry to his/her own culture and organizational headquarters on completion of an overseas assignment.

15.8 Exercise

Assume that your organization (place of work or management school) is an overseas subsidiary of an organization headquartered in one of the following countries (if your own country is listed, do not choose it):

- *Japan*
- *The Netherlands*
- *Brazil*
- *Hong Kong*
- *Sweden*

Headquarters decides to post one of its staff to manage your subsidiary.

1. Write a job description for the manager, taking into account

    - the manager's role; needs for managerial and technical exper-
      tise, relevant experience;
    - perceptions of cultural difference;
    - headquarters needs to control the subsidiary;
    - the subsidiary's needs for communication with headquarters.

2. Assume that the manager is male, and will be accompanied by his
    wife and two children.

    Design a support package that will facilitate their adjustment,
    taking into account that

    - the manager is male, 37 years old, with average education and
      experience for the post;
    - he has previous expatriate experience, lasting two years, in a
      culture very different to both the headquarters country and yours;
    - the wife is a qualified administrative assistant and experienced
      writer;
    - she has no previous expatriate experience;
    - she wishes to continue working, on a part-time basis;
    - the children consist of a girl, aged 14, and a boy, aged 10;
    - the children need schooling, if possible in their own language;
    - possibly, no one in the family speaks your language but all are
      prepared to learn.

3. Now assume that the organization is headquartered in one of the
    other countries listed above (but again, not your own). Revise your
    answers to 1 and 2 where necessary.

Notes

1. Thomas O'Boyle, "Grappling with the expatriate issue," *Wall Street Journal,*
    December 11, 1989.
2. John Schwartz et al., "The 'salaryman' blues," *Newsweek,* May 9, 1988; and
    Brian O'Reilly, "Japan's uneasy U.S. managers," *Fortune,* April 25, 1988.
3. Schwartz et al., "The 'salaryman' blues," op. cit., n. 2.
4. A 1982 survey by the *Japan Economic News,* cited by Tung (1987).
5. "Musical Chairs," *The Economist,* July 17, 1993. OECD figures.
6. Jolie Solomon, "Women, minorities and foreign postings," *Wall Street
    Journal,* June 2, 1989.
7. Joann S. Lublin, "Warning to expats: maybe you can't go home again,"
    Asian Wall Street Journal, August 27–8, 1993.
8. Ibid.

9. Robin Pascoe, "Employers forsake expatriate spouses at their own peril," *Asian Wall Street Journal*, February 27, 1992. See also Pascoe (1992).

10. Agence France Presse, "Not where *they* go when they die," *International Herald Tribune*, October 30, 1991.

11. "Florida and chips," *The Economist*, February 8, 1992.

12. E. S. Browning, "Unhappy returns," *Wall Street Journal*, May 6, 1986.

13. Ibid.

Training for an Expatriate Assignment

16.1 Introduction

Hari Bedi tells the story:[1]

> A Thai manager for an international company got tired of his regional boss calling him an eastern potentate – which he would invariably do whenever he saw his secretary serving coffee on her knees. So when a franchised "self-assertiveness" course was being offered in Bangkok, the Thai executive sent his secretary along. A few days later, when the regional president was visiting again, the secretary asked him "Coffee, Bill?" He was astonished at the change and was still talking about it when she came back with the coffee and got down on her knees to serve it!

This story demonstrates the weakness of cross-cultural training that focuses on changing superficial behaviors and ignores the problems of changing attitudes at a deeper level. Power distances between boss and secretary are different in Thai and Western cultures, and are expressed differently. For her part, if the secretary had understood *why* it was inappropriate to kneel when inviting a Western manager to have coffee, she could have generalized from this to other activities – for instance, serving. For his part, the boss erred in mistaking her behavior (culturally appropriate within an all-Thai context) for a personal lack of assertiveness.

Training is a single element in the whole process of selecting and supporting the manager and his/her dependants at an overseas post. These other issues were dealt with in the preceding chapter. Here, we focus on the manager's various training needs – of which cross-cultural training is only one.

The manager may be expatriated to work in a subsidiary, an international joint venture, or in some other form of overseas operation.

The chapter is organized in the following sections:

16.2   Training Needs

A study by Tung (1982) shows that only 32 percent of the United States firms surveyed indicated that they had formalized training programs to prepare candidates for expatriate assignments. In contrast, 69 percent of the West European companies and 57 percent of the Japanese provided such training. Of the four job categories recorded (CEO, Functional Head, Trouble Shooter, Operative) the Japanese provided most training for Operatives, 76 percent claiming to give language training (compared with 24 percent of United States firms and 48 of Europeans). In general, the study showed that the more rigorous the training, the greater the likelihood of success.

The notion that employees should be trained to meet the specific problems posed by an expatriate assignment has been late-developing. In 1979, Lanier found that only 25 percent of multinationals offered extensive pre-departure training programs. Baker's 1984 survey conducted among the 1,000 largest United States industrial multinationals discovered that

- most of the programs offered lasted five days or less;
- less than half of the respondents' top managements believed that language facility was important, and only 20 percent of the companies required language for the overseas posting. But 36 percent of the expatriate employees questioned believed that a language facility was necessary and important, and more than 43 percent spoke the local language.[2]

This indicates a greater awareness of the need for at least language training by cross-cultural managers than by their headquarters controllers. It suggests that headquarters were unwilling to learn from the experience of repatriates in developing relevant orientation programs.

The point is substantiated by Domsch and Lichtenberger (1991). Their study of Germans working in the People's Republic of China and Brazil

> found that the companies are less certain than the expatriate managers themselves about the effective mix of preparatory training appropriate for foreign postings. (p. 43)

Expatriate managers benefit when headquarters staff with responsibilities for their selection, briefing and training have personal experience of working conditions in the other country.

16.2.1 Why training is ignored

Why do headquarters staff so often omit to properly train their managers before sending them on expatriate assignments?

Black and Mendenhall (1991a) conclude from their literature review that the most common reason given in United States companies is that top management does not believe cross-cultural training is necessary. And when we ask *why* top management thinks thus,

> the fundamental reason behind the lack of training seems to lie in the same assumption that causes American corporations to look only at domestic track records and to ignore cross-cultural-related skills when selecting expatriate candidates. The assumption is that good management is good management, and therefore, an effective manager in New York or Los Angeles will do fine in Hong Kong or Tokyo . . . (pp. 178–9)

But management practices are *not* the same everywhere, and the manager who understands the needs and values of the workforce in Culture X may be unable to recognize needs and values in Culture Y. A good domestic track record is not a good predictor of overseas success.

United States companies give a range of reasons for paying so little attention to this training (Tung 1982).

- The trend towards employment of local nationals.
  But this does not address the issue of how best to prepare the headquarters manager when the decision has been made to post him/her rather than appoint a local.
- The temporary nature of the assignments. Assignment length is always likely to influence the length and composition of the training program.
  But every assignment, no matter how short, can benefit from *some* training. Even if the assignment lasts for only a few days to negotiate

a contract, the manager who steps off an international flight capable of greeting his/her hosts in their own language is immediately a step ahead of competitors who have not mastered even this elementary skill.

- Doubts as to the effectiveness of such training programs.

    But some training is almost always better than none. (Black and Mendenhall (1990) review the evidence of success in cross-cultural training.) Some methodologies and programs will meet your needs; others may be inappropriate, or simply bad. The training manager is responsible for acquiring the training programs that best suit the organization's needs – just as when purchasing any other service.

    When some training has been attempted, doubts as to its effectiveness might reflect a failure to apply rigorous evaluation – discussed in section 16.4.3.

- The lack of time.

    But the organization should be appointing the expatriate manager in time to allow him/her adequate opportunities to obtain training before relocating. The organization that has a history of persistently giving its managers only a few months' or weeks' warning before transferring them needs to review its expatriate staffing policies.

In sum, the failure to train tends to reflect a clear-cut expatriation policy, and understanding of what training can – and cannot – achieve.

16.2.2   The training needed by the expatriate managers and spouse

Appropriate training for the expatriate manager and spouse falls into two broad areas:

- training to work in the new culture.
- training to live in the new culture (Black, 1988, p. 291).

The expatriate manager who adjusts in one area does not necessarily adjust in the other. Training should take into account both sets of needs.

The spouse's difficulty in adjusting to the new situation is a common cause of the manager's failure – as we saw in the previous chapter, section 15.2. This indicates the importance of giving the spouse whatever training can assist his/her adjustment.

Where appropriate, the manager and spouse are trained together; otherwise training is specialized.

Training and briefing may be needed in the six categories below. Categories (a) and (b) below relate only to working in the new culture; (c)–(f) relate to both working and living.

(a)   technical training;
(b)   management training;
(c)   domestic information;
(d)   counteracting culture shock;
(e)   cross-cultural training;
(f)   language training.

This section discusses (a) – (d). Cross-cultural training is taken up in section 16.2.3, and language training in section 16.3.

(a)   *Technical training*   The manager is briefed on

- technologies used by the foreign organization with which he/she is unfamiliar, including alternative technologies;
- local attitudes towards technology transfer and innovation;
- opportunities for technology transfer and innovation;
- constraints on the local implementation of new technology;
- culture as a constraint on technology transfer, innovation, implementation, etc.

(b)   *Management training*   specific to the post and the company. The manager is trained in

- the administrative responsibilities of the post;
- the company's organizational structure; strategies and opportunities for change; structures for control and communication; structures for planning, motivation, and conflict resolution; organizational climate; informal structures;
- procedures and issues in relations with the headquarters; the climate of control, communications;
- investment and treasury factors, including accounting and auditing procedures, relations with financial sources, protection of assets in the local country, procedures for repatriating capital and earnings;
- the company's relations withpublic-sector bodies;
- the business environment; local and international markets, competitors, distributors; relations with other subsidiaries; tariff and other barriers; economic indicators, political and governmental influences, political risk;
- marketing issues and strategy; product characteristics (e.g., life cycles, development, differentiation); R&D policy; pricing strategy; channels of distribution; advertising and promotional strategies; market research;
- human resource issues; labor markets and recruitment; labor relations and policies; relations with unions; salary and reward structures; training resources and policies;
- policies regarding ethical issues.

The headquarters functional manager who is being assigned to a general management role in the overseas organization may need a greater understanding of headquarters units than he/she normally acquires within the functional specialism. He/she needs

- an understanding of each unit's interests and competencies;
- a personal relationship with senior managers in each unit.

This means that he/she should be exposed to these headquarters departments before leaving for the expatriate post.

The spouse may need to know something of the foreign organization's scope of operations and the manager's general area of responsibility. Exactly how much the spouse needs to know will be is influenced by the degree of business entertainment that he/she is willing to undertake.

(c)   *Domestic information*   The manager and spouse are briefed on such issues as

- accommodation;
- details of schools, hospitals, medical professionals, social services, etc.;
- details of shopping facilities and availability of domestic goods and services including power and water;
- customs regulations and procedures;
- availability of cars; import regulations; insurance.

The spouse may have greater need for briefing on these topics than does the manager.

The information given must be practical and up-to-date. The manager who arrives at post and discovers that the briefing was inappropriate, inaccurate or outdated is immediately demoralized.

Before leaving for Libya in 1970, a British professional was told by his head office that electrical consumer goods could not be purchased in Benghazi. He therefore invested part of his relocation allowance in purchasing and shipping a refrigerator. On arrival, he discovered that in the two years since the briefing notes had been formulated, a number of Japanese makes were readily available in high-street stores.

Ideally, the manager and spouse are sent on information trips to the host country before the assignment. These give them opportunities not only to inspect the local organization but also to review their needs for domestic information.

(d)   *Overcoming culture shock*   Culture shock is never entirely overcome, but the worst effects can be mitigated. The manager and spouse are briefed on techniques, discussed in chapter 15, section 15.4.

16.2.3   Cross-cultural training

Successful cross-cultural training borrows from social learning theory. The training/learning process consists of three main stages:

- *Attention*   The learner is exposed to the behavior that is being taught.
- *Retention*   The behavior becomes encoded in the learner's memory in the form of "cognitive maps."
- *Reproduction*   The learner is able to reproduce the taught behavior and to check his/her performance against the model.

This model assumes a high degree of motivation on the part of the learner (the manager and/or spouse).

Cross-cultural training aims at achieving three related outcomes (Black and Mendenhall, 1990). It teaches

(a)   *about* the other culture;

- values within the other culture;
- shows the manager and/or spouse how to generalize beyond the models used in the training, to other and new situations;
- how the culture is reflected in significant historical, political and economic data.

(b)   *how to adjust to* the other culture;

- develops non-evaluative attitudes towards the culture;
- develops a capacity for predicting when culture will be a factor in determining behavior;
- shows how cultural values are expressed in behavior;
- develops a capacity for weighing the significance of culture as against other factors in determining behavior.

(c)   factors relating to *job-performance* within the other culture;

- how the culture affects attitudes towards work; e.g., performance standards, degree of personal involvement, motivation, concepts of responsibility and authority, conflict and its resolution, organizational climate;
- how the culture influences formal interactions; e.g., organizational structures and systems, roles and relationships, planning needs and procedures, communication systems;
- how culture influences relations between organizations; e.g., development of commercial and professional associations, negotiation practice, ethical norms.

The spouse may have a greater need for cross-cultural training than the manager, at least in areas (a) and (b) above. He/she may be forced into a wider range of interactions with the local culture. Often, the manager follows routines set by headquarters, works primarily with other employees posted from headquarters or local employees indoctrinated in the organizational climate. His/her contacts with the local culture are channeled and restricted. But when the spouse is responsible for dealing with domestic servants and trades people, he/she may be forced into a wider range of contacts with the culture, and have greater needs for some aspects of the training program described above.

Non-working spouses have greater need for training in how to live in the new culture than in how to work there. Their different priorities are reflected in the focus and content of the training given.

16.3   Language Training

Here we consider one form of acculturation training, language and communications training, in more detail.

The expatriate always benefits from knowing something of the local language – and the manager on an expatriate assignment is particularly aware of this need. The German managers researched by Domsch and Lichtenberger (1991) placed longer and more intensive language training at the top of their list of training priorities. However, the majority of companies still resist making significant investments in this area.

Here are some reasons given by organizations for *not* providing language training – in addition to those listed in section 16.2.1:

- A belief that communication in the other language is better managed by interpreters. True, you are unlikely to approach even a very narrowly defined functional fluency in less than several hundred hours' training. But some knowledge of the language gives you a corresponding check on the accuracy of your interpreter, and in a negotiation inhibits the other side from commenting upon your proposals in asides among themselves when they think you are ignorant of the language. A balance between learning some of the language yourself and otherwise depending on professional interpreters may be most practical. The balance you reach depends upon such factors as your linguistic proficiency, the business at hand, the situation, and the skill of your interpreter and your trust in him/her.
- Fears that the linguistically proficient manager commands a greater price on the job market, and will be lured away by competitors willing to pay more generously for his/her services. Where this applies, the interests of the manager and the organization are in conflict. The manager may prefer not to work for an employer who deliberately constrains his/her development in this manner.

- A belief that the language used at headquarters is "international," and therefore the manager has no need to learn "national" languages. This point is now examined.

16.3.1   Learning the national language

International languages, spoken by significant groups in more than one country as a first or second language include Arabic, Chinese (Cantonese and Mandarin), English, French, Malay, Portuguese, Russian, Spanish. The European Community uses English, French, and German as working languages, although the growing use of English is fast eroding use of the other two.[3]

In theory, this might appear good news for native English speakers, and for multinationals that use English as a working language. That is, a superficial reading of the situation would suggest that the native-speaker of an international language has no need to learn "national" languages, and that the onus is on local managers and negotiation partners to learn his/her language. In practice, this is not the case, and in many respects, the native-speaker is at a disadvantage.

In colonial days, the colonizer enjoyed an advantage by using an international language.

> It strengthened the grip of the colonizer on the colonized, helping him sell his unlovely goods, with unchanged instruction-books, in his dominions. What he said loudly in English mattered. What they replied softly in Hindi didn't. But in these days of frightful commercial rivalry, it is what the customer says that counts. You make your sales-pitch in English. The buyers discuss it politely in Korean. "This guy is sleep-walking: let's take him to the cleaners," they murmer, while you beam at them encouragingly.[4]

Nowadays, the manager who speaks his/her own national language *and* English is far better placed than the manager restricted to the international language of English. And the multinational that uses English as its headquarters language and for communicating between headquarters and its foreign branches may also expect them to use the local national language in their day-to-day affairs. Kuin (1972) writes

> Operations usually are, and should be, conducted in the vernacular. The need to learn the local language may vary in importance for managers in different categories (accounting, marketing, production, personnel, and so on), but he who cannot or will not learn languages always remains a stranger in any part of the business but "home." From the viewpoint of job rotation, such a man needs a special tab on his card.

16.3.2   The focus of language training

The problems of designing and organizing language training for managers are complex (see Mead, 1990, chs 11–12). These points may need to be considered.

- You (probably) cannot invest in learning the language up to general fluency. However, you can gain a working competence in specialized language skills.
- The language/communication-needs analysis defines the communicative skills needed by the expatriate and his/her dependendents. The output of the needs analysis influences the content of the syllabus – although at beginner levels all learners are likely to require a foundation in the same basic grammar and vocabulary.
- The needs analysis distinguishes between

  - productive skills (speaking and/or writing) and receptive skills (comprehending and/or reading); for instance, some managers discover they have greatest needs to read in the other language;
  - occupational and social needs; for instance, you might decide that you should delegate your occupational and professional communications to an interpreter, and focus on learning sufficient "social" language to create good relationships with your local managers and negotiation partners;
  - communicative functions; for instance, greeting, welcoming, persuading, informing, etc.;
  - standards of language competency desired. And if you are organizing a teaching program for other people, you may need to specify desired entry and exit standards to/from the program;

- The alternatives to your learning more than the functional minimum; consider how to use interpreters, and whether it is practical to have local managers trained in your language;
- Contract a *professional* applied linguist to

  - conduct a needs analysis;
  - identify learner entry and target exit levels;
  - design a teaching syllabus;
  - design teaching and testing materials;
  - organize staff to teach the materials or teach them him/herself;
  - administer tests and advise you on the implications that test scores have for the learner's competence in the expatriate post;
  - design instruments to evaluate the program, and to revise the program for use with further learners.

The applied linguist does not need to be a native-speaker of the target language; but beware of hiring well-intentioned amateurs to design and teach your programs. Any native-speaker has fluent production skills, but this certainly does not guarantee his/her competence as a teacher, and even less as a program designer.

If the necessary skills are available in the country of the expatriate post, you may decide that some of the teaching should be conducted at site. But bear in mind that in his/her first few months, the expatriate is likely to be suffering from culture shock and to be otherwise overwhelmed by a host of professional, logistical and cultural problems. Such circumstances are not conducive to focused language study. However, there is an argument for teaching within the context of the language, where the learner has ample opportunities to practice the new skills within authentic situations.

In practice, the most satisfactory results are often achieved by teaching in both contexts. For instance, the absolute beginner studies up to an intermediate level before leaving headquarters to take up the post. (Skills needed to qualify as "intermediate" proficiency are defined by the initial needs analysis.) When he/she arrives at post, additional training is given to brush up these intermediate skills and show the learner how to apply them in authentic situations.

Both manager and spouse require the same beginner's level training, at which a common grammatical and vocabulary core is taught. But beyond that, their tuition might have to be differently planned. They interact in different communicative situations and needs analyses will indicate how these needs should be serviced.

16.4 Training Programs

The alternatives for the company are to

- contract out cross-cultural training to a consultant;
- make this an in-house responsibility of the training department.

It is assumed here that your organization decides to embark on its own training program. Training must be consistent with the organization's strategy and policies, and have clear and consistent goals. The full process comprises the stages shown in Figure 16.1, discussed below.

16.4.1 Research, and needs analysis

Research proceeds in two stages. First, an investigation is made of

Resource analysis: availability of and needs for trainers, materials, technology, etc.

Research ⟶ needs analysis ⟶ syllabus design ⟶ materials design
⟶ implementing the program ⟶ program evaluation (⟶ research).

Figure 16.1   Stages in a training program.

- *The objectives of training*   How does headquarters describe the job? How does the subsidiary describe the job?
- *The skills needed*   (for both working in the new organization and living in the new culture), as specified by headquarters and the subsidiary.

The priorities given to headquarters and subsidiary objectives and specifications reflect the degree of centralized control exerted by headquarters, and the freedom given to the subsidiary to manage its own affairs.

In addition, this basic investigation examines

- evaluation output from previous programs.

What lessons can be learned? What mistakes can be avoided and what planned and unplanned benefits can be applied in the new program?

The resources available and needed to develop the program are investigated as early as possible. At this early stage, it may not be possible to specify in anything other than broad terms the availability and needs for

- financing;
- personnel (researchers, resource persons such as repatriates, program designers, materials writers, trainers, briefing staff, secretarial and ancillary staff, etc.);
- rooms and other facilities;
- equipment;
- time; hours allotted for training.

The second major research stage consists of making a detailed needs analysis of the manager's actual target performance. It answers such questions as:

- What roles will the manager perform, when both working and living in the new culture and organization?
- What roles will dependants perform when living in the new culture?

- At what standards must roles be performed?
- What criteria are applied to role performance?
- How much weight should be given to different roles?
- With whom are the roles performed? Who else is affected by their performance?
- What outcomes are expected from role performance?

The answers to these questions can only be translated into a set of syllabus specifications when they also take into account the manager's background. This includes his/her

- professional qualifications;
- standards already achieved in the target skills;
- experiences of learning other languages and cultures;
- experiences of working and living in other cultures;
- domestic status; dependants;
- personal needs and expectations;
- level of motivation; to train, to work in the other organization, to live in the other culture.

The needs analysis goes into as much detail as is practical – that is, as much as can be applied in a training syllabus and materials (the supplementary exercise in chapter 16 of the Instructor's Manual shows how a language needs analysis is developed).

In order to make an accurate and detailed needs analysis, the organization may decide to send the analyst to the post, in order to conduct this basic research. This is particularly important when the purpose is to design a language-training syllabus. If this option is not available, the organization gives the analyst access to recent repatriates, who can give up-to-date information on the needs of their successors.

A needs analysis based on research conducted with headquarters staff, subsidiary staff, present expatriates (at post) and recent repatriates reflects a range of opinions. It reflects the interests both of headquarters and of the subsidiary; of prescriptive norms (roles that the manager should perform), and of descriptive norms (roles that the manager actually performs).

When the syllabus is designed, these different perceptions and goals, practice, and need have to be reconciled. Difficulties in agreeing priorities – for instance, when headquarters and subsidiary cannot agree on expatriate goals, or analysis of practice is at variance with goals – may indicate structural problems. Perhaps communications between headquarters and the subsidiary, are inadequate and need to be improved, or the manager's job description should be rewritten.

16.4.2 Syllabus and materials design and implementation

At its most basic, the syllabus lists the topics and skills to be covered in the training course and is derived from the research and needs analysis stages. But the derivation is indirect, and a number of other problems have to be resolved before a list can be transformed into a set of teaching materials;

- How should the topics be ordered? In terms of ease of teaching? Ease of learning? Perceptions of importance? (From most important to least important, or vice versa?) Or randomly, to be selected by either trainer or trainee as they progress through the program?
- How much time is available for teaching? The less time, the fewer topics can be covered, or the less time can be allotted to each topic.
- What other resources are available? For instance, budgetary constraints determine how many trainers and other persons can be involved. The choice of materials writers and trainers (who have particular areas of expertise) constrains the range of topics that can be prepared and taught. Thus the syllabus specification is influenced by the analysis of resources available for developing the program. In turn, the syllabus gives more precise information on the resources needed; for instance, it tells you whether the allotted resources are adequate.
- What is the composition of the trainee group? A syllabus prepared for a large group of mixed-ability trainees with widely varying levels of experience, expertise, motivation, etc., is bound to differ from a syllabus tailor-made to suit a single individual;
- What techniques and methodologies will be used? The choice influences the selection of topics and how they are treated by materials writers. And in turn, it is influenced by the selection of trainers (a particular trainer may have a strong preference for a particular technique) and by physical resources of classroom space and equipment available.

Tung (1981) classifies some of the most popular techniques used to train staff for cross-cultural postings. She includes:

- documentary programs/area studies, which teach the country's history, economy and culture through written materials;
- cultural assimilators: programmed instruction that exposes the trainee to specific incidents targeted as critical within the new culture (for example, see Edge and Keys, 1990);
- field experiences;
- sensitivity experiences;
- language training.

A range of methodologies have been developed and materials produced. The US Peace Corps have been responsible for much pioneering work in acculturation training (Henry, 1971). These and others' techniques are discussed by Harris and Moran (1979, 1987). But in general these are designed for Americans and may be less appropriate for cross-cultural managers belonging to other cultures and bringing other priorities to the training. A range of textbooks present techniques, exercises, and case studies for teaching culture, all of which may be useful; see, for instance texts by Brislin et al. (1986). Miller discusses 36 techniques specifically used by international trainers in business and industry (1979); and for small-group teaching methodologies, see Abercrombie (1974).

Research by Earley (1987) compares forms of documentary and interpersonal training (using both sensitivity training and field experience). He found that the two were comparably effective in adjusting his experimental population for entry to the new culture (see also the discussion of this paper in Howe et al., 1990).

In general, the criterion for all materials and techniques, and so for all training, is that it should

- teach real skills, which the trainee can use in real situations;
- teach skills that cannot be otherwise acquired so economically;
- generate meaningful changes in behavior;
- be motivating: the trainee perceives intrinsic rewards in training – which answer the question "What's in it for me?"

16.4.3 Evaluation

Evaluation is important because it tells the organization whether or not it is using its training resources to optimal advantage. It indicates areas in which training could be improved. Efficient evaluation resolves doubts about the values of the training and of the particular techniques used.

Program evaluation and the resources necessary to conduct it are planned at the earliest stages of program development.

All evaluation of training programs has functions of

- specifying and comparing programs goals and achievement;
- showing how far achievement has met program goals, given the resources available;
- assessing performance of trainers, trainees, and other persons involved;
- showing how far the program has given value for money;
- providing feedback, that can be applied in the development of future programs.

Evaluation made during the *research, needs analysis,* and *design stages* focuses on the goals of training, plans for program development, resources needed and available, and plans for later evaluation. Evaluators might include program developers and trainers, repatriates (perhaps who have been trained by an earlier version of the program), human resource personnel, managers of the candidate trainees. If at all feasible, top management of the subsidiary should be brought into the process; this gives them a point of comparison for making evaluation after program termination. Candidate trainees involved at this stage are more likely to be motivated when the training starts. Try to involve top management, and at least keep them informed of evaluation objectives and outcomes; this helps build top level support for the program.

The selection of evaluators will be constrained by cultural factors. Where power distances are high, subordinates cannot be expected to evaluate activities conducted by superiors (as program organizers, trainers, or trainees). In highly collectivist cultures and where organizational units identify themselves in opposition to other units, you may have difficulties in using persons from unit to evaluate training conducted by some other. These points apply equally below.

Evaluation made during *training* focuses on what learning is taking place, and the factors that help and detract from learning; and it also keeps a check on costs. Mid-training evaluation reviews completed stages, shows how far the training process corresponds to the original plan, demonstrates on-going progress to trainees and trainers, and aims to motivate them. Possible evaluators include the persons listed above; the candidate trainees are now actual trainees, and their feedback is invaluable.

Evaluation made at *program termination* gives immediate feedback on how far achievement has met the program's goals. It tells trainers and trainees what learning has taken place and gives the participants and top management feedback on how far the program has given value for money. Lessons learned about the effectiveness (or otherwise) of the materials, teaching and organization, are applied to planning further programs. It reports on the activities of staff involved and gives a final accounting of costs. Accounts staff will need to be included as evaluators.

Evaluation made at *periodic intervals after project termination,* and when the trainees are at their expatriate posts, gives long-term feedback on how far achievement has met goals. It shows how much learning has been short-term and how much long-term. This evaluation is largely summative, but has formative influences on the development of future programs. Evaluation is contributed by ex-trainees, who comment on the value of their training to working and living within the expatriate environment. Cultural and organizational factors permitting, evaluation is also made by the ex-trainees' at-post managers, who assess the capacity of the ex-trainees capacity to adjust to expatriate conditions, and the apparent effectiveness of the training.

Training program evaluation is conducted by such instruments as

- tests;
- questionnaires;
- interviews;
- observation;
- control group testing;
- accounting and financial data.

The selection of instrument is determined by such factors as

- the purpose of the training;
- the purpose of the evaluation;
- the materials and techniques used in training;
- the identity and status of evaluators;
- the identity and status of trainers;
- the identity and status of trainees;
- cultural factors;
- organizational constraints.

16.5   Training Other Staff Categories

This chapter has focused on the training needs of the expatriate manager and his/her spouse who are expected to make a long-term commitment to the overseas organization. But it should be clear that other groups can also benefit from different aspects of the training programs proposed. These groups include:

- headquarters staff with responsibilities for selecting and posting the expatriate manager;
- other headquarters staff with specific interests in the overseas organization;
- headquarters staff with professional interests in international development; for instance, marketing staff;
- headquarters staff sent on short-term assignments; for instance, negotiating staff;
- local staff in the overseas organization.

Sections 16.2.2, 16.2.3, and 16.3.1 distinguished between the needs of the manager and his/her spouse. And similar distinctions need to be made when identifying and meeting the needs of each of the groups listed above.

Section 16.5.1 below focuses on the needs of the last group listed, local staff.

16.5.1   Training local staff

In addition to training in managerial and technical fields, local staff can also benefit from cross-cultural training that enables them to operate at maximum efficiency when dealing with foreign clients and also with expatriated headquarters staff.

Expatriate assignments can fail because local staff are unwilling to modify their behavior in relationships with the visitors. This refusal to concede may result from not understanding the culture of the head-quarters country – at any significant level.

Subsidiaries usually specify in job advertisements for local managers that applicants should have reasonable fluency in the language of the multinational and/or in English. And local managers tend to "self-select" their foreign employers; that is, the manager only chooses to apply to a United States company because he/she has a prior sympathy with and some knowledge of United States culture. But that may not be sufficient, and headquarters may decide that local managers would benefit from further language training and a deeper understanding of the cultural values practiced in the national environment of the headquarters.

This training may be provided locally, for instance on a formal class-room basis, or by rotating local managers back to headquarters. In many contexts, the opportunity to work at headquarters or attend training there carries status, and can be a useful incentive to performance.

Training local managers in the headquarters language and culture may be more economical than investing heavily in training headquarters staff in the local language and culture, particularly when the headquarters manager is likely to be posted on a short-term basis to a range of sub-sidiaries in the course of his/her career. But for some firms this might suggest a problem; the more sophisticated the local managers grow in operating within the national culture of the headquarters, the greater their mobility on the international job-market and the wider their oppor-tunities for finding alternative employment with the firm's competitors.

The larger the power distances between senior and junior staff, the greater the problems of involving persons of different rank in the same training program or class. Senior managers may perceive that they lose face by being seen to be trained, and may have to be trained off premises, perhaps on a one-to-one basis by a trainer of comparative age. Where collective loyalty to the unit is equaled by rivalry with other units within the same organization, difficulties may arise in training different units together. Qualitative research conducted in Thailand discovered both these problems in firms trying to introduce information technology (Hughes, 1991).

16.6   Organizational Support for Training

The greater the support that the organization gives the training effort, the more likely that the training will meet its objectives.

The training officer builds organizational support by canvassing support from and regularly communicating with

- top management and other decision-makers;
- actual and potential trainees and their managers;
- persons involved in developing the program, including trainers.

The training officer tries to ensure that

- top management is fully supportive, and make their support obvious to the participants (trainers, etc., and trainees);
- resources, including finance, are committed;
- training constitutes part of the manager's regular duties, and is conducted during office hours;
- the managers is rewarded for taking training; unmotivated trainees learn little;
- training sessions are undisturbed; this means that sessions are not interrupted by phone messages, calls from the shop floor, etc.;
- so far as possible, the training is tailored to meet the manager's individual needs;
- the manager's spouse and other dependants are trained;
- adequate time is devoted to training;
- standards are maintained; the organization is committed to providing training that is thorough and rigorous.

16.6.1   Adequate time for training

The importance of devoting adequate time to training is often overlooked, and the great majority of organizations could benefit from devoting far more time to training that at present.

The amount of time reserved for training is influenced, on an extensive basis, by the time allowed between the manager's selection for a post and his/her departure from headquarters in order to take up the post.

A study conducted mainly with German expatriates on foreign assignments in the People's Republic of China and Brazil discovered that of 16 companies, only one gave preparation of two years "as defined by professional expertise" (Domsch and Lichtenberger, 1991, p. 50).

Eighteen percent gave a maximum of 16 months; 18 percent gave less than two months; and "the preparation time for sales managers was often limited to two weeks."

Managers in many Anglo companies might count themselves lucky to be given even 18 months to make the psychological and intellectual preparations necessary. But the general point stands. A manager given insufficient notice of a lengthy assignment cannot obtain the training he/she needs; for instance, language training restricted to a two-month period is unlikely to be effective. The earlier that selection can be made, the better for trainers and manager alike.

16.7　Implications for the Manager

Review the policies followed by your organization in training for cross-cultural assignments.

1. What acculturation training is given to each of the following categories of expatriate staff and spouses, for both working living in the culture?

    (a)　CEOs;
    (b)　functional heads;
    (c)　trouble-shooters and short-term consultants;
    (d)　operatives;
    (e)　spouses of each of (a)–(d).

    Answer, using these training categories:

    - technical training;
    - management training;
    - domestic information;
    - counteracting culture shock;
    - cross-cultural training;
    - language training.

2. How successful is training in each of the categories listed above?

    - In which training categories, and for which staff categories, should the training be improved?
    - What improvements should be made?
    - How much time is allotted to training, and should this be increased? If so, by how much, and in what staff and training categories?

3. How are training needs modified by the country of posting?

    - How do existing training programs take country-specific conditions into account?

4. What organizational support is given to training expatriate staff and dependants?

    - the support of top management;
    - adequate resourcing;
    - incentives;
    - (other support)?

5. How far does your organization

    (a) hire outside consultants (etc.) to train expatriate staff and dependants?
    (b) employ internal resources to train?

    - Can the present combination of external and internal training be improved? If so, how?

6. What proportion of cross-cultural (and other) training is given before reaching the expatriate post? What proportion is given at post?

    - Should these proportions be modified? If so, how?

7. How are cross-cultural training programs organized? How much weight is given to each of these stages?

    (a) background research;
    (b) needs analysis;
    (c) syllabus design;
    (d) materials selection and design;
    (e) implementating the program;
    (f) program evaluation.

    - What adjustments at each of these stages might improve the development of training programs? (If necessary, reconsider your answer for each of the training categories listed in 1 above.)

8. What cross-cultural and other training is given to

    (a) other headquarters staff groups?
    (b) local staff in the foreign organization?

    - in the case of local staff, what additional training (including language training) would help them adjust to working with expatriates?

In addition
Assess needs for language learning (see also Mead, 1990, chs 10–11).

- Estimate the advantages of the cross-cultural manager learning the other language as against opportunity and training costs. Take into account the level of proficiency he/she needs to be effective in (a) managerial roles, and (b) non-work social roles.

- Estimate the advantages of employing only local staff who speak the manager's language.
- Estimate the advantages of training local staff to speak the manager's language as against opportunity and training costs, and their enhanced mobility in the job market.
- Estimate the advantages of hiring *interpreters* as against the disadvantages.
- Calculate the optimal mix between

  (a) the manager's learning and using (some of) the local language;
  (b) local staff learning and using (some of) the manager's language;
  (c) hiring *interpreters*.

16.8 Summary

This chapter has discussed training for cross-cultural postings. Section 16.2 dealt generally with *training needs*. At present, much training is inadequate, both in terms of duration and content. Expatriate managers and their spouses have varying needs for training and briefing in technical, managerial, domestic topics; in counteracting culture shock; cross-cultural topics; language. Section 16.3 focused on issues of *language training*. Arguments *against* learning something of the local language were discussed and found wanting. The final part of the section reviewed the complex problems of designing and organizing language programs.

Section 16.4 took up general issues involved in organizing *training programs*. It examined planning and implementing stages; background research, needs analysis, syllabus design, materials design, implementation, and program evaluation – which provides feedback needed for the development of further programs. Section 16.5 pointed out that *other staff categories* beside the manager and his/her spouse can benefit from aspects of cross-cultural (and other) training, and focused on the needs of staff locally employed in the overseas organization. Section 16.6 emphasized the importance of full *organizational support for training*. Training is unlikely to succeed unless given the energetic support at the most senior levels.

16.9 Exercise

This exercise asks you to analyse the professional roles that you perform in your job, and to apply this analysis to designing training priorities.

1. Suppose that you have to brief your successor for the job you currently hold (or last held). What information does he/she need in order to perform the job effectively? Assume that he/she

    *   comes from the same culture as yourself;
    *   has the same level of technical and managerial expertise that you had on starting the job.

    Write a list of five topics, in order of importance. Restrict your list to topics concerning relationships within the organization, sources of power and influence, motivators, sources of conflict and conflict resolution.

2. Suppose that you have been posted to a similar post (at the same managerial level and requiring the same technical skills) in *one* of these countries:

    *   Switzerland;
    *   Nigeria;
    *   Australia;
    *   or some other country that you have not visited before.

    What information do you need from your predecessor? List five topics.

3. Prepare a short presentation (between five and ten minutes) based on at least two of the points you listed in 1 above. Your objective is to brief your successor. Explain the behavior that you are describing, and give examples. If necessary, prepare supporting visual and text materials.

Notes

1. Hari Bedi, "Off-the-track training," *Asiaweek*, June 21 1987.
2. Baker's findings are also discussed in Baliga, Gurudutt, and Baker (1985).
3. "Jetzt wird Deutsch Gesprochen," *The Economist*, August 17, 1991.
4. "Lingua franca, lingua dolorosa," *The Economist*, August 24, 1991.

Part V

Culture and Change

17

Shifts in the Culture

17.1 Introduction

The model Japanese office-worker, or "salary man," is conventionally pictured as loyal to his boss and the organization to the point of giving up evenings, weekends, and even vacations in order to serve organizational needs. But a new generation of employees, called *shinjinrui* (new human beings), do not fit this model. A *shinjinrui*

> is more direct than the traditional Japanese. He acts almost like a Westerner, a gaijin. He does not live for the company, and will move on if he gets the offer of a better job. He is not keen on overtime, especially if he has a date with a girl. He has his own plans for his free time, and they may not include drinking or playing golf with the boss.[1]

It is not only the well-educated young and junior level employees who adopt these new attitudes to work. Older defectors can escape from the system by joining foreign multinationals. The story goes on to report that the Keidanren, an employers' association, reported on a survey that showed only 3 percent of the 250 managers surveyed still favored such traditional practices as insisting on long hours and arbitrarily transferring employees to new posts where they might be separated from their families.

If these attitudes really reflect deeply held values, then Japanese culture has shifted, so that old values of unconditional hard work and collective loyalty are disappearing. In Hofstede's terms, the *shinjinrui's* involvement with the company is becoming less moral and more calculative – perhaps reflecting a move towards higher individualism (Hofstede 1984a). (The increased borrowing of English language pronouns "my" and "I" supports this; see Sherry and Camargo, 1987, p. 178.) Loyalty to the employer is seen less as a virtue; does this indicate lower needs to avoid uncertainty? Does increased respect for personal freedom and rejection of the company's interference in the individual's private life show less masculinity?

This and the final chapter deal with the imponderables of change. Here we examine different explanations for how and why shifts occur in a national culture, and how these affect the organization. Chapter 18 sees how far culture influences techniques for planning and implementing change in the organization.

When the culture shifts significantly, members of the organization bring new values to the workplace. They look for new relationships with peers, superiors and subordinates. They expect new satisfactions from their work. They are no longer challenged by old motivators.

The organization alienates its members when it continues to operate procedures and structures that reflect outmoded values, just as it loses customers when it goes on producing outmoded goods and services. On the other hand, it risks making an equally expensive mistake when it overcommits in order to accommodate shifts that later prove superficial and short-lived.

Even for a member of the culture group, problems arise in identifying real and significant movement. The problems is much more severe for the manager who is a cultural outsider.

The chapter is organized as follows:

17.2 Recognizing Significant Shifts in the Culture
17.3 Environmental Factors
17.4 Which Environmental Factors Are Significant?
17.5 The Cultural Conditions for Shift
17.6 Implications for the Manager
17.7 Summary
17.8 Exercise

17.2 Recognizing Significant Shifts in the Culture

This section deals with the problems of identifying and explaining

- significant shifts in values, to which the organization should respond;
- short-lived trends.

The cross-cultural manager can never afford to take apparent manifestations of change at face value. For instance, the introductory case might suggest that Japanese culture is undergoing a massive realignment with

Anglo cultures; but other evidence suggests that the deep meaning of the process is considerably more subtle. And the effects of an environmental factor, economic recession, soon demonstrated that an apparently significant shift was in practice less straightforward.

It had seemed that perceptions of appropriate roles for men and women were in flux, and hence that perceptions of what constituted valid achievements in society might be evolving.

> Three years ago, the success of the Iron Butterfly, Takako Doi, the Socialist Party leader, created a "Madonna Boom" in Japanese politics, with parties rushing to enlist women candidates . . .[2]

The private sector followed suit. The financial press warned that, at senior levels, the labor shortage could only be solved by hiring more women managers, and it seemed certain that women would soon take their places in the top boards of directors. (At low levels the problem was resolved by hiring illegal immigrants; Japan has one of the highest rates of illegal labor.) In addition, companies eager to impress their foreign clients made a point of dispatching women managers to overseas posts. Because many overseas postings are still unpopular and regarded as akin to banishment, the companies perhaps welcomed the excuse not to send their male managers, and thus kill two birds with one stone.

All this suggested that Japan was moving away from its heavily masculine values towards a more foreign culture, in which sex roles were less strictly differentiated.

However, these expectations would have been premature. By 1992 the recession and stock-market collapse meant that firms were shedding staff and making fewer new appointments; and women suffered disproportionately.

> Toyota Motor will reduce its intake this year of young male high school graduates by 7.4 percent to 1,580, while the number of women graduates is to fall by 25.6 percent to 570. Nomura Securities will halve its annual intake of women from last year's [1991] 800 and the total number of women workers is likely to fall to 3,000 in 1997 from the present 5,000.[3]

A further newspaper story about the *shinjinrui* indicates why their seeming revolt against traditional practice in the workplace cannot be taken at face value, and also seeks to explain why cultural fundamentals so often resist modification.

Some scholars doubt whether this new middle class is, at heart, any less group-oriented than other Japanese. They argue that although the *shinjinrui* may claim to be "individualist," at heart they still identify with the group.

> That will not change, say anthropologists such as Oxford University professor Joy Hendry, unless the current generation of shinjinrui departs radically from child-rearing methods that have become the norm in Japan.
>
> Unlike in the U.S. or Europe, where children are encouraged to be independent, Japanese mothers still rear their children to be totally dependent on home and family by continually warning them of the dangers that lurk without ... Ultimately, this is expanded to include the "group" and eventually the "country," both of which offer protection from the "dangers" that exist "out there" ...[4]

And, the writer argues, this need is illustrated by Japanese travelers abroad; they seldom venture far on their own, away from the collective security of a Japanese tour group.

This suggests, first, that the emergence of the *shinjinrui* generation and their preference for owning foreign cars and dressing in chic Western clothes demonstrates superficial fashion rather than real change in Japanese values. And the Anglo manager who decided to structure a Japanese operation on the assumption that Japanese values now equated to Anglo values, and that his/her Japanese workforce showed high individualism, weak masculinity, and low needs to avoid uncertainty, might be making an expensive mistake.

17.2.3 Explaining slowness to shift

Second, this story underlines the central importance that child-rearing has in fixing individual and group values. The group passes on the fundamentals of its culture from one generation to the next in the education it gives its children in the first few years of life. At this age, familial influences are most powerful in forming the individual's value system.

But this point applies generally across cultures, and so does not explain why Japanese culture should be any more more resistant to change than others. To understand that, we need to examine the focus of child-rearing in that society.

The Japanese mother's chief function is to stay at home and bring up the children, and almost always this means giving up her career. This reflects Hofstede's (1984a) perception of masculinity in Japanese culture as a division of roles between men and women. It also explains why Japanese companies are so unwilling to recruit and train women to managerial posts. Given the unlikelihood of their continuing long in work after marriage, some other non-conventional investment must be made – for instance, day care or job sharing.

One alternative, that parents should switch their traditional roles and the father take on that of house-husband and child-rearer while the mother develops her career, is meeting acceptance in Scandinavia and beginning to be recognized in the United States. (See, for instance, Brian Basset's widely syndicated cartoon strip, "Adam.") But it is most unlikely in Japan.

Again in Scandinavia and increasingly elsewhere in Western countries, even very young children are sent out to child minders, crèches and play groups. This has the effect that they are learning culture from a variety of sources – and perhaps from members of different sub-groups. But in Japan, where child-rearing continues to be the mother's main responsibility and prerogative, learning the culture is a much more focused process. And hence we should not be surprised that values transmitted by the mother are so resistant to change.

17.3 Environmental Factors

The organization and its culture operates within an external environment, which includes such factors as

- international relations;
- multinational company policies;
- local political and legislative factors;
- market and industry factors;
- economic conditions;
- conditions in the natural environment;
- technology.

All these factors are unstable, and particularly so in societies undergoing rapid development.

These factors interrelate, and change in one factor has effects elsewhere. Rapid growth in the developing economies creates new markets and forces companies to revise their strategies for established markets. For instance, the success of the green revolution means that many countries which previously found it difficult to feed themselves are now able to export food. Countries which once enjoyed near-monopolies in certain food exports now have to compete. They are forced to adopt higher controls on quality and to invest more in processing, packaging, and marketing. This affects demand for skilled labor.

The multinational company stimulates organizational change when headquarters lays down policy to be implemented in its branches. Headquarters policy also affects staff representing the company in joint ventures, and this may have knock-on effects, influencing behavior within the other joint venture parent.

The organization is directly affected by shifts in the labor market. First, economic growth creates new demands for labor, both quantitatively and qualitatively; new skills are needed and old skills are needed at higher levels. Second, economic growth depends in part on the supply of a sufficiently educated workforce – increasingly a problem in both the United States and Europe.

More highly educated employees have different expectations of their relations with management and the degree of responsibility that they should be permitted. Close supervision is less tolerated, and may be less effective in securing positive outcomes – for instance, when the workforce have greater relevant expertise than do their supervisor.

17.3.1   The environment and culture

A shift in values is reflected by new behaviors in the culture group, which in turn may affect the environment. But what generates this shift in values? A process model of culture views culture as always changing, yet a community is unlikely to jettison a feature of its value system for no reason. Wilkins and Dyer (1988) argue that the more stable the culture, perhaps

> only a major environmental crisis could produce enough impetus for culture change. (p. 527)

That is, some event must occur which forces members of the group to adopt a new perception of the world and of their relationships. But the reverse may also be the case, and a major crisis can paralyze a culture, thus inhibiting change and causing disintegration.

Here are two examples of how an event in the environment can influence the culture – and how a subsequent shift in values rebounds to affect the environment.

- In the richer countries, the decline of the traditional "smoke-stack" industries, which demanded physical rather than mental qualities in the workforce, is slowly eroding traditional distinctions between "man's work" and "woman's work." In newer industries, such as electronics, physical brawn counts for less than manual dexterity and mental alertness. Labor costs in the United States have grown to the point that American electronics producers have moved their manufacturing facilities to Mexico. Because women are perceived as more dexterous and docile, they make up the bulk of the new labor force. This causes role reversal and disruption, and forces men to emigrate in order to find work.

- Since the nineteenth century, new forms of transportation (railway, car, plane) and communication (radio, telephone, television) have made persons steadily less dependent on their local communities. The opportunities for rapid physical mobility and communication across wide distances encourage a decline in collectivist loyalties and a rise in individualism. The individual is increasingly willing to distance him/herself from the immediate group, for instance, by seeking promotion, and by training in the new skills that secure promotion. The new availability of skilled labor leads multinational companies to make new investments within the community.

It follows from this that the manager needs to develop a sensitivity towards significant factors in the environment, and to identify

- *which* factors guarantee stability;
- *which* factors are most likely to affect fundamental values;
- *how* they might affect fundamental values.

17.4 Which Environmental Factors Are Significant?

Here we deal with three significant environmental variables, and examine conditions under which changes in these variables affect the national culture.

The problem of explaining how cultures reflect both stability and change has occupied scholars for many years. Conflict theorists such as Marx, Mills, Dahrendorf, and others perceived all social systems to be in continual conflict, hence change is continual. Functionalists such as Parsons and Merton described change as an adjustment process, and focused on the natural capacity of social systems to adapt to strains and stresses, and to find a new stability (Parsons, 1966; Parsons, 1971). Social systems are functional in the sense that all parts are related and integrated (Merton, 1967).

The sub-sections below look at three factors in the environment, and examine the circumstances under which these may impact upon the culture;

- deliberate intervention from the external environment;
- change in economic conditions;
- technological innovation.

17.4.1 Deliberate intervention from the external environment

Here we deal with deliberate intervention, such as forced entry, invasion, and occupation, made by some other social group.

Invasions by Western colonialists profoundly influenced the indigenous cultures of the less developed world before and during the nineteenth century. But the changes that were wrought seldom corresponded with the expectations of the colonialists and contemporary observers. And even now, many years after the critical events, their significance may be unclear.

Serious difficulties arise in trying to predict culture shift from changes in international alliances, and even foreign intervention. This was demonstrated during the 1990–91 Gulf War. Saudi Arabia was a front-line antagonist and host to a massive allied army. And as foreign troops flocked in during the run-up to war, many Saudi and non-Saudi citizens were convinced that changes in social values were imminent.

The three stories, (a), b), and (c) below, appeared between September 5, 1990 and September 4, 1991.

> (a)   Saudi Arabia, in facing up to the Iraqi military challenge, is undergoing fundamental changes in its social . . . doctrines.
>   King Fahd . . . has called upon government authorities to make it easier for women to participate in the fields of nursing, civil and medical assistance programs. . . .[5]

Besides ordering the expansion of the armed services, the King called for greater participation of Saudi women in the strictly segregated labor market, where it was expected that they would replace foreign women in roles of nurses, clerks, and medical technicians.

> [A local newspaper editor noted] "the rise of social consciousness and activism . . . The crisis is making us aware that we have to depend primarily on ourselves."
>   "The situation is tragic but it is stirring things in a way many of us never dreamed could happen," said Rabaa Khatib, a Saudi woman scholar of English literature . . .[6]

But eight months later, after the fighting in which Saudi Arabia had played an important part on the winning side, the country returned to routine:

> (b)   "Life has returned to normal," said Teymour Alireza, a prominent businessman. "Almost nothing has changed."

... the lack of immediate change has depressed many middle-class, well-educated Saudis who had hoped that the confrontation with Iraq and the vast American presence here would prompt the Saudi ruling family to side more openly with those who favor modernization and liberalization, including religiously mandated social restrictions and political restraints.[7]

There had been a period of openness to Western media; but this proved to be brief. After the war, broadcasts of Cable News Network at major hotels were discontinued, and Saudis were no longer so willing to offer their opinions to Western journalists. The ultra-religious morals police, or *mutawah*, returned to harassing both those Saudi and foreign women they considered insufficiently covered in public places, and the authorities seemingly reneged upon promises to employ women in a wider range of occupations.

"It's always a very careful balance here [between progressive and conservative factions]," said a Saudi professor. "Part of the ruling family's genius is maintaining that balance over time. Things will change, but slowly. . . ."[8]

And a third story, published a year to the day after story (a), reflected upon hopes aroused by the foreign invasion, and disappointments for the progressives.

(c)   In particular, they hoped that the example of [Western] women soldiers, serving alongside their male colleagues to defend the kingdom against attack from Iraq, would loosen the ancient binds on Saudi women. . . .[9]

But one year later, the country appeared largely unaffected.

The . . . *mutawah* [religious police] patrol the shopping centres scolding women who have dropped their veils or exposed their hair. . . .
The cultural impact of the troops "was just about nil," said a Western diplomat.
[However, a Saudi diplomat] said "Saudi Arabia is really undergoing real change."
"But," he added, "Americans flatter themselves if they think they provoked it. The change in Saudi Arabia is working on its own dynamic."[10]

Why were expectations of change disappointed? The following points appear significant:

• Predictions were made that the values expressed by foreign troops would influence local values. It was expected that differences between traditional local and modern "imported" value systems would lead to a crisis in the culture, from which new values would eventually emerge from the process of adjustment.

- These predictions were made both by outsiders and by some "expert" insiders (who presumably knew their culture).
- The crisis did not occur. Temporal, locational, and cultural factors were significant:

  i.   the presence of foreign troops, in large numbers, was short-lived – less than a year.
  ii. The troops were quarantined away from large urban centers, contacts between Saudis and troops were restricted, and there was no cultural contamination.
  iii. This quarantining was deliberate and planned; uncontrolled change was feared by both Saudi and United States authorities.
  iv. Saudi political structures are capable of integrating tribal and social differences. If a sufficient number of Saudis had understood and supported the "progressive" cause, and if the contradiction between traditional and modern value sets had been acute, the situation might have been different. But as things stood, existing values were never seriously challenged.

- Hence the question of adjustment between alternative, or conflicting value sets did not arise.
- Because opposition to the ruling family was insignificant, the authorities were able to shrug off the temporary inconvenience of playing host to so many outsiders, and Saudi society very quickly adapted back to its previous state.
- The question is left open as to whether real change was in process. It is implied that change would be generated by internal imbalances between progressive and conservative factions, not by pressure applied from external interests.

Given the puritanical and traditional nature of Saudi society, the unsympathetic Westerner is tempted to overlook the possibilities of internally generated change (as suggested by story (c)). But Lacey (1981) pointed us how much had already changed. A short time ago one of today's television singers could perform only in secret, cigarette smoking was forbidden in public and cigarettes could only be purchased under the counter in plain brown envelopes. Only in 1981 did a committee of Islamic legal scholars rule that a Saudi woman must be allowed to unveil in front of her prospective bridegroom.

> "Any man forbidding his daughter or sister to meet her fiance face to face will be judged as sinning," the committee declared. (pp. 512–13)

Even the direction of this slow change is uncertain, and there is no reason to suppose that the mass of Saudi Arabians want to move closer to the Anglo cultures.

> It is a peculiarly Western way of looking at the world to assume that every problem must have a solution. There are some uncertainties one must learn to live with, and if you ask a young Saudi Arabian cosmic questions about his own future and the future of his Kingdom, he will try to answer for a time, and then give up. (Lacey, 1981, p. 521)

17.4.2 When intervention is decisive

This case of Saudi Arabia in the Gulf War suggests that outsider intervention is unlikely to have long-term consequences. But this may not always be the case, and a much earlier example shows the opposite.

In 1853, Japan had defended itself from Western cultural influences for almost 300 years; foreign visitors were forbidden, and no Japanese who left the islands could claim readmittance. This self-imposed isolation was only ended when an American sailor, Commander Perry, entered Tokyo Bay and refused to leave. Perry's "black ships" profoundly shocked the value system. His mission precipitated the Meiji restoration and the collapse of Japanese feudalism.

Why did this intervention serve as a catalyst for culture shift within Japan, when the Gulf War appears to have had no corresponding effect in Saudi Arabia? Change was possible only because there already existed an organized opposition to the Shogunate, and a sense of moral revulsion towards the values that it represented. And the failure of the Allied forces to play a similar role in Saudi Arabia is partly explained by the relative absence of any such political and moral contradictions among the mass of the Saudi people.

In sum, an intervention is most likely to affect the culture when internal conditions for movement are already in place.

This has implications for the cross-cultural manager. The manager's ability to secure a long-term change process within an organization rooted in some other culture depends upon his/her capacity to secure the support of significant numbers of insiders, or insiders with significant power. In the absence of a supportive constituency and key brokers willing to negotiate between the outsider and insiders, his/her freedom to introduce fundamental innovations to the organization is severely restricted. This point is developed in the next chapter.

17.4.3 Change in economic conditions

A very general correlation occurs between wealth and individualism. The precise relationship is a matter of debate. Drucker (1958) argued the case for marketing as a catalytic agent in the economic development process; in response, Dholakia and Sherry (1987) reviewed conceptions of development and suggested that too little is known about the marketing-development relationship, particularly in Third World countries, to yet make definitive statements.

Despite such exceptions as Japan and Israel, the wealthier countries tend to be more individualist and the poorer countries more collectivist. And it also seems to be the case that as a country becomes more developed, it shifts towards greater individualism.

How does economic advancement modify the person's dependence on the group – and in the long run, modify the culture so that collectivist values give way to individualist values? First, when private-enterprise capitalism offers rewards to individual effort, more innovative members of the society are tempted to rely on themselves in order to secure wealth. And when sufficient numbers share this perception of opportunity, become aware of common interest, and have access to capital, an entrepreneurial middle class is developed. Their growing economic power buys them freedom from collectivist norms of conformity and group consensus in making decisions, and they are able to ignore social sanctions imposed on those who transgress these norms. In time, the values expressed by the new class create new norms.

This function of breaking down collectivist values may also be served by ethnic enclaves who serve as mediators between the host society and the outside world; for instance, Chinese in South-east Asia, Ibos in West Africa, Indians in East Africa.

Figure 17.1 gives Hofstede's (1983b) evidence of a correlation between individualism/collectivism and GNP in 1970. At this date, the poorer countries tended to be more collectivist, and collectivist cultures tended to be poorer. For instance, Indonesia and Colombia suggest a positive correlation between collectivism and poverty, and the United States, Canada, and Sweden the correlation between individualism and a high GNP per capita.

However, these data do not prove what causal relationship holds between economic values and economic development. That is, they do not prove conclusively

- *whether* the drift towards individualism is causal; this generates more profitable economic activity;
- *or* economic development is causal; this generates more individual behavior.

But there is circumstantial evidence. Cases of poor countries enriching themselves and becoming more individualist supports the second of these two hypotheses. For instance, Hofstede's 1970 GNP data shows the

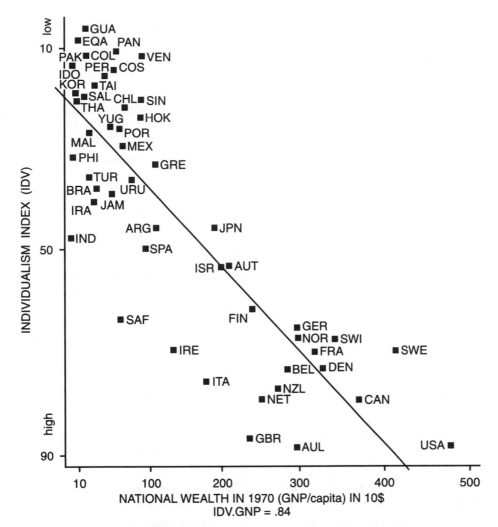

Figure 17.1 Individualism index (IDV) vs 1970 national wealth (per capita GNP) for 50 countries.

Asian countries of Taiwan, Korea, Singapore, and Hong Kong among the poorest. Since then, these "four little dragons" have all successfully exploited their access to Pacific basin markets and their proximity to Japan, and have massively increased their per capita incomes. In February 1988 the United States judged them to have industrialized to the extent that preferential trade agreements were no longer justified.

This example shows effects of economic development in one of these countries, South Korea. Employees at all levels used to feel a strong need for loyalty to the organization and strikes were rare. But by the end of the 1980s, economic development had brought increased material rewards; wages rose 13.5 percent in 1987, 14 percent in 1988, and about 12 percent in 1989. This coincided with a decline in values associated with organizational unity and an increase in union militancy.

A 1989 newspaper story explained that unions, previously suppressed, had developed new power and influence, and like many of their Anglo equivalents, become confrontational.[11] A strike at Hyundai Heavy Industries had recently ended in violent confrontation. Unlike in Japan where unions are company-based and in general committed to working with management, South Korean unions are industry wide.

> Wages have risen at a mind-boggling pace – 13.5 percent in 1987, 14 percent in 1988 and a predicted 12 percent this year [1989] . . .
>
> While the number of strikes is falling, they are lasting longer – from an average 5.3 days in 1987 to more than 15 days so far this year. . . .
>
> Government and corporate officials are aware that authoritarian traditions no longer have a hold over workers. In this Confucian society, society founders gave workers a job, clothes, housing, meals and wages in return for their labor and obedience. But employees feel no emotional ties to the new corporate management. . . . "The old value system is being dismantled," says [a labor relations professor].

17.4.4 Longitudinal evidence of a shift

Hofstede (1983a) repeated his research four years after the first study and his data led him to the conclusion that in all the 50 countries under investigation except Pakistan, an increase was found in individualism, and this seemed to follow an increase in wealth. Although the extremes of individualism and collectivism were converging, those that had achieved fast economic growth were shifting most noticeably towards individualism.

In general, the question of cultural convergence is still undecided. Child (1981) found that one group of scholars were arguing that the world was becoming more similar, while another group, equally reputable, were claiming that organizations were maintaining their differences. Most of the studies showing convergence were focused on issues like structure and technology, while most of those demonstrating the opposite dealt with the behavior of people in organizations.

There is certainly no suggestion that Japan is likely to match or outstrip Anglo and Scandinavian countries in individualism, despite the relatively greater success of the Japanese economy. It seems that periods of economic recession in these countries do not drive these cultures back to collectivism or to inhibit the drift towards greater individualism; the next decade may provide more evidence to test this hypothesis.

A move towards individualism in Japanese culture may have comparatively little importance to Japanese relations with other countries, because their cultures will have also shifted. Hofstede (1991) comments "the cultures shift, but they shift together, so that the differences between them remain intact" (p. 77).

Longitudinal changes on other of Hofstede's (1983a) dimensions are less easily explained by economic factors. On the dimension of uncertainty avoidance, stress seemed to be increasing in the vast majority of countries; the tendency was towards divergence of countries at extremes. Most masculine cultures appeared to be becoming more masculine, and most feminine more feminine. On the dimension of power distance, an overall divergence of countries could again be traced, although the trend is complex.

17.4.5 Technological innovation

But the level of gross national productivity is not the only factor to influence whether or not the culture evolves. There are bound to be other factors involved.

Saudi Arabia exemplifies a society that has shot from dire poverty to phenomenal wealth in a few years; the first oil revenues were earned in 1933, and by 1981 the Kingdom enjoyed a daily income of $320 million. Section 17.4.1 made clear that some fundamental values have evolved; nevertheless, changes appear to be far less than in the Asian Pacific region for instance, where financial growth, though substantial, lags far behind Saudi Arabia.

Financial growth and economic activity may cause a breakdown in traditional values when members of the culture group are unable to resist its effects. Contact with Europeans after 1492 provoked large-scale dislocations to indigenous cultures in America. When other factors are in place, economic activity can have positive effects, and cause cultural evolution. There must also be a willingness to innovate technologically, and members must be willing to accept the social and cultural consequences of innovation. And the precise impact of economic development is influenced

- on a macro level, by the extent of the investment in appropriate technology;
- on a micro level, by the impact that the new technology has upon the values of those implementing it.

The case of Japan shows how the extent of the investment is a factor at the macro level. It also shows how existing social and cultural priorities influence what technologies are selected and developed.

Exports were relatively low-tech into the 1970s, and typified by steel, ships, and textiles. A fear of over-dependence on a single (United States) market prodded Japanese companies to moving many of these industries off-shore and investing at home in high technology. And more and more it is

> the jobs of middle-aged generalist white-collar workers and skilled blue-collar workers in the sea-coast heavy industries which will disappear, while the new jobs will be for young specialists in the new information service industries in the big cities.[12]

This switch in technological focus, coupled with the far shorter shelf-life of technological skills in the new industries, has the following effects.

- Increasing numbers of workers are made technologically obsolete when still in mid-career.
- In order to stay in the workforce, they are obliged to retrain for other industries.
- Fewer employees are guaranteed lifetime employment (that is, employment until retirement). The extent of lifetime employment has probably been exaggerated in the past, and certainly never extended to all workers. Sullivan and Peterson (1991, p. 94) show that permanent job security was still on offer to "well over 50 percent of employees" in the firms they investigated. This may seem high; nevertheless the system is in decline – both for economic reasons, and because fewer employees wish to commit themselves to the relationship.
- As lifetime employment declines, there is a corresponding effect to the cultural values that the practice reflects (long-term commitment, loyalty between employer and employee, loyalty between peer groups hired contemporaneously).
- And, as an expression of this modification to the culture, job-hopping between employers increases. And job-hopping is associated with an apparently distinct social group, the *shinjinrui* – as we saw in sections 17.1 and 17.2.

The implemention of innovative technologies always promises to modify employer–employee values and also values associated with work itself. Lebas and Weigenstein (1986) discuss evidence that in Japan, as much as in the United Kingdom, the United States, and France, younger managers are less prepared to devote their lives to work for its own sake and instead demand careers that offer "self-fulfilment" – defined in Western terms.

17.4.6   How technology influences values

At a micro level, how does a technology influence the values of individuals directly associated with its implementation? Briefly, it creates the conditions for members of the organization

- to create old products or services in new ways;
- to create new products or services in new ways.

These new production methods create the conditions for new relationships between peers, superiors, and subordinates. These new relationships are expressed by new priorities in reporting and communicating – as chapter 6, section 6.5.1, demonstrated.

For instance, if your boss understands less about the new technology than do you – a specialist – you may find yourself spending more time in explaining to him the implications and applications, and less time in listening to his instructions.

These new production priorities influence the members' expectations of the workplace, both within the organization of employment and within other organizations. And by a slow process – measured in part by the speed and extent of technological development through society – the culture is modified.

The cross-cultural manager learns to recognize how members of the other culture are best able to re-adjust themselves to technological innovation. He/she cannot infer that work processes and relationships are modified in the same way in all different cultures. That is, other aspects of Japanese culture *not* present in the cultures of the United Kingdom, the United States and France explain how far the *shinjinrui* phenomenon is peculiar to Japan and how far it parallels youth subcultures elsewhere in the world.

If Japan and other East and South-east Asian communities appear willing to accept the cultural implications of economic development, Saudi Arabia demonstrates the other side of the coin. There, a massive increase in the GNP per capita has fueled an appetite for new technology, but technology transferred from elsewhere rather than generated within the country. Given the caution with which the Saudi community approaches any development which threatens to challenge essential values, a causal relationship may be hypothesized between the will to innovate and a readiness to accept cultural change.

17.4.7 Cultural conservatism in agricultural communities

The importance of technology is also demonstrated by its absence – where the absence of new productive methods and machinery acts as a brake upon change. Agricultural communities, for instance, may have very little access to technical development. Some respond to pressures from the city by erupting in peasant revolt – for instance, in Cuba,

Mexico, China. Some are among the most conservative. In the Balkan states of

> Albania and Romania, two thirds of the population lives in rural poverty, deeply suspicious of urban "intellectuals" pushing change. Communists find it easy to exploit pervasive fears of land reform and lost jobs, and they are adept at harnessing the region's strongest political force, nationalism, to their own ends. . . . uniquely in Europe, communism in Albania, especially in rural areas, is synonymous with the very existence of the state.[13]

And the Communists, who represented the forces of conservativism and the status quo, won the subsequent national election in 1991.

Farmers, like any other business people, resist new technology until they perceive a reasonable chance of making a profit on it. Writing about Thailand, Mingsarn Kaosa-Ard et al. (1989) write:

> Farmers do not adopt a new technology on a full scale as soon as they come across it. Innovative farmers generally experiment with the new technology on a small plot first. If incremental gains do not exceed incremental costs in terms of management, labor, or capital, then this new technology is not adopted. (p. 136)[14]

The writers make the point that adoption is a gradual process, and point to one technology that was only fully adopted after a 15-year period of modification and adjustment. Success depends not only on the intrinsic qualities of the technology and the profits it creates but also on such factors as

- access to information about the technology;
- patterns of communication and influence within the agricultural community;
- communication and access (including transportation) with markets.

Where these factors are absent, the new technology is unlikely to be adapted, and thus cannot play a part in the change process.

17.5 The Cultural Conditions for Shift

Thus far we have seen how shifts in the culture may be generated by factors within the environment, and we have noted the importance of economic and technological factors. But even when these factors are in place, some cultures resist change. The case of Iran before the 1978 revolution showed the dangers of attempting to force the pace of cultural evolution in the face of traditional values. The Shah's policy of channeling the new oil wealth into paying for superficial modernization eventually proved futile. He was overthrown in part because his subjects, mostly Shi'ite Muslims, would no longer tolerate political repression and attacks upon the religious culture.

This section deals generally with the issue of cultural conditions and why some cultures are more adaptable, and then focuses on educational systems as a channel for cultural evolution.

In many developed countries the culture appears to be in a constant state of flux. The United States is a prime example – and exemplifies Hall's (1976) notion of the low-context culture in which cultural patterns can change quickly. This is supported by Hofstede's (1984a) model, which shows a relatively low emotional resistance to change – a connotation of low needs to avoid uncertainty. And Americans are relatively tolerant of proposals for change.

In this example, an American lawyer writing on the prestigious op-ed page of the *New York Times* argues that "polygamy is good feminism":

> I married a married man.
>
> In fact, he had six wives when I married him 17 years ago. Today, he has nine. . . . At first blush, it sounds like the ideal situation for the man and an oppressive one for the women. . . . [However,] It offers men the chance to escape from the traditional, confining roles that often isolate them . . . More important, it enables women, who live in a society full of obstacles, to fully meet their career, mothering and marriage obligations. Polygamy provides a whole solution. I believe American women would have invented it if it didn't already exist.[15]

She spells out in some detail her daily schedule, and how her relationships with her husband and his other families benefits her and their daughter. This endorsement of polygamy is not radical in terms of religion. (Although the writer appears to be a Mormon – a long established religious sect that traditionally practices polygamy – she is not proselytizing for her faith.) But it is radical in terms of mainstream feminism. And the last two sentences quoted make an implicit appeal to other American women, regardless of their religious beliefs, to experiment with the same "solution" to lifestyle problems.

But such experimentation is relatively unlikely in a low-context culture where cultural patterns are ingrained and slow to change. Chilcott's (1968) study of United States citizens of Mexican descent shows that even second- and third-generation Americans held Mexican values that differed significantly from mainstream American values.

A further example is provided by Saudi Arabia. It is past-oriented in terms of the Kluckhohn and Strodtbeck (1961) model, and members' actions are more likely to be guided by the lessons of experience rather than aspirations for a different future. In 1963, King Faisal explicitly denied that modernization could be achieved only at the cost of destroying the past. Lacey (1981) summarizes the King's attitude:

> the surest progress comes through tradition, for, though it might make change slower, it makes it surer. . . .
>
> Sa'udi tradition dictated, for example, that women's social activities outside the family should be segregated from those of men. But this did not prevent – rather, it encouraged – the formation of women's co-operative groups, and these women's collectives are today among the most active private associations in Sa'udi life. (p. 368)

That is, modifications to behavior and hence to the value system are tolerated only when they do not contradict tradition and existing norms.

17.5.1 Change and education

The country's educational system is a formal structure by which the cultural values of the community are disseminated to its new members, its children and young adults. In addition, educational structure and methodology

- indicate the conditions under which the culture may be legitimately modified;
- indicate what modifications to the culture are possible;
- create conditions for and against change; on the one hand, the educational system aims to produce model citizens; on the other, it aims to create agents of change – of such changes as the society thinks it needs.

For instance, in Saudi Arabia, all education beyond primary levels is segregated, and relatively few women progress beyond secondary levels. Throughout the system all methodologies are heavily influenced by Islamic values.

Islam teaches that language has divine origins, is precise, and hence no useful distinction can be drawn between the dictionary definition of a word and its significance (Laffin, 1975, pp. 56, 72–6). This means that schools and universities rely on rote learning in order to teach the conventional meaning of a text. Children are educated to accept conventional truths, and neither to enter into a dialogue with text and teacher, nor to develop ideas for change that deviate from received wisdom. These methodological tendencies are apparent elsewhere in the Islamic world, including such non-Arab countries as Pakistan and Malaysia (Taib and Ismail, 1982; Mead, 1988).

Whereas Islamic culture is idealistic and prescriptive, the Confucian cultures of Asia (South Korea, Taiwan, Singapore and Hong Kong) are essentially pragmatic (Oh, 1991). Confucianism teaches lessons for the here-and-now rather than for an after-life. It focuses on the task of harmonizing human relationships, and involves a system of subordination and social order. Hence questions of how to demonstrate appropriate respect to other persons are central within these cultures – and in this aspect, they appear most conservative.

Respect for seniority is expressed in relations to educators and educational qualifications. But the increased demand for skilled labor is matched by a corresponding demand for credentials. And throughout the region, both state and private universities are degenerating to the status of paper mills, servicing a demand for certification at the expense of standards (Clad, 1989).

Innovations in syllabus and methodology occur in South-east Asia, but these are often influenced by imported ideas in preference to indigenous experiences. (Bloom (1987) argues this in the case of the United States – a position execrated by his "politically correct" adversaries.) For instance, the conventional American MBA syllabus stands as a powerful symbol of modernity, and exerts enormous influence on management training in the region. And those aspects of local management practice which do not belong in this syllabus tend to be ignored – for instance, patronage.

Educational school systems in the developed countries pride themselves on developing skills in free expression and creative problem-solving. But in practice they often have a hard job keeping up with the rate of change, and in producing both teachers and pupils able to cope with cultural shifts arising from economic and technological innovation.

17.5.2 Education, and the case of the United Kingdom

Rajan notes four weaknesses in the educational systems of the European Community countries:[16]

- inadequate schooling – for instance in Greece, Italy, Ireland, Portugal, Spain, and the United Kingdom;
- irrelevant and elitist curriculum; "With the exception of Denmark, Holland, France and West Germany, the curriculum is organized round the pupil as a 'product' and not as a putative worker;"
- lack of complementarity (that is, lack of connection between education provided by the state and subsequentially by employers);
- higher education restricted to a select few; the United Kingdom shows lower rates of pupils proceeding to "A" level or equivalent examinations, and hence on to universities.

The United Kingdom still fails to provide a sound basis for continuous and relevant education throughout the individual's schooling and working life. The culture pays great respect to the notion of "learning from experience," and fosters a suspicion of formal education and educators, and of technology.

Education at all levels suffers from this antipathy, even in areas that vitally affect technological development. Figures cited by Prais (1989) show how Britain lagged behind its main trade rivals in training engineers and technologists. For every 14 bachelor degrees in Britain, there were 15 in France, 19 in the United States, 21 in Germany, and 30 in Japan; for every 35 craftsmen, 44 in Japan, 92 in France, 120 in Germany (United States figure not available; original figures for Japan and the United States reduced in proportion to the British population).

An education journalist argued that

> anti-intellectualism appears to be a particularly British disease. . . . [This is explained by a] profound cultural gap separating British business and most of the rest of the developed world. The heads of major French and German firms routinely possess advanced degree-level qualifications. The Japanese and the Americans are well known for closely established links between business and education. They take intellectual ability seriously, in sharp contrast to the entrepreneur traditionally made in Britain.[17]

The writer went on to distinguish between the British manufacturing sector, which contributed relatively generously to university R&D, and the service sector. Financial markets, for instance, focused entirely on quarterly results and have no interest in long-term research. So at a time when

> the Japanese are busying themselves analysing the potential of global markets in the year 2010, their British counterparts consider projections two years hence to be, frankly, purely academic.[18]

The British preference for "muddling through" is antagonistic to the development of planned change and long-term innovation. It also militates against the development of a culture positive to fundamental modifications in values, as distinct from superficial modernism.

17.6 Implications for the Manager

Under some conditions, environmental changes may affect behavior, and eventually lead to shifts in cultural values.

1. Identify significant economic and other events that have occurred within *your own* culture during the previous few years (for instance,

political changes, economic recession or boom, technological innovations).

- How have these affected people's behavior – if at all?
- How have these affected your relationships with

  (a) other persons in your organization?
  (b) business acquaintances?
  (c) family, friends and social acquaintances?

2. Do you expect these behavioral changes (if any) to modify values in
    your own culture?

    - If you *do* expect a modification in values, in what direction?
    - What effects do you expect these changes to have on the culture
      of your organization?

3. Identify significant economic and other events that have occurred
    within *some other* culture that you know well during the previous few
    years (for instance, political changes, economic recession or boom,
    technological innovations).

    - How have these affected the behavior of members of *the other*
      culture – if at all?
    - Do you expect these behavioral changes (if any) to modify values
      in *the other* culture?
    - If you *do* expect a modification in values, in what direction?

5. Identify significant shifts of values within *your own* culture over the
    past few years.

    - Describe these shifts in values.
    - How did these shifts in values affect your industry? Your organ-
      izational culture?

6. Identify significant shifts of values within *the other* culture over the
    past few years.

    - Describe these shifts in values.
    - How did these shifts in values affect an industry that you know in
      that culture? An organization?

7. In what respects does the educational system within *your own* culture
    facilitate change in cultural values?

    - In what respects does it inhibit change?

8. In what respects does the educational system within *the other* culture
    facilitate change in cultural values?

    - In what respects does it inhibit change?

17.7 Summary

This chapter has dealt with the problems of identifying significant shifts in culture and predicting how events in the environment will affect values.

Section 17.2 discussed the problems of *evaluating change*. Real shifts in values profoundly affect how members of the organization feel about their work and working relationships, and usually demand a response from the manager. Section 17.3 showed why cultural values evolve in response to *factors* in the *environment*. This led to the question, taken up in section 17.4, *which environmental factors are significant?* Evidence suggests that economic development will have a decisive effect, but is likely to be associated with technological innovation. An intervention from the external environment is likely to affect fundamental features of the culture when supported by an internal demands for change. Section 17.4 dealt with *the cultural conditions for shift*, and asked why some cultural systems are preconditioned to more radical developments than others.

17.8 Exercise

This exercise helps you practice predicting the effects of economic change on cultural values.

- The Kingdom of Darana is landlocked and historically of little interest to the outside world (the Kingdom was never colonized). The United Nations lists it among the world's 20 poorest countries. It has a population of six million, of whom about 500,000 live in the capital, Daranaville. There are no other large cities.
- Social and political life in the Kingdom is controlled by a traditional elite of 16 families who derive their power from extensive land holdings. They are proud of their country's history and independence, and their custom of giving lavish hospitality to strangers. Those families who can afford to, send their children to Western countries for secondary and university education.
- Primary education is good; 87 percent of males and 63 percent of females are literate. The only university teaches humanities. Technical studies are taught in a vocational school.
- The largest single employer is the civil service. Seventy-seven percent of the workforce is employed in the agricultural sector. There is a small clay mining industry. Otherwise, the private sector consists of small family businesses, mostly involved in trading.
- The typical company is marked by wide power differentials between

ownership, middle management, and the workforce. Females are occasionally employed in junior secretarial functions.

- Other than among the elite, 91 percent of the female workforce in Daranaville is employed in the production of domestic ceramics (an all-female specialization), other craft occupations, and as house-wives and domestic servants.

Then it is discovered that the local clay has unusual qualities of heat-resistance and tensile strength, of major value not only to producers of kitchenware but also to the auto, aero, and space industries. This clay is unknown elsewhere in the world. An economic boom is promised; one prediction foresees average per capita income growing by 20 percent every year for the next ten years. The government is inundated by requests for business licenses from a range of foreign companies, in extraction, manufacturing and service industries.

(a) Predict how this bonanza might affect Daranese values.
(b) What policies should the government follow in order to protect Daranese interests while exploiting this bonanza to the national advantage?
(c) What human resource policies should a foreign company adopt, assuming that it expects to have a long-term presence in the Kingdom (of at least 10 years)? Assume a particular industry, and consider policies for

- recruitment;
- training;
- structural organization;
- motivating, rewarding, and disciplining.

Notes

1. "Free, young and Japanese," *The Economist*, December 21, 1991. But note that this article also cites the case of an employer sacked by Hitachi in 1967 because he refused to do overtime. Only by 1992 did the Supreme Court decide the case – and ruled for the company; "employees are obliged to work overtime, even against their will, if the request is reasonable." So how far does the Court represent true and contemporary values?
2. Robert Thomson, "Future dims for Japanese women," *Bangkok Post*, August 31, 1992.
3. Ibid.
4. Ronald E. Yates, "Juppies," *Chicago Tribune*, April 24, 1988.
5. Youssef M. Ibrahim, "Saudis: major change in rigid society," *International Herald Tribune*, September 5, 1990.
6. Ibid.

7. Judith Miller, "Storm over, Saudis revert to routine," *New York Times*, May 8, 1991.
8. Ibid.
9. Rone Tempest, "Change comes, at its own pace, in Saudi Arabia," *International Herald Tribune*, September 4, 1991.
10. Ibid.
11. Damon Darlin, "Korea's unions, suppressed for decades, become stronger, more confrontational," *Wall Street Journal*, 12 April 1989.
12. "A job for life no more," *The Economist*, December 5, 1987.
13. Robin Knight et al., "Communists prevail in the Balkans, for now," *US News and World Report*, April 15, 1991.
14. For an interesting discussion of how changing conditions in rural Thai communities affect values, see Turton (1988).
15. Elizabeth Joseph, "My husband's nine wives," *New York Times*, May 23, 1991.
16. Amin Rajan, "Poor education puts Britain on the skids", *Sunday Times*, 6 May, 1990. The writer presents the key arguments in his book, *1992: A Zero Sum Game*, The Industrial Society, Birmingham (1990).
17. Alison Utley, "Never mind a fee, enjoy the lunch," *The Times Higher Education Supplement*, October 25, 1991.
18. Ibid.

18

Planning Change

18.1 Introduction

Change is painful, and people tend to resist it. Although medical science has demonstrated the consequences of continuing to smoke, drink excessively, and engage in unsafe sexual practices, millions of people across the world refuse to modify these behaviors.

In politics and business, proponents of radical change are often treated with suspicion. Moderation is generally preferred. A 1992 United Kingdom survey of electors' perceptions of the Prime Minister and Leader of the Opposition revealed that "Cautious" was seen as desirable, along with "Likeable as a person," "Competent," "A good team player," "Can be trusted," etc.; whereas its opposite, "Willing to take risks" belonged with "Not likeable," "Incompetent," "A loner," "Cannot be trusted":

> Some people, including Mr Major [the Prime Minister], approve of risk-taking. However it is probably also to [his] advantage that he is widely seen as being "cautious." It cannot be good for Mr Kinnock that so many people see him as a man "willing to take risks."[1]

The previous chapter examined movement in the environment, and saw how a culture might shift. This chapter asks how the organization can be made to change in response to these pressures. When change is painful, proposals for change encounter resistance. Hence, getting organizational change accepted is a difficult political process of changing people's minds. The chapter is organized as follows:

18.2 Planning Change in the Organization
18.3 The Values of Planning
18.4 Culture and Timescales

18.2   Planning Change in the Organization

This section first examines a change model and then looks at the needs to communicate effectively in order to have the change accepted.

It is normally assumed that change is managed most effectively when it is planned and the plan is properly implemented. (Alternative strategies, reflecting a world in which the environment is increasingly unpredictable and the manager has increasingly few opportunities for reflective and systematic planning, are dealt with in section 18.6.) The classic model for planning change has been developed and discussed by a range of scholars (see Zaltman, Duncan, and Holbeck, 1973). The basic version consists of these eight stages:

1.   identifying a need for change; defining the goal of the plan;
2.   collecting relevant information;
3.   analysing the information and projecting past and present conditions into the future;
4.   designing alternative strategies to meet the need;
5.   selecting the best strategy;
6.   implementing the selected strategy;
7.   monitoring and reviewing the implementation stage;
8.   making necessary modifications, based on stage 7 output.

This model is "ideal" and may not be fully implemented at every stage. In practice, strategies have to be designed and implemented without access to comprehensive information and perhaps only one strategy is ever worked out in full. Nevertheless, it is accepted here for the time being; the problems of trying to plan within an unstable environment are discussed in section 18.6.

18.2.1   Communicating change plans

A change plan is unlikely to have practical consequences unless it is effectively communicated. In short, this means that its usefulness must be persuasively demonstrated to those groups and individuals whose support is needed for implementation. They include those who

- have the power to authorize it;
- implement it;
- will live with its consequences.

Support for change is created by appropriate communication. And employees who contribute to the planning and implementation processes are less likely to feel their jobs at the mercy of forces beyond their control. Persons who feel some ownership over the process are more disposed to accept it as a contract (Allaire and Firsirotu, 1990).

Delays in involving the workforce in planning change cause real dissatisfaction. One study of the British auto industry showed that workers' organizations were usually approached only at the early implementation stage (that is, after a strategy had been selected) and even then management imposed qualifications on their capacity to participate (Whipp and Clark, 1986). This resistance to worker participation played a significant part in causing the troubles that afflicted the British industry during the 1980s. In contrast and at the same time, the managements of the Japanese auto industry were involving their workforces in real decision-making as early as possible.

18.2.2 Communicating change plans in different cultures

Cultural factors influence what communicative style is most appropriate. In a flat organization, the change plans are communicated with an eye to building a broad consensus, and this means inviting suggestions and comments. Informal channels may be as least as important as formal ones (Schon, 1963). In a hierarchical organization, only senior members are consulted, and subordinates are informed of change plans. Where power distances are small, it may be necessary to communicate very widely and include all those whose interests are directly and indirectly affected. Where power distances are great, junior subordinates may not expect to be informed in any great detail, and may be confused if an inappropriate style is used. But even here it is possible to cascade the decision to change down, allowing the lower ranks to plan details of implementation.

In standard management theory, a participative style invites employee participation in the planning process, and the greater this is the greater their sense of "ownership" of the change process, and their commitment to it, and hence the greater the success of the change process.

But in some cultural contexts, the notion of worker participation may be little understood and little appreciated – at least when the workforce have not been trained to participate. Chapter 6, section 6.4.1 noted an example from Puerto-Rica where attempts to involve the labor force so disconcerted them that they left the organization (Woodworth and Nelson, 1980).

The cross-cultural manager has particular need to focus on communication issues, where

- different cultural values are associated with the concept of planning;
- locals do not share the manager's perceptions of the issue as a strength, weakness, etc.

Cultural factors determine

- *with whom* you communicate at each stage;
- *how* you communicate;

    (i)   the communicative style: at one extreme, giving directions; at the other extreme, consultative;
    (ii) the selection of channel and mode;

- *what* aspects of the plan you communicate.

18.2.3 The political process

Because plan communications must be persuasive in order to be effective, and are intended to generate action (in terms of support, enthusiasm, implementation activities, etc.), they are political in nature and building support is a political process (see Watson, 1971; Duncan, 1979).

A proposal for organizational change is most likely to succeed when those persons who are likely to be affected are convinced that all the following conditions apply (derived from Dutton and Duncan, 1987):

1. levels of dissatisfaction with present circumstances are intolerably high;
2. senior (and other influential) members of the organization believe that change is possible;
3. specific changes can be formulated;
4. these proposed changes are welcomed;
5. initial implementation procedures can be identified;
6. resources for implementing the changes are available – including change agents, training facilities and capital;
7. environmental forces are supportive of change, or at worst neutral;
8. the likely cost of change appears less than the cost of continuing under present conditions.

When any one of these conditions is *not* present, the odds are stacked against implementing change successfully. Or, to put this another way, change plans are unacceptable when the perceived cost of making the change is less than the expected benefit.

For instance, many Poles explain the failure of national movements against Communist rule by the fact that the then Soviet Union continued to support the government against the vast mass of the Polish people. But in 1989, the Soviet Union discovered that its interests were better served by creating a Polish window to the Western world, and hence relaxed its controls. A successful revolution soon followed.

Because affected persons have to be certain of these conditions for the plans to succeed, the proponents of change have the task of convincing them – a question of communicating persuasively.

18.2.4 Building support

Who proposes change? Where power distances are large, for instance in a Latin American or Asian family company, a proposal is legitimated when it comes from the top. A suggestion from a lower level may be taken to imply criticism (that a problem exists, that no one in authority noticed it, etc.).

Where power distances are small, the idea may spring from a lower level – at least in theory; Burgelman and Sayles (1986) suggests that the middle-ranking manager can take on the role of corporate strategist. In practice, industrial, functional and organizational culture factors may qualify lower-level involvement. Rothwell's (1984) study of 23 British companies discovered that original technology planning was organized at the initiative of the Board of Directors, the Managing Director, or the Marketing Director.

The political aspects of implementing a change plan include the following.

- *Identifying supporters* among superiors, peers and subordinates, and reinforcing their support; winning neutrals to a position of support; moving opponents to a position of neutrality. The manager cannot take for granted the same constituency within different cultural contexts.
- *Identifying a champion* He/she is a person with authority and influence in the organization – in a bureaucracy, the CEO or an entrepreneurial senior departmental head with an instinctive "primal" drive (Lessem, 1989, p. 114).

  In a traditional South-east Asian family company, where only those ideas generated by at the top level are acceptable, the owner champions his/her own proposals.

  In a cross-cultural situation, a change plan is given additional credibility when associated with a member of the local culture as champion;

- *Identifying change agents* and building their enthusiasm. Who will be responsible for communicating and leading the change in each affected unit? Within this culture, what are the implications of involving only senior people? People at subordinate levels? Do supervisors need training?
- *Involving affected persons* Have persons expected to be affected by the change been adequately involved? Do they understand why it is necessary for the organization, and in their long-term interests? Do they understand what short-term difficulties may arise, and how these can be overcome? How far can they be involved in planning and implementing processes – and so given some ownership over the process?

18.2.5 Transplanting systems

This sub-section deals briefly with the issue of meeting needs for change by borrowing management systems from another cultural context.

Borrowing practices is attractive when the other country copes successfully with management problems that seem beyond the capacity of your own country. Applications made around the world of the American-style syllabus in management education (in particular the MBA), and America's own interest in Japanese practices show that borrowing is rife (Johnson, 1988).

Schein (1981) contributed to the debate over importing Japanese practice by warning against "quick fix" solutions that do not fully recognize the differences in the cultural environments within which Japanese and American organizations operate.[2] Japanese cultural practices cannot be transplanted to an American setting as though they were rice seedlings.

It is often forgotten that many Japanese techniques – including the Quality Circle – are not indigenous but were invented in the United States (Griffin, 1988). The more successful Japanese firms did not attempt the "quick fix." They analysed the cultural implications of the technology and the conditions under which it could be grafted to their existing structures and within the cultural context (Goldstein, 1988).[3] And in transplanting they adapted. Since then many other countries have tried to follow their example – such as the United States, where firms have "reimported" the Quality Circle with very varying success.

When a management process is borrowed inappropriately, or the conditions for its successful application within the local culture have not been met, one of three things happen:

- the process is rejected; it fails to work as efficiently within the new context as it does within its indigenous context;

- the process functions as planned, but its operation results in the problem being transferred elsewhere in the total system – just as a new road designed to alleviate traffic pressure at one spot creates a new pressure point elsewhere;
- the process functions as planned, but its operation causes new problems. For instance, new technology is introduced within one unit. This unit perceives itself, and is perceived by others, as preferred. The resulting inter-group tensions between the units offset the improvements offered by the technology.

In sum, a management system originated for a different context should be applied only after careful analysis and comparison of the situations, and any necessary modifications have been made.

18.3   The Values of Planning

This section sees how culture affects priorities in planning, and why planning processes vary across cultures.

Planning is made in response to moderate uncertainty about future events. No planning is necessary in conditions of absolute certainty, nor feasible in conditions of absolute uncertainty (Mintzberg, 1988, p. 86). Individuals and cultures vary in their perceptions of moderate uncertainty when planning may serve useful ends.

By investing time and resources in planning, the planner demonstrates

- a belief in the reality of future time;
- optimisim: a belief in his/her capacity to dominate and model future time.

And so a culture that invests heavily in planning fits these orientations of the Kluckhohn–Strodtbeck (1961) model:

- (the temporal focus of human activity) future;
- (the person's relationship to nature) dominant.

Planning is an optimistic activity in that it presupposes that the future can be made better than the present and that positive change is possible. The optimist plans radical changes to the organization, expecting that these can be implemented; the pessimist accepts the status quo. But here is an exception:

Workers asked to find cost savings in the accounts department of one of Britain's biggest companies [Rover] found a dramatic if effective solution: they sacked themselves. . . .

> [W]ithin nine months of being set new productivity targets by management, staff in a main accounts department produced their own novel solution: a plan to slim down their office from 174 people to 111 with no loss of output of invoices and accounts.
>
> Those who had thought themselves out of jobs have moved on to other companies or to other areas within Rover.[4]

This story makes news because it goes against common sense. We do not expect employees to plan their own redundancies. In fact, this situation is so unusual that one looks for a deeper explanation; who planned, those made redundant or those who survived? How generous were redundancy payments? Had those who moved elsewhere in the company been promised these positions before the process began?

18.3.1 Planning as symbolic action

All planning is symbolic in the sense that it claims to assert control over significant variables where little or none is possible; future events cannot be accurately predicted and the number of possible variables that influence the future are infinite. This symbolism has value (including economic value) to the extent that it relieves individuals' anxieties over the future, and satisfies their needs for the illusion of control over the future – and is therefore motivating.

Although planning aims to establish areas of certainty in the unknown future, in practice it is based on only what *is* known – past and present conditions, and succeeds only to the extent that future events conform to present projections made of events that have already been experienced. The planner stumbles when the unexpected occurs. Planning based on projections of existing conditions did not help governments and companies foresee the oil crisis of 1973 and the Iranian revolution of 1980, and when these events occurred existing plans needed to be scrapped.

Different cultures express the need to plan in very different ways. They make different assumptions about *what* can be planned, *how* plans should be made and implemented, *what information* is relevant, and *who* plans.

18.3.2 What is planned?

All cultures plan to exploit perceived strengths and opportunities and to protect themselves against perceived weaknesses and threats. They vary in terms of what factors they perceive as strengths, opportunities, etc.

Hofstede (1984a, p. 264) argues:

- where needs to avoid uncertainty are small, planning is less detailed and more long-term;

- where needs to avoid uncertainty are larger, the opposite conditions apply. Specialists are made responsible for detailed planning. Because uncertainties need to be resolved as quickly as possible, an emphasis is placed on short-term feedback systems.

This associates small needs to avoid uncertainty with less emotional resistance to change. But it does not follow that in such cultures all proposed changes are equally welcomed and more than that all changes are equally feared where needs are large.

An organization is likely to be more accepting of changes that more closely reflect dominant cultural values. For instance, a proposal for formal participation in works councils and boardroom representation is far more likely to be acceptable where power distances are small than large (Hofstede, 1984a, p. 82).

Uncertainty about performance factors is reflected in planning of control systems and operating procedures; and about personal factors in retirement plans and health policies.

18.3.3 How is planning conducted?

Illustrations from Asia show that different cultures approach the process differently.

Redding and Martyn-Johns' (1979) study of companies based in Indonesia, Hong Kong, Malaysia, the Philippines, Singapore, Thailand, and (originally) South Vietnam discovered either less formal planning systems and/or planning systems with fewer variables than in equivalent Western companies. Monitoring, performance evaluation, and feedback was less rigorous. All this resulted in less integration of planning and control systems.

But no single model holds for all Asia. Studies discussed by Fukuda (1983) show that Hong Kong Chinese companies plan very differently to Japanese. The Chinese demand more detailed information and place greater reliance on developing an effective Management Information System (MIS). Both the Japanese and Chinese managers give subordinates the responsibility for developing alternative plans. But the Chinese keeps more information to him/herself, and is more likely to take the final decision. He/she behaves more like the classic model of the Western "decision-maker" and the process is less collectivist.

In Japan, planning is treated more deliberately as a formal process, at least at lower levels of the organization. A comparison of Japanese and United States management attitudes found that junior Japanese managers favored formulating strategies by the classic model of analysing the issue and finding the most appropriate solution (Sullivan and Nonaka, 1986). But their seniors follow a process which is "partial, tentative, fragmented, incremental, empirical, inductive, messy, individualistic and pathfinding." The two processes can be followed simultaneously, each augmenting rather than competing with the other.

In practice, market and industry factors significantly influence what style is appropriate, regardless of culture. Where the market is in a state of turmoil and up-to-date information is unavailable, the classic model becomes increasingly unworkable – see section 18.6.

18.3.4   What is required for planning?

The decision to plan for or against a particular eventuality assumes not only that the planned change can be implemented, but that the data inputs are available and can be analysed.

The classic Western planning model depends upon such "hard" information as financial data and computer predictions of market change. Elsewhere, different emphasis is placed upon historical data, "best guesses," and superstition. In Hong Kong when starting a business venture, business people may gamble heavily on "lucky numbers" – for instance, eight, which in Cantonese translation sounds like *faat*, or "prosperity." Sarachek et al.'s (1984) study of middle level managers in Malaysia discovered that the "modern" notion that "time can be predicted and planned" was qualified in Chinese eyes by "respect for superstition." (Their Muslim Malay compatriots perceived success leading to enhanced social status as a reward for devoutness.)

Culture is not the only significant variable. The developed economies are information rich economies. Data is easily accessed – perhaps at a price – from data banks, research facilities, consultants and specialists, and the media. Advanced communication systems ensure that this information is available and can be rapidly accessed. The planner exploits a wide range of modern technologies in searching for up-to-date and verifiable data with which to support the rationale of the plan.

Very different conditions exist in poor economies where these data sources are not available. The situation is made worse by political instability, and a lack of standardization in marketing, accounting, and other systems.

Haines (1988) gives an example from Nigeria, where two prominent brewing companies commissioned a report on total demand for beer in the country. Their sales turnovers ammounted to well over £100 million, and they had sophisticated accounting systems.

> Yet the marketing function had to operate without the normal starting point of marketing analysis, that is, of total size in terms of demand whether expressed in monetary or volume terms. (p. 92)

Calculating supply presented no problems. The total capacity of the six brewers active in the 1960s was easily estimated. And even 20 years later, when the total had increased to 15 or 16 companies, a reliable estimation could still be made. But far greater difficulties were found in calculating total demand.

> For more than 20 years, the beer market was never in a "free supply" position. For all this period the salesmen of these companies were not selling their products at all, but allocating them to their distributors. It was thus impossible to assess what sales and at what prices beer would be sold if the supply exceeded the demand. (p. 92)

Although culture influences perceptions of what data are needed, economic, technological, and political factors determine whether or not they are available.

18.3.5 Who plans?

Where power distances are large, the top manager takes responsibility for planning, and for directing implementation. Hofstede (1984a) suggests that planning tends to support the short-term "political" ends of the superior rather than the strategic ends of the organization. Because subordinates can be little trusted to make effective plans, planning is left to specialists – which, in a family company in Latin America or Southeast Asia, means the owner and perhaps his/her close family members. But where power distances are small, subordinates are more likely to be trusted, and this is reflected in planning systems.

18.3.6 Organizational culture and planning responsibilities

Planning styles and responsibilities vary across organizational cultures. Table 18.1 (derived from material in Kono, 1990) sums up differences between three types:

- the entrepreneurial business;
- the family-owned business;
- the full bureaucracy.

The model of an *entrepreneurial* culture is idealistic and this approach to planning is risky. Structures must be fluid and employees feel confident in communicating across structural boundaries. Nevertheless some companies, particularly in Japan, have worked to build this type of culture, with considerable success; Toyota is an example.

Table 18.1 Differences in planning styles and responsibilities in three types of organizational culture

Culture	Entrepreneurial	Family-owned	Full bureaucracy
Needs	Innovation oriented	Owner orented	Rule-bound; safety first
Planner	Innovative planning group	The owner	'Expert' planning group
Risk-taking	Not afraid of failure	Failure the responsibility of the owner	Afraid of failure; failure is 'de-legitimated'
Status of the plan	Flexible	Determined by the owner	'Legal'
Communication	Ideas and counter-ideas presented and invited throughout	Only as directed by the owner; no counter-ideas	Formalized and rule-governed; ideas presented as policy

Source: adapted from Kono (1990)

In a *family-owned* business that is owner-oriented, the owner may do all the planning. Members are emotionally and occupationally dependent upon him/her, even when nominal responsibilities are taken by other persons in the family. Because he/she is bound to take responsibility for failures, members risk less and stand to gain less, and are less challenged to participate in the planning process.

When the owner has championed the plans for change, it may be expecting too much that he/she should openly admit to error. In this context, systems for monitoring implementation may be largely redundant.

Planning procedures in *full-bureaucracies* are governed by impersonal bureaucratic rules. All plans must meet covert objectives of ensuring the organization's survival. Planning is made the responsibility of a nominated group of experts, and other members are not normally expected to contribute. Established procedures are followed at each stage of the planning process.

Monitoring and feedback processes may be restricted to checking that these procedures have been correctly followed. Failure is routinely blamed on circumstances outside the planners' control. Before the collapse of communism, Soviet central planners blamed food shortages on the activities of Western enemies or on unexpected climatic conditions.

When British Rail ground to a halt during the 1990–1 winter, British Rail planners countered complaints that they had (still) failed to plan for winter by pointing out that, on the contrary, all rolling stock had now been equipped to operate in snow; however, "the wrong sort of snow had fallen."

Planning styles in these three cultures can be cross-cut. The large company that wishes to break out of its bureaucratic mode and adopt a more receptive posture in relation to its environment may license its planners to develop "intrapreneurial" initiatives (Lessem, 1988). In describing his experiences planning with Royal Dutch Shell, De Geus (1988) defines the planner as a "facilitator, catalyst, and accelerator of the corporate learning process" who has the role of playing with models in order to educate senior managers and change their minds.

Similarly, the family-owned company may adopt an entrepreneurial dash when first established, then gradually move towards a traditional family model as markets mature and management issues proliferate. The entrepreneurial or family company engaged in a joint venture with, say, a full bureaucracy, may be pressured to develop systems that come closer to that model.

18.3.7 Centralized planning

A range of countries have experimented with some centralized control of planning and production – in 1972 Benveniste noted capitalist France, and the mixed economies of India and Pakistan (p. 739). But before the collapse of communism, the most noteworthy cases were found in the Marxist states of Eastern Europe and the Soviet Union, which all had centralized "command" economies. These demonstrated bureaucratic planning in an extreme form.

The same planning models were used for the Soviet Union and the various satellite countries, regardless of the differences in their cultures and natural environments. Winiecki (1988) shows that all these countries developed industrial structures that were nearly identical; figures in 1980 showed a 0.99 correlation between resource-poor and unsophisticated Bulgaria and the resource-rich and relatively sophisticated Soviet Union.

The planners were responsible only for making the plans indicated by their political masters. They had no responsibilities to consumers. Persons responsible for implementing the plans might have very little communication with the planners – almost all planning was conducted in Moscow. They had no incentive to do more than they were directed, however ill-conceived the plan. Certainly they were unmotivated by any desire to innovate, and might be punished for proposing modifications. The results were sometimes catastrophic:

> [o]n becoming Kremlin boss [in 1986], Gorbachev expressed the hope that better planning might produce an extra two percent growth in Soviet industry. As examples of poor planning, he authorized an exhibition of shoddy and defective goods produced by Soviet workers, including a whole consignment of boots with high heels attached to the toes. (Hay, 1988, p. 183)

This dependence upon centralized planning exerted powerful long-term influences upon the managers in these countries. In 1990 (after the collapse of communism) Fogel discovered that Hungarian managers were unable to understand how an auditor could provide an independent valuation without government interference (p. 14).

By 1991 the People's Republic of China was one of the few remaining command economies (along with Cuba, Vietnam and North Korea). The leadership still insisted upon centralized planning in order to safeguard political orthodoxy.

> At a meeting hosted by [Premier] Li to discuss financial reforms, [an] economist proposed that the People's Construction Bank of China, which advances loans for infrastructural projects, be vested with power to veto projects. He argued that such decentralization of power would result in more prudent loan decisions because the loan officer would be held accountable. Currently, these decisions are made by the powerful State Planning Commission.
>
> The premier's response was curt: "Our comrades at the planning commission have the expertise and training to make the right decisions."[5]

The certainties of economic and political centralization were preferred to the uncertainties of market competition; and market competition had not yet reached the point at which centralized planning was no longer politically feasible.

None of this implies that a poor developing country can dispense with centralized planning altogether. Choguill (1980) noted the serious consequences for Bangladesh when the country boasted no more than a few dozen planners in total.

18.4 Culture and Timescales

Contextual and cultural factors influence the timetable for planning and implementing change. Moving too slowly carries two dangers:

- pockets of resistance have a chance to grow and finally undermine the radical change process (Tushman et al., 1986, 1987);
- the proposal becomes bogged down by bureaucratic inertia.

It is possible to outflank the opposition by introducing the change quickly, and "routinizing" it before they can mobilize their forces. But then members of the organization are unlikely to be committed, and may actively resist both your sleight of hand and the policing necessary to safeguard an unwanted reform. Moving too fast can also be a mistake if it means increasing people's insecurity. Rousseau (1989) argued that

> [e]ffective management of change means "no surprise." Telling people about change well in advance gives them an opportunity to psychologically adjust to it before it happens. (p. 42)

Drawing on her United States experience, she implies that potential supporters should be involved as early as possible – when the technology has been selected. But this may be too early in other contexts.

Giving time is important in situations where you expect resistance to fade as more people become used to the notion of change and more understanding of how they can benefit. In such cases the manager focuses on communicating goals and allaying anxieties.

Where a climate of change and experimentation is welcomed, and where uncertainty-avoidance needs are lowest, your audience is more receptive to the message. Time spent in teaching new routines is reduced and the change can be introduced comparatively quickly.

A less obvious problem arises in allowing members of the organization time to forget the old behavior which has been replaced. If the old behavior has become automatic, perhaps because it directly reflects values in the culture, a longer time is spent in their forgetting it and learning the new.

18.4.1 Cultural differences in timing

Cultures vary in the emphasis they give to short-term and long-term planning. For instance, Negandhi (1979) analysed organizational practices in US parent companies, US subsidiaries in three Latin American countries (Argentina, Brazil, and Uruguay) and three Far Eastern countries (India, the Philippines, and Taiwan), and local companies in these six countries. The subsidiaries commonly followed US timescales (planning five or ten years ahead), and lower-level managerial and technical personnel were consulted before final decisions were taken by top management.

The planning orientation of the local firms tended to be medium- or short-term.

> The typical firm in this category planned for a horizon of one or two years. The resulting plans were less comprehensive and detailed. Review

procedures, as well as strict adherence to planned targets, were taken less seriously than in the US subsidiary. There was relatively less participation by other echelons of managers in the planning activities. (Neghandi, 1979, p. 325)

The Latin American local companies engaged even less in long-range planning than did the Far Eastern companies.

These finding are substantiated in part by Neghandi et al. (1985) who compared management practices in local Taiwanese firms, and Japanese and United States subsidiaries in Taiwan. In the first two the emphasis was on medium- to short-term planning, looking one to two years ahead; and in the United States subsidiary, long-range planning, looking five to ten years ahead.

The relatively short timescales for Japanese planning times apparently reflects a readiness of the Japanese companies to adapt to local practice. They contradict the popular notion that all Japanese planning is long-term. In practice, a distinction needs to be drawn between the long-term strategic planning of top management, and middle-management planning designed to interpret top-management thinking in the light of the immediate situation.

The individual's psychological make-up also affects his/her planning horizons. Research by Das (1991) conducted in a major American bank discovered that executives with a "distant" future orientation preferred long-term planning, while those with a "near" future orientation preferred shorter planning horizons (p. 53). CEOs with longer "future" orientations used more impersonal strategic information sources, such as trade journals, reports, conferences, than those with shorter orientations.

18.4.2   Strategic planning

The implications of strategic thinking may be long-term but this does not mean that strategy and planning can be neatly differentiated on a temporal basis. Quinn (1988) defines strategy as

the pattern or plan that integrates an organization's major goals, policies, and action sequences into a cohesive whole. A well formulated strategy helps to marshall and allocate an organization's resources into a unique and viable posture based on its relative internal competencies and short-comings, anticipated change in the environment and contingent moves by intelligent opponents. (p. 3)

The greater the range of variables brought into play, the more strategic planning loses formal precision.

The development of strategic planning targets and skills has been perceived as as an evolutionary process. Gluck, Kaufman, and Walleck (1980) identified four stages in the planning process:

1. budget-based planning;
2. forecast-based planning;
3. externally oriented planning;
4. strategic management.

This concept of an evolutionary process was applied by Ali and Shaw's (1988) study of 48 large Australian organizations. This single-culture study examined the conditions under which some had progressed beyond financial planning and to increasingly adopt strategic planning concepts. Environmental factors, for instance opportunities to develop operations throughout the Asian Pacific region, were the most significant stimulants.

The concept has also to be applied across cultures. In comparing managerial practices in the United States and India, Joseph (1973) found that the American companies typically planned in corporate, production, finance, marketing, and manpower areas; the Indians in corporate, production, and finance. The Indian companies showed relatively little capacity for long-term strategic planning. Like the Americans they used budgeting and sales forecasting techniques; unlike them they made relatively very little use of cash forecasting and statistical techniques. In terms of the model presented by Gluck et al. (1980), the typical Indian company had progressed little beyond the second stage.

18.5   Culture and Change

Thus far, the chapter has described decisions to change as linked with the classic planning model. This and the next section look at environmental conditions in which this relationship may not apply.

A willingness to accept and generate change does not necessarily reflect commitment to formal planning. Family companies in South-east Asia, for instance, invest in little formal planning, yet in some respects may be highly entrepreneurial. This capacity for making entrepreneurial changes appears to reflect aspects of the culture, as we now see.

18.5.1   The Confucius connection and entrepreneurship

Hofstede and Bond (1988, p. 16) explain the rise of East Asia by the fact that their cultures almost perfectly fitted these countries to world-market conditions in the last years of the twentieth century. After 1955, they argue, a global market arose for the first time in history. A common Confucian heritage equipped the region to adapt to the pace of change in a way unlike that of any other countries.

The research instrument differed significantly from that used by Hofstede (1984a) in the original IBM project. This original questionnaire had been designed exclusively by Westerners, and hence the choice of items and research findings had inevitably reflected Western values. Bond designed the new project with an eye to rectifying this cultural bias, and asked a number of Chinese social scientists to prepare a list of basic values for Chinese people. And so the 40 questions in the Chinese Values Survey (CVS) reflected the priorities of Eastern rather than Western minds – and thus differed significantly from the IBM model, and from almost all other instruments used in cross-cultural research.

This questionnaire was then translated into English and the languages of the respondents, and administered to 100 students in each of 22 countries.

Three of the dimensions in the CVS (and based on the values suggested by Bond's Chinese experts) probed three aspects of social behavior; behavior towards seniors and juniors, behavior towards the group, and the expected roles of the sexes. As such they overlapped with those three dimensions in the IBM survey investigating power distances, collectivism/individualism, and masculinity/feminity.

No questions in the CVS reflected the uncertainty avoidance dimension in the IBM survey. Hofstede and Bond suggest that this dimension reflects Western preoccupations with Truth. The Westerner is analytic in his/her thinking and accepts the possibility of only one Truth; if my point of view (logical, religious, ethical, aesthetic) is true, and yours differs, then yours by definition is untrue (Hofstede, 1991). And this mind set reflects the three great Western religions of the Book, Judaism, Christianity, and Islam. But the Eastern mentality, and its ethical systems, are essentially synthetic. Confucianism and the major Asian religions all value Virtue rather than Truth and find Virtue in behavior (ritual, meditation, ways of living) rather than belief. So Virtue may be found in contradictory and even antagonistic behaviors and beliefs.

18.5.2 Long-term orientation

Hofstede and Bond (1988) found evidence of a fifth dimension, missing from the IBM survey, which they call the "Confucian Dynamism." They distinguished between long- and short-term orientations. The connotations of the former include a capacity to adapt tradition to new situations, a willingness to amass and a thrifty approach in using scarce

Table 18.2 Long-term orientation index ranking of countries

LTO rank	
1	People's Republic of China
2	Hong Kong
3	Taiwan
4	Japan
5	South Korea
6	Brazil
7	India
8	Thailand
9	Singapore
10	Netherlands
11	Bangladesh
12	Sweden
13	Poland
14	Germany FR
15	Australia
16	New Zealand
17	USA
18	United Kingdom
19	Zimbabwe
20	Canada
21	Philippines
22	Nigeria
23	Pakistan

Source: Hofstede (1991), p. 166

resources, a willingess to persevere over the long term and to subordinate one's own interests in order to achieve a purpose, a concern with Virtue. On the contrary, a short-term orientation reflects the opposites, including a lesser savings quote, an expectation of quick results, and a concern with "face" and with Truth (see Hofstede, 1991, pp. 170–3). Hofstede (1991) ranks countries in the Long-term orientation (LTO) index as shown in Table 18.2.

Hofstede (1991) claims that, in general, "the values at the LTO poll are very Confucian *and* support entrepreneurial activity" (p. 168). A willingness to adapt tradition, practice thrift, persevere, and when necessary, subordinate self-interest all foster a capacity for innovation. On the other hand, overmuch respect for tradition, unconditional respect for social and status obligations, lack of thrift, and emphasis on the short-term, all impede deep-rooted innovation.

18.5.3 Evaluating the Hofstede-Bond (1988) model

This model tries to measure a culture's capacity for change and helps explain the current appetite for entrepreneurial innovation in East Asian countries. But it interprets the concept of "change" in only a narrow sense; and a desire to modernize the economic system and to innovate productive capacity does not guarantee a willingness to innovate social organizations.

For instance, the Communist government of the People's Republic of China strictly distinguishes between economic and political liberalizations. By 1991, the private sector had grown enormously, and state enterprises were responsible for only 52.8 percent of the country's industrial output, compared with well over 80 percent in 1981.[6] On the basis of world-leading rates of growth during the 1980s and early 1990s, many observers expected China to emerge as a superpower in the first years of the twenty-first century (see Kennedy, 1988, ch. 8). But this development of the private sector had no parallel in political and social institutions, and the Communist Party's control was unchallenged – at least in the open.

Throughout the region, a willingness to innovate in terms of productive and technological resources and in relations with the environment (including the market place) does not mean that the owner of a family business (for instance) is equally willing to experiment with relationships and roles. Economic and political uncertainties, large power distances, and a Confucian stress on a stable hierarchy and complementarity of roles, inhibits organizational innovation. Even when further growth may be dependent upon modifying the structure, the owner may well decide *not* to expand when the company can only accumulate the resources needed by making a public flotation and hence introducing outsiders.

Westerners may have as many problems "reading" these research categories and findings as have Chinese reading the IBM categories and findings. To the Western mind, a "respect for tradition" indicates caution, and the introductory case indicates that caution in public life is welcomed in at least one Anglo culture. Also, concern for "face" is conventionally thought of as an Asian characteristic; but the writers remind us that the Index measures the *relative* value of one side against the other – in this case, "face" as against a willingness to subordinate oneself.

The model offers three significant advantages. First, it enables the cross-cultural manager to differentiate short- and long-term orientations to events in the future and in appetite to make short- and long-term investments. For instance, it helps explain why United States companies cannot ask for a career commitment from their employees – and vice versa – as can Japanese companies. Second, it demonstrates national differences in saving patterns. Third, to the extent that family companies in these cultures are innovatory, the conventional wisdom that change cannot be easily achieved in a climate of high status and power differentials is discredited (see Griffiths, 1964). Where top management – and even the owner – champions the process, change gives rise to little or no overt conflict and may be quickly accomplished.

18.6 Proactive planning

Earlier sections examined how the process of making change is managed by utilizing formal planning tools. This section sees why today's business environment increasingly restricts applications of the classic model.

Early management theory took for granted that planning must always be a deliberate process. In 1916, the French industrialist Henri Fayol described the functions of the manager as planning, organizing, co-ordinating, and controlling.

The classic model presupposes

- control over the organization;
- access to reliable information;
- the capacity to predict likely developments within the environment.

The model encapsulates the ideal situation. Lorange and Roos (1991), for instance, stress the importance of potential joint venture partners making thorough assessments of the strategic match and operational details before cementing the alliance. They refer to a number of matches (for instance, Yokogawa Electric and General Electric Medical Systems, Nippon Steel, and IBM) in which analysis has been exhaustive.

But the model is inadequate to the extent that change in the environment is discontinuous and unpredictable. Thompson (1962) quotes from an interview with the CEO of a "good-sized, fast-growing" company; in response to a question as to whether he has planning in his company, the CEO replies

> If you are asking me, "Do you do a lot of planning?" my answer is "Yes."
> If you are asking me whether we print a number of papers about it, headed Planning, the answer is "No."
>
> I am engaged in planning, 12 hours a day, every day. I don't know how you could run a business without thinking of the three- to five-year implications of everything you do today. . . . We do not have a formal ritual for planning. But, believe me, our planning gets an enormous amount of attention, continuous attention, even though it is not formalized. (p. 47)

Mintzberg (1975) cites more evidence (from Canada, the United States, Sweden, and Britain) to show that the modern manager has little time for reflective and systematic planning:

> Study after evidence suggests managers work at an unrelenting pace, that their activities are characterized by brevity, variety, and discontinuity, and that they are strongly oriented to action and dislike reflective activities. (p. 5)

Planning is becoming increasingly pragmatic and incremental, a distillation of reactions to numerous short experiences. There may not be sufficient time to make a complete market analysis. The manager rarely generates more than two or three realistic options, and rarely follows the implementation plan:

> the best strategies are usually already half implemented and those parts that have not been implemented are so uncertain that planning more than one or two steps ahead is wasteful. (Campbell, 1991, p. 108)

In sum, the modern manager recognizes the problems that arise from depending on formal analysis and instead develops his/her intuitive sense of vision and "feel." Mintzberg argues that a test of intuition is that it should meet three criteria:

1. it is deeply, often passionately, felt;
2. it is rooted in experience of the context, even if the learning is subconscious;
3. it emerges as a conscious choice and direction.

> Unless all three elements are present, then it is probably not intuition; it may just be prejudice. (Campbell, 1991, p. 109)

18.6.1   A post-modernist world

Why are applications of the classic model increasingly restricted? Some scholars argue that we now live in a post-modernist world; the links of cause and effect, which mankind utilized to develop the modern world, have snapped. This theory argues that our vision of future events has become significantly reduced. The future has been uncoupled from history. Past experience no longer influences what is going to happen in the future, and our technologies no longer guarantee controlled and predictable results. If the organization can no longer impose certainty, it must develop alternative models for coping within a world of uncertainty (Johnson, 1992).

The organization able to adapt to these circumstances is structured so that the manager does not becomes overburdened with operating decisions which could easily be delegated. It must be capable of continuously transforming itself and creating its own opportunities rather than waiting for them to emerge from the environment. The organizational strategist must be open to new influences, new information, and new signs of change. Rather than developing fully formed plans, he/she acts as change agent, a facilitator who helps managers plan (Raimond and Eden, 1990).

Nonaka (1991) writes that

[i]n an economy where the only certainty is uncertainty, the one sure source of lasting competitive advantage is knowledge. When markets shift, technologies proliferate, competitors multiply, and products become obsolete almost overnight, successful companies are those that consistently create new knowledge, disseminate it widely throughout the organization, and quickly embody it in new technologies and products. (p. 96)

By knowledge creation he means the process of making explicit concepts that are tacit, and then finding ways to express them in figurative language. For instance, Honda top management pushed down to a lower level (a group of young designers) the responsibility for expressing a vague dream (an entirely new car) in concrete plans (Nonaka, 1988).

Mintzberg and McHugh (1985) focused on how strategies develop in contemporary organizations. In contrast to the deliberately structured planning process, a strategy emerges as "a pattern in a stream of decisions or actions." It is formed from precedents set by groups that eventually enter the collective thinking of the organization and lead to its adopting a radically different posture to the world. Most importantly, strategy develops from an openness to what is happening in an increasingly unstable business environment and a willingness to learn from this experience.

18.6.2 Practical solutions

The point about proactive planning in an age of uncertainty is that there is no single copy-book solution to either the planning process or the solution.

Environmental pressures push companies in different directions. When markets seem likely to disappear and competition increase, cost-cutting is one answer. In 1991, Philips, the Dutch electronics giant, shed some 45,000 workers. In the same week in July 1993, Toyota announced plans to trim its United Staff salaried force for the first time ever, by five percent over two years, and Proctor and Gamble decided to eliminate 13,000 jobs because of rising production costs, despite record earnings over the previous year. Daimler eliminated two layers of management and reduced the workforce, and showed a profit.[7]

Other companies worry about overreacting to boom-bust cycles; in 1991, Royal Dutch Shell, Glaxo, and Hutchinson Whampoa all said that they would not cut capital expenditure.[8] In the case of Royal Dutch Shell, this decision was reached through detailed macroenvironmental analysis using competing strategies. The process was intended to be both protective in a time of recession, and entrepreneurial:

> Scenarios, at least as they are used at Royal Dutch/Shell, are fundamental aids in changing the mental models and altering the corporate micro-cosms in ways that allow managers to generate options for the future while assuming acceptable levels of risk. (Ginter and Duncan, 1990, p. 97)

Hutchinson's major headache was their US$387 million expansion into mobile communications in Britain, and in 1993 the firm decided to search for a equity partner, possibly supplanting the mother company as majority shareholder of Hutchison Telecommunications (UK).[9]

A further strategy is to invest in increased manufacturing and market-ing flexibility – a route taken by Peugeot and Nissan in 1990. Many companies try to subcontract production in order to offset increased risk, although by 1993 IBM discovered that this can be taken to extremes. Geographical diversification in manufacturing was adopted by ICI.

ICI is an example of a company that deliberately set out to design systems able to propose change in advance of shifts in the environment. Turner (1984) described how a team of eight executive directors, not involved in the operating units, were made responsible for

- economic and environmental assessment;
- comparison of ICI's performance with that of its competitors;
- formulation and implementation of planning models.

The team implemented a planning process that provided a long-term vision of the future business environment.

18.7 Implications for the Manager

Compare an organization that you know well in *your own* culture and a similar organization in *some other* culture.

1. In the two organizations, who normally proposes change and de-fines objectives? Answer in terms of

(a)   organizational rank;

(b)   functional and occupational responsibilities.

2.   In each organization, what are the implications for planning and implementing a change strategy?

- Examine the implications for

  (a)   identifying supporters;
  (b)   identifying a champion;
  (c)   identifying change agents;
  (d)   involving affected persons;
  (e)   building monitoring and feedback systems;
  (f)   implementing the change plan;
  (g)   monitoring and feedback;
  (h)   making revisions.

- How should each of these stages be communicated?
- How should the process of change be timetabled?
- At what points do your answers for *your-own-culture* organization and the *other-culture* organization differ?
- What implications do any differences have for an innovator moving from *your-own-culture* organization to the *other-culture* organization, and hoping to implement change strategies there?

3.   In each organization, how much emphasis is laid on formal planning? How much on informal and intuituive planning in response to events and external forces?

- To what extent do plans represent firm commitments, or intentions subject to reformulation in response to events?

4.   Review your answers to 1–5 above.

- At what points do your answers for *your-own-culture* organization and the *other-culture* organization differ?
- How far can these differences be explained by differences in

  (a)   organizational cultures?
  (b)   other factors internal to the organizations?
  (c)   national cultures?
  (d)   other factors in the external environment?

- What implications do any differences have for an innovator moving from *your-own-culture* organization to the *other-culture* organization, and hoping to implement change strategies there?

18.8   Summary

This chapter has examined how cultural values associated with change influence the formulation and implementation of planning systems.

Section 18.2 summarized the main features of formal models designed to *plan change in the organization.* A plan depends upon support from members of the organization in order to succeed. Creating this support is a communicative and political process. Cultural factors help determine what communicative style is appropriate at what stage of the plan. Section 18.3 dealt more broadly with *culture* as a factor influencing how formal *planning* models are applied. Culture influences what can be planned, how plans are made and implemented, what information is relevant in formulating a plan, and who plans. The culture of the organization is a further significant influence. Section 18.4 saw how *culture* and other factors influence the *timetabling* of planning and implementing change.

Section 18.5 examined the 1991 Hofstede–Bond model, and asked how far the distinction between long- and short-term orientations in *culture* explain attitudes towards *change.* Finally, section 18.6 examined the implications of post-modernist theory for planning. The concept of *proactive planning* takes account of circumstances in which cause and effect have become dislocated. The environment is increasingly unpredictable, and for some planning activities, formal models may be of declining relevance.

18.9   Exercise

This exercise practices planning change.

Identify an organizational structure or system (for instance, systems for appraisal, for compensation) at your place of work or study that you think needs changing; then answer these questions.

Wherever appropriate, show how features of the culture influence your answer – in a different cultural context, why might you plan your strategy differently?

(a)   What is the objective of the change proposal? Describe present conditions and how they will be changed.

(b)   How will the change affect

- established roles, relationships, and procedures?
- support functions, such as recruitment and training?
- other structures and procedures within the total system?
- costs? What new expenses will be incurred?

(c)   What groups will be affected directly and indirectly by the change? Consider the interests of formal and informal groups, pressure groups (such as unions), and groups in the external environment (such as customers, government bodies).

(d)   How will each group benefit or lose from the change? Who can you count on to

- support the proposal? why?
- be neutral to the proposal? why?
- oppose the proposal? why?

(e)   Who can you ask to champion your proposal? Why is he/she the best person?

(f)   Who will be your change agents, assisting you and/or the champion in implementing the change?

(g)   How will the change be implemented?

(h)   How will the process be communicated, by whom and to whom? Plan to communicate

- needs for change and objectives;
- long-term advantages in changing – and short-term problems – that will be overcome;
- implementation plans and procedures;
- monitoring and feedback plans.

(i)   Show how your strategy

- strengthens your supporters;
- wins the neutrals round to your cause;
- neutralizes your opponents.

(j)   Describe the timetable for the process.

(k)   What can go wrong? (Because something will!)

Notes

1.   Anthony King, "Major's 'grey' personality proves a hit with voters," *Daily Telegraph*, March 7, 1992.
2.   Schein (1981) reviews Ouchi (1981); and Pascale and Athos (1981). Both texts are optimistic about transplanting Japanese models.
3.   Goldstein (1988) argues that the organizational structure rather than the culture determine whether a new process is accepted or rejected; and structures can be more easily modified.
4.   Kevin Eason, "Rover workers plan themselves out of jobs to reduce costs," *The Times*, April 18, 1992.

5. Julia Leung, "China faces growing economic polarity," *Asian Wall Street Journal*, July 30, 1991.

6. James McGregor, "China pursues policy of the bottom line," *Asian Wall Street Journal*, March 2, 1992.

7. "Business: dreaming of butterflies," *The Economist*, June 26, 1993.

8. "Managing in an age of anxiety," *The Economist*, January 19, 1991.

9. Craig S. Smith, "Hutchison's UK strategy: call in help," *Asian Wall Street Journal*, July 21, 1993.

Bibliography

Abercrombie, M. L. J. 1974: *Aims and Techniques of Group Teaching*, Society for Research into Higher Education, London.

Abudu, F. 1986: Work attitudes of Africans, with special reference to Nigeria, *International Studies of Management and Organizations*, **16**(2), 17–36.

Adler, Nancy J. 1979: Women as androgynous managers: a conceptualization of the potential for American women in international management, *International Journal of Intercultural Relations*, **3**(4), 407–35.

Adler, Nancy J. 1983: A typology of management studies involving culture, *Journal of International Business Studies*, Fall, 29–47.

Adler, Nancy J. 1984: Women in international management: where are they? *California Management Review*, **26**(4), 78–89.

Adler, Nancy J. 1986, 1991: *International Dimensions of Organizational Behavior*, Kent, Boston MA.

Adler, Nancy J. 1987: Pacific Basin managers: a *gaijin*, not a woman. *Human Resource Management*, **26**(2), 169–91.

Adler, Nancy J., Campbell, Nigel, and Laurent, André 1989: In search of appropriate methodology: from outside the People's Republic of China looking in, *Journal of International Business Studies*, Spring, 61–74.

Agar, Michael H. 1980: *The Professional Stranger*, Academic Press, New York.

Aiken, Michael and Bacharach, Samuel B. 1979: Culture and organizational structure and processes: a comparative study of local government administrative bureaucracies in the Walloon and Flemish regions of Belgium. In Cornelis J. Lammers and David J. Hickson (eds), *Organizations Alike and Unlike: International and Institutional Studies of the Sociology of Organizations*, Routledge & Kegan Paul, London, 215–303.

Alexander, Jeffrey C. and Seidman, Steven (eds) 1990: *Culture and Society: Contemporary Debates*, Cambridge University Press, Cambridge, 183–195.

Ali, M. Yunus and Shaw, Robin N. 1988: Strategic planning and management in Australian organizations, *Asia Pacific Journal of Management*, 105–28.

Allaire, Yvan and Mihaela Firsirotu 1990: Strategic plans as contracts, *Long Range Planning*, **23**(1), 102–15.

Alter, S. L. 1980: *Decision Support Systems: Current Practices and Continuing Challenges*, Addison-Wesley, Reading, Mass.

Anderson, Erin 1990: Two firms, one frontier: on assessing joint venture performance, *Sloan Management Review*, **31**(2), 19–30.

Anderson, Lynn R. 1983: Management of the mixed-cultural work group, *Organization Behavior and Human Performance*, **31**(3), 303–30.

Anti-Slavery Society 1985: Child labour in Morocco's carpet industry. In Ray Bromley (ed.), *Planning for Small Enterprises in Third World Cities*, Pergamon Press, UK, 171–80.

Atkinson, John W. (ed.) 1958: *Motives in Fantasy, Action, and Society: A Method of Assessment and Study*, D. Van Nostrand, Princeton, NJ.

Austin, Clyde N. (ed.) 1986: *Cross-cultural Reentry: A Book of Readings*, Abilene Christian University, Abilene, Tex.

Azumi, K. and McMillan, C. J. 1981: Management strategy and organizational structure: a Japanese comparative study. In D. J. Hickson and C. J. McMillan (eds), *Organization and Nation*, Gower, Farnborough, 155–72.

Badr, H. A., Gray, E. R. and Kedia, B. L. 1982: Personal values and managerial decision making: evidence from two cultures, *Management International Review*, **22**, 65–73.

Bahrami, Homa and Evans, Stuart 1987: Stratocracy in high-technology firms, *California Management Review*, Fall, 51–66.

Baker, James C. 1984: Foreign language and pre-departure orientation training in U.S. multinational industrial firms, *Personnel Administrator*, **29**, 68–70.

Baliga, Gurudutt M. and Baker, James C. 1985: Multinational corporate policies for expatriate managers: selection, training, evaluation, *SAM Advanced Management Journal*, Autumn, 31–8.

Barnes, L. B. and Hershon, S. A. 1976: Transferring power in the family business, *Harvard Business Review*, July–Aug., repr. in *Harvard Business Review. Small Business*, Part 3, No. 21187, 84–93.

Barrett, C. V. and Frank, R. H. 1969: Communication preference and performance: a cross cultural comparison, *MRC Technical Report*, No 29.

Bartlett, Christopher A. and Ghoshal, Sumantra 1987: Managing across borders: new strategic requirements, *Sloan Management Review*, Summer, 7–17.

Bartlett, Christopher A. and Ghoshal, Sumantra 1988: Organizing for worldwide effectiveness: the transnational solution, *California Management Review*, Fall, 54–73.

Bartlett, Christopher A. and Ghoshal, Sumantra 1989: *Managing across Borders: The Transnational Solution*, Hutchinson Business Books, London.

Bartmess, Andrew and Cerny, Keith 1993: Building competitive advantage: a capability-centred approach, *California Management Review*, **35**(2), 78–103.

Bazerman, Max H., Magliozzi, Thomas, and Neale, Margaret A. 1985: Integrative bargaining in a competitive market, *Organization Behavior and Human Performance*, **34**, 294–313.

Beamish, P. W. and Calof, J. L. 1989: International business education: a corporate view, *Journal of International Business Studies*, Fall, 553–64 at 561.

Beamish, P. W. and Wang, H. Y. 1989: Investing in China via joint ventures, *Management International Review*, **29**(1), 57–63.

Becker H. and Fritzsche, D. 1987: Business ethics: a cross-cultural comparison of managers' attitudes, *Journal of Business Ethics*, **6**, 289–95.

Benedict, Ruth 1946, 1974: *The Chrysanthemum and the Sword: Patterns of Japanese Culture*, New American Library, New York.

Benveniste, Guy 1972: *The Politics of Expertise*, Boyd & Fraser, San Francisco.

Bernard, H. Russell 1988: *Research Methods in Cultural Anthropology*, Sage, Newbury Park, Cal., 150–1.

Berry, John W. and Cavalli-Sforza, L. L. 1986: Cultural and genetic influences on Inuit art, unpublished report.

Berry, John W., Poortinga, Ype H., Segall, Marshall H., and Dasen, Pierre R. 1992: *Cross-cultural Psychology*, Cambridge University Press, Cambridge.

Bhalla, A. (ed.) 1991: *Small and Medium Enterprises*, Greenwood Press, New York.

Bies, Robert J. and Moag, Joseph S. 1986: Interactional justice: communication criteria of fairness, *Research on Negotiation in Organizations*, **1**, 43–55.

Black, J. Stewart 1988: WorkRole transitions: a study of American expatriate managers in Japan, *Journal of International Business Studies*, **19**(2), 277–94.

Black, J. Stewart and Gregerson, Hal B. 1991a: The other half of the picture: antecedents of spouse cross-cultural adjustment, *Journal of International Business Studies*, 3rd quarter, 461–77.

Black, J. Stewart and Gregerson, Hal B. 1991b: When Yankee comes home: factors related to expatriate and spouse repatriation adjustment, *Journal of International Business Studies*, 4th quarter, 671–94.

Black, J. Stewart and Mendenhall, Mark 1990: Cross-culture training effectiveness: a review and theoretical framework for future research, *Academy of Management Review*, **15**, 113–36.

Black, J. Stewart and Mendenhall, Mark 1991a: A practical but theory-based framework for selecting cross-cultural methods. In Mark Mendenhall and Gary Oddou (eds), *International Human Resource Management*, PWS-Kent, Boston, 177–204.

Black, J. Stewart and Mendenhall, Mark 1991b: The U-curve adjustment hypothesis revisited: a review and theoretical framework, *Journal of International Business Studies*, 2nd quarter, 225–47.

Black, J. Stewart and Mendenhall, Mark 1993: Resolving conflicts with the Japanese: mission impossible? *Sloan Management Review*, Spring, 49–59.

Black, J. Stewart, Mendenhall, Mark, and Oddou, Gary 1991: Towards a comprehensive model of international adjustment: an integration of multiple theoretical perspectives, *Academy of Management Review*, **16**(2), 291–317.

Black, J. Stewart and Porter, Lyman W. 1991: Managerial behaviors and job performance: a successful manager in Los Angeles may not succeed in Hong Kong. *Journal of International Business Studies*, 1st quarter, 99–113.

Black, J. Stewart and Stephens, Gregory K. 1989: The influence of the spouse on American expatriate adjustments and intent to stay in Pacific Rim overseas assignments, *Journal of Management*, **15**(4), 529–44.

Blau, Peter M. 1968: The hierarchy of authority in organizations, *American Journal of Sociology*, **73**, 453–67.

Blodgett, Linda Longfellow 1991: Partner contributions as predictors of equity share in international joint ventures, *Journal of International Business Studies*, **22**(1), 63–78.

Blodgett, Timothy R. 1968: Showdown on "business bluffing," *Harvard Business Review*, May–June (reprint no. 68302).

Bloom, Allan 1987: *The Closing of the American Mind*, Simon & Schuster, New York.

Boisot, Max 1986: Managing with Chinese characteristics: socialist enterprise in a period of reform, *European Management Journal*, **4**(3), 164–70.

Bork, David 1986: *Family Business, Risky Business*, AMACOM (American Management Association), New York.

Boyacigiller, Nakiye 1990: The role of expatriates in the management of interdependence, complexity and risk in multinational corporations, *Journal of International Business Studies*. 3rd quarter, 357–81.

Boynton, Andrew C. 1933: Achieving dynamic stability through information technology, *California Management Review*, **35**(2), 58–77.

Brandt, Steven C. 1982: *Entrepreneuring: The Ten Commandments for Building a Growth Company*, Addison-Wesley, Reading, Mass.

Brenner, M. 1988: *House of Dreams*, Random House.

Brislin, Richard W., Cushner, Kenneth, Cherrie, Craig, and Yong, Mahealani 1986: *Intercultural Interactions: A Practical Guide*, Sage, Beverly Hills.

Bromley, Ray (ed.) 1985: *Planning for Small Enterprises in Third World Cities*, Pergamon Press, Oxford, 171–180.

Brooke, M. and Remmers, H. L. 1970: *The Strategy of Multinational Enterprise*, Longman, London.

Brown, R. and Gilman, A. 1960: The pronouns of power and solidarity. In T. A. Seboek (ed.), *Style in Language*, MIT Press, Mass., 253–76.

Brummelhuis, Han Ten 1984: Abundance and avoidance: an interpretation of Thai individualism. In Han Ten Brummelhuis, Han Ten and Jeremy H. Kemp (eds), *Strategies and Structures in Thai Society*, Antropologisch-Sociologisch Centrum, Universiteit van Amsterdam, 39–54.

Brummelhuis, Han Ten and Kemp, Jeremy H. (eds) 1984: *Strategies and Structures in Thai Society*, Antropologisch-Sociologisch Centrum, Universiteit van Amsterdam.

Bryson, L. (ed.) 1947: *Conflicts of Power in Modern Cultures: Seventh Symposium*, Harper & Brother, New York.

Buera, A. and Glueck, W. F. 1979: The needs satisfactions of managers in Libya, *Management International Review*, **19**(1), 113–21.

Burack, Elmer H 1991: Changing the company culture: the role of human resource development, *Long Range Planning*, **24**(1), 88–95.

Burgelman, Robert A. and Sayles, Leonard R. 1986: *Inside Corporate Innovation*, The Free Press, New York.

Burke, R. J. 1970: Methods of resolving superior–subordinate conflict: the constructive use of subordinate differences and disagreements, *Organizational Behavior and Human Performance*, **5**, 393–411.

Burns, L. R. 1989: Matrix management in hospitals: testing theories of matrix structure and development, *Administrative Science Quarterly*, Sept., 349–68.

Burns, L. R. and Wholey, D. R. 1993: Adoption and abandonment of matrix management programs: effects of organizational characteristics and inter-organizational networks, *Academy of Management Journal*, **36**(1), 106–38.

Business International 1974: *151 Checklists: Decision Making in International Corporations*, Business International, New York.

Campbell, Andrew 1991: Brief case: strategy and intuition – a conversation with Henry Mintzberg, *Long Range Planning*, **24**(2), 108–10.

Campbell, Nigel C. G., Graham, John L., Jolibert, Alain, and Meissner, Hans Gunther 1988: Marketing negotiations in France, Germany, the United Kingdom, and the United States, *Journal of Marketing*, **52**, 49–62.

Carr, Albert Z. 1968: Is business bluffing ethical?, *Harvard Business Review*, Jan.–Feb. (repr. no. 68102).

Carroll, Archie B. 1987: In search of the moral manager, *Business Horizons*, Mar.–Apr., 7–15.

Casson, M. and Nicholas, S. 1989: Economics of trust: explaining differences in organizational structure between the United States and Japan, Discussion Paper in Economics, No 217, University of Reading, UK.

Caudron, Shari 1992: Preparing managers for overseas assignments, *World Executive Digest*, Nov., 72–3.

Chandler, Alfred D., Jnr 1962: *Strategy and Structure*, MIT Press, Cambridge, Mass.

Chandler, D. L. 1988: *The Binghams of Louisville*, Crown, New York.

Chee Peng Lim, Puthucheary, M. C. and Lee, Donald 1979: *A Study of Small Entrepreneurs and Entrepreneurial Development Programmes in Malaysia*, University of Malaya Press, Kuala Lumpur.

Chee Peng Lim 1990: *Development of Small-scale Businesses in Developing Asian Countries*, International Department, Institute of Small Business, University of Gottingen.

Chilcott, John G. 1968: Some perspectives for teaching first generation Mexican Americans. In John G. Chilcott, Norman C. Greenberg, and Herbert B. Wilson (eds), *Readings in the Socio-Cultural Foundations of Education*, Wadsworth, Belmost, Mass.

Chilcott, John G., Greenburg, Norman C. and Wilson, Herbert B. (eds) 1968: *Readings in the Socio-Cultural Foundations of Education*, Wadsworth, Belmost, Mass.

Child, J. 1981: Culture, contingency and capitalism in the cross-national study of organizations. In L. L. Cummings and B. M. Straw (eds), *Research in Organizational Behavior*, JAI Press.

Child, John 1987: Information technology, organization, and the response to strategic challenges, *California Management Review*, Fall, 33–49.

Child, John and Kieser, Alfred 1979: Organizational and managerial roles in British and West German companies: an examination of the culture-free thesis. In Cornelis J. Lammers and David J. Hickson (eds), *Organizations Alike and Unlike: International and Institutional Studies of the Sociology of Organizations*, Routledge & Kegan Paul, London, 251–71.

Choguill, Charles L. 1980: Toward a theory of implementation in planning based on the Bangladesh experience, *Journal of Administration Overseas*, 148–59.

Chow, Irene Hau-siu 1988: Work related values of middle managers in the private and public sectors, *Proceedings of the 1988 Academy of International Business Southeast Asia Regional Conference*, Bangkok, June 23–5, A14–25.

Chung, Chen H., Shepard, Jon M.,and Dollinger, Marx J. 1989: Max Weber revisited: some lessons from East Asian capitalistic development, *Asia Pacific Journal of Management*, **6**(2), 307–21.

Church, A. T. 1982: Sojourner adjustment, *Psychological Bulletin*, **9**, 540–72.

Clad, James 1989, 1991: *Behind the Myth: Business, Money and Power in Southeast Asia*, Grafton Books, London.

Clapham, P. 1985: *Small and Medium Enterprises in Southeast Asia*, Institute of Southeast Asian Studies, Singapore.

Cole, Robert E. and Deskins, Donald R., Jnr 1988: Racial factors in site location and employment patterns of Japanese auto firms in America, *California Management Review*, Fall, 9–22.

Connerton, Paul 1989: *How Societies Remember*, Cambridge University Press, Cambridge, 79–82.

Contractor, Farok J. 1990: Ownership patterns of U.S. joint ventures abroad and the liberalization of foreign government regulations in the 1980s: evidence from the benchmark surveys, *Journal of International Business Studies*, **21**(1), 55–73.

Contractor, Farok J. and Lorange, Peter 1988: Competition vs. cooperation: a benefit/cost framework for choosing between fully-owned investments and cooperative relationships, *Management International Review*, **28**, 5–18.

Cooke, R. A. and Ryan, L. 1988: The relevance of ethics in management education, *Journal of Management Development*, **7**(2), 29–30.

Cooper, Gary L. and Cox, Charles J. 1989: Applying American organizational sciences in Europe and the United Kingdom: the problems. In Yg Osigweh and A. B. Chimezie (eds), *Organizational Science Abroad: Constraints and Perceptives*, Plenum Press, New York/London, 57–65.

Copeland, Lennie and Griggs, Lewis 1985: *Going International: How to Make Friends and Deal Effectively in the Global Marketplace*, Random House, New York.

Coulthard, Malcolm 1977, 1991: *An Introduction to Discourse Analysis*, Longman, London.

Cox, Taylor H., Jnr and Blake, Stacy 1991: Managing cultural diversity: implications for organizational competitiveness, *Academy of Management Executive*, **5**(2), 45–56.

Cox, Taylor H., Jnr, Lobel, Sharon A. and McLeod, Poppy L. 1991: Effects of ethnic group cultural differences on cooperative and competitive behavior on a group task, *Academy of Management Journal*, **34**(4), 827–47.

Crozier, Michel 1964: *The Bureaucratic Phenomenon*, The University of Chicago Press.

Cummings, L. L. and Straw, B. M. (eds) 1981: *Research in Organizational Behavior*, JAI Press.

Czarniawska, Barbara 1986: The management of meaning in the Polish crisis, *Journal of Management Studies*, **23**(3), May, 313–31.

Daft, Richard L. and Weick, Karl E. 1984: Toward a model of organizations as interpretation systems, *Academy of Management Review*, **9**(2), 284–95.

Danco, L. A. 1981: *Outside Directors in the Family Company*, The University Press, Cleveland, Ohio.

Daniels, Tom D. and Spiker, Barry K. 1991: *Perspectives on Organizational Communication*, 2nd edn, Wm C Brown, Dubuque, Iowa.

Das, T. K. 1991: Time: the hidden dimension in strategic planning, *Long Range Planning*, **24**(3), 49–57.

Davis, Stanley M. and Lawrence, Paul R. 1977: *Matrix*, Addison-Wesley Publishing Co., Reading, Mass.

De Geus, Arie P., 1988: Planning as learning, *Harvard Business Review*, Mar.–Apr., 70–4.

De la Torre, Jose and Toyne, Brian 1978: Cross-national managerial interaction: a conceptual model, *Academy of Management Review*, July, 462–74.

De Leon, Corinna T. 1987: Social categorisation in Philippine organizations: values towards collective identity and management through intergroup relations, *Asia Pacific Journal of Management*, Singapore, **5**(1), 28–37.

Deal, Terrance and Kennedy, Allen 1982, 1988: *Corporate Cultures*, Penguin Books, London.

Dean, J. P., Eichorn, R. L. and Dean, L. R. 1967: Fruitful informants for intensive interviewing. In J. T. Doby (ed.), *An Introduction to Social Research*, Appleton-Century-Crofts, New York, 285.

Dennison, D. 1984: Bringing corporate culture to the bottom line, *Organizational Dynamics*, **13**(2), 5–22.

Dholakia, N. and Sherry, John F. Jnr 1987: Marketing and development: a resynthesis of knowledge, *Research in Marketing*, **9**, 119–43.

DiPrete, Thomas A. 1987: Horizontal and vertical mobility in organizations, *Administrative Science Quarterly*, **32**, 433–44.

Dobbert, Marion L. 1982: *Ethnographic Research*, Praeger Publishers, New York.

Dobkin, James A. 1988: Negotiating an international technology joint venture, Part ll, *Newsaction*, Northwestern University, **3**(1), 34–5.

Doby, J. T. (ed.) 1967: *An Introduction to Social Research*, Appleton-Century-Crofts, New York.

Dolores, M 1976: The process of teaching decision-making through values clarification and its effects on students, *Dissertation Abstract International*, **37**, Oct.

Domsch, M. and Lichtenberger, B. 1991: Managing the global manager: predeparture training and development for German expatriates in China and Brazil, *Journal of Management Development*, **10**(7), 41–52.

Donaldson, Thomas 1985: Multinational decision-making: reconciling international norms, *Journal of Business Ethics*. **4**(4), 357–66.

Donnelley, Robert 1964: The family business, *Harvard Business Review*, July–Aug., repr. in *Harvard Business Review, Small Business*, Part 1, No. 21185, 43–55.

Douma, Sytse 1991: Success and failure in new ventures, *Long Range Planning*, **24**(2), 54–60.

Downing, Hazel 1983: On being automated, *ASLIB Proceedings*, **35**(1), 40.

Drake, Bruce H. and Moburg, Dennis J. 1986: Communicating influence attempts in dyads: linguistic sedatives and palliatives, *Academy of Management Review*, **11**(3), 567–84.

Drucker, Peter 1958: Marketing and economic development, *Journal of Marketing*, **22**(3), 252–59.

Drucker, Peter 1981: What is business ethics?, *The Public Interest*, **63**, Spring.

Drucker, Peter 1988: The coming of the new organization, *Harvard Business Review*. Jan.–Feb., 45–53.

Dubinsky, Alan J., Jolson, Marvin A., Kotabe, Masaaki, and Chae Un Lim 1991: A cross-national investigation of industrial salespeople's ethical perceptions, *Journal of International Business Studies*, 4th quarter, 651–70.

Duncan, Robert 1979: What is the right organization structure? decision tree analysis provides the answer, *Organizational Dynamics*, Winter.

Dunnette, Marvin D. (ed.) 1976: *Handbook of Industrial and Organizational Psychology*, Rand McNally, Chicago.

Dutton, J. E. and Duncan, R. B. 1987: The creation of momentum for change through the process of strategic issue diagnosis, *Strategic Management Journal*, **8**(3), 279–95.

Dyer, W. Gibb, Jnr 1986: *Cultural Change in Family Firms*, Jossey-Bass, San Francisco.

Eagly, A. H. 1974: Comprehensibility of persuasive arguments as a determinant of opinion change, *Journal of Personality and Social Psychology*, **4**, 525–31.

Earley, P. Christopher 1987: Intercultural training for managers: a comparison of documentary and interpersonal methods, *Academy of Management Journal*, **30**(4), 685–98.

Earley, P. Christopher 1993: East meets West meets Mideast: further explorations of collectivistic and individualistic work groups, *Academy of Management Journal*, **36**(2), 319–48.

Edge, Al and Keys, Bernard 1990: Cross-cultural learning in a multinational business environment, *Journal of Management Development*. **9**(2), 43–9.

Efron, D. 1941: *Gesture and Environment*, New York.

Eisenberg, Eric M. 1984: Ambiguity as strategy in organizational communication, *Communication Monographs*, **51**, 227–42.

Eisenstadt, S. N. and Lemarchand, Rene (eds) 1981: *Political Clientism, Patronage and Development*, Sage, Beverly Hills.

Eisenstadt, S. N. and Roniger, Luis 1981: The study of patron–client relations and recent developments in sociological theory. In S. N. Eisenstadt and Rene Lemarchand (eds), *Political Clientism, Patronage and Development*. Sage, Beverly Hills.

Elgström, Ole 1990: Norms, culture and cognitive patterns in foreign aid negotiations, *Negotiations Journal*, **6**(2), 147–60 at 157–8.

England, George W. 1967: Personal value systems of American managers, *Academy of Management Journal*, Mar., 53–68.

England, George W. 1986, National work meanings and patterns: constraints on management action, *European Management Journal*, **4**(3), 176–84.

England, G. W., Neghandi, Anant R. and Wilpert, B. (eds) 1979: *Organizational Functioning in a Cross-Cultural Perspective*, Comparative Administration Research Institute, Kent State University Press, Ohio.

Etzioni, Amitai 1964: *Modern Organizations*, Prentice-Hall, Englewood Cliffs, New Jersey.

Evan, William M. 1974: Culture and organizational systems, *Quarterly Journal of Management Development.* **5**(4), 1–16.

Evans, Sybil 1992: Conflict can be positive, *HR Magazine,* **37**(5), 49–51.

Falk, G. 1982: An empirical study measuring conflict in problem-solving groups which are assigned different decision rules, *Human Relations,* **35**, 1123–38.

Farson, Richard E. 1963: Praise reappraised, *Harvard Business Review,* Sept.–Oct., repr. in *Motivation: Part 1, Harvard Business Review,* 111–16.

Fisher, Roger and Ury, William 1981, 1983: *Getting to Yes,* Penguin, Harmondsworth.

Fisk, E. K. and Osman-Rani, H. (eds) 1982: *The Political Economy of Malaysia,* Oxford University Press, Kuala Lumpur.

Fogel, Daniel S. 1990: Management education in central and eastern Europe and the Soviet Union, *Journal of Management Development,* **9**(3), 14–19.

Francis, June N. P. 1991: When in Rome? the effects of cultural adaptation on intercultural busienss negotiations, *Journal of International Business Studies,* **22**(3), 404–28.

Franke, Richard H., Hofstede, Geert, and Bond, Michael H. 1991: Cultural roots on economic performance: a research note, *Strategic Management Journal,* **12**, 165–73.

Frankenstein, John 1986: Trends in Chinese business practice: changes in the Beijing wind, *California Management Review,* **29**(1), 148–60.

Franko, L. G. 1971: *Joint Ventures Survival in Multinational Corporations,* Praeger, New York.

Franko, L. G. 1974: Joint venture divorce in the multinational company, *Columbia Journal of World Business,* **6**(3), 13–22.

Franko, L. G. 1989: Use of minority and 50–50 joint ventures by United States multinationals during the 1980s: the interaction of host country policies and corporate strategies, *Journal of International Business Studies,* Spring, 19–40.

Fujita, Akihisa 1990: Creating new corporate culture through organizational fusion process in overseas operations, *Review of Economics and Business,* Kansai University, **18**(2), Mar., 65–88.

Fukuda, K. John 1983: Japanese and Chinese management practices: uncovering the differences, *Mid-Atlantic Journal of Business,* Seton Hall University, **21**(3), Summer, 35–44.

Fukuyama, Francis 1991: *The End of History and the Last Man,* Hamish Hamilton, London.

Galbraith, J. 1971: Matrix organization designs: how to combine functional and project forms, *Business Horizons,* **14**, 29–40.

Gan See Khem 1988: Comparative analysis of the effect of organization structure and personnel management practices on bank employee job satisfaction, *Proceedings of the 1988 Academy of International Business Southeast Asia Regional Conference,* June 23–5, 1988, Bangkok, A72–A100.

Geertz, Clifford 1973: Thick description: toward an interpretative theory of culture. In Clifford Geertz, *The Interpretation of Cultures,* Basic, New York 3–30.

Geertz, Clifford 1973: *The Interpretation of Cultures,* Basic, New York.

Geringer, J. Michael 1991: Strategic determinants of partner selection criteria in international joint ventures, *Journal of International Business Studies*, **22**(1), 41–62.

Geringer, J. Michael and Hebert, Louis 1989: Control and performance of international joint ventures, *Journal of International Business Studies*, Summer, 235–54.

Geringer, J. Michael and Hebert, Louis 1991: Measuring performance of international joint ventures, *Journal of International Business Studies*, **22**(20) 249–63.

Gibson, Jane W. and Hodgetts, Richard M. 1991, *Organizational Communication: A Managerial Perspective*, 2nd edn, HarperCollins, New York, 225–7.

Gillespie, K. 1989: Political risk implications for exporters, contractors and foreign licensors: the Iranian experience, *Management International Review*, **29**(2), 41–50.

Ginter, Peter M. and Duncan, W. Jack 1990: Macroenvironmental analysis for strategic management at Royal Dutch/Shell, *Long Range Planning*, **23**(6), 91–100.

Gladwin, Thomas N. 1980: *Multinationals under Fire*, John Wiley, New York.

Glenn, E. S., Witmeyer, D. and Stevenson, K. A. 1984: Cultural styles of persuasion, *International Journal of Intercultural Relations*, Summer, 11–22.

Glenny, Misha 1990: *The Rebirth of History: Eastern Europe in the Age of Democracy*, Penguin Books, London.

Gluck, F. W., Kaufman, S. P. and Walleck, A. S. 1980: Strategic management for competitive advantage, *Harvard Business Review*, **58**(4), 154–61.

Gluskinos, U. M. 1970: Management and union leaders' perception of worker needs as compared with self-reported needs, Proceedings of the 78th APA Convention. Findings tablified in M. Smith, J. Beck, C. Cooper, C. Cox, D. Ottaway, and R. Talbot 1982: *Introducing Organizational Behaviour*, Macmillan Education, Basingstoke, 49.

Goffman, E. 1956: On face-work: an analysis of ritual elements in social interaction, *Psychiatry*, **18**(3), 213–31.

Goldstein, S. G. 1988: Cultural fit or structural fit: the case of quality circles, *Proceedings of the 1988 Academy of International Business Southeast Asia Regional Conference*, Bangkok, June 23–25, 1988, E366–70.

Gomes-Casseres, Benjamin 1989: Joint ventures in the face of global competition, *Sloan Management Review*, **30**(3), 17–26.

Goodman, Robert S. and Kruger, Evonne Jonas 1988: Data dredging or legitimate research method? Historiography and its potential for management research, *Academy of Management Review*, **13**(2), 315–25.

Gordon, George G. 1991: Industry determinants of organizational culture, *Academy of Management Review*, **16**(2), 396–415.

Graham, J. L. 1985: The influence of culture on the process of business negotiations: an exploratory study, *Journal of International Business Studies*, Spring, 81–96.

Graham, J. L. and Herberger, R. A. 1983: Negotiators abroad: don't shoot from the hip, *Harvard Business Review*, July/Aug., 160–8.

Greenbaum, S., Leech, G. and Svartvik, J. (eds) 1980: *Studies in English Linguistics for Randolph Quirk,* Longman, London.

Greenley, Gordon 1989: *Strategic Management,* Prentice-Hall, UK.

Gregory, Kathleen L. 1983: Native-view paradigms: multiple cultures and culture conflicts in organizations, *Administrative Science Quarterly,* **28,** 359–76 at 364.

Griffin, Ricky W. 1988: Consequences of quality circles in an industrial setting: a longitudinal assessment, *Academy of Management Journal,* **31**(2), 338–58.

Griffiths, D. 1964: Administrative theory and change in organizations. In M. Miles (ed.), *Innovation in Education,* Columbia University, New York.

Haine, Mason, Ghiselli, E. E. and Porter, L. W. 1966: *Managerial Thinking: An International Study.* Wiley, New York.

Haines, W. R. 1988: Making corporate planning work in developing countries, *Long Range Planning,* **21**(2), 91–6.

Hall, Edward T. 1960: The silent language in overseas business, *Harvard Business Review,* May–June, 87–96.

Hall, Edward T. 1976: *Beyond Culture,* Anchor Press/Doubleday, New York.

Hall, Edward T. 1983: *The Dance of Life,* Anchor Press/Doubleday, New York.

Hall, Edward T. 1987: *Hidden Differences,* Anchor Press/Doubleday, New York.

Hall, Edward T. and Whyte, W. F. 1961: Intercultural communication: a guide to men of action, *Human Organization,* **19**(1), 5–12.

Hallen, L., Johanson, J. and Mohamed, N. S. 1987: Relationship strength and stability in international and domestic industrial marketing, *Industrial Marketing and Purchasing,* **2**(3), 22–37.

Hamill, Jim 1989: Expatriate policies in British multinationals, *Journal of General Management,* **14**(4), Summer, 18–33.

Hammersley, M. (ed.) 1983: *The Ethnography of Schooling: Methodological Issues.* Nafferton, Driffield.

Hammersley, M. and Atkinson, P. 1983: *Ethnography: Principles in Practice,* Routledge, London.

Hanami, Tadashi 1979: *Workers and Employers in Japan,* Kodansha International, Tokyo.

Handy, Charles B. 1976, 1985: *Understanding Organizations,* Penguin Books, London.

Harnett, D. L. and Cummings, L. L. 1980: *Bargaining Behavior: An International Study,* Dame Publications, Houston, Tex.

Harpaz, Itzhak 1990: The importance of work goals: an international perspective, *Journal of International Business Studies,* 1st quarter, 75–93.

Harrigan, K. R. 1983: Research methodologies for contingency approaches to business strategy, *Academy of Management Review,* **8,** 398–405.

Harris, Philip R. and Moran, Robert T. 1979, 1987: *Managing Cultural Differences,* Gulf, Houston, Tex.

Hartmann, Donald P. 1982: Assessing the dependability of observational data. In Donald P. Hartmann (ed.), *Using Observers to Study Behavior,* Jossey-Bass, San Francisco 51–66.

Hartmann, Donald P. (ed.) 1982: *Using Observers to Study Behavior,* Jossey-Bass, San Francisco.

Haworth, Dwight A. and Savage, Grant T. 1989: A channel-ratio model of intercultural communication: the trains won't sell, fix them please, *Journal of Business Communication*, **26**(3), 231–54.

Hay, Peter 1988: *Harrap's Book of Business Anecdotes*, Harrap, London.

Hayes, Robert H. and Jaikumur, Ramchandran 1988: Manufacturing's crisis: new technologies, obsolete organizations, *Harvard Business Review*, Sept.–Oct., 77–85.

Heller, Jean E. 1980: Criteria for selecting an international manager, *Personnel*, May–June.

Henry, E. R. 1971: What business can learn from Peace Corps selection and training, *Personnel*, **42**(4), 40–6.

Herzberg, Frederick, Mausner, Bernard, and Snyderman, Barbara Bloch 1959: THE *Motivation to Work*, Wiley, New York.

Herzberg, Frederick 1968: One more time: how do you motivate employees?, *Harvard Business Review*, **46**, 53–62.

Hickson, D. J. and McMillan, C. J. (eds) 1981: *Organization and Nation*, Gower, Farnborough, 155–72.

Higgins, Richard B. and Diffenbach, John 1989: Communicating corporate strategy – the payoffs and the risks, *Long Range Planning*, **22**(3), 133–9.

Hilton, Margaret 1991: Sharing training: learning from germany, *Monthly Labor Review*, **114**(3), 33–7.

Hirokawa, Randy Y. and Poole, Marshall Scott (eds) 1986: *Communication and Group-Decision Making*, Sage, Beverly Hills.

Hitchcock, G. 1983: Fieldwork as practical activity: reflections on fieldwork and the social organization of an urban, open-plan primary school. In M. Hammersley, (ed.), *The Ethnography of Schooling: Methodological Issues*, Nafferton, Driffield, 30.

Hines, George H. 1974: Sociocultural influences on employee expectancy and participative management, *Academy of Management Journal*, June, 334–9.

Hofstede, Geert 1980a: *Culture's Consequences: International Differences in Work-Related Values*, Sage, Beverly Hills.

Hofstede, Geert 1980b: Motivation, leadership, and organization: do American theories apply abroad? *Organizational Dynamics*, Summer, 42–63.

Hofstede, Geert 1983a: National cultures in four dimensions, *International Studies of Management and Organization*, **13**(1–2), 46–74.

Hofstede,Geert 1983b: The cultural relativity of organizational practices and theories, *Journal of International Business Studies*, **14**, Fall, 75–89.

Hofstede, Geert 1984a: *Culture's Consequences: International Differences in Work-Related Values*, abridged edn, Sage, Beverly Hills.

Hofstede, Geert 1984b: Cultural dimensions in management and planning, *Asia Pacific Journal of Management*, **1**(2), 81–99.

Hofstede, Geert 1985: The interaction between national and organizational value systems, *Journal of Management Studies*, **22**(4), 347–57.

Hofstede, Geert 1989: Cultural predictors of national negotiation styles. In F. Maunter-Markhof (ed.), *Processes of International Negotiations*, Boulder, Colo., 193–202.

Hofstede, Geert 1991: *Cultures and Organizations: Software of the Mind,* McGraw-Hill, London.

Hofstede, Geert and Bond, Michael Harris 1988: The Confucian connection: from cultural roots to economic growth, *Organizational Dynamics,* **16**(4), 4–21.

Hofstede, Geert, Neuijen, Bram, Ohayv, Denise Daval, and Sanders, Geert 1990: Measuring organizational cultures: a qualitative and quantitative study across twenty cases, *Administrative Science Quarterly,* **35**, 286–316.

Hollingsworth, David S. 1988: Building successful global partnerships: an interview with Hercules CEO David S. Hollingsworth, *Journal of Business Strategy,* Sept./Oct., 12–15.

Hoogvelt, Ankie, Puxty, Anthony G. and Stopford, John 1987: *Multinational Enterprise,* Macmillan, London/Basingstoke.

Howe, Irene Chew Keng, Tsai-pen Tseng, Anthony, and Teo Kim Hong, Adrian 1990: The role of culture in training in a multinational context, *Journal of Management Development,* special issue: *Management Development in Asia,* **9**(5).

Hsu, F. L. K. 1963: *Clan, Caste and Club,* Van Nostrand, Princeton NJ.

Huff, Anne Sigismund 1988: Politics and argument as a means of coping with ambiguity and change. In Louis R. Pondy, Richard J. Boland Jnr, and Howard Thomas (ed.), *Managing Ambiguity and Change,* John Wiley, Chichester 79–90.

Hughes, Graeme C. 1991: Culture and the application of information technology, ms, Department of Management Sciences, University of Waterloo, Canada.

Hulbert, James A. and Brandt, William K. 1980: *Managing the Multinational Subsidiary,* Holt Rinehart & Winston, New York.

Humble, John and Jones, Gareth 1989: Creating a climate for innovation, *Long Range Planning,* **22**(4), 46–51.

Hung, C. L. 1991: Canadian strategic business alliances in Southeast Asia: motives, problems, and performance, *Journal of Southeast Asia Business,* **7**(3), 46–57.

Hunt, J. G. and Blair, J. D. (eds) 1986: *Yearly Review of Management* of the *Journal of Management,* **12**(2).

Huo, Y. Paul and Steers, Richard M. 1993: Cultural influences on the design of incentive schemes: the case of East Asia, *Asia Pacific Journal of Management,* **10**(1), 71–85.

Imai, M. 1975: *Never Take Yes for an Answer,* Simul, Tokyo.

Insko, C. A., Lind, E. A. and La Tour, S. 1976: Persuasion, recall and thoughts, *Reports of Research in Social Psychology,* **7**, 66–78.

Irwan, Alexander 1989: Business patronage, class struggle, and the manufacturing sector in South Korea, Indonesia and Thailand, *Journal of Contemporary Asia,* **19**(4), 398–434.

Ishizumi, Kanji 1985, 1990: *Acquiring Japanese Companies,* Blackwell, Oxford.

Jaeger, Alfred M. 1983: The transfer of organizational culture overseas: an approach to control in the multinational corporation, *Journal of International Business Studies,* Fall, 91–114.

Jaeger, Alfred 1986: Organizational development and national culture: where's the fit?, *Academy of Management Review,* **11**(1), 178–90.

Jaggi, Bikki 1979: An analysis of perceived need importance of Indian managers, *Management International Review,* **19**(1), 107–12.

Jain, S. C. and Puri, Y. 1981: Role of multinational corporations in developing countries: policy makers views, *Management International Review*, **21**, 57–66.

Johnson, Chalmers 1988: Japanese-style management in America, *California Management Review*, Summer, 34–45.

Johnson, Gerry 1992: Managing strategic change – strategy, culture and action, *Long Range Planning*, **25**(1), 28–36.

Johnson, J. L., Sakano, Tomaaki, and Onzo, Naoto 1990: Behavioral relations in across-culture distribution systems: influence, control and conflict in U.S.–Japanese marketing channels, *Journal of International Business Studies*, **21**(4), 639–55.

Johnston, W. B. and Packer, A. 1987: *Workforce 2000: Work and Workers for the 21st Century*, Hudson Institute, Indianapolis.

Joseph, P. M. 1973: A cross-cultural comparison of managerial practices: India and the United States, *Quarterly Journal of Management Development*, Kent State University Press, Ohio, June, 73–82.

Kahn, Joel S. 1988: Ideology and social structure in Indonesia. In John G. Taylor and Andrew Turton (eds), *Sociology of Developing Societies: Southeast Asia*, Macmillan Education, Basingstoke, 181–90.

Kanter, Donald L. and Mirvis, Philip H. 1989: *The Cynical Americans*, Jossey-Bass. San Francisco.

Kanter, Rosabeth Moss 1991a: Transcending business boundaries: 12,000 world managers view change, *Harvard Business Review*, May–June, 151–64.

Kanter, Rosabeth Moss 1991b: In search of a single culture, *Business*, UK, June 58–66.

Kanungo, Rabindra N. and Wright, Richard W. 1983: A cross-cultural comparative study of managerial job attitudes, *Journal of International Business Studies*, Fall, 115–29.

Kaosa-Ard, Mingsarn, Rerkasem, Kanok, and Roongruangsee, Chaiwat (eds) 1989: *Agricultural Information and Technological Change in Northern Thailand*, Thailand Development Research Institute Foundation, Thailand.

Kapoor, A. and Grub, P. D. (eds) 1972: *The Multinational Enterprise in Transition*, Darwin, Princeton.

Kelly, Joe 1969: *Organizational Behavior*, Richard D. Irwin, Illinois; adapted as (no date) Make conflict work for you, *Harvard Business Review: Dealing with Conflict*, Cambridge, Mass. (reprint 70407) 130–40.

Kelley, Lane, Whatley, Arthur, Worthley, Reginald, and Lie, Harry 1986: The role of the ideal organization in comparative management: a cross-cultural perspective of Japan and Korea, *Asia Pacific Journal of Management*, **3**(2), 59–75.

Kennedy, Charles R. 1993: *Managing the International Business Environment*, Prentice-Hall, New Jersey.

Kennedy, Paul 1988: *The Rise and Fall of the Great Powers*, Unwin Hyman, London.

Kent, David H. 1991: Joint ventures vs. non-joint ventures: an empirical investigation, *Strategic Management Journal*, **12**, 387–93.

Killing, J. Peter 1982: How to make a global joint venture work, *Harvard Business Review*, May–June, 120–7.

Kim, W. Chan and Mauborgne, Renée A. 1993: Making global strategies work, *Sloan Management Review*, Spring, 11–27.

Kimmel, M. J., Pruitt, D. G., Magenau, J. M., Konar-Goldband, F. and Carnevale, P. J. D. 1980: Effects of trust aspiration and gender on negotiation tactics, *Journal of Personality and Social Psychology*, **38**, 9–23.

King, Ambrose Y. C. and Leung, D. H. K. 1975: The Chinese touch in small industrial organizations, occasional paper, Social Research Centre, Chinese University of Hong Kong.

Kitch, K. J. 1967: Capitalism and the Reformation. In H. F. Kearney (ed.), *Problems and Perspectives in History*, Longman, London.

Kluckhohn, C. and Kluckhohn, F. 1947: American culture: generalized orientation and class patterns. In L. Bryson (ed.), *Conflicts of Power in Modern Cultures: Seventh Symposium*, Harper and Brother, New York.

Kluckhohn, Florence Rockwood and Strodtbeck, Fred L. 1961: *Variations in Value Orientations*, Peterson, New York.

Kobrin, S. J. 1988: Expatriate reduction and strategic control in American multinational corporations, *Human Resource Management*, **27**(1), 63–75.

Kohl, John P., Miller, Alan N., and Barton, Laurence 1990: Levi's corporate AIDS programme, *Long Range Planning*, **23**(6), 31–4.

Kohls, L. Robert 1979, 1984: *Survival Kit for Overseas Living*, Intercultural Press, Yarmouth, Maine.

Kono, Toyohiro 1988: *Corporate Culture under Evolution*, Kodansha, Japan.

Kono, Toyohiro 1990: Corporate culture and long-range planning, *Long Range Planning*, **24**(40), 9–19.

Kovach, Kenneth A. 1987: What motivates employees? Workers and supervisors give different answers, *Business Horizons*, Sept.–Oct., 58–65.

Kroeber, A. L. and Kluckhohn, Clyde 1963: *Culture: A Critical Review of Concepts and Definitions*, Vintage/Random House, New York.

Kuin, P. 1972: The magic of multinational management, *Harvard Business Review*, Nov.–Dec., 89–97.

Kunio, Y. 1988: *The Rise of Ersatz Capitalism in South-east Asia*, Oxford University Press, Singapore.

Lacey, Robert 1981: *The Kingdom*, Harcourt Brace Janovich, New York.

Laffin, John 1975: *The Arab Mind*, Cassell, London, 56, 72–76.

Laffin, John 1982: *Fight for the Falklands*, St Martin's Press, New York.

Lammers, Cornelis J. and Hickson, David J. (eds) 1979: *Organizations Alike and Unlike: International and Institutional Studies of the Sociology of Organizations*, Routledge & Kegan Paul, London.

Lanier, Allison 1979: Selecting and preparing personnel for overseas transfer, *Personnel Journal*, **58**, March 160–3.

Lansing, Paul, and Ready, Kathryn 1988: Hiring women managers in Japan: an alternative for foreign employers, *California Management Review*, Spring, 112–27.

Lasser Tax Institute, J. K. 1989: *How to Run a Small Business*, McGraw Hill Book Co., New York.

Laurent, André 1981: Matrix organizations and Latin cultures, *International Studies of Management and Organization*, 101–14.

Laurent, André 1983: The cultural diversity of western conceptions of management, *International Studies of Management and Organization*, **13**(1–2), 75–96.

Laurent, André 1986: The cross-cultural puzzle of international human resource management, *Human Resource Management*, **25**(1), 91–102.

Lawrence, P. R. and Lorsch, J. W. 1967: *Organization and Environment*, Harvard University Press, Boston, Mass.

Lebas, Michel and Weigenstein, Jane 1986: Management control: the roles of rules, markets and culture, *Journal of Management Studies*, **23**(3), 259–72.

Leech, Edmund 1976: *Culture and Communication*, Cambridge University Press, Cambridge, UK.

Legg, Keith R. no date: Patrons, clients, and politicians, Working Papers on Development 3, Institute of International Studies, University of California, Berkeley.

Lessem, Ronnie 1988: *Intrapreneurship: How to Be an Enterprising Individual in a Successful Business*, Wildwood House, Hampshire.

Lessem, Ronnie 1989: *Global Management Principles*, Prentice-Hall International, Hemel Hempstead.

Leung, Kwok 1988: Some determinants of conflict avoidance, *Journal of Cross-Cultural Psychology*, **19**(1), 125–36.

LeVine, Robert and Campbell, Donald 1972: *Ethnocentrism*, John Wiley & Sons, New York/London.

Levinson, Harry 1971: Conflicts that plague family businesses, *Harvard Business Review*, Mar.–Apr., repr. in *Harvard Business Review, Small Business* Part 2, No. 21186, 22–30.

Levinson, Harry 1976: The abrasive personality, *Harvard Business Review*, July–Aug., repr. in *Harvard Business Review: Dealing with Conflict*, Cambridge, Mass., repr. 78307, 111–19.

Limlingan, V. 1987: *The Overseas Chinese in Asean: Business Strategies and Management Practices*, Vita Development Corporation, Manila.

Lincoln, James R. 1989: Employee work attitudes and management practice in the U.S. and Japan: evidence from a large comparative survey, *California Management Review*, Fall, 89–106.

Lincoln, James R., Hanada, Mitsuyo, and McBride, Kerry 1986: Organizational structures in Japanese and U.S. manufacturing, *Administrative Science Quarterly*, **31**, 338–64.

Litterer, J. A. 1966: Conflict in organization: a re-examination, *Academy of Management Journal*, **9**, 178–86.

Lofland, John 1971: *Analyzing Social Settings*, Wadsworth, Belmost, Cal.

Lorange, Peter and Roos, Johan 1991: Why some strategic alliances succeed and others fail, *Journal of Business Strategy*, Jan./Feb., 25–30.

London, M., Wohlers., A. J. and Gallagher, P. 1990: A feedback approach to management development, *Journal of management development*, **9**(6), 17–31.

Lopreato, Joseph 1970: *Italian Americans*, Random House, New York.

Lynch, Frank 1970: Social acceptance reconsidered. In Frank Lynch and Alfonso de Guzman ll, *Four Readings on Philippine Values*, Quezon City, Philippines: Ateneo de Manila University Press, 1–64.

Lynch, Frank and de Guzman, Alfonso ll (eds) 1970: *Four Readings on Philippine Values*, Quezon City, Philippines: Ateneo de Manila University Press.

Lyons, Michael Paul 1991: Joint ventures as starategic choice: a literature review, *Long Range Planning*, **24**(4), 130–44.

Mabry, B. and Srisermbhok, Kundhol 1985: Labour relations under martial law: the Thailand experience, *Asian Survey*, **25**(6), 613–37.

Madden, Carl H. (ed.) 1977: *The Case for the Multinational Corporation*, Praeger, New York.

Mahoney, John 1990: *Teaching Business Ethics in the U.K., Europe and the U.S.A.*, Athlone Press, London.

Malinowski, Bronislaw 1964: *A Scientific Theory of Culture and Other Essays*, Oxford University Press, London.

Mann, J. 1989: *Beijing Jeep: The Short, Unhappy Romance of American Business in China*, Simon & Schuster, New York.

Marett, Pamela C. 1984: Japanese-owned firms in the United States: do they resist unionism? *Labor Law Journal*, April. Repr. in Jagdish Sheth and Golpira Eshgi 1989: *Global Human Resources Perspectives*, Southwestern Publishing Co., Cincinatti.

Masaaki Imai 1975, *Never Take Yes for an Answer*, Simul Press, Tokyo.

Maslow, Abraham H. 1943: A theory of human motivation, *Psychological Review*, (July) 370–96.

Maslow, Abraham H. 1954: *Motivation and Personality*, Harper and Brothers, New York.

Mason, R. Hal 1974: Conflicts between host countries and the multinational enterprise, *California Management Review*, **17**(1), 5–14.

Maunter-Markhof, F. (ed.) 1989: *Processes of International Negotiations*, Boulder, Colo.

McCann, Robert M. 1992: A behavioral pattern analysis of Thai university students studying English as a foreign language. Unpublished MA(TESL) dissertation, University of California, Los Angeles.

McCaskey, Michael B. 1988: The challenge of managing ambiguity and change. In Louis R. Pondy, Richard J. Boland Jr, and Howard Thomas (eds), *Managing Ambiguity and Change*, John Wiley, Chichester 1–15.

McClelland, David C. 1965: Achievement motivation can be developed, *Harvard Business Review*, Nov.–Dec., repr. in *Motivation: Part 1, Harvard Business Review*, 64–70.

McClelland, D. C. 1976: *The Achieving Society*, revised edn, Irvington, New York.

McDonald, Gael M. and Zepp, Raymond A. 1989: Business ethics: practical proposals, *Journal of Management Development*, **8**(1), 55–66.

McGrath, J. E. 1984: *Groups: Interaction and Performance*, Prentice-Hall, Englewood Cliffs, New Jersey.

McGuinness, Norman, Campbell, Nigel, and Leontiades, James 1991: Selling machinery to China: Chinese perceptions of strategies and relationships, *Journal of International Business Studies*, 2nd quarter 187–207.

McLean, A., Sims, D., Mangham, I. and Tuffield, D. 1982: *Organizational Development in Transition: Evidence of an Evolving Profession*, Wiley, Chichester.

Mead, D. 1982: Small industries in Egypt: an explanation of the economies of small furniture producers, *International Journal of Middle East Studies*, **14**(2).

Mead, Richard 1980: Expectations and sources of motivation in English for academic purposes, *ELR Journal*, **1**, Birmingham University.

Mead, Richard 1988: *Malaysia's National Language Policy and the Legal System*, Monograph Series 30, Yale University Southeast Asia Studies, Yale Center for International and Area Studies, New Haven, Conn.

Mead, Richard 1990: *Cross-Cultural Management Communication*, John Wiley, Chichester.

Mead, Richard 1992: Perceptions and experiences of conflict: cross-cultural management in Thailand. Conference paper presented to *Seminar on Cross-Cultural Management in the Asia-Pacific Region toward the Year 2000* (APEC-HRD-BMN and NESDB: Sasin GIBA, Thailand, Sept. 22–3 (Proceedings in press).

Mendenhall, Mark E., Dunbar, Edward, and Oddou, Gary R. 1987: Expatriate selection, training and career-pathing: a review and critique, *Human Resource Management*, **26**(3), 331–46.

Mendenhall, Mark, and Oddou, Gary 1985: The dimensions of expatriate acculturation: a review, *Academy of Management Review*, **10**(1), 39–47.

Mendenhall, Mark and Oddou, Gary (eds) 1991: *International Human Resource Management*, PWS-Kent, Boston, 177–204.

Merton, Robert K. 1967: Manifest and latent functions. In Robert K. Merton, *On Theoretical Sociology*, Free Press, New York, 73–138.

Merton, Robert K. 1967: *On Theoretical Sociology*, Free Press, New York.

Miles, M. (ed.) 1964: *Innovation in Education*, Columbia University, New York.

Miller, E. L., Beechler, S., Bhatt, Bhal, and Nath, R. 1986: The relationship between the global strategic planning process and the human resource management function, *Human Resource Planning*, **9**(1), 9–23. Reprinted in Jagdish Sheth and Golpira Eshgi 1989: *Global Human Resources Perspectives*, Southwestern Publishing Co., Cincinatti.

Miller, Vincent A. 1979: *The Guidebook for International Trainers in Business and Industry*, American Society for Training and Development, WI/Van Nostrand Reinhold, New York.

Mintzberg, Henry 1975: The manager's job: folklore and fact, *Harvard Business Review*, July–Aug., 4–16, reprint No. 75409.

Mintzberg, Henry 1988: Strategy making in three modes. In James B. Quinn, Henry Mintzberg, and Robert M. James (eds), *The Strategy Process*, Prentice Hall, Englewood Cliffs, New Jersey, 82–9.

Mintzberg, Henry and McHugh, Alexandra 1985: Strategy formation in an adhocracy, *Administrative Science Quarterly*, **30**, 160–97.

Moran, Robert T. 1986: Who makes the rules in cross-cultural conflicts? *International Management*, **41**(1).

Moran, Stahl, and Boyer Inc. 1987: *International Human Resource Management*, Moran, Stahl, and Boyer Inc., Boulder, Colo.

Morgan, Ronald B. 1993: Self- and co-worker perceptions of ethics and their relationships to leadership and salary, *Academy of Management Journal,* **36**(1), 200–14.

Moris, Jon R. 1976: The transferability of the western management tradition into the public service sectors, an East African perspective, *Management Education in Africa,* East African Community Management Institute, Tanzania, Nov., 50–85.

MOW International Research Team 1986: *The Meaning of Working: An International Perspective,* Academic Press, London/New York.

Mulligan, Thomas M. 1987: The two cultures in business education, *Academy of Management Review,* **12**(4).

Munchus, George, lll 1983: Employer–employee based quality circles in Japan: human resource policy implications for American firms, *Academy of Management Review,* **8**(2), 255–61.

Mutiso, G-C. 1974: *Socio-Political Thought in African Literature,* Barnes & Noble, New York.

Nahavandi, Afsaneh and Malekzadeh, Ali R. 1988: Acculturation in mergers and acquisitions, *Academy of Management Review,* **13**(1), 79–90.

Napley, David 1975: *The Technique of Persuasion,* Sweet & Maxwell, London, 2nd edn.

National Foreign Trade Council 1968: Foreign Service Personnel Compensation, NFTC.

Naumann, Earl 1993: Organizational predictions of expatriate job satisfaction, *Journal of International Business Studies,* **24**(1), 61–71.

Neghandi, Anant R. 1973: *Management and Economic Development: The Case of Taiwan,* Martinus Nijhoff, The Hague.

Neghandi, Anant R. 1979: Convergence in organizational practices: an empirical study of industrial enterprises in developing countries. In Cornelis J. Lammers and David J. Hickson (eds), *Organizations Alike and Unlike: International and Institutional Studies of the Sociology of Organizations,* Routledge & Kegan Paul, London, 323–45.

Neghandi, Anant R. 1983: Cross-cultural management research: trend and future directions, *Journal of International Business Studies,* Fall, 17–28.

Negandhi, Anant R. 1987: *International Management,* Allyn & Bacon, Boston.

Neghandi, Anant R. and Baliga, B. R. 1979: *Quest for Survival and Growth,* Praeger, New York.

Neghandi, Anant R., Eshgi, Golpira S., and Yuen, Edith C. 1985: The management practices of Japanese subsidiaries overseas, *California Management Review,* **27**(4). Reprinted in Jagdish Sheth and Golpira S. Eshgi (eds) 1989: *Global Human Resource Perspectives,* Southwestern Publishing Co., Cincinatti, 86–98.

Neghandi, Anant R. and Prasad, S. B. 1971: *Comparative Management,* Appleton-Century-Crofts, New York.

Nevis, Edward C. 1983: Cultural assumptions and productivity: the United States and China, *Sloan Management Review,* Spring, 17–29.

Nicholson, Nigel and West, Michael 1988: *Managerial Job Change,* Cambridge University Press, Cambridge.

Nonaka, Ikujiro 1988: Toward middle–up–down management: accelerating information creation, *Sloan Management Review*, Spring, 9–18.

Nonaka, Ikujiro 1991: The knowledge-creating company, *Harvard Business Review*, Nov.–Dec., 96–104.

Northcraft, Gregory B. and Neale, Margaret A. 1990: *Organizational Behavior*, Dryden, Chicago.

Oh, Tai K. 1991: Understanding managerial values and behavior among the Gang of Four: South Korea, Taiwan, Singapore and Hong Kong, *Journal of Management Development*, **10**(2).

Omar, Asmah Haji 1979: *Language Planning for Unity and Efficiency*, Penerbit Universiti Malaya, Kuala Lumpur.

Onedo, A. E. Ojuka 1991: The motivation and need satisfaction of Papua New Guinea managers, *Asia Pacific Journal of Management*, **8**(1), 121–9.

Ong, Aihwa 1987: *Spirits of Resistance and Capitalist Discipline*, State University of New York Press, New York.

O'Reilly, Charles 1989: Corporations, culture, and commitment: motivation and social control in organizations, *California Management Review*, Summer, 9–25.

Osigweh, Chimezie, A. B. (ed.) 1989: *Organizational Science Abroad: Constraints and Perspectives*, Plenum Press, New York.

Ouchi, W. 1981: *Theory Z: How American Business Can Meet the Japanese Challenge*, Addison-Wesley, Reading, Mass.

Parsons, Talcott 1966: *Societies: Evolutionary and Comparative Perspectives*, Prentice-Hall, Englewood Cliffs, NJ.

Parsons, Talcott 1971: *The System of Modern Societies*, Prentice-Hall, Englewood Cliffs, NJ.

Pascale, R. T. and Athos, A. G. 1981: *The Art of Japanese Management: Applications for American Executives*, New York: Simon & Schuster.

Pascale, Richard T. 1990: *Managing on the Edge: How the Smartest Companies Use Conflict to Stay Ahead*, Simon & Schuster, New York, 263.

Pascoe, Robin 1992: *Surviving Overseas: The Wife's Guide to Successful Living Abroad*, Times Publishing, Singapore.

Paul, William J. Jnr, Robertson, Keith B., and Herzberg, Frederick 1969: Job enrichment pays off, *Harvard Business Review*, Mar.–Apr.

Perlmutter, Howard V. and Heenan, David A. 1974: How multinational should your top managers be?, *Harvard Business Review*, Nov.–Dec., 121–32.

Peters, Tom J. 1990: Get innovative or get dead, part 1, *California Management Review*, **33**(1), 9–26.

Peters, Tom J. 1991: Get innovative or get dead, part 2, *California Management Review*, **33**(2), 9–23.

Pfeffer, Jeffrey 1981: Management as symbolic action: the creation and maintenance of organizational paradigms, *Research in Organizational Behavior*, **3**, JAI Press Inc., 1–52.

Pinchot, G. 1984: *Intrapreneuring*, Harper & Row, New York.

Pinder, C. C. and Schroeder, K. G. 1987: Time to proficiency following transfers, *Academy of Management Journal*, **30**, 336–53.

Pitt, L. F. and Abratt, R. 1986: Corruption in business: are management attitudes right? *Journal of Business Ethics*, **5**, Feb., 39–44.

Pondy, Louis R., Boland, Richard J. Jnr, and Thomas Howard (eds) 1988: *Managing Ambiguity and Change*, John Wiley, Chichester.

Porter, Michael E. 1990: *The Competitive Advantage of Nations*, Free Press, New York.

Poterba, James and Summers, Lawrence 1991: Time horizons of American firms: new evidence from a survey of CEOs. Unpublished ms.

Poulsen, Per Thygesen 1988: The attuned corporation: experience from 18 Scandinavian pioneering corporations, *European Management Journal*, **16**(3), 229–35.

Pradhan, Prachanda 1978: Management challenges and institutions in Nepal. In Seshan, Suresh A. (ed.), *Professionalization of Management in Developing Countries*, Indian Institute of Management, Ahmedabad.

Prais, Sig 1989: Productivity, education and training: Britain and other countries compared, *National Institute Economic Review*, National Institute of Economic and Social Research, London.

Preece, David A. 1989: *Managing the Adoption of New Technology*, Routledge, London.

Pruitt, Dean G. 1983: Strategic choice in negotiation, American behavioral scientist, **27**(2), 167–94.

Pruitt, Dean G. and Rubin, Jeffrey Z. 1986: *Social Conflict: Escalation, Stalemate and Settlement*, Random House, New York.

Putnam, Linda 1986: Conflict in group decision making. In Randy Y. Hirokawa and Marshall Scott Poole (eds), *Communication and Group-Decision Making*, Sage, Beverly Hills, 175–96.

Pye, Lucian 1982: *Chinese Commercial Negotiating Style*, Rand/Air Force, Santa Monica.

Quinn, James B. 1988: Strategies for change. In James B. Quinn, Henry Mintzberg, and Robert M. James 1988: *The Strategy Process*, Prentice Hall, Englewood Cliffs, New Jersey, 2–9.

Quinn, James B., Mintzberg, Henry, and James, Robert M. (eds) 1988: *The Strategy Process*, Prentice Hall, Englewood Cliffs, New Jersey, 82–9.

Radnor, Rebecca 1991: U.S.–Japanese negotiation: an exploration in cross cultural conflict. Ms: Northwestern University, Anthropology Department.

Raimond, Paul and Eden, Colin 1990: Making strategy work, *Long Range Planning*, **23**(5), 97–105.

Rajan, Amin 1990, 1992: *A Zero Sum Game*, The Industrial Society, Birmingham.

Rajan, Mahesh N. and Graham, John L. 1991: Understanding the Soviet commercial negotiation process, *California Management Review*, Spring, 40–57.

Raiffa, Howard 1982: *The Art and Science of Negotiation*, Harvard University Press, Cambridge, Mass.

Ratiu, Indrei 1983: Thinking internationally: a comparison of how international executives learn, *International Studies of Management and Organizations*, **13**(1–2), 139–50.

Ray, Carol Axtell 1986: Corporate culture: the last frontier of control?, *Journal of Management Studies*, **23**(3), 287–95.

Redding, S. G. and Martyn-Johns, T. A. 1979: Paradigm differences and their relation to management, with reference to South-East Asia. In G. W. England, Anant R. Neghandi, and B. Wilpert (eds), *Organizational Functioning in a Cross-Cultural Perspective*, Comparative Administration Research Institute, Kent State University Press, Ohio 103–25.

Redding, S. G. and Ng, Michael 1983: The role of "face" in the organizational perceptions of chinese managers, *International Studies of Management and Organization*, **13**(3), 92–123.

Reddy, Prakash 1989: *Saadan er Danskerne*, Grevas Forlag, Aarhus. Engl. lang. version, Danes Are Like That, unpublished as of Jan. 1992.

Reeves, Edward B. 1990: *The Hidden Government: Ritual, Clientelism, and Legitimation in Northern Egypt*, University of Utah Press, Utah.

Reid, John B. 1982: Observer training in naturalistic research. In Donald P. Hartmann (ed.), *Using Observers to Study Behavior*, Jossey-Bass, San Francisco, 37–50.

Rieger, Fritz and Wong-Rieger, Durhane 1990: A configuration model of national influence applied to Southeast Asian organizations, *Research Conference on Business in Southeast Asia: Proceedings*, May 12–13, 1990, Southeast Asia Business Program, University of Michigan 1–31.

Roberts, K. H. and Boyacigiller, N. A. 1984: Cross-national organizational research: the grasp of the blinded men, *Research in Organizational Behavior*, **6**, 425–75.

Robinson, R. 1983: Book reviews: Geert Hofstede, *Culture's Consequences, Work and Occupations*, **10**, 110–15.

Robinson, R. 1986: *Indonesia: The Rise of Capital*, Allen & Unwin, Sydney, 310.

Root, F. R. 1972: Analyzing political risks in international business. In A. Kapoor and P. D. Grub (eds), *The Multinational Enterprise in Transition*, Darwin, Princeton.

Rosen, B. 1959: Race, ethnicity, and the achievement syndrome, *American Sociological Review*, Feb.

Rosenzweig, Philip M. and Singh, Jitendra V. 1991: Organizational environments and the multinational enterprise, *Academy of Management Review*, **16**(2), 340–61.

Ross, Harold, Bouwmeesters, Jan, and other Institute staff 1972: *Management in the Developing Countries*, UN Research Institute for Social Development, Geneva.

Rosten, Keith A. 1991: Soviet–U.S. joint ventures: pioneers on a new frontier, *California Management Review*, Winter, 88–108.

Rothwell, S. G. 1984: Company employment policies in new technology in manufacturing and service sectors. In M. Warner (ed.) *Microprocessors, Manpower and Society*, Gower, Aldershot.

Rousseau, Denise M. 1989: Managing the change to an automated office: lessons from five case studies, *Office: Technology and People*, **4**, 31–52.

Saffold, Guy S. lll 1988: Culture traits, strength, and organizational performance: moving beyond strong culture, *Academy of Management Review*, **13**(4), 546–58.

Salacuse, Jaswald W. 1988: Making deals in strange places: a beginner's guide to international business negotiations, *Negotiations Journal*, **4**(1), 5–14.

Salacuse, Jaswald W. and Jeffrey Z. Rubin 1990: Your place or mine?, *Negotiations Journal*, **6**(1), 5–10.

Sarachek, Bernard, Hamid, Aziz Abdul, and Ismail, Zakaria Bib 1984: An opinion survey of Malaysian middle level managers and professionals, *Asia Pacific Journal of Management*, **1**(3), 181–9.

Schein, Edgar H. 1969: *Process Consultation: Its Role in Organization development*, Addison-Wesley, Reading, Mass.

Schein, Edgar H. 1981: Does Japanese management style have a message for American managers?, *Sloan Management Review*, Fall, 55–68.

Schein, Edgar 1987: *Organizational Culture and Leadership*, Jossey-Bass, San Francisco, Cal.

Schellekens, Leo 1991: Foreign direct investments, transnational corporations and management training options in Africa, *Management Education and Development*, **22**(1), 31–45.

Schlegelmilch, Bodo 1989: The ethics gap between Britain and the United States: a comparison of the state of business ethics in both countries, *European Management Journal*, **7**(1), 57–64.

Schlegelmilch, Bodo and Houston, J. 1988: Corporate codes of ethics in large U.K. companies: an empirical investigation of use, content and attitudes, *European Journal of Marketing*.

Schmitz, Hubert 1990: Small firms and flexible specialisation in developing countries, *Labour and Society*, **15**(3), 257–85.

Schneider, Susan C. 1988: National vs corporate culture: implications for human resource management, *Human Resource Management*, **27**(2), 231–46 at 239.

Schon, D. A. 1963: Champions for radical new inventions, *Harvard Business Review*, Mar.–Apr.

Schrage, Michael 1989: A Japanese giant rethinks globalization: an interview with Yoshihisa Tabuchi, *Harvard Business Review*, July–Aug., 70–6 at 74.

Scott, W. Richard, Dornbusch, Sanford B. and Utande, Emmanuel A. 1979: Organizational control: a comparison of authority systems in US and Nigerian organizations. In Cornelis J. Lammers and David J. Hickson (eds), *Organizations Alike and Unlike: International and Institutional Studies of the Sociology of Organizations*, Routledge & Kegan Paul, London, 168–82.

Sekaran, Ulma and Snodgrass, Coral R. 1989: Organizational effectiveness and its attainment: a cultural perspective. In Chimezie Osigweh, A.B. Yg (ed.), *Organizational Science Abroad: Constraints and Perspectives*, Plenum Press, New York, 269–92.

Selmer, Jan 1987: Swedish managers' perceptions of Singaporean work related values, *Asia Pacific Journal of Management*, **5**(1), 80–8 at 87.

Semler, Ricardo 1991: *Maverick!*, Century, UK; Warner Books, USA.

Sengenberger, Werner 1988: Economic and social perspectives of small enterprises, *Labour and Society*, **13**(3), 249–60.

Seshan, Suresh A. (ed.) 1978: *Professionalization of Management in Developing Countries*, Indian Institute of Management, Ahmedabad.

Shan, Weijan 1991: Environmental risks and joint venture sharing arrangements, *Journal of International Business Studies*, **22**(4), 555–78.

Shane, Scott A. 1993: The effects of cultural differences in perceptions of transactions costs on national differences in the preference for international joint ventures, *Asia Pacific Journal of Management*, **10**(1), 57–69.

Shaw, M. E. 1983: Group dynamics, *The Psychology of Small Group Behavior*, McGraw-Hill, New York.

Shenkar, Oded and Zeira, Yoram 1987: Human resources management in international joint ventures: directions for research, *Academy of Management Review*, **12**(3), 546–57.

Shelby, A. 1986: The theoretical bases of persuasion: a critical introduction, *Journal of Business Communication*, **21**(1), 5–29.

Sherry, John F. Jnr and Camargo, Eduardo G. 1987: "May your life be marvellous:" English language labelling and the semiotics of Japanese promotion, *Journal of Consumer Research*, **14**, Sept., 174–88.

Sheth, Jagdish and Eshgi, Golpira S. (eds) 1989: *Global Human Resource Perspectives*, Southwestern Publishing Co., Cincinatti.

Siddall, Peter, Willey, Keith, and Tavares, Jorge 1992: Building a transnational organization for BP oil, *Long Range Planning*, **25**(1), 37–45.

Simon, Denis Fred 1990: What is the future for foreign business in China?, *California Management Review*, Winter, **32**(2), 106–23.

Simon, Jeffrey D. 1982: Political risk assessment: past trends and future prospects, *Columbia Journal of World Business*, Fall, 62–71.

Sinclair, J. McH. 1980: Discourse in relation to language structure and semiotics. In S. Greenbaum, G. Leech, and J. Svartvik (eds), *Studies in English Linguistics for Randolph Quirk*, Longman, London, 110–24.

Singh, Paras Nath and Wherry, Robert J. Snr 1963: Ranking of job factors by factory workers in India, *Personnel Psychology*, **16**, 29–33.

Sirota, D. and Greenwood, J. M. 1971: Understanding your overseas work force, *Harvard Business Review*, **49**(1), Jan.–Feb., 53–9.

Skinner, C. Wickham, 1964: Management of international production, *Harvard Business Review*, Sept.–Dec., 132.

Smircich, Linda 1983: Concepts of culture and organizational analysis, *Administrative Science Quarterly*, **28**, 339–58.

Smith, M., Beck, J., Cooper, C., Cox, C., Ottaway, D. and Talbot, R. (eds) 1982: *Introducing Organizational Behaviour*, Macmillan Education, Basingstoke.

Smith, Tasman 1982: *Cross-Cultural Management Effectiveness*, Oxford University Press East Asia, Thailand.

Spradley, James P. 1979: *The Ethnographic Interview*, New York: Holt, Rinehart & Winston.

Stark, Andrew 1993: What's the matter with business ethics?, *Harvard Business Review*, May–June, 38–48.

Steers, Richard M. and Porter, Lyman W. 1991: *Motivation and Work Behavior*, 5th edn, McGraw-Hill, New York.

Stewart, E. C. 1972: *American Cultural Patterns: A Cross-Cultural Perspective*, Intercultural Press, Chicago.

Sullivan, Jeremiah J. and Nonaka, Ikujiro 1986: The application of organizational learning theory to Japanese and American management, *Journal of International Business Studies*, Fall, 127–47.

Sullivan, Jeremiah J. and Peterson, Richard B. 1991: A test of theories underlying the Japanese lifetime employment system, *Journal of International Business Studies*, 1st quarter, 79–96.

Sullivan, Jeremiah, Peterson, Richard B., Kameda, Naoki, and Shimada, Justin 1981: The relationship between conflict resolution approaches and trust: a cross cultural study, *Academy of Management Journal*, **24**(4), 803–15.

Sullivan, Jerry and Snodgrass, Coral 1991: Tolerance of executive failure in American and Japanese organizations, *Asia Pacific Journal of Management*, **8**(1), 15–34.

Sviokla, John Julius 1986: Planpower, XCON, and Mudman: an in-depth analysis into three commercial expert systems in use. PhD dissertation, Harvard University.

Taib, Abdullah and Ismail, Mohamed Yusoff 1982: The social structure. In E. K. Fisk and H. Osman-Rani (eds), *The Political Economy of Malaysia*, Oxford University Press, Kuala Lumpur, 104–24.

Taylor, John G. and Turton, Andrew (eds) 1988: *Sociology of Developing Societies: Southeast Asia*, Macmillan Education, Basingstoke, 181–90.

Terpstra, Veern and David, Kenneth 1985: *The Cultural Environment of International Business*, South-Western Publishing, Cincinatti.

Terrill, Ross 1984: *The White-Boned Demon*, William Morrow & Co. New York.

Thomas, Kenneth W. 1976: Conflict and conflict management. In Marvin D. Dunnette (ed.), *Handbook of Industrial and Organizational Psychology*, Rand McNally, Chicago.

Thompson, Allan G. 1989: Cross-cultural management of labour in a Thai environment, *Asia Pacific Journal of Management*, **6**(2), 323–38.

Thompson, James D. 1967: *Organizations in Action*, McGraw-Hill, New York.

Thompson, Stewart 1962: *How Companies Plan*, American Management Association, New York.

Torbiorn, Ingemar 1982: *Living Abroad*, Wiley, New York.

Torbiorn, Ingemar 1985: The structure of managerial roles in cross-cultural settings, *International Studies of Management and Organization*, **15**(1), 52–74.

Toulmin, Stephen, Rieke, Richard, and Janik, Allan 1984: *An Introduction to Reasoning*, Macmillan, New York.

Triandis, H. C. 1982: Review of culture's consequences: international differences in work-related values, *Human Organisation*, **41**, 86–90.

Trice, Harrison M. and Beyer, Janice M. 1984: Studying organizational cultures through rites and ceremonials, *Academy of Management Review*, **9**(4), 653–69.

Trompenaars, Fons (no date): *The Organization of Meaning and the Meaning of Organizations*, Social Systems Sciences Department, The Wharton School of the University of Pennsylvania, Philadelphia.

Tung, Rosalie L. 1981: Selection and training of personnel for overseas assignments, *Columbia Journal of World Business*, **16**, 68–78.

Tung, Rosalie L. 1982: Selection and training procedures of U.S., European and Japanese multinationals, *California Management Review*, **25**(1), 57–71.

Tung, Rosalie L. 1987: Expatriate assignments: enhancing success and minimizing failure, *Academy of Management Executive*, **1**(2), 117–26.

Tung, Rosalie L. 1991: Motivation in Chinese industrial enterprises. In Richard M. Steers and Lyman W. Porter (eds), *Motivation and Work Behavior*, 5th edn, McGraw-Hill, New York, 342–51.

Turner, Graham 1984: ICI becomes proactive, *Long Range Planning*, **17**(6), 12–16.

Turton, Andrew 1988: Ideological commodity production. In John G. Taylor and Andrew Turton (eds), *Southeast Asia*, Macmillan Education, Basingstoke, 207–10.

Tushman, Michael N., Newman, William H. and Elaine Romanelli 1986: Convergence and upheaval: managing the unsteady pace of organizational evolution, *California Management Review*, **29**(1); 1987, special reprint.

Tyebjee, Tyzoon 1988: A typology of joint ventures: Japanese strategies in the United States, *California Management Review*, Fall, 75–86.

UNECOSOC 1978: *Transnational Corporations in World Development: A Re-examination*, United Nations, New York.

United States Department of Commerce 1982, 1980: *Census of Population (General Population Characteristics: Florida)*, United States Government Printing Office, Washington DC, 11–71.

Vaupel, J. W. and Curhan, J. P. 1969: *The Making of Multinational Enterprise*, Harvard University, Boston.

Vernon, Raymond 1977: The power of multinational enterprises in developing countries. In Carl H. Madden (ed.), *The Case for the Multinational Corporation*, Praeger, New York.

Vicere, Albert A. and Freeman, Virginia T. 1990: Executive education in major corporations: an international survey, *Journal of Management Development*, **9**(1).

Vogel, David 1992: The globalization of business ethics: why America remains distinctive, *California Management Review*, Fall, 30–49.

Vroom, C. W. 1981: Indonesia and the West: an essay on cultural differences in organization and management, *Majalah Management and Usahawan Indonesia*, Indonesia, 25–31.

Ware, James P. and Barnes, Louis B. 1983: Managing interpersonal conflict. In Leonard A. Schlesinger, Robert G. Eccles, and John J. Gabarro (eds), *Managing Behavior in Organizations*, McGraw-Hill, New York, 196–209.

Warner, M. (cd.) 1984: *Microprocessors, Manpower and Society*, Gower, Aldershot.

Watson, Goodwin 1971: Resistance to change, *American Behavioral Scientist*, **14**, 745–66.

Watson, Warren E., Kumar, Kamalesh, and Michaelson, Larry K. 1993: Cultural diversity's impact on interaction process and performance: comparing homogenous and diverse task groups, *Academy of Management Journal*, **36**(3), 590–602.

Weber, Max 1947: *The Theory of Social and Economic Organizations*, transl. and ed. A. M. Henderson and T. Parsons, Free Press, New York.

Weber, Max 1968: *Economy and Society*, ed. G. Roth and C. Wittich, New York.

Wenburg, John H. and Wilmot, William W. 1973: *The Personal Communication Process*, Wiley, New York.

Wertheim, W. F. 1965: *East-West Parallels*, Quadrangle Books, Chicago.

Westwood, Robert G. and Everett, James E. 1987: Culture's consequences: a methodology for comparative management studies in Southeast Asia, *Asia Pacific Journal of Management*, Singapore, **4**(3), 187–202.

Whipp, R. and Clark, P. 1986: *Innovation and the Auto Industry*, Francis Pinter, London.

Whipple, Thomas W. and Swords, Dominic F. 1992: Business ethics judgements: a cross-cultural comparison, *Journal of Business Ethics*, **7**(9), 671–8.

Wiener, Yoask 1988: Forms of value systems: a focus on organizational effectiveness and cultural change and maintenance, *Academy of Management Review*, **13**(4), 534–45.

Wilkins, Alan L. and Dyer, W. Gibb Jnr 1988: Toward culturally sensitive theories of culture change, *Academy of Management Review*, **13**(4), 522–33.

Wille, Edgar 1989: Management skills group book summary 9: Bartlett and Ghoshal (1989). Unpublished ms, Ashridge Management College, UK.

Williams, J. E. and Best, D. L. 1982: *Measuring Sex Stereotypes: A Thirty Nation Study*, Sage, London.

Williams, L. K., Whyte, W. F. and Green, C. S. 1966: Do cultural differences affect workers' attitudes?, *Industrial Relations*, **5**, 105–17.

Willis, Paul 1979: Masculinity and factory labor. In Jeffrey C. Alexander and Steven Seidman 1990: *Culture and Society: Contemporary Debates*, Cambridge University Press, Cambridge, 183–95.

Wilmot, William 1975: *Dyadic Communication: A Transactional Perspective*, Addison-Wesley, Reading, Mass.

Winiecki, Jan 1988: *The Distorted World of Soviet-type Economics*, Routledge & Kegan Paul, London.

Winterbottom, M. R. 1958: The relation of need for achievement to learning experiences in independence and mastery. In John W. Atkinson *Motives in Fantasy, Action, and Society: A Method of Assessment and Study*, D. Van Nostrand, Princeton, NJ, 453–78.

Wolfe, Art 1993: We've had enough business ethics, *Business Horizons*, **36**(3), 1–4.

Wolters, Willem 1983: *Politics, Patronage and Class Conflict in Central Luzon*, Institute of Social Studies, the Hague.

Woodward, David G. and Liu, Boris C. F. 1993: Investing in China: guidelines for success, *Long Range Planning*, **26**(2), 83–9.

Woodworth, W. and Nelson, R. 1980: Information in Latin American organizations: some cautions, *Management International Review*, **20**(2), 61–9.

Wong Siu-lun 1986: Modernization and Chinese culture in Hong Kong, *China Quarterly*, No. 106, 306–25.

Wright, Robert G. and Werther, William B. Jnr 1991: Mentors at work, *Journal of Management Development*, **10**(3), 25–32.

Wu Tianzu 1991: Technological transformation of small enterprises in Zhejiang Province, China. In A. Bhalla (ed.), *Small and Medium Enterprises*, Greenwood Press, New York, 139–51.

Wuthnow, Robert and Witten, Marsha 1988: New directions in the study of culture. *Annual Review of Sociology*, **14**, 49–67.

Yau, Oliver H. M. 1988: Chinese cultural values: their dimensions and marketing implications, *European Journal of Marketing*, **22**(5), 44–57.

Yeager, E. 1980: Quality circles: a tool for the 80's, *Training and Development Journal*, **134**, 60–2.

Yeh, Ryh-Song 1988: Values of American, Japanese and Taiwanese managers in Taiwan: a test of Hofstede's framework. *Academy of Management Best Papers Proceedings, 1988*, 106–10.

Yeh, Ryh-Song 1989: On Hofstede's treatment of Chinese and Japanese values, *Asia Pacific Journal of Management*, **6**(1), 149–60.

Yeh, Ryh-Song 1991: Management practices of Taiwanese firms: as compared to those of American and Japanese subsidiaries in Taiwan, *Asia Pacific Journal of Management*, **8**(1), 1–14.

Yorks, Lyle 1976: *A Radical Approach to Job Enrichment*, Amacom, New York.

Zaltman, G., Duncan, R. and Holbek, J. 1973: *Innovations and Organizations*, John Wiley, New York, 23–32.

Zeira, Yoram and Banai, Moshe 1985: Selection of expatriate managers in MNCs: the host-environment point of view, *International Studies of Management and Organization*, **15**(1), 33–51.

Zeira, Yoram and Harari, Ehud 1977: Managing third-country nationals in multinational corporations, *Business Horizons*, Oct., 83–8.

Zenoff, David B. 1971: *International Business Management*, Macmillan, New York.

Zuckerman, Alan S. 1979: *The Politics of Faction: Christian Democratic Rule in Italy*, Yale University Press, New Haven and London.

Index